D1522992

MOBILE MODERNITY

CULTURES OF HISTORY

CULTURES OF HISTORY
Nicholas Dirks, series sditor

The death of history, reported at the end of the twentieth century, was clearly premature. It has become a hotly contested battleground in struggles over identity, citizenship, and claims of recognition and rights. Each new national history proclaims itself as ancient and universal, while the contingent character of its focus raises questions about the universality and objectivity of any historical tradition. Globalization and the American hegemony have created cultural, social, local, and national backlashes. Cultures of History is a new series of books that investigates the forms, understandings, genres, and histories of history, taking history as the primary text of modern life and the foundational basis for state, society, and nation.

SHAIL MAYARAM
Against History, Against State: Counterperspectives from the Margins

TAPATI GUHA-THAKURTA
Monuments, Objects, Histories: Institutions of Art in Colonial and Postcolonial India

CHARLES HIRSCHKIND
The Ethical Soundscape: Cassette Sermons and Islamic Counterpublics

MOBILE MODERNITY

Germans, Jews, Trains

TODD SAMUEL PRESNER

WITHDRAWN

COLUMBIA UNIVERSITY PRESS   NEW YORK

Columbia University Press
Publishers Since 1893
New York   Chichester, West Sussex

Library of Congress Cataloging-in-Publication Data

Presner, Todd Samuel.
  Mobile modernity : Germans, Jews, trains / Todd Samuel Presner.
    p. cm. — (Cultures of history)
  Includes bibliographical references and index.
ISBN13 978-0-231-14012-6 — ISBN10 0-231-14012-6 (cloth : alk. paper)
ISBN 0-231-51158-2 (ebook)
1. Jews—Germany—Intellectual life—19th century.
2. Jews—Germany—Intellectual life—20th century.
3. Jews—Germany—Identity. 4. Jews—Cultural assimilation—Germany.
5. German literature—Jewish authors—History and criticism.
6. Technology—social aspects. 7. Technology and civilization. I. title. II. Series.

DS135.G33P67   2007
303.48'320943—dc22   2006029198

Casebound editions of Columbia University Press books are printed
on permanent and durable acid-free paper.
Printed in the United States of America
c 10 9 8 7 6 5 4 3 2 1

For Hinrich

CONTENTS

ACKNOWLEDGMENTS

THIS PROJECT BEGAN among the ruined railway stations of Berlin in the fall of 1996. It ended more than a decade later in Los Angeles after having traveled on tracks—both literal and intellectual—which led me across several academic disciplines, languages, and homes. In between, I had the fortune of meeting many extraordinary people who helped shape my ideas and hone my arguments. I would like to express my gratitude to those who have embarked on this journey with me.

Let me begin in the present. I would like to thank my departmental colleagues at UCLA, especially Jim Schultz and Andrew Hewitt, for their serious engagement with my work. I would also like to thank Carol Bakhos, Gil Hochberg, Eleanor Kaufman, David Myers, Ken Reinhard, and Mark Seltzer, who have all listened to or read various parts of "the railway project." Over the years, I have had the pleasure of presenting parts of this book at various conferences, including many of the annual meetings of the German Studies Association. I have greatly benefited by the comments and critiques of my colleagues in the field. Foremost among these, I would like to thank Julia Hell, who has generously offered me numerous forums for presenting my work over the years and who has been one of my most critically engaged interlocutors. My thinking on Sebald, Freud, Arendt, and Heidegger is imprinted by her intellectual friendship. I would also like to single out Leslie Adelson, Kevin Amidon, Esther Gabara, Bluma Goldstein, Atina Grossman, Andreas Huyssen, Pamela Lee, John Maciuika, Frank Mecklenburg, Leslie Morris, Jeffrey Peck, Andy Rabinbach, Gabriella Safran, Scott Spector, Benjamin Ward, Liliane Weissberg, Meike Werner, and Meg Worley for their support of my work and their constructive critiques of my ideas.

At Stanford this project took shape with the tremendous support of Russell Berman, Steven Zipperstein, John Felstiner, Valentin Mudimbe, Hayden White, Jeffrey Schnapp, Sepp Gumbrecht, and Amir Eshel. I thank Russell for prompting me to return to literature before theory; I thank Steven for sharing his fascination with railway maps in the East; I thank John for teaching me to listen to Celan; I thank Valentin for teaching me continental philoso-

phy; I thank Hayden for pushing me to develop a theory of history; I thank
Jeffrey for modeling a rigorously interdisciplinary practice of material history; I thank Sepp for the productivity and futurity of the German-Jewish
dialectic itself; and, finally, I thank Amir for his unflagging support of my
intellectual work and his genuine friendship. This book owes a significant
debt to Amir for his gift of conversation over the years.

I would like to thank Jonathan Hess for his extraordinarily detailed reading of the entire manuscript and his remarkable openness to my project.
His critiques of the penultimate draft helped me significantly improve the
final version. Of course, any errors or shortcomings are entirely my own. Finally, I thank my editors at Columbia University Press, Jennifer Crewe and
Susan Pensak, for their wisdom guiding this project through publication.

Over the years my family has been wonderfully supportive of all my work
and shared—sometimes vicariously, sometimes among the very ruins—in
the intellectual excitement of this project. I thank my brother Brad and his
wife Kiesha for always helping me keep it real; I thank my parents, Harvey
and Susan, for their patience, support, and faith in my academic work; I
thank my grandmother, Bess, who passed away my first year at UCLA, for
her genuine openness and sensitivity. She also taught me the joy of Yiddish.
And I thank my life partner, Jaime, who has traveled alongside me from
the very first day that I embarked on this project and has been there in
ways that I cannot even describe. This project would not have been possible
without his tireless support and love. Thank you, Jaime.

My book is dedicated to Hinrich Seeba, for it is his project as much as it
is mine. I first met Hinrich in the winter of 1997 as a student in his "Berlin
Cityscape" graduate seminar at Berkeley. I had just returned from Berlin's
Brach-Gelände. We shared our enthusiasm for Berlin and for a new kind of
German/Jewish cultural studies. Over the years that followed, I would come
to know him as a magnanimous mentor and true intellectual beacon who
modeled the kind of *Kulturkritik* I hoped to write. He embodied the values
I hoped—and still hope—to emulate. I have followed, with only some suc-
cess, in his footsteps.

Earlier versions of three of the chapters were previously published. Chapter 2 first appeared as "Traveling Between Delos and Berlin: Heidegger and
Celan on the Topography of 'What Remains,'" *German Quarterly* 74.4 (Fall
2001): 417-29. It is reprinted with permission of the Association of Teachers

of German. A scaled-down version of chapter 4 was published as "Jews on Ships; or, How Heine's *Reisebilder* Deconstruct Hegel's Philosophy of World History," *Publications of the Modern Language Association (PMLA)* 118.3 (May 2003): 521-38. It is reprinted by permission of the copyright owner, the Modern Language Association of America. Finally, a shorter version of chapter 6 was published as "'The Fabrication of Corpses': Heidegger, Arendt, and the Modernity of Mass Death," *Telos* 135 (Summer 2006): 84-108. It is reprinted with permission of Telos Press.

MOBILE MODERNITY

1. DIALECTICS AT A STANDSTILL

The onlookers go rigid when the train goes past.   —Franz Kafka, *1910*

1.1 Franz Schwechten, Anhalter Bahnhof, Berlin (1881). *Courtesy of the Granger Collection, New York*

AS THE TERMINUS of the first major, long-distance railway line to open in a German state, the Anhalter Bahnhof has always had more than just an incidental connection to the city of Berlin and its liminal geography as a point of entry to eastern, western, and southern Europe. From the moment it opened in 1840 until its destruction more than a hundred years later, the station served as a testament to the dizzying arrival and violent departure of German/Jewish modernity. In its built forms one could discern the triumph of technologies of modernization, the emergence of Prussian expansionism, the national hopes invested in a unified Germany, the primacy placed on transcendent size and speed, the ideals of cosmopolitanism coupled with fears of transmigration, the reality of an interconnected world of commerce and material exchange, and this world's destructive capacities. Even in its present ruin it is a witness to both the volatility of the twentieth century and the hopes and fears of the nineteenth. Its history runs straight through German/Jewish modernity, and, recursively, the history of German/Jewish modernity runs straight through its history.

Walter Benjamin certainly recognized the railway station's significance when he immortalized its technological greatness and immense scale in recollecting his childhood in Berlin: "The 'Anhalter' refers to the name of the mother cavern of all railways; it is where the locomotives are at home and the trains have to stop. No distance was further away than when fog gathered over its tracks."[1] To Benjamin the Anhalter Bahnhof was the reality of that marvelous and equally dubious nineteenth-century dream of progress characterized by, among other things, the possibility of connecting to a faraway place. It was where Franz Kafka arrived from Prague when he visited Felice Bauer in Berlin; it is also where Paul Celan stopped over on his way to Paris from Czernowitz on the day after November 8/9, 1938. In the 1930s thousands of Jewish children were sent on trains from Berlin's Anhalter Bahnhof to safety outside of Germany; in 1941–42 the station was used to gather elderly Jewish "transports" who were deported to the concentration camp of Theresienstadt.

If the "arcade" counts as the best material witness to nineteenth-century Paris, as Benjamin famously argued in his massive historiographic fragment, *The Arcades Project*, surely the railway—perhaps Berlin's Anhalter train station—would have to count as the best material witness to German/Jewish modernity. It was, after all, the railway that literally unified Germany in the late nineteenth century and connected Berlin to Western and Eastern Europe in the twentieth—in splendor, emancipation, and horror. In fact, the history of the very first railway line constructed in a German state is punctuated by the entanglement of German modernity and Jewish modernity. In 1835, the year in which a six-kilometer railway track opened between Nuremberg and Fürth, Jews were not allowed to reside in Nuremberg, although they could do business in the town, provided they were accompanied by a German citizen and did not stay overnight. At this time Jews comprised nearly 20 percent of the population of Fürth, a town that also boasted a Jewish university, two synagogues, and a Hebrew press. Encouraged by their local rabbi, Jews from Fürth invested in the railway construction project and became the first commercial travelers to take the train to work in the German town that barred them citizenship. German and Jewish, modernity and mobility became wed to one another.

Over the course of the next century, the railway emerged as an embodied, transitional space emblematic of both the emancipatory hopes and the destructive nightmares of an epoch. Not unlike the latent mythology of the arcade, the rapid expansion of the railway was driven by its unprecedented capacity to produce capital and facilitate transnational material transport. It became a "dream space" of modernity, displaying and exchanging the fetishized objects of a capitalist economy. Both the railway and the arcade thus became the symbols and proof of their epochs: Railways represented progress because they were the technological realization of mobility, speed, and exchange. They also became the first mode of transportation to move the masses, from the formation of mass politics to the implementation of mass deportations. And, finally, both the arcades and the railways eventually fell out of favor, overtaken by some other formation imagined to be faster, more fashionable, more progressive, more opulent, and more destructive.

The heady heydays of the arcades and the railway may be over, but their constitutive dreams are still legible in the surviving remains. The physical ruins of the Anhalter Bahnhof and its varied cultural testimonies may be all we are left with, but it is from these remains that we can map the cultural geographies of German/Jewish modernity. The Anhalter Bahnhof represents a paradigm of modernity, one that is already grafted, as a dialectical image, onto these cultural geographies. In its ruins "German" and "Jewish" are inextricably bound to one another, stretching far beyond the space of Berlin or the German nation, and "modernity" betrays itself as a persistent dialectic of enabling and checking mobility. Through the multiple encounters, strange tensions, and mediated interactions between German and Jewish, the cultural geography of this book emerges on the trains traveling on the tracks running to and away from the Anhalter Bahnhof.

WHAT IS GERMAN/JEWISH?

German/Jewish modernity begins with the slash, the cut, the decision, the divider. The separatrix refers to the line between the two words *German* and *Jewish*, the cut that separates them. The meaning of the separatrix is ambiguous: it may locate an opposition, as in German versus Jewish, it may signify simultaneity, as in both German and Jewish, and it may call upon a choice, as in German or Jewish. At the same time that the separatrix announces a kind of distinction, the relationship between the distinguished terms is characterized by an unresolved tension, a back-and-forth that is never subdued or sublated into a third term. Instead the two terms exist in permanent tension, moving with respect to one another, but never turning into something higher. In every case the separatrix indicates the dialectical movement of a finitely structured relationship that must be articulated according to its historical specificity.

Jacques Derrida first articulated the logic of the separatrix in his early attempts to explain the processes of deconstruction.[2] The work of deconstruction is to mercilessly search out the operations of the separatrix—the divider between text and context, inside and outside, primary and ancillary—and undercut its attempts to ground meaning, establish foundations, and stabilize truth by exposing the presuppositions and ideologies behind the very distinction. As Jeffrey Kipnis points out, Derrida attempts to "twist" the separatrix, "turn it back on itself, and poke holes in order to expose the inseparability of those terms that it separates."[3] For Derrida the enactment of a division or separation is always suspect because it is through such divisions that truth claims are grounded.

In the case of German/Jewish we find the two terms consistently "contaminated" by one another. They overlap; they become blurred; they switch places. One of the terms cannot be adequately articulated without the other. In fact, one of my contentions in this book will be that "the Jewish"—that which is supposedly differentiated from, outside of, or somehow opposed to "the German"—is actually within, if not constitutive of, that which is German. What this means is that the Jewish is entangled with and already "too close" to the German, despite the long and violent history, laced with anti-Semitism, of attempts to definitively separate the two. Hegel's attempt, for example, to confine the Jews to the first stage of world history is just one instance in which the two terms are given a structuring relationship in the form of an ontological separation imposed by a strict historical-developmental hierarchy. For Hegel the German is valorized as the pinnacle of world history while the Jewish is dismissed as outside its movements. But it is here, particularly for certain German thinkers, that the Jewish is actually constitutive—in a strange, sometimes even obsessive way—of the German. And it is the project of a thinker like Heinrich Heine to take the Hegelian logic of the progress of world history, repeat it with a Jewish difference and thereby betray both the limits of the Hegelian system and the inseparability of German/Jewish.

Much like Heine, Kafka also performed a kind of deconstruction of the separatrix between German/Jewish. He did this in a little speech on the Yiddish language that he gave in 1912 to an audience of German speakers at the Jewish Town Hall in Prague.[4] In his brief reflection on the history of the Yiddish language, Kafka suggests that Yiddish deterritorializes the German language through both its untranslatable closeness to and difference from the latter. He begins the short speech by assuring his German-speaking audience that they "understand much more Yiddish [*Jargon*] than they may believe" and that the "anxiety" they have toward Yiddish is actually unjustified (Y 421–22). He proceeds by enumerating some facts about the Yiddish language: that it is "the youngest European language," that it is unique because it has "no grammatical structure," and that it "consists entirely of foreign words" (Y 422).[5] He then points out that mobility is a critical part of the language: "The migration of peoples runs through Yiddish from one end to the other. German, Hebrew, French, English, Slavic, Dutch, Romanian, and even Latin are contained within Yiddish with ease and curiosity" (Y 422–23). But it is the German language, Kafka indicates, that historically has had the closest affinities to Yiddish. In fact, German is so close to Yiddish that not only can speakers of German understand Yiddish but "Yiddish cannot be translated into German" (Y 425). Kafka insists, "the connections between Yiddish and German are so gentle and significant" that to translate Yiddish into German or even "trace it back" to German would be to "destroy it" (Y 425). Kafka gives some examples: "*toit* [Yiddish for "dead"] for instance, is very close to but not *tot* [German for "dead"] and *blüt* [Yiddish for "blood"] is very close to but not *Blut* [German for "blood"]" (Y 425).

What is significant about Kafka's characterization of Yiddish vis-à-vis German is his recognition that the two languages are too close to be translated into one another. Translation presupposes a fundamental difference, a space or a gap between which something can be mediated. German and Yiddish are already contaminated by one another: German speakers can understand spoken Yiddish, and Yiddish speakers can understand spoken German. The fear of Yiddish is not simply that it can (almost) pass for German but that German can (almost) pass for Yiddish.[6] In effect, what we might interpret Kafka as saying is that Yiddish is the "dangerous supplement" of German, that which is rigorously excluded—because it is a bastard language, because it is not standardized, because it is the language of "crooks" and "thieves," because it is "uncultured," because it is a mere "dialect" of a "backward" people—but is actually already within German.[7] Yiddish essentially deterritorializes German by turning it eastward and making it Jewish. As Deleuze and Guattari astutely remark about Kafka's relationship to Yiddish: "He sees it [Yiddish] less as a sort of linguistic territory for the Jews than as a nomadic movement of deterritorialization that reworks German language."[8] After all, Kafka's examples—*toit* and *tot*, *blüt* and *Blut*—are differences uttered by the subaltern, which take the place of and enrich the plenitude of German. Through the operations of *différance*, barely recognizable in spoken language, Yiddish adds itself to, enriches, and replaces German. Yiddish is feared and perhaps dangerous because it undermines the authority, geography, and plenitude of the German language.[9]

As Kafka indicated by his attempt to valorize the oft-besmirched Yiddish language, a structuring hierarchy seems to govern the relationship between German and Jewish. German is supposedly the language of authority and nationality, grounded in the stability of geography and enduring cultural forms. Yiddish, on the other hand, is the language of Jewish "wanderers," a language composed of foreign words because it has no geographic or cultural home. While this may be true at many times, I do not want to reduce the complex interactions of German/Jewish history to a strict, hierarchical relationship of such valuations and enforced normativity. Although "Jewish" may emerge as the devalued or non-normative underside of this relationship, there is—I contend—no pure "German" or timeless geography of "Germany." The significance of this is that German modernity is always "contaminated" and, hence, means something else: namely, "German/Jewish" modernity.

To demonstrate this claim, my book is structured geographically around a group of dialectical encounters between German and Jewish thinkers: Heidegger/Celan, Goethe/Kafka, Hegel/Heine, List/Herzl, Heidegger/Arendt, and Freud/Sebald. An encounter does not necessarily refer to an actual meeting or a "dialogue," especially if the term is limited to a conversation between two people who, in the critical words of Gershom Scholem, "listen to each other, who are prepared to perceive the other as what he is and represents, and to respond to him."[10] The encounters that I am tracking here did not occur on even ground, nor were they dialogical in the sense that one learns from and comes to terms with the other. My primary concern, however, is not with the debate about whether the German-Jewish dialogue actually took place.[11] Indeed, dialogue is actually too narrow a description for the German/Jewish relationships that I am analyzing here, and a real, physical encounter or meeting of the minds is not a prerequisite for my argument. Sometimes the thinkers in question did actually meet or correspond, sometimes one thinker "reads"—and in so doing reworks—the other, and sometimes there are discursive conditions of possibility or intellectual commonalities that enable certain chiasmic, transhistorical, conceptual affinities.[12] In each case the separatrix between German and Jewish marks the relationship as dialectical and entangles them within one another.

In the introduction to *The German-Jewish Dialogue Reconsidered*, Klaus Berghahn argues that despite "the contradictions, illusions, and failures of Jewish emancipation and/or assimilation in Germany, there is still the possibility of historicizing the German-Jewish experience and restoring the German Jews as key figures in German culture."[13] While I agree with this assessment and its implicit negation of the model of failed dialogue, I go much further than simply "historicizing" the Jews in German modernity and "restoring" their place, something that essentially amounts to a retrospective project of historicization and commemoration. My argument is more fundamental: German modernity, I argue, is always already German/Jewish modernity. The two are inextricably and fundamentally linked. To reinsert the Jews into "German culture" would be to imply that they can be truly removed.

In terms of methodology, I position my thinking about German/Jewish modernity closer to the work of Michael Brenner and Peter Eli Gordon, the latter of whom explored what he calls "the intimacy of the relationship between Germans and German Jews" through the philosophies of Martin Heidegger and Franz Rosenzweig.[14] Both Brenner and Gordon focus on the richness of German-Jewish intellectual and cultural history in Weimar Germany without foreshadowing (or ignoring) the catastrophe that ensued. Like Gordon, I do not believe that we can maintain that the "richness and reality of intellectual exchange between Germans and Jews" did not occur because of the Holocaust; and, at the same time, I do not believe we should restrict ourselves to a narrowly conceived notion of dialogue, as Scholem insists. In Gordon's words: "For such [German/Jewish] dialogue one needn't understand the interlocutors as engaged in actual conversation. While Rosenzweig and Heidegger remained strangers in life, much of what they wrote bespeaks an intimate commonality of ideas" (xxiii), so much so that Gordon not only places Rosenzweig and Heidegger in contact with the philosophical traditions of German Idealism but, more significantly, concludes by entertaining "the startling possibility that Heidegger's philosophy itself might somehow derive from Judaism" (313).

While Gordon analyzed a snapshot of the German/Jewish dialectic
through his pairing of Heidegger and Rosenzweig, Paul Mendes-Flohr has
examined the ways in which certain German-speaking Jews struggled to
articulate hybrid identities torn between "German" and "Jewish."[15] Indeed,
the tensions between Jewish faith and German culture within the intellectual and spiritual composition of German-Jewish thinkers must not be un-
derestimated since the conjunctions and disjunctions between *Judentum*
(Jewishness) and *Deutschtum* (Germanness) were far from consistent and
clear-cut. After Mendelssohn, most German Jews, Mendes-Flohr argues,
found "their identities and cultural loyalties fractured" because they were
forced to struggle with and often choose between a "plurality of identities
and cultures" (GJ 3). Although Rosenzweig optimistically imagined Germany as a "land of two rivers" (*Zweistromland*), one German and one Jewish, both flowing together "*within* the soul of the German Jew" (GJ 23–24),
most German Jews saw their souls, in Benjamin's word, as "bifurcated" (GJ
59). Therefore, we must be cognizant of the operations of more than one
dialectic: that of German and Jewish within the soul of the German Jew[16]
and that of German and German-speaking Jew within the broader intellectual and cultural sphere. Mendes-Flohr examined the former dialectic
in his study of German Jews; I will attempt, not unlike Gordon, to map out
signposts for the geography of the latter dialectic here.

This, then, is the seemingly straightforward claim of my book: there is
no such thing as German modernity pure and simple; instead "German" is
always mixed together, for better and for worse, in splendor and in horror,
with "Jewish." I propose the signifier German/Jewish as a way of characterizing the movements, slippages, and tensions of this modernity and arrange
the chapters of my study as snapshots of moments when the German/Jewish
dialectic comes to a standstill. Here I will apply Benjamin's famous concept
of "dialectics at a standstill" to characterize my antidevelopmental historiography, which is organized according to constellations of tension between
past and present, near and far, German and Jewish. It is not simply that the
figure of the Jew is important for German thinkers; the idea of German—in
the cultural sense of "what is German?"—is also a Jewish project. This is not
to say, as Moritz Goldstein would famously argue in his article of 1912, "The
German-Jewish Parnassus," that Jews do, in fact, "administer" the "spiritual
property" of the German nation;[17] however, it is to say that German modernity—in its intellectual, cultural, and social forms—cannot be studied
apart from Jewish modernity. The modernity that I am studying here breaks

down into German/Jewish dialectics, and it is these inseparable tensions, encounters, relationships, and movements between German and Jewish which, recursively, constitute what I will term the dialectic of modernity.

The concept of the dialectic of modernity, as I use it here, certainly accords with the seminal work of Max Horkheimer and Theodor Adorno, although I offer a significantly different account of historical processes, which I will need to explain. Written in exile during the final years of World War II and published shortly thereafter, *Dialectic of Enlightenment* is an attempt to explain fascism by tracking down the regressive, totalitarian elements of the Enlightenment's dream of the rationalization of the world, the dissolution of myth, and the spread of knowledge.[18] The concept of enlightenment does not, despite its claims to the contrary, simply mean the progressive illumination of the world through demythologization, knowledge, and mastery; it also means the ruthless dominance of this world through the leveling power of universal concepts, abstraction, and totalization. "The fully enlightened earth radiates disaster triumphant" (DE 3) because progress is always bound up with sublimation and domination. According to Horkheimer and Adorno, the absolutism of the Enlightenment consumes everything, like a totalitarian system, such that "nothing at all may remain outside, because the mere idea of outsideness is the very source of fear" (DE 16). In the final analysis, "none can feel safe" (DE 23).

With the triumph of reason over myth (a triumph that can only happen completely when *ratio* becomes mythological), the fate of mimesis plays a particularly important role in articulating the dialectic, especially in Horkheimer and Adorno's explanation of anti-Semitism. Mimesis does not simply mean the imitation of an object, but it also means the appropriation of it and is, therefore, part and parcel of the domination of nature: "the capacity of representation is the vehicle of progress and regression at one and the same time" (DE 35). Civilization is characterized by the "organized control of mimesis," "rational practice," and "work" (DE 180); anything or anyone that does not need this "organized control" is, by definition, outside of civilization. Because of the Jewish taboo on mimesis—the so-called *Bildverbot*, the ban on making graven images of God—Jews carried forward the processes of Enlightenment by themselves and, hence, did not need to be "civilized." Hatred of the Jews, they argue, originated here and has thus become "a deeply imprinted schema, a ritual of civilization" (DE 171).[19]

Like Horkheimer and Adorno, I see the dialectic of modernity as simultaneously engendering opposing possibilities: On the one side of the coin,

construction, progress, and emancipation, and, on the other side of the
coin, destruction, regression, and enslavement. This dialectic is betrayed
at every moment in the cultural and material history of modernization:
The railway—the central example in my book—not only unified nations,
brought together people, and facilitated mass migration, but it also shored
up national borders, isolated people, and facilitated mass deportations. Or,
as Walter Benjamin famously maintained, with respect to the "cultural treasures" of a civilization: "There is no document of civilization which is not
at the same time a document of barbarism."[20] Culture and barbarism are
not simply opposed; rather, they comprise a contradictory unity. But, unlike Horkheimer and Adorno, my project is not to explain historical phenomena such as fascism and anti-Semitism by tracing out long-term gene-
alogies. For them fascism is the telos of Enlightenment absolutism, while
anti-Semitism is tantamount to the very foundation and history of civilization. This is because Jews embody a "negative principle" and thus "must
be exterminated to secure happiness for the world" (DE 168). Although I
find their argument for the explanation of the persistence of anti-Semitism
ingenious, it problematically confines Jews to a pure negativity and thereby
fails to recognize the ways in which Jews contributed to the extension of
"civilization" from within.[21]

Equally significant, the dialectic of modernity, as I articulate the concept here, does not consider fascism and the Holocaust to be the telos of
the Enlightenment; rather, it considers them both to be historically specific possibilities of German/Jewish modernity. That is to say, the Holocaust did not end German/Jewish modernity or prove that the so-called
dialogue had failed; rather, I consider the Holocaust as the most extreme
dialectical expression of this very modernity. In this regard the dialectic of
modernity does not trace out a history of continuous regression, culminating in the brutal totality of the "fully enlightened world radiating disaster
triumphant," with the Holocaust representing the endpoint of a historical
succession. Instead I consider modernity to break down into German/Jew-
ish dialectics, blurred possibilities and overlapping tensions of the varie-
gated movements between German and Jewish. These movements—both
the literal movements of people and the conceptual-historical interactions
between German thinkers and Jewish thinkers—are neither additive nor
modal: They do not constitute a continuous history nor do they have a
definitive direction or teleology. For this reason I am wary of explaining the
Holocaust by modernity—what essentially amounts to using a metaphysi-

cal concept of history to endow the Holocaust with meaning. To apply the apposite critique of Derrida: "This is the concept of history as the history of meaning . . . developing itself, producing itself, fulfilling itself. And doing so linearly, as you recall, in a straight or circular line. . . . The metaphysical character of the concept of history is not only linked to linearity, but to an entire *system* of implications (teleology, eschatology, elevating and interiorizing accumulation of meaning, a certain type of traditionality, a certain concept of continuity, of truth, etc.)."[22] This is a concept of history that this book explicitly disavows.

I can now pose the central methodological question under investigation in this book: how might one map the German/Jewish dialectic of modernity? Rather than writing a cultural history of German/Jewish relations, I have opted to call my study a cultural geography in order to emphasize the significance of space and mobility for the history that I examine. While the discipline of cultural geography lies primarily outside of literary and cultural studies, there are a number of significant points of contact with my own work, not the least of which is the idea that culture is spatially constituted, which I need to clarify briefly. To overly simplify a complex field, cultural geography deals with the cultural and linguistic expressions of people in a particular place as well as their movements, patterns of development, urban environments, and cultural and social landscapes using tools that pull from geography, geology, anthropology, cultural studies, and ethnology.[23] Carl O. Sauer, the legitimate founder of the field, explains that classic cultural geography is "concerned with those works of man [*sic*] that are inscribed into the earth's surface and give to it characteristic expression. . . . The geographic cultural area is taken to consist only of the expressions of man's tenure of the land, the cultural assemblage which records the full measure of man's utilization of the surface."[24] For Sauer the expression of human agency in spatial terms—whether through the building of roads and railways or the carving of new trade routes and frontiers for colonization—is what cultural geographers study.[25]

As the introduction to the seminal anthology *Readings in Cultural Geography* succinctly states: "cultural geography is the application of the idea of culture to geographic problems."[26] In other words, cultural geography attempts to solve geographic problems by examining, distinguishing, classifying, and evaluating certain cultural expressions vis-à-vis their spatial articulations. Since 1962, when this anthology was first published, new appraisals and theoretical models have emerged that have significantly opened up the field beyond solving specifically geographic problems. As Peter Jackson points out in *Maps of Meaning*, the new cultural geography attempts to articulate the "spatial constitution" of culture and its "territorial expression."[27] Other geographers such as Dennis Cosgrove, Edward Soja, and David Harvey have examined the dialectical relationship between culture and geography by focusing on the ways in which space, human landscapes, and spatial relations are socially and culturally constituted.[28] While my study shares a number of conceptual and metholodological points of contact with the field of cultural geography, not least in my analysis of cultural expression in spatial terms, I am not interested in trying to solve any particular "geographic" problem. Instead I am using geography to solve, so to speak, a cultural problem. That is to say, I want to examine the spatial constitution of German/Jewish modernity by mapping its intellectual and cultural history onto a decidedly cultural-geographic surface: the railway system.

For my purposes here, cultural geography is the pendant to cultural history. While my attention to cultural geography betrays many of the same interests as cultural geographers—including the theorization of spatial relations, the centrality of place and landscape to understand cultural production, the attempt to map mobility, and the attention to migration and transnationality—I am much more interested in how cultural geography can help me articulate a theory of modernity. To this end, cultural geography is essentially a practice of history, a kind of historiography, which, as we will see, owes a particular debt to Walter Benjamin by virtue of its antihistoricist, materialist approach to studying cultural artifacts. The cultural geography of German/Jewish modernity presented in this book flattens chronology in order to highlight the mobility, contamination, and exchange between German and Jewish. Both the German language and the places of encounter between German and Jewish thinkers become deterritorialized and remapped according to new constellations, figures, and sites of contact. This has several important theoretical consequences: First of all, in shifting attention away from chronology, it becomes impossible to trace lines of development or continuities. Connections are not made according to the necessity of succession but rather according to the contingency of geography and the possibility of mobility. This means that a cultural geography is radically fractured and discontinuous; it resembles a pile of snapshots of a dialectic. At the same time that succession is given up, it also becomes impossible to assign modality or direction to historical events. Geographies of simultaneity or constellations of possibility are the result.

Concretely speaking, I do not proceed "from" a certain period "to" a certain period because the argument that I am presenting is not linear.[29] At the same time, I do not restrict myself to Germany as a preexisting territorial unit of reference because the argument that I am presenting is not based on nationality. The deterritorialized Germany that I am examining begins in Berlin and Delos and moves to Sicily, New York City, the North Sea, Nuremberg-Fürth, Palestine, Auschwitz, Vienna, Prague, Antwerp, and Paris. What emerges—through the multiplicity of places of contact, mobility, and contention—is a complicated cultural geography of German/Jewish modernity, not a national literary history. By way of an attentiveness to the specificity of geography and mobility, each chapter treats a certain problem in the dialectic of German/Jewish modernity: memory, subjectivity, historicity, nationality, death, and representation. Unlike the Hegelian dialectic, the German/Jewish dialectic is never sublated into something else. Instead, through the logic of the supplement, the dialectic is brought to a standstill at moments of tension: Celan adds to, enriches, and replaces Heidegger; Kafka adds to, enriches, and replaces Goethe; Heine adds to, enriches, and replaces Hegel; Herzl adds to, enriches, and replaces List; and Arendt adds to, enriches, and replaces Heidegger. In the cultural geography that I present here, the hierarchy overturns itself one time, becoming Jewish/German, as Sebald adds to, enriches, and replaces Freud. In effect, I am positing that German modernity cannot be understood without its Jewish other *and* that Jewish modernity cannot be understood without its German other.

The methodological differences between cultural histories and cultural geographies underscore another important issue in German-Jewish studies, namely, the "place" of the Holocaust in such narratives. Nowadays, within the field of German-Jewish cultural history, there is general agreement that the Holocaust was not the inevitable telos of a long-term historical development, although there may still be certain continuities (for example, concerning the history of anti-Semitism) worth investigating. Like Amos Elon, for example, I believe that it makes little sense to see "German Jews doomed from the outset" by tracing out "an inexorable pattern in German history preordained from Luther's day to culminate in the Nazi Holocaust." Elon continues: "I have found only a series of ups and downs and a succession of unforeseeable contingencies, none of which seems to have been inevitable. Alongside the Germany of anti-Semitism, there was a Germany of enlightened liberalism, humane concern, civilized rule of law, good government, social security, and thriving social democracy."[30] And, at the same time that it makes little sense to trace forward the "inevitability" of destruction, it makes just as little sense to "backshadow" the Holocaust by emplotting our retrospective knowledge into the past and judging historical agents "as though they too should have known what was to come."[31]

Both of these problems, however, are particular to a mode of cultural study in which the successive logic of temporality is the structuring principle. In a cultural geography one cannot "foreshadow" or "backshadow" the Holocaust because temporality is flattened in favor of the dialectics of mobility and spaces of exchange. Traditional cultural histories allow us to productively investigate long-term cultural problems (such as the history of the "Jewish question" in German culture or the history of anti-Semitism) by giving us, more or less, synthetic histories with a beginning, a middle, and an end. Depending on how far these cultural histories are taken, the Holocaust enters the horizon—and rightly so—as a definitive end. It conditions the possibility of asking urgent questions such as "What happened?" "What went wrong?" and "Could it have been prevented?" But within the framework of a cultural geography, such questions cannot be asked or answered. Any sort of long-term, explanatory questions that seek to elucidate the development of a certain "track" or the emergence of a "history of mentality" are disallowed as soon as one gives up chronology, lines of influence, teleologies, modalities, and origins. Far from a simple binary, the dialectic of German/Jewish modernity is analyzed within discontinuous spaces of possibility, mobility, contingency, and connectivity, thereby enabling a new topology of concepts and problems to surface.

Over the past few years, the field of German-Jewish studies has moved in such a direction through the work of scholars such as Barbara Hahn, Scott Spector, Jonathan Hess, and Peter Gordon, even if their individual methodological claims are not expressed under the rubric of cultural geography. In her book on Rahel Levin Varnhagen, Bertha Badt-Strauss, Hannah Arendt, Margarete Susman, and other Jewish intellectuals, Hahn, for example, patently refuses to sketch out a "survey" of the history of "the Jewess Pallas Athena"; instead she divides her book into "constellations in which similar figures and similar positions continually reappear," resulting in "a network of references, sometimes difficult to decode, sometimes almost lost to sight."[32] It does not add up to something as comprehensive as a cultural history of German-Jewish modernity. In his *Prague Territories*, Spector explicitly grounds his analysis in a spatial matrix, mapping out cultural expression and problems of nationality through a multiplicity of "circles" around Prague and, more expansively, the "territories" of central Europe.[33] And while Hess and Gordon are not primarily concerned with questions of space and geography, both are concerned with the agency and even partnership of German and German-Jewish intellectuals in shaping the philosophical and cultural landscape of modernity in all its dialectical expressions.[34] For all of these critics a new set of terms, priorities, and methodological investments have emerged for tracking and mapping out the complexity of German-Jewish modernity, ones that differentiate these studies from the commemorative conventions of earlier cultural histories.

In my book the dialectic of German/Jewish modernity is analyzed by investigating the cultures in transit—in short, what might be called mobility studies. The railway—arguably the most iconic association of both the splendor and horror of German/Jewish relations—is not only an important part of the *cultural history* of German/Jewish modernity, something which I indicate by the dialectical images of the Anhalter Bahnhof preceding each chapter, but it also allows us to formulate a theory of *cultural geography* by drawing our attention to the spatial fundament of the dialectic of modernity. I study this dialectic by mapping out German/Jewish modernity—that is to say, by studying the cultural forms in which mobility was imagined, experienced, narrated, and variously expressed. The railway system represents the organizing principle, the material reality, and the cultural metaphor for understanding how German and German-Jewish thinkers construct modernity as a story of mobility. To put it in Benjamin's terms, the (German/Jewish) railway system is the "crystallization" of (German/Jewish) modernity, the distillation of its essential dialectics, "of the total event."[35]

The railway system thus provides the organizing principles of this cultural geography: Stations are infinitely connectable; the tracks are, by definition, bidirectional; the system is nonlinear, acentric, and open-ended; connections are based on the contingency of contiguity; and movement is synchronous. With the rejection of developmental models of history, connections cannot be made by chronology; instead, derived from the cultural geography of the railway system, they are made through new constellations of contiguity: Celan's Berlin is connected to the island of Delos for Heidegger's travels of memory; Sicily, New York City, and Baranovich Station provide the transnational itinerary for the creation of the German/Jewish subject in Goethe, Kafka, and Sholem Aleichem; the North Sea is the locale for mapping Hegel and Heine's movements of Spirit; the first German railway line between Nuremberg and Fürth is connected to Palestine via the national fantasies of Friedrich List and Theodor Herzl; the singularity of Auschwitz represents the site of modernity's transformation of death for Heidegger and Arendt; finally, the modern railway system connecting Vienna, Rome, Prague, Antwerp, and Paris is the basis of conceptualizing new practices of representation for Freud and Sebald. In every case the territorial unit of the German nation cannot be presupposed as a starting point. Nationality and national literary histories are replaced by transnational spaces of encounter, which have the effect of deterritorializing the authority of the German language. Rather than proceeding from the nation, one inquires into the conditions of possibility for nationality, and, in so doing, the German/Jewish dialectic is brought to a momentary standstill in order to articulate the nexus between modernity and mobility.

I would now like to clarify dialectics at a standstill, a concept derived from Walter Benjamin that I use to describe these snapshots of German/Jewish modernity. In the drafts he made for his uncompleted magnum opus, *Das Passagen-Werk*, known in English as *The Arcades Project*, Benjamin coined the term *dialectics at a standstill* to characterize the practice of historical materialism attentive to both the flow and the arrest of historical phenomena. Although it remained a notoriously murky and underdeveloped concept in Benjamin's oeuvre, the concept is important for this study because it contributes, first, to the creation of a discontinuous, nondevelopmental practice of history derived from material culture and, second, to a reconsideration of German/Jewish modernity as a complex interplay rather than a simple opposition. Unlike conventional historiographic practices that aim at reproducing the fullness of the past and are motivated by the belief that the past is worthy in and of itself of being preserved, Benjamin sought to articulate the contingency of the relationship between a given present and a given past as a dialectical image that comes together in a flash: "It's not that what is past casts its light on what is present, or what is present its light on what is past; rather, image is that wherein what has been comes together in a flash with the now to form a constellation" (AP 462). He calls this constellation "dialectics at a standstill" (AP 462). By contrast, he reviled historicism—the idea that the past can be represented "as it really was" such that eventually, over time, with careful and methodical accumulation, the reality of the past could be written, reconstructed, and finally rehabilitated—to be "the strongest narcotic of the nineteenth century" (AP 463).[36] Rather than attempting to produce a "homogenous" or "continuous exposition of history" (AP 470), historical materialism, Benjamin suggested, aimed at a kind of thinking that "comes to a standstill in a constellation saturated with tensions" (AP 475). This thinking "blasts the epoch out of the reified 'continuity of history'" (AP 474), thereby exposing the claims of the losers and the "refuse of history" (*Abfall der Geschichte*; AP 461). These claims and refuse represent what had to be left out, covered up, or forgotten in conventional accounts of history in order to evoke the semblance of progress, continuity, or homogeneity.

Rather than the necessity of chronology, the relationship between what is past and what is present is marked by contingency, "the now of a particular recognizability" (AP 463). This means that the past is not a timeless domain amenable to narrative rehabilitation but always subject to present legibility and recognizability. In the sixteenth thesis on the philosophy of history, Benjamin underscores the significance of the present for the historical materialist: "A historical materialist cannot do without the notion of a present which is not a transition, but in which time stands still and has come to a stop. For this notion defines the present in which he himself is writing history."[37] Unlike the historicist who attempts to produce "the 'eternal' image of the past," the task of the historical materialist is to "blast open the continuum of history" through a kind of thinking that "involves not only the flow of thoughts, but their arrest as well."[38] The historical materialist "[brushes] history against the grain"[39] in order to interrupt the seemingly inexorable flow of "history" and salvage some of the refuse that has been subsumed, lost, or edited out. The cultural geography of this book is an attempt to brush the history of modernity against the grain.

Although Rolf Tiedemann considered the "dialectical image" and "dialectics at a standstill" to be "without a doubt, the central categories of the *Passagen-Werk*," Benjamin, he notes, never completely fleshed out how these concepts would inform a philosophy of history nor did he ever use them with "any terminological consistency."[40] According to Tiedemann, the concept "dialectics at a standstill" first surfaced in a 1935 exposé in which Benjamin "localized dialectical images as dream and wish images in the collective subconscious."[41] Here the collective dreams its successor while referring back to "Ur-history" and the utopian ideal of a classless society: "Ambiguity is the manifest imaging of dialectic, the law of dialectics at a standstill. The standstill is utopia, and the dialectical image, therefore, dream image. Such an image is afforded by the commodity per se: as fetish."[42] After criticism from Adorno, Tiedemann notes that Benjamin dropped this line of thought in favor of an understanding of dialectics at a standstill that "seems to function almost as a heuristic principle, a proce-dure that enables the historical materialist to maneuver his objects."[43]

According to Max Pensky, Benjamin's concept of the dialectical image, despite "all the permutations and variations [had] . . . a remarkable degree of consistency," which revolved around a few key terms: "dream and waking, myth and critical insight, historical continuum and shocking interruption, phantasmagoria and image, fetish and historical object."[44] At the intersec-tion of these axes, as Susan Buck-Morss has demonstrated, is the dialectical image, the crystallization of ostensibly antithetical elements, in which "the 'fundamental coordinates' of the modern world" can be recognized.[45] For my purposes here, I am particularly interested in how Benjamin's concept of dialectics at a standstill can be used, first, to generate a critical, materialist historiography and, second, to articulate some of the fundamental coordi-nates, so to speak, of German/Jewish modernity. But rather than attempt-ing to clarify or further explicate the concept, I will attempt to perform or enact it in the chapters that follow.

In terms of a critical materialist historiography, Benjamin conceived of the dialectical image, as Michael Jennings has pointed out, "as a powerful antidote to the concept of progress, for him the most dangerous ideologi-cal weapon in the capitalist arsenal."[46] The critic's juxtaposition of images is invested with a revolutionary power to transform consciousness, some-thing that results in a concept of history decidedly unlike the progressive logic of the Hegelian dialectic. Benjamin's dialectics are at a standstill pre-cisely to halt the forward-moving progress of history such that particular-ity is no longer inexorably subsumed into the universal. The result is an antidevelopmental practice of history in which what is past enters into and out of legibility according to the contingency of a given present. Unlike the "additive" method of any sort of universal history, which "musters a mass of data to fill the homogeneous, empty time,"[47] a materialist historiogra-phy freezes the dialectic, if only for a moment, in order to blast the image "from the continuum of historical process" (AP 475). As such, "history breaks down into images, not into stories" (AP 476; translation slightly altered), and it is in these configurations of dialectics at standstill that the historical materialist finds "a revolutionary chance in the fight for the op-pressed past."[48]

The following six chapters of this book, each preceded by a dialectical image of the Anhalter Bahnhof, represent a moment in which the move-ments of the German/Jewish dialectic have come to a standstill. These chapters do not add up to produce a "history" but rather, through the ways in which mobility is variously mapped by the thinkers under consideration, blast apart any claims to continuous development or narrative rehabilitation. German/Jewish modernity does not lead anywhere; instead it opens up a radically deterritorialized cultural and linguistic geography. The task of this study is to map out and salvage some of the remains of this modernity.

I can now say something about the overall ambition of the project and the status of the German/Jewish pairings in each chapter. In terms of ambition, Benjamin's concept of dialectics at a standstill provides the materialist grounding and historiographic impetus for my cultural geography, which attempts to track some of the movements, tensions, and expressions of German/Jewish modernity. In terms of the status of the pairings, the concept provides a way of reconceiving the relationship between German and Jewish beyond a simple binary opposition or a normative orientation of the "German" (which is "bad") and a normative orientation of the "Jewish" (which is "good"). My argument is that the one cannot be understood without the other, and that both are in a productive tension, which takes many different forms, valuations, and expressions. It is not that the German simply stands for one thing and the Jewish for its opposite; rather, the separatrix between German and Jewish means that the relationship is ambiguous and coconstitutive, a dialectic marked by undecidability, movement, slippage, and contamination. Far from mere oppositions, then, List and Herzl, for example, are both concerned with nationality; Sebald and Freud are both concerned with how contingency became the defining attribute of modernist practices of representation. And even in cases where the German "side" of the dialectic comes to stand for something normative (such as Hegel's conception of world history or Heidegger's "groundedness" of memory), it can only be recognized as such by way of the Jewish "side" of the dialectic (Heine's ghost stories or Celan's layered topographies), adding to, enriching, and productively engaging with the German "side." What emerges is not a simple opposition but a dialectic at a standstill, a moment in which a new image or constellation emerges that allows us to reassess and reinterpret the culture from which the thinkers, ideas, and objects came. This is only possible, to invoke Benjamin, because the historical materialist or cultural geographer makes choices from the perspective of the present about what texts and authors to bring together in a productive, potentially explosive tension.

The Geography of Cultural Studies

Because the separatrix simultaneously separates two (or potentially more) concepts and brings them together in a dialectical unity, the fact
of a separatrix is the starting point for any study of mobility. The undecidability of the relationship between the terms conditions their movement,
slippage, and tension. As in German/Jewish, it is a relationship characterized by contamination, exchange, hybridity, connection, transnationality,
and displacement. An attempt to definitively separate them only reveals the
extent to which the one is constitutive of the other. And just as significantly,
the terms cannot be sublated into something else, as if the particularity of
German and Jewish could be synthesized into something like a universal
modernity. The modernity that I am studying here breaks down into dialectical encounters between German and Jewish, images of enabling and
checking, facilitating and arresting mobility. This book constructs a cultural geography of German/Jewish modernity by mapping snapshots of
this dialectic at a standstill. In this respect, it shares something of Adorno's
assessment of Benjamin's thought, namely, "the obligation to think at the
same time dialectically and undialectically."[49]

In providing one of its first theoretical reflections, Stephen Greenblatt
described mobility studies as the tracking of the "restless and often unpredictable movements" of language and literature.[50] According to Greenblatt,
the primary concern of literary history and the study of literature and languages can no longer be the charting of progress, the analysis of organic
development, or the security of origins; instead literary studies, conceived as
the study of mobility, examines the contingent interactions and sometimes
bloody encounters between people on the move. In his words, "We need to
understand colonization, exile, emigration, wandering, contamination, and
unexpected consequences, along with the fierce compulsions of greed, longing, and restlessness, for it is these disruptive forces, not a rooted sense of
cultural legitimacy, that principally shape the history and diffusion of languages."[51] At the core of mobility studies is a recognition of contingency, that
things could have been otherwise. Any sort of historicist assumptions about
inevitable teleologies, transcendental units of analysis, or the unbleached
recovery of "how it really was" are rejected out of hand. This does not mean
that everything goes, that every story is as good as every other story, or that
history is reduced to randomly chosen events.[52] Rather, it means that we
must create modes of writing cultural criticism in which the contingency

of location, language, and transmission—all things that make the borders of any language and national literature, not to mention what constitutes the literary, far from clear—comes to the forefront of our analyses.

Although the purpose of this book is not to propose something as comprehensive, grandiose, or as highly structured as a new literary history, it might be useful to mention some of the conventional organizational premises of historical emplotment. If temporality is taken to be the raw material, so to speak, of literary history, questions of chronology (designations of before and after or not yet and no longer), origins, end points, modalities (history as direction), teleologies (history as an inevitability), and periodization are generally the privileged terms of analysis.[53] If, however, mobility is taken to be the raw material of historical analysis, a new emphasis on the relationship between space and time informs the investigation, allowing us to focus on the complexities of intercultural transmission, contamination, exchange, translation, migration, and transgression. An account of the relationship between space—both the space in literature and of literature in space, to use Franco Moretti's distinction[54]—and temporality—both diachronic changes and synchronic events—becomes a central part of the study of culture. Indeed, these are the kinds of premises that have informed the fragmentary geographies of the "new histories" of French and German literature.[55]

In addition to the work of Moretti, a significant body of work on literary geography and mobility studies has emerged in recent years, particularly within the fields of cultural studies of transnationality and globalization.[56] It is here that the limitations of national literatures have been critically assessed with a view toward reexamining the complexity of cultural production by exposing structures of hegemony and discourses of exclusivity. Somewhat less attention, however, has been given to the problem of how to write such a cultural geography—that is to say, to what it might look like in practice. In her afterword to *The Literary Channel*, an anthology of essays examining the international cultural production and transmission of the novel between France and England, Emily Apter indicates three studies that begin to imagine what such models might look like. Here, she cites Rey Chow's "diaspora studies," Moretti's "distant reading," and Perry Anderson's "new cartography" as being "representative of a new kind of literary history that circumvents nation-based criticism even as it recognizes that no general theory of literature can dispense with the nation as a crucible of historical and aesthetic comparison."[57] My own work builds on and shares certain conceptual affinities with these new geographical approaches to studying cultures in transit.

Given the importance of mobility—whether diaspora or exile, emigration or dislocation, travel or deportation—within Jewish history, it may be surprising to learn that the vast majority of work in the fields of cultural geography and mobility studies has been done by scholars far removed from Jewish studies.[58] Within the field of geographically oriented cultural studies, the attention to mobility and space goes back to James Clifford's seminal essay "Traveling Cultures," in which he attempted to shift the field of cultural anthropology away from privileging relations of "dwelling" to investigating the complexities of movement, encounter, and cultural exchange.[59] For Clifford, the study of mobility allows us to recognize new types of agency that constitute "discrepant cosmopolitanisms" across cultural, social, national, and linguistic borders. These movements, encounters, and exchanges always take place in space and are mediated by certain temporal and spatial practices,[60] which, according to Clifford, require us "to rethink cultures as sites of dwelling *and* travel."[61]

Not unlike Clifford, Homi Bhabha situates the "location of culture" within a postcolonial framework in which geography and mobility also come to the foreground. Bhabha argues that culture must be understood as both transnational and translational

> because contemporary postcolonial discourses are rooted in specific histories of cultural displacement, whether they are the "middle passage" of slavery and indenture, the "voyage out" of the civilizing mission, the fraught accommodations of Third World migration to the West after the Second World War, or the traffic of economic and political refugees within and outside the Third World . . . [and] because such spatial histories of displacement—now accompanied by the territorial ambitions of "global" media technologies—make the question of how culture signifies, or what is signified by *culture*, a rather complex issue.[62]

This question of signification is complex precisely because of "the transnational dimension of cultural transformation"—that is to say, because of mobility and its consequences of cultural hybridity, plurality, and contingency, particularly in an age of globalized media.[63] For Bhabha the analysis of culture from a postcolonial perspective requires a resistance to any sort of "unifying discourse" or "holistic forms of social explanation" and the embrace of "forms of dialectical thinking that do not disavow or sublate the otherness (alterity) that constitutes the symbolic domain of psychic and social identifications."[64] The snapshots of the fractured, discontinuous dialectic of German/Jewish modernity offered here are an attempt to produce an analysis of culture attentive to both the transnational and translational effects of mobility.

Within the field of cultural studies perhaps the most important work to examine the problems of modernity within a transnational, intercultural framework explicitly against "nationalist or ethnically absolute approaches" is Paul Gilroy's *The Black Atlantic*.[65] Gilroy takes "the fatal junction of the concept of nationality with the concept of culture" as his starting point for addressing "the stereophonic, bilingual, or bifocal cultural forms originated by, but no longer the exclusive property of, blacks dispersed within the structures of feeling, producing, communicating, and remembering ... the black Atlantic world" (BA 2, 3). Breaking from the conventions of English and American cultural studies, which, at the time his book appeared, were still ensconced in rigidly eurocentric models of nationality, Gilroy's study of modernity derives from the transcultural, international formation he calls the black Atlantic. As a "rhizomorphic, fractal structure" (BA 4) for representing the complexity of both cultural and human transport, the black Atlantic, "continually crisscrossed by the movements of black people—not only as commodities but engaged in various struggles towards emancipation, autonomy, and citizenship—provides a means to reexamine the problems of nationality, location, identity, and historical memory" (BA 16). In effect, Gilroy introduces a new cultural geography, derived from the dialectics of mobility, to articulate the counterculture of modernity.

For Gilroy the organizing image for the black Atlantic is the ship—with its various kinds of cargo—moving across the water separating Europe, the Americas, Africa, and the Caribbean. As Gilroy indicates and as I will discuss in more detail in the chapters that follow, ship travel is a central paradigm of Western cultural existence. It calls upon a wide range of experiences such as voyages of discovery, conquest, and enslavement as well as a wealth of metaphors, including journeys of progress, enlightenment, and education. And, materially, ships "were the living means by which the points within [the] Atlantic world were joined. They were mobile elements that stood for the shifting spaces in between the fixed places that they encountered. Accordingly they need to be thought of as cultural and political units rather than abstract embodiments of the triangular trade" (BA 16–17). As Gilroy underscores through the image of the ship on the black Atlantic, mobility must always be considered dialectically, as moving simultaneously in two directions: emancipation and enslavement, discovery and destruction. In this regard, building off the work of Bakhtin and Clifford, he sees the ship as a new "chronotope" for rethinking the cultural study of modernity beyond the boundaries of both conventional historiographies and traditional nation-states (BA 17).

Analogous to travel by ship, travel by train cannot be circumscribed to preexisting national borders. With the construction of an interconnected, international railway system at the end of the nineteenth century, travel by train was, by definition, transnational and translational, in the sense described by Bhabha; but, perhaps paradoxically, it was precisely the railway that played a significant part in German national unification by literally connecting together the fragmented space of the "dormant nation." This paradox will be examined in detail in chapter 5 under the rubric of "some assembly required" when I discuss List and Herzl. In this respect, my study of mobility, following Apter's admonition, cannot dispense with the nation "as a crucible of historical and aesthetic comparison." At the same time, I will argue that these geographies of mobility—whether the black Atlantic or the transcontinental railway—deterritorialize the nation by opening up new social and political spaces for cultural exchange and encounter. Like the black Atlantic, such spaces emerge beyond the binaries of nationality and diaspora and, therefore, require new approaches to cultural and literary studies that are not strictly nation based or chronologically driven.[66]

In much the same way that Benjamin looked to the arcade to examine how the hopes, desires, dreams, and fears of an epoch lay buried in its architectural and cultural forms, I look to the materiality of the railway system to investigate the deterritorialized cultural geography of German/ Jewish modernity. As Benjamin suggested in *The Arcades Project*, a historical materialist must turn to the leftover remains—from architectural achievements to cultural ephemera, from railway stations to works of literature—to offer up the "physiognomy" of an epoch from the perspective of the contingency of the present. The trove of cultural sources under investigation here ranges from travel literature, poetry, philosophy, and photography to railway maps, train schedules, decrepit railway tracks, bombed out stations, and abandoned machinery. As both material witnesses to a bygone epoch and as figures for the finitude of any practice of cultural criticism, they all testify to the dialectics of mobility and thereby represent a starting and ending point for my reflections on the cultural geographies of German/Jewish modernity.

Ultimately, of course, the cultural forms do not add up to something whole. The cultural geography presented here is fractured and partial, representing just one possibility for mapping German/Jewish modernity. Other possibilities might focus on different thinkers or other relationships and produce a very different map of the "stations" where the dialectic comes to a standstill. Nevertheless, I think that my choice of examples allows me to construct a compelling account of this modernity by mapping the multiple and complex ways in which the separatrix between German and Jewish renders the two terms inseparably connected and indefinitely mobile. Furthermore, by focusing on the ways in which these thinkers variously map mobility, the problems of memory, subjectivity, historicity, nationality, death, and representation—all critical terms for understanding any modernity—are given a new cultural genealogy. The payoff is not only a new cultural genealogy of German/Jewish modernity but also an interdisciplinary methodology—cultural geography—for writing about cultures in transit.

Let me now say something about the chapters that follow. All of the chapters begin with the assumption that there is something irreducibly anthropological about the study of modernity. How else can the plans, hopes, anxieties, and answers built into its material objects and written into its texts and discourses be studied, if not by examining modernity's remains, by finding and piecing together some of its fragments? As the art historian T. J. Clark has recently indicated in his episodic history of modernism, the visual forms that modernity gave rise to—that is to say, its answers—are no longer readily comprehensible to us today because we have arrived on the scene too late, after both its realization and self-destruction, what Clark sees as the complementary horrors of modernization.[67] We know what happened, and no amount of philosophical bracketing will deliver—at least not in good faith—the pure forms of modernity in and on their own terms. The "pure form" is but a pretext for horror. And no amount of historical reconstruction will patch together the pieces into a former whole. In that sense, studying the objects, discourses, and documents of modernity is an exercise in futility because, paradoxically, the pieces do not add up yet cry out for unity.

I begin and end my study with the remains of the Anhalter Bahnhof, the wasteland of scattered industrial debris and architectural ruins that bear witness to a former whole. As a culturally stratified site, the dialectics of

German/Jewish modernity can be traced in the material remains of the Anhalter Bahnhof. The task, however, is not to reconstruct the station or its history; instead, as I suggest in chapter 2, it is to construct a philosophy of history, an approach to cultural criticism, out of its materiality. As Adorno wrote in *Negative Dialectics*, "We are not to philosophize about concrete things; we are to philosophize, rather, out of these things."[68] The wastelands of the Anhalter Bahnhof—its concrete, material remains—disrupt the homogenizing processes of "historicization" because they are "out of joint" with respect to both historical time and the time of the present. They are ruins that have not yet been decided, not yet subsumed into a discourse of historical intelligibility. In a word, they represent the unmastered remains of German/Jewish modernity.

As I show in the second chapter, it is precisely this undecidability that Celan preserves in his poetry but that Heidegger seeks to overcome in his philosophy. Both turn to material remains—for Celan it is the ruins of Berlin's Anhalter Bahnhof, whereas for Heidegger it is the ruins of ancient Greece—in order to articulate the urgency of the concept of memory after the destruction of World War II. I bring Heidegger and Celan together as a snapshot of the German/Jewish dialectic of modernity by examining two autobiographical travel narratives composed in 1962: Heidegger's account of his voyage to the Greek island of Delos, *Aufenthalte* (Stopovers), and Celan's train travels through Europe in the poem "La Contrescarpe." Whereas Heidegger pursues the rootedness of place to ground the concept of memory, Celan envisions a kind of topographical memory in which the stratified remains of the past are encountered, however briefly, in the contingency of the present.

This chapter also serves to introduce the two paradigms of mobility under consideration in this study: travel by ship and travel by train. For Heidegger the sea voyage to Delos is a voyage of confirmation, in which he attempts to locate, in the most literal sense of the word, the groundedness of Greco-German being. As we will see in my subsequent discussion of Goethe, Hegel, and Herzl, the "meta-epistemology of the ship" (something exemplified by Heidegger's travel narrative) is a long-standing ideological configuration, which is consistently linked with the production of a strong, nationally grounded subject with a safe, transcendental perspective on the world "out there." By contrast, the railway system—as a horizontally differentiated, third-order network—is a structure of mobility that fundamentally prevents such a perspective and thereby gives rise to a less aggregated form of subjectivity as well as different possibilities of representation. Taking Heine's famous observation that railways have killed space and time as my entry point, I analyze the "meta-epistemology of the railway" in Kafka, List, Freud, and Sebald as a dialectical configuration of contingency specific to modernity.

In chapter 3 I consider the question of the German/Jewish subject by looking at the meta-epistemology of mobility in Goethe's *Italienische Reise* (Italian journey), Kafka's *Der Verschollene* (The man who went missing), and Sholem Aleichem's *Railroad Stories*. The subject of German/Jewish modernity, I argue, emerges in the deterritorialized, non-national spaces of encounter—between Sicily, New York City, and the Baranovich Station—in which mobility is variously experienced and mapped in these travel narratives. Whereas Goethe's *Italienische Reise* and his novel of education, *Wilhelm Meister*, narrate the formation of a German subject without a nation by mapping the spaces of geographic, linguistic, and political privilege, the travels of Kafka's fictional figure, Karl Rossmann, map the desubjectification of the immigrant as a dislocated mass object of modernization. As a figure of abjection, he is severed from all geographies of nationality, citizenship, religion, and language. I place Kafka's novel within the context of Jewish travel writing in Yiddish, particularly Sholem Aleichem's contemporaneous *Railroad Stories*, in order to show how the modernist Jewish subject emerges in the dialectical and disaggregated network of the railway. The formation of the German/Jewish subject is illustrated in the conceptual, cultural, and material spaces of encounter between German and Jewish mobility.

Chapter 4, "The North Sea," examines the concept of historicity by articulating a nautical space of encounter between Hegel and Heine. I show how Hegel's lectures on the philosophy of world history can be read as a travel narrative of World Spirit and that Heine's *Reisebilder* (Pictures of travel), although ostensibly "images" from his travels through Germany and Italy, deconstruct Hegel's all-consuming philosophy by repeating it with a Jewish difference. Heine transforms the travel narrative into a critique of history by taking the grand historical narrative, with its investment in the "Greek" trope of seafaring, and deconstructing its systematic claims of national belonging and teleological development. Through an analysis of the "North Sea" poems, I show how Heine reworks both the genre of travel literature as self-discovery and Hegel's geographically determined movement of "World Spirit." The result is a nonsystematic Jewish conception of historicity, which, in its embrace of particularity, subverts the absolutism of Hegel's philosophy of history by exposing the very metaphors upon which its progressive development relies.

Not without irony, Hegel's philosophy of world history as a sea voyage of World Spirit had a significant afterlife in the early Zionist imaginary. Jewish thinkers such as Max Grunwald and Theodor Herzl elevated the seafaring Jew into a historical paradigm of national and colonial rejuvenation. The result, as I show in chapter 5, is that Jews—far from being a landlocked people condemned to wander from nation to nation—actually set sail and thus have a claim, in Hegel's sense of the word, to be world-historical people. In fact, the Zionist idea of nationality was consistently articulated as a politics of mobility: Seafaring and train travel not only provided the practical means of transporting the Jews of Europe to Palestine, but it also helped solidify a Jewish national consciousness, something that Herzl underscored in his own travels and writings about Zionism in *Der Judenstaat* (The Jewish state) and his Jewish bildungsroman, *Altneuland* (Old-new land).

By looking to the relatively recent model of German unification, Herzl argued that the age-old Jewish question needed an analogous solution, which he considered to be the establishment of a modern Jewish nation. In chapter 5 I focus on two discursive periods in which the future-directed fantasies of German and Jewish nationality, respectively, conditioned one another dialectically: The period around 1835, emblematically represented by the ideas of German railway pioneer Friedrich List, and the period around 1900, emblematically represented by the ideas of Theodor Herzl, the founder of modern Zionism. Here the German/Jewish dialectic of modernity paralleled another dialectic, namely, that of nationality and globalization. By examining a range of cultural expressions—including Fichte's speeches to the German nation, List's railway plans, the Young Germany controversy, and the development of national literary histories—I show how inwardly directed fantasies of German nationality were dependent upon encoding the Jew as global. Then, in the second part of this chapter, I show how the outwardly directed fantasies of Jewish nationality were dependent upon the inward history of German national unification. In both cases the fantasy of German/Jewish nationality needs its other for self-legitimation. My cultural geography thereby links the first German railway line between Nuremberg and Fürth—historically and conceptually—to Palestine.

Chapter 6 turns to the destruction of the other and the modernity of mass death. Significantly, both this chapter on Heidegger and Arendt and the next on Freud and Sebald do not "follow" from the previous chapters in the developmental sense that one might expect from a linear cultural history. It is here that one recognizes the fractured possibilities of a cultural geography: there is no attempt to anticipate, explain, or historicize the Holocaust because it is not situated chronologically as a kind of end point or telos of a history of meaning; instead it is broached as a dialectical possibility of German/Jewish modernity. I begin this chapter by grounding the deportation of German Jews in the specificity of the Anhalter Bahnhof and the transports of elderly Jews from Berlin who were sent to the concentration camp of Theresienstadt from this station. But, rather than analyzing the deportations as an instance of mobile modernity, I focus on the immobilization of the German/Jewish dialectic itself—that is, the Nazi attempt to absolutely destroy the Jewish other. The modernity of mass death, I suggest, represents the core of this immobilization.

Although both Heidegger and Arendt use the same phrase—"the fabrication of corpses"—to describe this destruction, the concept of death and, hence, the concept of life are far from congruous in the two thinkers. To explicate the essential differences, I compare Arendt's reflections on totalitarianism, particularly her discussion of mass death in *The Origins of Totalitarianism* (1949/51), with Heidegger's reflections on authenticity and mass death in his Bremen lectures of 1949. Although Arendt adopted Heidegger's critique of modernity into her political theory, I show the divergence of their thought with regard to the Holocaust and the significance of mass death to philosophy. While Arendt traces the transformation of human nature with the historical achievement of state-sponsored mass death, Heidegger never gives up the paradigm of authenticity for understanding death as one's most individualizing possibility and will, therefore, insist that the victims of mass death never "died." In the final analysis, I suggest, Heidegger's thinking—not just about death but also about memory—fundamentally precludes the thought of mass death, something that not only prevents him from thinking the Holocaust but even redeems the Nazi's failure to absolutely immobilize the German/Jewish dialectic.

In chapter 7 I turn to the construction of the railway system across Europe and use Freud and Sebald to reflect on the problem of representation in German/Jewish modernism. As my final stop of the German/Jewish dialectic, Sebald, I argue, shares an important conceptual and epistemological connection with the early thought of Freud: The railway system is the condition of possibility for modernist modes of representation. After abandoning the logocentrism of the so-called seduction theory in late 1897,

Freud, particularly in *The Interpretation of Dreams* and his essay on "Screen Memories," opens up the possibility that memory is not set down once and for all but rather subject to various movements through the open-ended processes of rearrangement, retranscription, connection, displacement, and contingency. Memory, like history, does not correspond to the replication of the past but rather calls upon the mobile interpretation of what remains in the space of the present. For Freud it is the modernity of the railway system that offers—through its seemingly infinite connectivity, contingency, and open-endedness—not only a model for the mobility of memory but also the conceptual basis of modernist practices of representation and the interpretative work of psychoanalysis itself. By mapping his most famous "Jewish" dream of Rome, "My Son, the Myops," I show how his interpretation of the dream follows the logic of an acentric railway system in which the free play of associative links expands indefinitely into a complex, open-ended, horizontally differentiated network of mobility.

While the mobility of the railway system offers the conditions of conceptuality for both Freud and Sebald's theories of representation, I argue that Sebald also sees the railway as the material embodiment of the dialectic of modernity. The stratified remains of the railway figure significantly in both his critique of the dialectic of German/Jewish modernity and his practice of historical representation. By divorcing the representation of the past from a literalist replication of what happened, Sebald, following Freud, introduces a new possibility to historical emplotment, namely, a cultural geography of the present. Here the remains of German/Jewish modernity are shown—once again—to be inextricably entangled in one another. His novels, particularly *Austerlitz,* are extended meditations on the present possibilities of representing the modernity of the German/Jewish catastrophe, and I illustrate this through the layered cultural geographies connecting Sebald and Freud via Vienna, Rome, Prague, Antwerp, and Paris. Through their artificial closures, ruptures, periscopic narration, and simultaneous histories, Sebald's works, with their modernist roots in Freudian theories of representation, offer a materialist history of the present as a dialectical site of uncertainty. In so doing, he transforms history into an investigation of cultural geography, in which the conceptual, material, and cultural remains of German/Jewish modernity are forever "contaminated" by one another.

2. BERLIN AND DELOS
Celan's No-Places and Heidegger's Homecomings
Philosophy and Poetry Out of Material History

2.1 Fenced-off ruins of the Anhalter Bahnhof, Berlin (1997). *Author's photograph*

I FIRST SAW the ruins of the Anhalter Bahnhof a number of years ago, as I was walking north along Möckernstrasse toward Berlin's Potsdamer Platz. I came upon a densely forested region on the left-hand side of the street that was enclosed by a fence several meters high. Heeding the numerous warning signs of "no trespassing," like any well-behaved urban flaneur, I stood on the cement ledge encircling the land and peered through the metal slats of the fence. Buried by the jungle of trees and thick shrubbery, I discerned an urban wasteland of trash, industrial debris, and railway tracks. As I continued north for a couple of hundred meters along Möckernstrasse, I arrived at a well-manicured, grassy flatland about the size of a soccer field—and found people using it for exactly that purpose. Along the periphery was a group of saplings, outlining the rectangular field; in its center, at the far end of the field, stood the architectural ruins of a portal with three entryways. Realizing it was part of a bombed-out building from World War II, I asked someone what it was. "Those are the remains of the Anhalter Bahnhof." The empty space where we stood, surrounded by saplings, was the ground upon which the gigantic train station once sat. The fenced-off area, now overgrown by some forty years of vegetation, is what is left of the railway tracks leading south out of the city of Berlin.

2.2 Field with the remains of the entrance portal to the Anhalter Bahnhof, Berlin (1997). *Courtesy of the Granger Collection, New York*

It is hard to imagine that this urban wasteland of tracks, this grass-covered field, and these ruined pieces of the entrance hall could have inspired Walter Benjamin to celebrate the station's greatness. Yet during its legendary heyday in the 1920s and 1930s, a newspaper once mythologized the station like this: "Berlin-Anhalter Bahnhof! One ought to say these words very slowly: Anhalter Bahnhof! For this railway station opens up a world, a separate world, unparalleled and peerless; like hardly another, it is a gateway of entry and exit, a point of entry to the South, to Italy, France, and Spain."[1] I sensed that these hopes and desires, dreams and fantasies, fears and anxieties from a bygone epoch lived on—just barely—as a ghostly presence in the Anhalter Bahnhof's surviving ruins.

Today only the station's north entrance portal, standing at a fraction of its former height of nearly 35 meters, remains as a testimony to its former greatness. Since 2002 the formerly empty land behind the ruined entrance portal has become the permanent home of Tempodrom, a world-famous, international music theater and cultural festival. About 200 meters south of the portal, one encounters the *Brach-Gelände* (wasteland) of the train station, consisting of multiple, split train tracks, decrepit machinery, ruined buildings, and other urban detritus. The *Brach-Gelände* have been closed-off for years, and, since at least 1987, enclosed by fences and restricted by government order, presumably because the region is dangerous, being over-run by dilapidated tracks, construction debris, and some fifty years of vegetation. The remains are thus held in (temporary) check, spatially bound and separated from the surrounding land, suspended (*épochè*), awaiting a decision, perhaps awaiting a sort of redemption.

THE GERMAN/JEWISH SPECTERS OF HISTORY

On May 8, 2005, the sixtieth anniversary of Germany's defeat, the Berlin Holocaust memorial—a massive sea of twenty-seven hundred concrete columns of varying size—was officially dedicated after years of public debate and controversy. When the ground for the memorial was first broken, some seven years earlier, two closely related news stories broke in Germany, just days apart, both of which demonstrated how unsettled, entangled, and present the German/Jewish past remained. The first story concerned the confession of a former Gestapo member and the subsequent discourse of understanding and adjudicating his crimes more than fifty years after they occurred. The second story concerned the material space of the memorial itself and the excavation of the remains of several Nazi buildings from the ground where it was to be built. When the memorial was officially dedicated in 2005, both of these stories from the past were regrafted onto the present. I will use them to situate the materiality of the German/Jewish dialectic of modernity.

On March 4, 1998, German prosecutors announced the arrest of a suspected Nazi war criminal, a seventy-eight-year-old man residing in Stuttgart who acknowledged personally killing five hundred camp prisoners, primarily Jews, at the concentration camp Maidanek. He was further implicated

by German authorities in organizing the slaughter of up to eighty thousand
Jews in 1943 during the so-called Operation Harvest Festival, a major Nazi
operation in Poland involving prisoners from Maidanek and the Ukrainian
city of Lvov.[2] The same day the story broke, Josef Joffe, the prominent political commentator, writer, and then editor of the *Süddeutsche Zeitung,* gave
a provocative interview about the story on National Public Radio (NPR).
He reacted to the so-called haunt of the fascist past returning so unpredictably in its most gruesome and raw form through the living confession of a
Gestapo member toward the end of his life. Joffe speculated that perhaps
the man sought a sort of earthly "redemption," waiting and living more
than fifty years before making his confession. Joffe further reacted to the
inevitable generational gaps in "coming to terms with" the Holocaust: the
third generation is temporally "further" from the event and can "safely" and
openly deal with the Nazi past without "repressing" its burdens. He concluded by saying, "It's been more than fifty years since the Holocaust. . . .
The monster is safely caged, and, therefore, it is easier to look at it."[3]

The second story concerns a similar specter from the Nazi past, but,
rather than a living perpetrator, it concerns the living-on of the material
ruins of Nazi buildings. The debate about building a National Holocaust
Memorial in Berlin—a debate that has proceeded almost unabated in the
press since 1988, the year in which Lea Rosh galvanized the Citizen's Initia-
tive to build a memorial in Berlin,[4] and has continued right up through the
unveiling of the memorial—became embroiled in an impossible historical
materiality: On the site where the memorial was to be erected, the bunker
of Joseph Goebbels was excavated. The twenty thousand square meters of
land allotted in 1992 by Helmut Kohl had been an empty wasteland for
nearly fifty years. It laid just north of the former Gestapo Headquarters (the
so-called Topography of Terror) and the monumental building projects on
Potsdamer Platz, directly south of the Brandenburg Gate, and next to the
eastern border of the Tiergarten. On March 9, 1998, one of Berlin's chief
newspapers, the *Berliner Morgenpost,* described an aerial photograph of the
recently excavated region:

> The gigantic grounds of the former ministerial garden, to the right of
> Ebertstraße, are still a desolate wasteland. Here, on the upper third, the
> Holocaust memorial is to be built. On historically fraught land. An aerial
> photograph still shows the relics from the Nazi period, relics that excava-
> tors are removing little by little. On the top left (on Behrenstraße), in the

former garden of the Ministry of Nutrition and Agriculture, the recently discovered bunker of Goebbels is recognizable. His villa laid to the left of it, connected to the garden of the Reich's president. The remains still exist of a number of smaller buildings for adjutants, built between 1939 and 1944, and the air-raid shelters still exist in the middle. At the bottom of the picture are the former grounds of the Reich's Chancellery. To the left, the foundations of guardhouses complete with their underground garages and workshops. To the right, the foundational orangery wall, also called Hitler's palm house.[5]

In both cases the haunt of the fascist past returns as a disruptive force in the present-day historical, political, and cultural landscapes of Germany. As Joffe alluded, no one could have speculated that this former Gestapo member would have confessed to his crimes when he did; similarly, no one openly knew that the land where the memorial for the Jewish victims of the Holocaust is being erected would be found, upon excavation, to be the final hiding place of Joseph Goebbels and numerous other high-ranking Nazi officials headquartered in Berlin.

But it is precisely because of this disruptive uncertainty that it is premature to say that "the monster [of fascism] is safely caged." For, in so doing, Joffe has to appeal to a linear temporal span that has elapsed—more than fifty years—to mark, suspend, and temporally "cage" a bygone epoch. The problem, as both the coming forward of the Gestapo guard and the discovery of Goebbel's ruined bunker indicate, is that a disjuncture exists between this measured and elapsed segment of time (its distance as fifty plus years) and the spatial proximity, the intimate neighborliness of ruins, relics, ghosts, and living specters of the past in the urban space of the present. The fact of survivors (whether victims, bystanders, or perpetrators) and the fact of contaminated ruins in the city spaces of Germany disrupt the integrity of the distinction between "the past" and "the present." The experience of safety is thus misleading because all the specters from the Nazi past, whether people or material spaces, have not been (perhaps cannot yet, or ever, be) conjured, placated, and buried.[6]

In trying to conceptualize such disjunctures in historical experience, Ernst Bloch introduced the concept of "die Gleichzeitigkeit des Ungleichzeitigen," in his book, *Heritage of Our Times*.[7] This term, variously translated as the "simultaneity of the nonsimultaneous" or the "contemporaneity of the noncontemporaneous," is predicated on the idea that different times, specifically different speeds of development and disintegration, contribute to the experience of a given present. It is a term that has gained favor by historians of Germany, such as David Blackbourn and Geoff Eley, who have been hard-pressed to account for the "uneven, and potentially explosive, juxtaposition of the old and the new, of what has been superseded and what is still in the process of taking shape."[8] Reinhart Koselleck, for example, appropriated the term in his conceptual-historical account of the effect of modernity, or *Neuzeit*, as betraying a multiplicity of coexisting times and spaces that were only subsequently organized diachronically for the sake of charting progress.[9]

If we turn to material space, we might say that Berlin's disjointed topography is simultaneously haunted by the material remains of two of Germany's nonsimultaneous pasts, Communism and Fascism. Examples of this are, of course, not hard to find. The debate over the Palace of the Republic—whether the building should be condemned because of its supposed asbestos toxicity, whether it should be preserved as a relic of the DDR, or whether the Royal Palace should be rebuilt in its place—is just one instance of how the materiality of the past lives on in Berlin's present. After a decade of contentious debate, the city of Berlin recently opted to "unbuild" the Palace of the Republic and rebuild part of the Royal Palace. The last traces of the Berlin Wall are still detectable, even while the formerly empty spaces in the city center are almost completely filled in with postmodern department stores, office spaces, and museums. One need only look below the surface to see the uncanny ways that remains from the past survived: Located at the edge of Potsdamer Platz, the underground safe of Wertheim, the largest Jewish-owned department store of the 1920s, became one of Berlin's most successful techno clubs after reunification. Or, one could mention the 1985 excavation of the nearby Gestapo Headquarters on the fortieth anniversary of Germany's capitulation, and, more ominously, the discovery of the remains of Goebbel's bunker at the site of the Holocaust memorial.

The simultaneity of these disjunctures presents a difficulty to realist historical practices that seek to assign stable "resting-places" to particular times, as in Joffe's discourse of caging. That is to say, the unpredictable haunt of the past within the space of present-day experience complicates the rendering of history into something safely distant, bygone, and beyond. Here the risk is not so much the "forgetting" of the Holocaust or the relativizing of its centrality to German history (since it is reliably assigned to a specific place in a temporal span or chronological narrative), but rather the risk concerns its objectification into something that can be safely seen from a distance, controlled, and, finally, mastered.[10] However, as these stories indicate, the marking of time as distance traversed is undermined by the very proximity of remains and ruins, not to mention the unsettled memories of survivors and perpetrators. And, more than that, the stories underscore the inseparability of the German/Jewish dialectic of modernity: The memory of the German Gestapo member is still contaminated by his Jewish victims, and the site of the memorial to the murdered Jews is still contaminated by German Nazis. This is not simply a statement about the politics of memory but rather indicates something more fundamental about conceptualizing and historicizing the relationship between German and Jewish.

Not unlike Benjamin who drew upon the widest possible range of cultural ephemera to imagine the material history of modernity and thereby conceptualize his philosophical approach to constructing its history, I would like to look more carefully at the logic of present remains in order to think philosophy and poetry out of material history. As Susan Buck-Morss aptly characterized Benjamin's method in *The Arcades Project*: he sought to "construct philosophy out of history ... to reconstruct historical material as philosophy."[11] Through a reflection on the materiality of the German/Jewish past, I will show how Heidegger and Celan construct philosophy and poetry, respectively, out of the ruins of history in order to articulate, in their very different ways, a concept of memory. As we will see, this concept of memory only makes sense when the German and the Jewish come together to form a dialectic saturated with tension.

Ruins, remains, and survivors place us within the Derridean logic of ghosts, the revenant or the specter, that which cannot be so easily vanquished with the passing of time or with the writing of history but continues to return (*revenir*), haunt, and, most important, obstruct and refuse final mastery. The *Brach-Gelände* near the Holocaust memorial and the Anhalter Bahnhof, for example, represent precisely these kind of "out of joint" ghosts,[12] living on (*sur-vivre*) in the middle of the most widespread, urban foundation (re)laying program of arguably any city in Europe this century. These remains are testimonies to the multilayered, nonsimultaneous pasts, which are simultaneously sedimented in the time of the present. Their indeterminacy points us to the paradoxical definition of the very concept of remains as that which both remains behind and that which is dead. Indeed, *to remain* is to stay behind or back, to dwell, and is etymologically related to a spatial economy, namely, a manor. The verb refers to that which lives on, endures, and continues to persist. Remains are also what is dead, specifically corpses, and refer to that which does not continue to endure or persist. In this indecisiveness the *Brach-Gelände* remain and are remains, both living on and dead.

Remains live on by evoking specters of the past in the present; they haunt because of their undecidability. If specters indicate the frequency of a visibility or an appearance (such as of a ghost or of a memory-jarring trace), the temporal project of conjuring and coming to terms with remains must proceed by suspending and bracketing them off from the present. To say Fascism or the Cold War are bygone epochs that ended in 1945 and 1990, respectively, and then to do everything in one's power to "treat" the material remains (by putting them in a museum or disposing of them) would be to contain the past as finally over, bound, and suspended. Etymologically, an *epoch* is a temporal suspension, and, as such, remains are suspended in time and specters are driven away. The problem is that exorcisms, like attempts to cage the past, are never so easy.

The *Brach-Gelände* are unique precisely because of their historical uncertainty: They testify to the difficulty of containing "the past" as such. However, this uncertainty will not last forever. The *Brach-Gelände* are finite, and, one day, these landscapes of ruins will be cleaned up, determined, and assigned meanings. Indeed, in the not too distant future, the last material remains of the Holocaust will be settled: Some of the remains will be placed in museums or archives, some will be intentionally disposed, and others will simply be handed over to oblivion with the passing of time. All the memorials or monuments to the dead will have been built, the number of dead tallied and named (or resolved to be undeterminable and thus fixed as a ballpark figure), the last of the reparations paid out, and the historical accounts settled. The Berlin Holocaust memorial is the most obvious example of this discourse of settling accounts. All the survivors, the eyewitnesses, perpetrators, and bystanders contemporaneous with the Holocaust will have passed away. No one alive will have direct memories of the events; our understandings, ideas, and commitments will be formed primarily by the way in which images of mass death are represented, historicized, and passed-down—that is to say, the ways in which they are considered to be important for our culture, our ethics, our history, and ourselves. Anniversary rituals will become a part of the historical consciousness of countries or peoples who value the presence of the past and, perhaps, also become a part of their self-understandings and ethical obligations. The third and fourth generations, the children of the children, will be seen as somehow living a kind of redemption because they embody, in Helmut Kohl's deeply ambivalent terms, "the grace of late birth" and faraway place. Temporal distance—eventually—brings safety.

But, because of the living specter of the perpetrator and the survivor, because of the haunt of material remains of the past in the ground of memorials for the future, because of the survival of the *Brach-Gelände*, because of the vigorous debates over reparations as well as debates over the public commemoration of the Holocaust, this safety has not yet arrived. The past has not yet been caged. And for this reason, before the ethical and political questions about what "should be done" with the material remains of the Holocaust, there is still the even more basic question for any historical and memorial practice: What *might* be done with the material remains of the Holocaust? That is to say, what is possible? What might happen?

At least three possibilities seem evident. First, remains can simply be disposed and eliminated to make way for new urban projects or, perhaps more symbolically, to distinguish past ruins (byproducts of violence or terror) from the present and its hopes for the future by not having to be constantly bombarded by their claims and demands or just their silent testimony.[13] Understandably, such projects of disposal are often impugned as *Entsorgung der Vergangenheit* (disposing of the past), an especially acute charge in reunified Germany today given the emphasis on urban renewal and the architectural impulse toward a second *Gründerzeit*. This term has had a certain public currency since Jürgen Habermas used it in his May 8, 1985, anniversary article published in the newspaper *Die Zeit*, "Entsorgung der Vergangenheit."[14] *Entsorgung* presupposes both waste and the mechanisms of waste disposal. It is a term usually utilized with respect to nuclear waste, particularly remains of such toxicity that "normal treatment" is not sufficient. The physical remains of the Fascist (and, later, Communist) past—from Gestapo buildings to concentration camps, deportation stations to places of mass death—are treated as uncommonly toxic, and procedures of disposal and waste containment work to bury, dispose, correct, and, finally, detoxify. After forty years the discourse was containment and disposal: One need only wait out the passage of time, which would naturally bring about the treatment of waste and the detoxification of remains. But by May 8, 1995, Habermas' fiftieth anniversary article now diagnosed the drive as the time of *Befreiung,* or "liberation."[15] The next stage would be Martin Walser's critique of Germany's "memorial culture" and his call "to look away" or *wegschauen.*[16]

Second, remains can be contained in a museum, integrated into a broader historical narrative commenting on, accounting for, and sometimes justifying their coming into existence, or simply the fact of their desistance. The risk of remains being put into a museum calls upon the perennial (but nonetheless important) criticism of reification, the musealization (*musealisierung*) of the past as a static, even mastered object to be occasionally encountered, contemplated from a distance, and perhaps periodically mourned.[17] In this conventional sense the museum is the spatial pendant to Joffe's temporal discourse on caging.

Third, remains can be more or less let be, more or less left alone, the decision of what exactly to do with them deferred until some other seemingly more propitious time and circumstances. I say more or less because they are never completely ignored or unencountered, only that they are not unequivocally participating within the signifying system of an enclosed institution (such as a museum) or a specific political/social discourse making claims to a somewhat stable referent outside of itself (such as "the history of Germany"). My concern here is not primarily the disposal or museological preservation of remains but rather this third possibility: the *Brach-Gelände* as "not yet" anything, ruins that have *not yet been decided*. In postunification Berlin these regions of ruins are primarily along the periphery of the Wall, since these lands comprised the so-called no-man's zone productive of the most crushing distinction of East/West. It is here, for example, that we find the "contaminated" space of the Holocaust memorial as well as the geographically stranded land of the Anhalter Bahnhof with its dilapidated tracks, overgrown with more than fifty years of vegetation, leading to nowhere.

What would it mean to think philosophy and poetry out of the material ruins of the Anhalter Bahnhof? In what ways can the German/Jewish dialectic of modernity be illuminated by picking through these *Brach-Gelände*? First, the fact that the *Brach-Gelände* are closed off and entry is forbidden is indicative of a certain anxiety of remains; theoretically, no bodies may enter, but, at the same time, the ruins appear to elicit a profound fascination, and many Berliners seem to have stories of roaming through the ruins as children.[18] Moreover, the *Brach-Gelände* are unsettled because they are the remainders of a past, which is not yet able or ready to be fixed; they are excess in the senses of both "too much" and of "trash" (*Abfall, Lumpen*). The remains of the Anhalter Bahnhof, like Benjamin's arcades, are material testaments to and figures of excess and ambiguity. In this respect, remains occupy the precarious no-man's position of "no longer" and "not yet"—*no longer* a railway station, but *not yet* a fixed concept, settled monument, or agreed history; they are not a determined expenditure in the productive sense articulated and criticized by Bataille or in the realist, rehabilitative sense of historicism derided by Benjamin.[19]

The "no longer" is especially important to the theory of the *Brach-Gelände* because it indicates the short-lived, transitory quality of remains: Remains decay, remains are buried, remains are disposed, remains are placed in the context of a museum. In effect, something happens or will happen to remains; the potential for their disposal or removal is always imminent. As such, the *Brach-Gelände* are finite. Claims to transcendence or demands invested in a historical discourse or set of referents standing outside the land only result when the remains are "decided," when they are subsumed in a monumental or realist history. But, until this happens, remains and their specters mock "liberation" by balking at the passage of chronological time periodically commemorated by the distance of an anniversary. Remains testify to how untreated, how toxic, how close, how irregular, how unmonumental, how haunted, and how unresolved the materiality of the present remains.

The disaster is certainly a prerequisite of remains—the remains refer (back) to the disaster, but this does not mean that the sum of the remains equals the disaster or that such a thing as "the history of the disaster" can ever be produced. The linchpin (or the punch line) then is not that museums do, in fact, have this kind of transcendent presence—a kind of bad infinity—or that realist histories can, in fact, resuscitate the past, but rather that these assertions themselves structure both the latter: a referent is imagined to exist (or have existed), outside of both the museum and the historical discourses, that is not only considered constant but also recoverable. The belief in the representability of this referent in the space of the museum and the time of history is what serves to ratify and justify the very claims and the very objects contained inside. Through the management of a totalized, settled, and fixed representational universe, the "contained remains" in a museum stand in for (by producing and participating in) a kind of presence posturing as "history itself." To this extent, the disaster is "forgotten" while the seemingly representative selection of remains is "remembered" all too well. Against such a figure of presence, however, the *Brach-Gelände* both differ from their surrounding land (a spatial distinction) and the decision of what to do with them has been deferred until some other time. The meaning of the *Brach-Gelände* has not yet arrived (a temporal distinction). Differing and deferring, the *Brach-Gelände* witness Derrida's nonword, nonconcept of *différance*[20]—for him a critique of classical ontology; here a critique of traditional historical and musealogical practices of realist representation.

As both the materiality and figures of undecidability, the *Brach-Gelände* are dangerous because their discursive meanings and historical understandings are ambiguous: neither this, nor that. Analogous to the forgetting of the "founding violence" from which systems of law are born, the refounding of Berlin will forget the *Brach-Gelände,* the ruins of another founding violence, that of the Third Reich. Just as survivors die (and, dying with them, their memories and their time as wholly otherwise from the memories and time of nonsurvivors), the *Brach-Gelände* will be "normalized" and settled, the content of history filled in and more or less fixed when the last of the pesky ghosts from the past quits haunting or is finally exorcised. If Berlin is being "founded" since 1990, as many commentators believe, the disposal of the remains of Nazism is central to this founding. The *Brach-Gelände,* as trash or remains, will be settled, normalized, and forgotten. Like refuse, the *Brach-Gelände* are either disposed, never to be seen again, or petrified like a souvenir, a *memento mori* in Benjamin's very accusatory sense of "cultural treasures."[21] In both cases the effect is coherence, historicization, and "caging."

By contrast to this process of historicization, Benjamin sees the task of the historical materialist to "brush history against the grain,"[22] to stir the detritus under the seemingly inexorable and unidirectional flow of "history." The historical materialist is a *chiffonier,* brushing backward and plucking remains from processes of leveling, salvaging alterity in order to redeem that which has been subsumed, edited out, or disregarded in the normative discourses of telling "the past." Derived from Benjamin's theory of history in *The Arcades Project,* my cultural geography of German/Jewish modernity is an attempt to think cultural studies from a nonsite of mobility, to produce a genealogy of modernity out of the nonplace of the ruined railway station and its overgrown train tracks. It is to brush history against the grain so as to make it appear different from itself, to rescue the trash, the remains, the alterity, and the strange dialectics of the past. This "other of history" is the German/Jewish dialectic of modernity: the forgotten, the trash, the refuse, the ruin, the obsolete passage, the destroyed railway station, and the *Brach-Gelände.* It is that which has to be concealed or expelled to produce the effect of historical coherence and unity but that also contaminates precisely such effects of coherence and unity from the very start. The *Brach-Gelände* still contaminate Germany by attesting to a *différance* in history, in time, in the organization of urban space, in memories, and on bodies that remain otherwise than history. German/Jewish modernity can be mapped by starting with its ruins, by walking through Berlin's finite *Brach-Gelände*. What we find in the ruins is that there is no such thing as German modernity pure and simple: There is only German/Jewish modernity, each adding to, enriching, and replacing the other.

To visualize this in practice, I would now like to turn to my first snapshot of the German/Jewish dialectic: Heidegger and Celan. I bring the "thinker" and the "poet" together in order to show how they both called upon the material remains of the past in order to articulate a concept of memory and historicity. Celan's engagement with Heidegger's work is, of course, quite well known, and intellectual historians have conscientiously documented Celan's encounters with Heidegger.[23] I will only briefly mention this history here. Although it is still not certain how much of Celan's work Heidegger knew, Otto Pöggeler gave Heidegger a copy of Celan's "Meridian Speech" in April 1961, and Celan paid Heidegger two visits, in which he gave the philosopher copies of his poetry. As some commentators such as Philippe Lacoue-Labarthe and Christopher Fynsk have argued, Celan's later poetry and his "Bremen" and "Meridian" speeches are largely dialogues with Heidegger's thought. Celan himself famously commemorated his 1967 visit to Heidegger's "hut" in the poem "Todtnauberg," in which he hopes "for a coming word [about the Holocaust] in the heart" of the thinker.[24]

While my discussion builds upon this body of scholarship, my concern lies elsewhere, namely, with how Heidegger and Celan use the material remains of the German/Jewish past to derive two different concepts of memory and historicity. In what follows I will perform a careful reading of two autobiographical travel narratives—both written in 1962, one on a ship and one on a train—in which Heidegger and Celan attempt to forge a relationship between physical remains and the production of memory after the Holocaust. Both attempt to articulate how the encounter with the remains of a historical place and the recollection of the past come together to form a present "site of memory." Whereas Heidegger seeks the groundedness of a Greco-German nationality on the Greek island of Delos in order to preserve memory, Celan turns to the "no-places" of mobility, particularly the ruins of Berlin's Anhalter Bahnhof. For Celan the physical remains of the Anhalter station function as a stratified site of mobility for the production of a kind of memory, which refuses the successive demands of linear histories. The consequence, as we will see, is that two different accounts of memory and mobility emerge: Although both are interested in the geography of memory, Heidegger's philosophy is motivated by a logic of nationality and groundedness, while Celan's poetry is motivated by transnationality and the contingency of historical and geographic simultaneity.

Although one could certainly read these two accounts of memory "in opposition" to one another, I am arguing that we cannot understand Heidegger without Celan, and, recursively, we cannot understand Celan without Heidegger. Celan adds to, enriches, and replaces Heidegger's concept of memory, thereby locking the poet and the thinker in a dialectical relationship saturated with tension. When critically juxtaposed in the present, they come together in a flash to form a new constellation and thereby produce a new historical image. This image "gains legibility only at a particular time" (AP 462), what Benjamin will call "the now of a particular recognizability" (AP 463). The now is our post-Holocaust present, and it is the cultural critic who makes the choice about what texts to bring together in order to form this new image, a dialectic at a standstill.

MEMORY AND MOBILITY

In 1962 both Heidegger and Celan took trips, which they subsequently described in terms of the memory of and present encounter with remains. Heidegger took a trip to Greece, the only one he ever took in his lifetime, in order, as he says, to confirm that his *Denkweg* (path of thinking) was no *Irrweg* (path of errors).[25] His autobiographical reflections—written in 1962 but not published until 1989—are those of the *Denker,* constantly invoking the *Dichter* (not Celan but rather Hölderlin), as he moves through, and briefly stays over at, various Greek islands. The reflections are appropriately entitled *Aufenthalte,* as in "stays" or "stopovers" on a journey. During the same year, Celan took a trip to Nyon, Switzerland, where he composed an important poem entitled "La Contrescarpe."[26] It is a deeply personal poem, in some ways like Heidegger's autobiographical-intellectual journey, but in other ways quite different in its urgency. Celan, too, makes references to Hölderlin, and his poem, much like Heidegger's travels into the past, is a journey for Celan into his past. Celan's poem is also a *Denkweg,* so to speak, but, as we will see, in marking his personal "detours" (*Umwege*) through Eastern Europe, Berlin, Switzerland, and, finally, Paris, Celan values the "sites" of a different kind of historical memory. In moving away from, back to, and through Germany, they both attempt to think through *what* and *where* memory can be after the Holocaust.

Heidegger's journey was motivated by a wish to confirm his idea of ancient Greece: he wants to go to the geographic origin—the *Ursprung,* meaning for Heidegger both the beginning and the primal leap into the past via the future—but fears being disappointed by what he might find. His topographical reflections begin by quoting the fourth strophe of Hölderlin's poem, "Bread and Wine," as he wonders why Hölderlin did not need to take such a trip to Greece: "Aber die Thronen, wo? die Tempel, und wo die Gefäße, / Wo mit Nectar gefüllt, Göttern zu Lust der Gesang? / Wo, wo leuchten sie denn, die fernhintreffenden Sprüche? / Delphi schlummert und wo tönet das große Geschick? [But the thrones, where are they? Where are the temples, the vessels, / Where, to delight the gods, brim-full with nectar, the songs? / Where, then, where do they shine, the oracles winged for far targets? / Delphi's asleep, and where now is great fate to be heard?]" (quoted in H 4).[27] Heidegger wants to know where the remains of his idea of ancient Greece are to be found. But his journey is not motivated by an attempt to find just any thrones and temples, any old songs and oracles, but rather those which speak to a certain way of being, now lost. We might say that his trip is actually motivated by a line just before the ones he quotes from Hölderlin's poem, a line he decides not to cite in his autobiographical reflections: "Seeliges Griechenland! du Haus der Himmlischen alle, / Also ist wahr, was einst wir in der Jugend gehört? [Happy land of the Greeks, you house of them all, of the Heavenly, / So it is true what we heard then, in the days of our youth?]."[28] Quite unlike other travel journeys predicated on the discovery of the unknown and the encounter with the foreign, such as Goethe's *Italienische Reise*, to which Heidegger makes passing reference, Heidegger is undertaking a voyage of confirmation. He already knows what he wants to find in Greece and essentially seeks to verify the truth of his pathway of thinking by moving through its present remains.

To do so, accompanied by his wife who painted three pictures of the Greek coast along the way, he took an organized cruise, on a "modern cruise ship" (H 4). The first stop was Corfu. But Heidegger—surprised and a little nervous—tells us that Corfu doesn't look like it should: "Is this really Greece? What I had sensed and expected did not appear. . . . Everything looks more like an Italian landscape" (H 5). Greece looks like Italy, and he wonders how Goethe could have possibly experienced "Greece" while journeying through Sicily, for not even Greece looks Greek. The next stop on

the following day was Ithaca, but it, too, doesn't look like he expected it
to look and his "doubts" increase. From there, via Pyrgos he takes a "bus"
to Olympia but only discovers "a barren town" with newly built American
tourist hotels (H 7). He is unimpressed by the museums and, once again,
thinks the ruined temples and other remains could just have likely been
found in Italy. As the journey proceeds day by day (he visits the Gulf of
Corinth but decides to stay on the ship; he forgoes seeing the Acropolis;
Crete doesn't appear Greek to him), he becomes more and more disappointed with present-day Greece. "Modern technology" [*moderne Technik*]
and "the power of the essence of technology" is probably to blame: "In view
of this state of the world, the remembrance of what is uniquely Greece is an
undertaking foreign to this world. At least it seems that way" (H 16). The remembrance (*Andenken*) of what is special about Greece can no longer take
place today because of the uprootedness caused by modern technology; the
experience of the Greek topography in 1962 is entirely alien to Heidegger's
idea of ancient Greece.

But on day five of the journey, when the traveling philosopher finally
disembarks at the island of Delos, everything has changed: The little island
is scarcely populated and is, instead, covered by ruins of temples and other
architectural remains. No American tourist traps, no modern technology
(save the cruise ship he arrived on). Heidegger is quick to point out that the
name of the island means "the manifest and the appearing" (*die Offenbare,
die Scheinende*), and it is the place where he experiences the truth of Greek
being. Delos is both origin and *Heimat* (home) for Heidegger, the manifestation of aletheia: Delos, he says, is where "all poeticizing and thinking
is looked at in advance" (H 20). The island is characterized by its "purity,"
and he experiences a "stay that reminds him of home," uncorrupted by any
sort of "calculative thinking" endemic to the modern world.[29] As an origin in the future, it is both the time before and the time after the loss of
being, *Seinsverlassenheit*, a loss that he sought to overcome at least since the
"Letter on Humanism" (1946).[30] For Heidegger the island turns "thinking
into memory" (*Denken zum Andenken*) because it offers the closeness of the
ground and preserves the rootedness of place (H 21).

A couple of years earlier, in his 1955 commemoration speech for the German composer Conradin Kreutzer, delivered on the date of the composer's
175th birthday, Heidegger clearly articulated this idea that memory is connected to place and groundedness.[31] In both discourses on memory he establishes the importance of *Bodenständigkeit* (groundedness) for any true

memorial practice: *Andenken* is necessarily grounded in the native soil, and is, hence, intimately connected with *Ortschaft* (place) and *Seßhaftigkeit* (the sedentary; H 27). It is in this respect that the Greeks have "created a world" (H 27), one which he seeks to return to via the topography of its present remains.

At the conclusion of his journey through Greece, Heidegger leaves satisfied, having "found what he sought" but not without first turning the memory of Delos into a decidedly German task of overcoming the "loss of being" caused by technology. As he returns to Germany, he quotes the final strophe of Hölderlin's "Gesang des Deutschen" (Song of the German): "Wo ist dein Delos, wo dein Olympia, / daß wir uns alle finden am höchsten Fest?— / Doch wie erräth der Sohn, was du den / Deinen, Unsterbliche, längst bereitest? [Where is your Delos, where is your Olympia / that we all find the most celebrated? / How does the son divine what you / have long prepared for yours, immortal one?]" (H 34). Upon turning back, his departure from Greece also becomes his arrival in Germany. Heidegger's Delos is the recovery of and return to an origin tied to the specificity of the German nation. He comes full circle: "The departure from Greece turned into the arrival" (H 33). For Heidegger it is the poets and the thinkers who mark out the path where leave-taking and arrival—Germany and Greece, Greece and Germany—become one and the same. In 1962 Heidegger's journey of memory was a geographically arranged, roundtrip narrative of confirmation: He went to the Greek origin, found what he was looking for, and returned back to the German nation.

I will now juxtapose Celan's poem, "La Contrescarpe." The fifty-one-line poem was published the year after it was written, as one of the last poems in his 1963 collection, *Die Niemandsrose*. It concerns, at least in part, a trip Celan took to Switzerland in 1962; however, it is also the condensation of many separate travels taken by Celan since 1938, some willingly, some under the force of circumstance. Rather than giving a line-by-line exegesis, I want to pay particular attention to the complex ways in which Celan figures the relationship between place, time, and memory in this poem. As we will see, Celan's movement, primarily by railway, through the topography of Europe produces a dialectically related but quite different practice of memory than the pathways of thought pursued by Heidegger in his sea voyage to Greece.

If we pause on some of the key words in the first lines of the poem, one certainly hears an echo of the topography of Greece as thought and poeticized by Heidegger and Hölderlin. Celan writes: "an der Kehre, / wo er dem Brotpfeil begegnet, / der den Wein seiner Nacht trank, den Wein / der Elends-, der Königs- / vigilie [On the turning, / where he encounters the bread-arrow, / which drank the wine of his night / of sorrow-vigil, of royal-vigil]" (lines 9–13). Words like *Brotpfeil* and *Wein* are not only clear allusions to the Eucharist, an embodied ritual of memory, but also allusions to the same Hölderlin poem that Heidegger used to begin and justify his own journey through Greece. But the term *Kehre*—a staple in Heideggerian reflections on Greece, often taking on the form of a *Rückkehre* (a "turning back") in his discussions of Hölderlin's poems, such as "Heimkunft" and "Andenken"—is for Celan connected to a different kind of movement: not a return to a past origin via a future pathway but rather a *Gegenverkehr* (counter-traffic) and *Umkehre* (turning around) in the space of the present. In both his Bremen speech and Meridian speech, as well as in the collection of notes he made for the latter, Celan imagines a kind of back-and-forth countermovement, distinct from Heidegger's doubled return to the Greek origin and the German nation. Celan is moving in a different direction, against the unidirectional "flow" of history, in order to draw out the complex sedimentation of topographical remains. It is a practice of memory and mobility that is intimately connected to marking, calling forth, and living with "disjunctures" in time and space.[32]

In his notes for the Meridian speech of 1960, Celan characterized a poem as a *Wortlandschaft,* a word landscape or topography composed of language.[33] The word landscape in "La Contrescarpe" moves from a street in Nyon, "Herzbuckelweg," to the spaces of Greek mythology, to the memory of a train trip Celan first took to Paris, via Cracow and Berlin, in November of 1938. These topographical points along his circuitous route make up the second to last, eighteen-line strophe, which is indented from the rest of the poem. Its first ten lines read as follows: "Über Krakau / bist du gekommen, am Anhalter / Bahnhof / floß deinen Blick ein Rauch zu, / der war schon von morgen. Unter / Paulownien / sahst du die Messer stehn, wieder, / scharf von Entfernung. Es wurde / getanzt. (Quatorze / juillets. Et plus de neuf autres.) [Via Cracow / you arrived at Anhalter / station / your gaze flowed into the smoke / which was already from tomorrow. Under / Paulownien / you saw the knives standing, again, / sharply from a distance. They / danced. (Fourteen / Julys. And nine more)]" (lines 29–38). Moving from East to West, via Cracow, Celan arrives at Berlin's Anhalter train station just after *Reichskristallnacht*, November 8/9, 1938. He sees smoke, possibly the train's smoke mixing with the smoke of burning Jewish synagogues and vandalized stores. His journey continues to Paris, and in the poem the temporal distance separating this first journey and the journey of 1962 is figured in French as "fourteen Julys. And nine more": in other words, counting from November 1938, adding fourteen years beginning with the next July of 1939 and nine more, we arrive at the present, 1962. But another date is embedded here, namely, the date of Celan's exile to Paris, July 14, 1948, Bastille Day— celebrated by "Es wurde getanzt" and marked in the poem by the inversion of "Juillet Quatorze." As a practice of memory, the word landscape is saturated with both the disjunctures of time and a kind of transnational mobility. The simultaneity of Celan's cultural geography moves between Cracow, Berlin, and Paris not in order to represent the singularity of a journey to an origin (like Heidegger) but rather to imagine a practice of memory that is derived from the sedimented and fractured spaces of mobility.

Celan's layered temporality refuses both any kind of circularity, such as a return to an origin, and any kind of linearity, such as the arrangement of historical time into a succession of years. He is not interested in marking the passage of time in order to "commemorate" the past as a unit of distance; nor is he concerned with collecting pieces of the past—the *Souvenirchen* (trinkets; line 44), as he diminutively calls the assembly of remains into something coherent or whole again. Rather his journey is an encounter in the present with the temporally stratified materiality of both language and space; it is a journey of memory as a kind of poetic vigil of what can be told about "what remains."

As a simultaneous word landscape composed in the nonsimultaneous space and time of the present, his poem is a form of language that is not motivated by or dependent upon conventional poetic tropes such as "metaphors" or "synonyms," let alone the production of "art" or "representation," but rather by the reality of present remains, both material and linguistic.[34] Unlike Heidegger's topographical journey of memory, Celan's practice of *Toposforschung*, as he famously called it in his Meridian speech, is not carried out by the localization of place (*Ortschaft, Heimat, Seßhaftigkeit*) but rather "in the light of u-topia" (M 199). The "no-places" that Celan finds are the nonexistent places of his own heritage, the landscapes that were once inhabited by Eastern European Jews like Karl Emil Franzos encountering Germans such as Georg Büchner. These places of encounter appear to have been largely destroyed: "None of these places can be found. They don't exist" (M 202). They are not approachable in the sense of a "return" to a historical origin but only as temporally layered topographical memories, in the same way that a "hesitant finger" points to a "child's map" (M 202). Reworking Heidegger's insistence on "return," Celan calls these ways (*Wege*) and detours (*Um-Wege*), "a kind of homecoming" (*Eine Art Heimkehr*; M 201) because—at least in Europe—there is no Jewish Delos to return to.

By contrast, for the philosopher of memory, the task of the poet is to mark out the path home, the return to the origin. Heidegger articulates this quite clearly in his explication of Hölderlin's poem "Heimkunft": "The poet's job is the home-coming, through which the home, as the land of the near, is first prepared [to become] the origin [Der Beruf des Dichters ist die Heimkunft, durch die erst die Heimat als das Land der Nähe zum Ursprung bereitet wird]."[35] The poet "arrives out the future," Heidegger says in his 1946 essay "What Are Poets For?" because the poet—rather than merely pointing toward the future or returning to the past—shows the pathway to a past origin that lies in the future.[36] In effect, the poets not only illuminate the way to the *Heimat* (an originary place) but also a return to a way of being, what he considers to be an originary rootedness in place.

As critics such as Véronique Fóti and Beda Allemann have indicated with respect to Heidegger's interpretation of Hölderlin's poems "Der Ister" and "Andenken," his concern lies with the illumination of "the destinal mandate of Germania."[37] Citing Hölderlin's own "patriotic turning" (*vaterländische Umkehr*), Heidegger seeks to overcome the atomizing uprootedness of modernity by returning—in his case via ship—to the originary ground of the German-Greek homeland.[38] And this is precisely why Celan is suspicious of Heidegger's insistence on any kind of originary rootedness: Celan's *Toposforschung* is not grounded in the locality of a country or homeland because *Seßhaftigkeit*, *Ortschaft*, and *Ursprung* are all too easily connected with the violent nationalization of place. While both are concerned with the cultural geography of remains, Heidegger's desire to turn the idealized origin of ancient Greece into a future Germania is quite different from Celan's desire for a *Toposforschung* undertaken in the light of utopia: A no-place cannot, by its very definition, be nationalized.

For Celan the localization of place is thus less important than the "ways" in which topographies are experienced in the present and narrated as stratified sites of memory. This practice of memory is forged through the relationship between the "word landscape" of the poem and the movement over a historically layered topography of material remains. To demonstrate this more specifically, I want to focus on two figures in the poem: the first being the military structure of the "contrescarpe" and the second

being the overdetermined sign for the dialectic of modernity, Berlin's Anhalter Bahnhof.

Celan's poem is suffused with references to the possibility of mobility,
not least of all from the title, which refers to a strategically sloping military wall positioned in such a way as to prevent movement. A contrescarpe
is generally built on land in order to prevent entry into a stronghold or
military fortification. But Celan connects two kinds of movement to this
martial figure of immobilization: movement through the air by carrier
pigeons and movement over sea. Celan writes: "Scherte die Brieftaube aus,
war ihr Ring / zu entziffern? (All das / Gewölk um sie her—es war lesbar.)
[The carrier pigeons broke away, was their ring / able to be deciphered?
(all that / clouds around—it was legible)]" (lines 20–22). Carrier pigeons,
of course, were used for military communication, and, in order not to reveal their national identity, they had decodable identity "rings." The point
is less the content of the letter transported by the pigeon and more the fact
that the "ring" is still legible: It was clear where the bird came from. And
four lines later, a message bleeds from the bulkhead of a ship: "Durch die
Schotten / blutet die Botschaft, Verjährtes / geht jung über Bord [Through
the bulkheads / the message bleeds, expired / goes recently overboard]"
(lines 26–28). Here the message is literally "yeared" (*verjährt*). That is to
say, the message has expired because its statute of limitations is up, too
much time has passed to still prosecute for past crimes. Altogether, then,
Celan moves from the foiling of movement, to the place of a message, to
the expiration of historical action. Just as Celan cautioned in his Meridian
notes that "Black milk of daybreak . . . is no [metaphor, but] . . . is reality,"[39] an allegorical or metaphorical reading is not necessary here. The
historical reality of the poem is that the Eichmann trial took place the
year before, in Jerusalem in 1961, and the Auschwitz trials began the year
after, in 1963.

Celan presents a temporally layered topography, in which time is not
spatialized as the progressive marking of a distance covered or a linear span
that has elapsed. This kind of chronologically spatialized time renders events
like the Holocaust as "caged" or "far away," able to be safely commemorated
by periodic anniversaries because the crimes have since become *verjährt*.
The topographical remains and the word landscapes that Celan encounters on moving trains are thus not about securing the nationality of place.
They are also not about the return to the groundedness of being or the
remoteness of times caged, past, and long gone. Instead he is interested in

the poem, as he calls it in his Meridian notes, as a kind of "vigil" or "encounter"—a relationship—with remains in the present.

In "La Contrescarpe" the dominant figure of present remains is the gigantic, bombed-out ruins of Berlin's legendary Anhalter Bahnhof. The train station was razed in 1960–1961, leaving behind only a small part of its entry portal, perhaps as a kind of testament to another time. As Celan knew and experienced first-hand, Berlin's Anhalter Bahnhof was once one of the most important train stations in all of Europe, the central arrival and departure point to Prague, Vienna, and many other southern and eastern destinations. Once again, Celan is not interested in artistry and metaphorical language but rather in the poem as a real "word landscape" and vigil of historical encounter. The topographical remains and language tracks—here literal train stations and railway tracks—are not metaphors, standing for or standing across from some originary place of figurative unity, wholeness, or presence. "The poem is the place where all synonyms . . . stop; where all tropes . . . are carried out ad absurdum; the poem has . . . an anti-metaphorical character."[40] Instead Celan's poems are concerned with the "here" and "now," the "places" and "hours" of present remains.[41] The word landscapes are as real as the physical landscapes: both are sites of memory and mobility embodying the German/Jewish dialectic of modernity.

When Celan first arrived from Cracow at the Anhalter Bahnhof in 1938, it was world renown as one of the most modern, most opulent, most efficient, and largest railway stations in Europe. Celan probably knew that shortly thereafter the Anhalter Bahnhof was used by the Nazis to collect, transport, and deport thousands of Berlin's Jews. By 1962, when he composed "La Contrescarpe," the historical structure had been razed and its tracks condemned to oblivion. For the next four decades the ruins of its north portal faced an empty landscape where its great hall once stood. There are still train tracks from the Anhalter Bahnhof that lead south out of Berlin, but they are overgrown by years of vegetation and in the past few years have begun to be removed by the city of Berlin. As a deeply stratified site of memory, the remains of the station and its tracks to no-where are a jarring, strange presence in the newly constructed landscape of a unified Berlin.

These *Brach-Gelände* are the *Abfall der Geschichte*, to use Benjamin's words, the remains or trash of history. Because of their finitude, contingency, and temporality, they enter into and out of legibility at specific times, under particular circumstances, in a given present. They are "bound to a time-kernel [*Zeitkern*],"[42] which prefigures their finitude. The material remains, like Celan's "word landscapes," balk at attempts at chronological historicization or spatial mastery. For Celan the poem is a relational site of memory, which emerges through the simultaneity of its multiple discontinuous times and spaces, rather than an object of beauty or historical representation suspended at a safe distance. The linguistic and material word landscapes of a poem or a railway station are dialectical encounters between what-has-been and the now. To this extent, remains disrupt the procession of chronology and thereby allow for the creation of a relational memory in the contingency of the present.

I would now like to conclude by moving back, so to speak, to the relationship between memory and mobility in Celan and Heidegger. For Celan places, people, buildings, landscapes, and languages, which, in the wake of the Holocaust, have fallen into a kind of *Geschichtslosigkeit* (historylessness) are not redeemed by returning to an ethos of national dwelling or rootedness but only encountered in the present as partial landscapes of material and linguistic remains.[43] Celan's "Gespräch im Gebirg"[44] (Conversation in the mountains) might be understood precisely along these lines: The "conversation" is an encounter between two languages, German and Yiddish (one national and one non-national), and two Jews (one "large" and one "small") who meet somewhere in the mountains to discuss what being Jewish might mean in 1959. The topography in which they encounter one another is impossible to "nationalize" or even locate in terms of a geographic rootedness. Not unlike Heine's linguistic doublings, Celan's slippage between the "Germanization" of Yiddish and the "Yiddishization" of German yields a "word landscape" as a present site of memory:

Ich bin dir begegnet, hier, und geredet haben wir, viel, und die Falten dort, du weißt, nicht für die Menschen sind sie da und nicht für uns, die wir hier gingen und einander trafen, wir hier unterm Stern, wir, die Juden, die da kamen, wie Lenz, durchs Gebirg, du Groß und ich Klein, du, der Geschwätzige, und ich, der Geschwätzige, wir mit den Stöcken, wir mit unsern Namen, den unaussprechlichen, wir mit unserm Schatten, dem eigenen und dem fremden, du hier und ich hier—ich hier, ich; ich, der ich dir all das sagen kann, sagen hätt können.

[I met you, here, and we've talked, a lot, and the folds there, you know, for humans they're not and not for us, who went walking and came on each other, we here under the star, we, the Jews who came here, like Lenz, through the mountains, you Gross and me Klein, you, the babbler, and me, the babbler, we with our sticks, we with our names, unspeakable, we with our shadow, our own and alien, you here and I here—I here, I; I, who can say, could have said, all that to you.][45]

In this chatty encounter the two Jews, with unpronounceable names, mark space not by means of "nationality" or "origins" but through the mixing of languages under the borderless no-place of the stars. Celan's translation of German into Yiddish and Yiddish into German emerges in a liminal zone of possible contact, transmitted within the nameless geographies where the conversation took place.

For Celan topographical and geographical spaces—whether the physical remains of Berlin's Anhalter train station or the linguistic word landscapes of the poem—present possible "Wege, Umwege . . . zu dir" (ways, detours . . . to you; M 201) and, hence, can participate in a dialogical ethics of memory. Like Heidegger, Celan is interested in pursuing the "ways" and "detours" of memory, but, unlike the philosopher of memory, these *Wege* yield a practice of ethical relationality, not the singularity of an origin. In fact, Celan will explicitly condemn Heidegger's *Du-Latenz* (you-latency) and the *Dulosigkeit* (you-lessness) of his thought.[46] He will also reject the grounding of language or literature in the space of the nation or the rootedness of the homeland.

For Celan the poem is not to be understood as figuring or representing something else, such the Anhalter Bahnhof or *Reichskristallnacht*; instead "the poem always remains a phenomenal form of language," a form of "being present" (*Gegenwärtigkeit*) and "materiality" (*Gegenständigkeit*)— that is to say, a word landscape.[47] The poem, like the ruined deportation station, leaves behind its own language tracks, namely, the reality of its topographical remains encountering a present *Du*. Quite unlike Heidegger's return to "sites of memory" for the sake of the nationalization of place, Celan's *Toposforschung* is a practice of memory as a kind of relational encounter with the disjointed time and space of present remains.

It is not necessary to confront Heidegger's most infamous "forgetting" of the Holocaust—that is, his scandalous agriculture remark of 1949—to see how differently the priorities of memory and historicity functioned after 1945 for the philosopher.[48] Nor is it necessary to scour Heidegger's prewar, interwar, and postwar philosophy in search of evidence to exonerate or

convict the philosopher on charges of Nazism.[49] Heidegger, in fact, had lots
to say about how modern technology uprooted peoples, jeopardized meditative thinking, endangered true memory, and "threatened [the rootedness]
of man . . . today at its core."[50] He also believed that the very concept of the
human being had changed, that being itself had been lost with the loss of
the *Bodenständigkeit* (rootedness) of place: In the atomic age, as Heidegger
calls it, "many Germans have lost their homeland, have had to leave their
villages and towns, have been driven from their native soil. Countless others
whose homeland was saved, have yet wandered off. They have been caught
up in the turmoil of big cities and have resettled in the wastelands of industrial districts."[51] The mass death of two world wars, the destruction of
the Eastern Front, the loss of the German homeland, the atomic bomb, the
"Americanization" of Europe: these are only the most recent disasters that
Heidegger cited time and again.[52]

But the point for Heidegger is not the memory of these disasters but
the very possibility of memory threatened by the disaster, which for him
is subsumed by another problem, namely, the loss of being. That is to say,
because these disasters force people from their homeland, from the stability
and nationality of the ground, memory—which is intimately a grounded,
national, and rooted kind of thinking and being—is also threatened. This is
why he makes a trip to Delos and why he ends his memorial speech with a
call to renewing, in this "changed age," something that Johann Peter Hebel
once said: "We are plants which—whether we like to admit it to ourselves
or not—must with our roots rise out of the earth in order to bloom in the
ether and bear fruit."[53] It is the same sentiment expressed in the "Letter on
Humanism": the "homelessness of modern man" can only be overcome by
a return to dwelling, a connection to the land, like "the furrows that the
farmer, slow of step, draws through the field."[54] And it is the same reason
why Heidegger's poets—whether Hölderlin, Trakl, or Rilke—elucidate the
pathway back home.

Memory and the disaster are thus completely incompatible, antithetical
terms for Heidegger: There is no writing the memory of the Holocaust because it is the uprooting of the disaster itself that nullifies memory. Memory is always connected with the rootedness of place, the recovery of the
Ortschaft, Seßhaftigkeit, and *Ursprung.* The task of the poets—"those who
remember"—is to help guide the philosophers safely back home. This is
why he ends his own travel narrative by highlighting the question posed
by Hölderlin in his "Gesang des Deutschen": "Wo ist dein Delos?" and not

"Wo ist dein Auschwitz?" Memory demands an originary place, a home to return to—not the destruction of place and the inability to go home. Heidegger's roundtrip chronicle of his journey to Delos is thus a practice of memory that secures the grounded nationality of place and is driven forward by a Greco-German cultural geography that marks the recovery of "being."

Celan's *Toposforschung* is somewhere else. The writing of the memory of the Holocaust is an encounter, in the simultaneously nonsimultaneous space of the present, with what remains. On the train, heading East to West in 1938 and West to East in 1962, Celan is never heading "home." His encounters are not nationally grounded or even about the desirability of finding ground; they are carried out "in the light of u-topia" and, in this respect, present a different kind of homecoming than Heidegger's memory. Celan both begins and ends with, departs from and returns to the remains of no-place. These are the remains of language and the remains of German/Jewish modernity: poetry and Berlin's Anhalter Bahnhof—after the Holocaust. Both the word landscapes and the physical landscapes are deeply ambivalent sites of memory, no-places of hope and horror, that we can still encounter in our own "here" and "now."

There is a single line about Kepler in the notes that Celan composed for his Meridian speech: "Kepler: Dreamed of a new star."[55] It is a dream of a new orientation, a new direction, a new way. Etymologically, *disaster* is the breaking apart of the star. As Blanchot writes, the disaster "means being separated from the star," to "break with the star."[56] For the thinker and the poet the ruins of modernity and the desire for a new orientation go hand in hand. Memory emerges in the tension between destruction and the dream of a new star. For both Heidegger and Celan the desires, dreams, and disasters of German/Jewish modernity become legible, however tentatively, in the ruined landscapes of the present. Recognizing this legibility is the start of what it means to write philosophy and poetry out of material history.

3. SICILY, NEW YORK CITY, AND THE BARANOVICH STATION
German/Jewish Subject Without a Nation
On the Meta-epistemology of Mobility and Mass Migration

3.1 Front of Anhalter Bahnhof (ca. 1885), Berlin. *Courtesy of the Landesarchiv, Berlin*

ON SEPTEMBER 1, 1840, the first part of the railway line that would connect Berlin to the German state of Anhalt was opened between Dessau and Köthen by the directors of the Berlin-Anhaltische Eisenbahn Gesellschaft.[1] The construction of Berlin's Anhalter Bahnhof was quickly completed, and by September of the following year daily service began running to Köthen via Wittenberg, Coswig, and Dessau. The line, which connected the German states of Prussia and Anhalt together, was the longest railway line in any German state at the time, stretching more than 150 kilometers.[2] By 1848 service from the Anhalter extended to Dresden and Halle and, from there, into Thuringia. Before German unification the Anhalter played a critical role in helping to expand the reach of the Prussian railway network.

The original railway station, designed and built between 1838 and 1841, was erected on what would become Askanischer Platz, directly on the outer edge of the old city of Berlin. It was to be accessible through a new gate leading into and out of the city. The three-story neoclassical "receiving building" was reached through a main entryway and was designed to rival the greatest English railway stations—only the Anhalter was to be larger and "more beautiful."[3] The station was a *Kopfbahnhof*, a terminal railway station, and constructed to connect the city of Berlin to places outside of Prussia. Its two main platforms, one for people and one for the transportation of goods, ran south out of the city along the newly constructed Militär-Strasse.

Immediately after German unification in 1871, the city of Berlin and shareholders of the Anhalter decided to rebuild the station to better service the rapidly industrializing nation. Beginning in 1872 the old station was torn down because it was deemed too small to handle the rising passenger and goods traffic and the main receiving building lacked in any sort of distinguishing monumentality appropriate to the dominance of Prussia. Between the summer of 1871 and August of 1878 the chief architect of the new station, Franz Schwechten, proposed no fewer than nine different, monumental designs.[4] Even though the final design would change several more times before the new station was completed, the orders for "one million well-browned building bricks" and "one and a half million red bricks" were placed in 1875, and construction officially began on September 7 of that year.[5]

The Anhalter was rebuilt on a colossal scale and reopened to the public in 1880. At the time, the new building was one of the largest "terminal railway stations" in the world, measuring 170 meters long, 60 meters wide, and nearly 35 meters high at its apex. The passenger station now had six main platforms, two ancillary platforms, and six additional platforms for baggage. The brightly illuminated building, complete with glass windows along the roof, was held together by the massive innovations of iron construction. All sorts of accolades were heaped upon the architectural innovation of the structure: Anhalter Bahnhof was now the largest, the fastest, and the most efficient railway station in Germany. But, more than that, it was also considered the most beautiful: more than eight hundred specially trained stone workers were employed to craft the extravagant ornamentation covering the entire structure, ranging from terra-cotta relief figures and sculpted arabesques to detailed friezes, ornate columns, and flowering capitals.[6] The terra-cotta ornamentation alone cost more than 1,500,000 marks, and the total cost of rebuilding the entire station was unprecedented in railway history, totaling 14,100,000 marks.[7] Indeed, all of its proportions were mythological. After all, the new nation needed to build new myths.

MODERNIST TRAVELS

Shortly after the opening of the Paris-Rouen and the Paris-Orleans railway lines in 1843, Heinrich Heine reflected on the "world-historical" significance of the railway from the perspective of his Parisian exile. Using some of the most hyperbolic rhetoric he could muster, Heine appealed to creation theology to describe the earthly impact of railway technology. He placed the railway in a historical lineage that included other key turning points in the history of human civilization: the invention of gunpowder, the discovery of America, and the spread of the printing press; the last had "sent the word of God into the world."[8] In quite the same way, the railway "is once again such a providential event," fundamentally transforming the way we live in the world and record our experiences of it. Heine wrote: "While the great mass of people stares astounded and dumbstruck at the outward manifestation of these great forces of mobility, the intellectual is seized by an uncanny horror, the way we always feel when the most monstrous, the most unheard of thing happens, the consequences of which are unforeseeable and incalculable."[9] He likens the construction of these two railway lines—the one extending northwest from Paris, the other southwest from Paris—to a "tremor" and an "electric shock" that instantaneously travels in a chain reaction through the "entire population of Paris."[10] No one is left untouched; everyone and everything is irrevocably changed.

In Heine's diagnosis the construction of railways monstrously broke with the order of pregiven experiences and expectations, inaugurating a new world and an unforeseeable future. Playing off the new metaphors generated by railway transportation, Heine, not one for understatement, underscored how the railways ruptured the world he knew by severing past expectations: "Let us simply say that our entire existence is being ripped up and hurled on new tracks [neue Gleise]; that new relationships, pleasures, and torments await us, and the unknown exerts its ghastly fascination, irresistible and, at the same time, fearful."[11] Here Heine draws our attention to the inability of deducing or deriving the future from the past. A circular continuity, what the philosopher of history, Reinhart Koselleck, will term the eschatological determination of the premodern world, is broken apart when experience no longer lines up with expectation.[12] For Koselleck the rupture between "the space of experience" and "the horizon of expectation" is the hallmark of a "new time" (*Neuzeit*), modernity. Time is no longer eschatological—the future already determined—but imagined as a space of possibility, openness, and unfixedness. Central to this reconfiguration of temporality was the generation of a form of historical time characterized by future-oriented concepts such as progress, acceleration, and revolution, the last no longer considered in terms of *revolutio* or "return" but now "rupture." Such a reorientation could only take place when Christian eschatological time, predicated on the definitive and determined arrival of the Second Coming and Judgment Day, was superseded by the unbinding of the future from the past such that something entirely new and unexpected could come about in this world. As Koselleck noted, progress could happen when "the expectations that reached out for the future became detached from all that previous experience had to offer."[13] For Heine the processes of modernization and industrialization, especially railway construction projects and the primacy placed on speed, offered the material proof of and justification for this radical temporal reorientation.[14]

Writing a number of years after the so-called *Sattelzeit* (saddle period) of 1780–1820, a span that Koselleck, among others, sees as the start of a modern experience of temporality,[15] Heine's mix of fear over and enthusiasm for the unknown bears witness to precisely this ongoing, structural reorientation of the modern world. Superlatives, in conjunction with a sense of inevitability—"the most monstrous," "the most unheard of," "irresistible"—are thus not only descriptors of the railway's transformative technology but are also the diagnosis of a new historical time. This is an age in which the fundamental prerequisites of being-in-the-world and narrating experience, namely, the ways in which space and time are known, organized, and related to one another, are completely reconfigured. In short, it is the age of an unprecedented mobility and unpredictable modernity.

The railways brought forth such a seemingly or potentially unbounded mobility because formerly faraway distances were bridged and formerly extended durations were shortened. As Heine foresaw the basic epistemological implications, more than a decade before anything close to a railway system was built on the mainland European continent, the ways in which we both intuit the world and represent our experiences of the world are structured by temporal and spatial life-world concepts that have now been rendered remarkably unstable: "Even the elementary concepts of time and space have become shaky. The railways have killed space, and only time still remains for us. If only we had enough money to respectfully kill time, too."[16] Although Heine did not flesh out the epistemological consequences of this new mobility, which I intend to do in this chapter by examining the new relationships between the experience of mobility and the formation of subjectivity, he consistently reacted—sometimes in horror—to the eradication of traditionally secured spatial distinctions and temporal markers. For instance, as early as 1831, after meeting the German railway pioneer, Friedrich List, in Paris, Ludwig Börne reports that Heine found it "a terrible idea" that he might, one day, be able to take a train from Paris to Germany in a mere twelve hours.[17] Although the first German railway line did not open until the end of 1835, Heine already feared the potential eradication of the geographic distinction between Germany and France, not to mention the relative safety that the distance of exile allowed. But by 1843, predicting that French railways would eventually connect Paris to any major city in Germany, Heine wrote on a more sanguine note: "I already smell the fragrance of the German Linden trees; the North Sea is knocking at my doors."[18] By 1856, the year Heine died, railway travel between Paris and Frankfurt was indeed possible.

In his jocular wish for "enough money" to properly kill time alongside space, Heine was undoubtedly raising a subtle critique of the dominance of certain railway magnates, particularly the Rothschild and Pereire families in France, for creating financially and politically driven railway monopolies. Indeed, as we will see in chapter 5, the role of industrial capitalism and the opening up of national economies to international finance is an important part of the modernization of Germany and the modernity of the German/Jewish dialectic. The (re)invention of German nationality in the early nineteenth century and the rise of German nationalism were, at least in part, internally directed reactions to the "global" expansion of capitalism and the development of technologies for both penetrating and securing national boundaries.

Since Heine did not look to England in the early 1840s, what he failed to see was that time had already been "killed" across the channel, in the first country in the world to have constructed a national railway system.[19] In November 1840 the directors of England's Great Western Railway ordered that standard London time be kept at all of its stations and used in all of its timetables. As early as 1842, articles began to appear in the English press calling for the end of the multiplicity of local times and the implementation of a nationwide uniform time.[20] The fact that every locality maintained its own time first presented a problem in the late eighteenth century for scheduling postal deliveries and, several decades later, presented an analogous, although decidedly more dangerous, problem for coordinating trains. The idea of reliably reconnecting experience and expectation, past departures and future arrivals, was made public in the May 14, 1842, edition of the *Illustrated London News* in an article entitled "Important to Railway Travelers. Uniformity of Clocks Throughout Great Britain."[21] Although a nationally standardized time (Greenwich time) was not formally adopted by the English railway industry until 1847, the need for a uniform time was recognized as early as 1840 when local times were first abolished by railway schedules. By "killing" local times, the English invented, by the forces of necessity, a standardized, "new time."

One need only compare the relative development of railways in England, France, and Germany in the early 1840s to recognize that, when Heine was writing, the experiences of both distance and duration were fundamentally different in England than in France or Germany. By 1840, with more than eleven primary railway lines connecting every major English city to one another and with scores of subsidiary lines extending from London, Manchester, Birmingham, Newcastle, and other nodal cities, English railway lines formed a complex, structurally differentiated system.[22] I use the term *railway system* to describe a third-order network comprised of multiple, interconnected railway nodes and segments. Second-order complexity refers to *railway nodes,* defined as cities with at least two railway segments, and first-order complexity refers to simple segments connecting only two cities together. If we compare the contemporaneous railway development in Germany or France, we quickly see that neither country had yet achieved anything close to a system and, hence, did not yet have to address the epistemological, let alone the practical, communicational problems that a railway system presented. In the 1840s, with the exception of Berlin, Leipzig, and Dresden, virtually no major German cities were connected by rail. The level of complexity was either first-order segments (for instance, segments between Nuremberg-Fürth, Augsburg-Munich, Wiesbaden-Frankfurt am Main) or second-order nodes around Berlin and Leipzig. Analogously in France, a few second-order nodes existed around Paris, but nothing like a nationwide railway system emerges until the late 1850s, about the same time as Germany developed a railway system.[23]

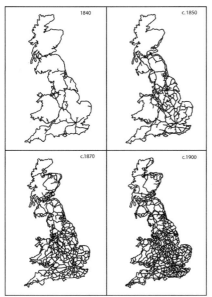

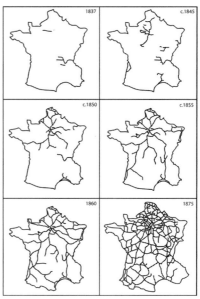

3.2 Railway development in England. *Author's drawing. Adapted from John Langton and R. J. Morris, eds.,* Atlas of Industrializing Britain, 1780–1914 *(London: Methuen, 1986), 89*

3.3 Railway development in France. *Author's drawing. Adapted from François Caron,* Histoire des chemins de fer en France, 1740–1883, *part 1 (Paris: Fayard, 1997), figure 11 (between 337–38)*

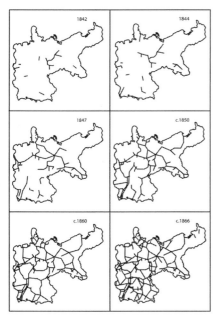

3.4 Railway development in Germany. *Author's drawing. Adapted from Hans-Henning Gerlach,* Atlas zur Eisenbahngeschichte: Deutschland, Österreich, Schweiz *(Zurich: Orell Füssli), xxi*

In this regard, to follow David Landes, we might say that the "making of the modern world"[24] brought about two complementary (and not irreconcilable) impulses. First, as Heine indicated by his diagnosis of the monstrous shock of the advent of the railway age, one of the consequences of modernity is the radical unbinding of experience from expectation; and, second, as indicated by the English institution of a national standard time, the new time of modernity necessitated the reconnection of experience and expectation through the strategic linking of past and future, the progressive coordination of tradition and anticipation. With regard to the latter, one might think of the history of the coordination of train schedules, analyzed by Wolfgang Schivelbusch as "temporal shrinkage,"[25] as due to what will become, several decades later, Greenwich mean time or uniform world time.[26] Or one might think of the organization of the "working day" or "factory time" whereby the determinate and precise linkage between experience and expectation yields surplus value.[27] Or one might think of Husserl's life-world (Lebenswelt), a structure he conceives as the reliable ground for all our activities precisely because expectations can be, more or less, derived from and based upon experiences.[28] Of course, with the making of the modern world, multiple "modern" possibilities for breaking out of these flowing and homogeneously connected temporal rhythms also emerged: Railway strikes, Marx's proletariat revolution, Bergson's individually experienced time (durée), Proust's memoire involuntaire, Sorel's general strike, Benjamin's Jetztzeit or now time, and, perhaps most ominously, the numerous messianisms that, all too often, look like and bring about the disaster.

The construction and regulation of the railway system as a third-order network of interconnected nodes and segments is thus a paradigmatic illustration of how this decidedly modern process of delinking and relinking experience and expectation looks in practice. On the one hand, the invention of the railway broke with the horizon of expectation because the political, social, and economic consequences could not be derived from the prior stock of experiences. And, on the other hand, the coordination of arrival and departure times for an international network of moving trains required a strictly predictable and derivable relationship between experience and expectation to regulate and prevent railway disasters as best as possible. Of course, contingency—most dramatically, the possibility of a crash—could never be entirely eliminated from the operation of the system, only turned into a manageable risk. This is partly because the system as a whole could not be surveyed all at once: there is no transcendental perspective on the railway system such that an observer could know, at any given time, precisely where all the trains were, in what direction they were heading, and at what speed. Despite the invention of elaborate tracking and telegraphic devices for communicating between stations and trains, railway accidents, strikes, and disasters still happened.[29] But contingency also exists because there are simply too many variables to relate to one another: a system of organized complexity means, according to Niklas Luhmann, that "it is no longer possible at any moment to connect every element with every other element,"[30] even though, within the railway system, every linked city may be eventually reached by way of a series of interchanges and connections. In other words, the railway system—as *the* material structure of modernity—is an interconnected, nonlinear whole in which experience and expectation are more or less coordinated, but no perspective exists to observe, encompass, or map its entire operation at any one time. Moreover, it is not possible to banish or master every contingency that might break apart the delicate balance; instead contingency is a defining attribute of mobile modernity.[31]

When Kafka was traveling with Max Brod through parts of southern Europe in the early 1910s and writing his first novel, *Der Verschollene* (The man who went missing, 1912), all the major cities in mainland Europe were completely connected together by a coordinated, transcontinental railway system running on a newly adopted world standard time.[32] Heine's enthusiasm for and fear over time and space being "killed" had thus in some sense come true, certainly in comparison with the prerailway life-world or in comparison with the second-order railway nodes that Heine himself experienced. While traveling by train, Kafka noted in a diary entry from September 29, 1911, that there was a fundamental difference between the modern experience of mobility on the railway and what he understood to be the experience of mobility in Goethe's prerailway life-world. Of course, Kafka did not (and could not) directly experience travel in Goethe's world; he did, however, read Goethe's accounts of his travels in the *Italienische Reise* (Italian journey) and in his novel of education, *Wilhelm Meister*. Goethe's stories are narrative renditions of his phenomenal experiences of mobility, structured by certain meta-epistemological and metaphorical structures specific to his mode of travel. More important, they document the creation of a particular kind of individualized subject whose spectatorship, subjectivity, sociality, and national identity are shored up through the narration of mobility.

Kafka lucidly recognized that different, historically specific technologies of transportation not only structure what travelers can see and know but also reveal the spatial and temporal limits, terms, and conditions of conceptualization for both narrative description and subject formation. Carriage and ship transportation supports a fundamentally different kind of spectatorship on and experience of the external world than railway travel does. In the most important consideration that he ever gave to this difference, he wrote in his diaries:

> Goethe's observations on his travels [*Reisebeobachtungen*] different from today's because made from a mail-coach, and with the slow changes of the region, develop more simply and can be followed much more easily even by one who does not know those parts of the country. A calm, so-to-speak pastoral form of thinking sets in. Since the country offers itself untouched in its innate character to the passengers in a wagon, and since highways also divide a country much more naturally than railway lines (to which the former perhaps stand in the same relationship as do rivers to canals), so too the observer need not do violence to the landscape, and he can see systematically [*systematisch sehn*] without great effort.[33]

Because of its closeness to both the landscape and the apparent rhythms of nature, carriage travel facilitates a different kind of observation on the world than that made possible by railways. Although Kafka does not show how travel by ship also contributes to the configuration of "systematic" spectatorship that he identifies with respect to Goethe's travels in a mail coach, he does draw our attention to the relationship between the natural stability of the realist landscape and the security of Goethe's masterful observations and transcendental views on the world. And, even more important, Kafka's diary entry also distills a crucial component of the meta-epistemology of the railway system, namely, that systematic seeing, or, in my words, spectatorship from an inviolable subject position on terra firma, is no longer possible when all frames of reference are contingent and in relative motion.

The narration of travel in Goethe's life-world, according to Kafka, proceeds according to a "calm," "pastoral" logic, which is "easy to follow," because the narrative, like the carriage itself, follows the "natural" rhythms and undisturbed topography of the landscape. Goethe's observations are thus linked with the "natural flow" of space whereby spectatorship emerges from the landscape's contours in a "slow" and "systematic" way. As we will see, Goethe's travels through Italy are not only systematic by virtue of the author's subject position and visual mastery over objects in the landscape, but the narrative is also systematically organized as both circular and telos driven. Precise times and exact locations provide reliable markers for the historical and geographic mapping of the narrative. Days and places follow in slow succession, while the narrative as a whole is always already connected together by a cycle of temporal continuity and return. Calling upon a well-established dichotomy between technology and nature, railways, according to Kafka, violently destroyed the natural environment and, following the logic of his reflections, not only produced new possibilities for mobility but also contributed to a new kind of narration of experience. But Kafka's reflections end here, and thus it is up to us to specify the nature of the transformation as well as the epistemological and narrative consequences for subject formation.

Although they bear witness to two very different experiences of mobility and two very different processes of subject formation, the narratives that Goethe and Kafka produced about their experiences of travel were both conceived and written from a perspective outside the German nation. In bringing Goethe and Kafka together in this chapter as a kind of conceptual-historical encounter, I am proposing that the subject of German/Jewish modernity emerges in a deterritorialized, non-national space in which mobility is variously mapped in the German language through narratives of travel.[34] Through an analysis of Goethe's *Italienische Reise*[35] and novel of education, *Wilhelm Meister*, I will argue that Goethe, in his desire to secure a transcendental or systematic perspective on safe ground for observing national differences, allows us to map the formation of a strong, individualized "German" subjectivity. The narration of mobility by carriage and ship contributes to the formation of a rationalized subject of the Enlightenment, who, despite (or perhaps precisely because of) the nonexistence of the German nation, desires the political privilege and geographic mooring of a nationally grounded subject. Building on Kafka's remark on the "systematic" nature of Goethe's observations, I show that Goethe's travel narratives and the genre of the bildungsroman itself are organized by what I call "the meta-epistemology of the ship," an episteme in which experience and expectation are never broken apart and world spectatorship is made possible by the absolute distinction between the knowing subject and the object known.

Whereas Goethe's travel narratives map the geographic, linguistic, and political privilege of a (future) national subject, Kafka's narratives of his own travels by railway as well as those of his fictional figure, Karl Rossmann, map the formation of an immigrant subject who is torn from the geography of the nation, severed from its linguistic expressions, and expelled from its political privilege. Through the figure of Karl Rossmann in the novel *Der Verschollene*, Kafka creates a "desubjectified" mass object who is ultimately disassociated from all geographies of nationality, citizenship, religion, and language. Far from an autonomous individual, Kafka's Rossmann is an abject figure of dislocation and anonymity, a byproduct of modernization, mass migration, and ineluctable systems of mobility. By examining the travels of Karl Rossmann and by placing Kafka's novel within the context of "Jewish" travel writing in Yiddish, particularly Sholem Aleichem's contemporaneous *Railroad Stories*, I show how the modern Jewish subject emerges within the deterritorialized and mediated spaces of encounter between German and Jewish mobility. Here, I suggest, the history of both the modern German subject and the modern Jewish subject—emblematically illustrated by Goethe, Kafka, and Sholem Aleichem—come together as a dialectic at a standstill in the conceptual, cultural, and material spaces of transnational mobility.

GOETHE STEERING TO PORT ON A TEMPESTUOUS SEA

On September 3, 1786, Goethe penned the first line on what was to become a nearly twenty-month long journey through Italy: "I stole out of Carlsbad at three in the morning, for otherwise I would never have gotten away."[36] Since July 27 of that year, he had been vacationing in Carlsbad with Charlotte von Stein, Duke Carl August, the Herders, and a number of other unnamed acquaintances. After most of his friends had left and after having secured an "indefinite leave" from the duke, Goethe escaped Germany in the middle of the night and began traveling incognito in a mail coach. He wanted to reach the Italian border as quickly and as quietly as possible. For years Goethe had been planning to take an extended trip to Italy, just as his father had done in 1740, but for one reason or another his plans had never materialized. In his haste to get to Italy, Goethe headed first to Innsbruck through the Bavarian cities of Regensburg, Munich, and Mittenwald, making it to the Tyrol in less than six days. Rushing through the Brenner Pass, Bolzano, and Trent, Goethe reached the town of Roveredo, "the language border," in the evening of September 11 (28). On September twelfth, "[writing] at the latitude of forty-five degrees and fifty minutes," he finds himself "truly . . . in a new land, in a completely foreign environment" (29). He remarks that doors have no locks, windows have no glass panes, and certain facilities for relieving oneself are entirely absent. This foreign land, "rather close to a state of nature" (29), is Italy. Goethe had finally arrived.

In both the retrospectively penned accounts of 1816–1817, *Reise I-II*, and to an even greater extent in the diary he kept during the journey itself and would periodically send to Charlotte von Stein, Goethe is always careful to inscribe a time and a place to his narration of the journey.[37] When he writes about leaving Roveredo for Torbole, for example, not only does he give a precise time (September 12 in the evening after five), he also gives a precise latitude (forty-five degrees and fifty minutes). As will we see, the ways in which Goethe experiences, describes, and specifies both temporality and geography are highly significant for his determination of national differences. Moreover, the emplotment of time and place in the narration of the journey is also revealing of the production of a particular kind of subject position, one that emerges through Goethe's ambitious spectatorship and political privilege as well as the larger epistemological structure of the travel narrative itself. I will discuss this below with respect to both the specific modes of mobility utilized by Goethe (carriage, foot, and ship) and the specific kinds of observations and patterns of knowledge these perspectives disclose about the places he visits.

But first let me be clear about the kinds of claims I want to make about Goethe's *Italienische Reise* and why I feel that I am justified in making certain claims about the text as a whole. As I already indicated, the text that Goethe composed about the actual journey that he undertook in Italy between 1786–1787 was only written and published retrospectively, with the distance of nearly thirty years for the first two parts (*Reise I-II*) and a distance of more than forty years for the final part (*Zweyter Aufenthalt in Rom*). Not only did an older, neoclassical Goethe intervene in the conceptualization and representation of Italy, Goethe revised, edited, and even altered the existing documents, primarily letters and diaries, that he had about the original journey. As Erich Schmidt first demonstrated, particularly for the third and final part of the *Italienische Reise*, Goethe added, crossed out, and omitted whole passages from the perspective of 1829.[38] For this reason Goethe scholars have consistently emphasized the cautionary grain of salt with which the entire "literary-historical text" should be taken. Gerhard Schultz perhaps put the admonition best:

> Whereas the author of the diaries and letters from Italy was in his thir-
> ties, that of the *Italienische Reise* was in his mid-sixties when he began
> the task of revision and just on eighty when he finally finished it. In
> other words, the traveler or "hero" of the *Italienische Reise* should not
> be equated with the actual traveler in Italy, Johann Wolfgang Goethe of
> the years 1786 to 1788; he is, rather, a fictitious character created by the
> author, a historicized version of himself.[39]

Clearly, the text of the *Italienische Reise* can be understood as more of an autobiographical-literary testament to the development of Goethe's career than it can be seen as an exact historical account of his actual trip to Italy.

These historical admonitions and critical interventions are unquestion-ably important if one wants to investigate the origins of the text and pre-vent simplistic biographical equations. My concern here, however, is not with comparing the *Italienische Reise* to Goethe's actual journey, nor is it with documenting Goethe's various deviations from the "raw" historical sources that he had before him. Additionally, I am not interested in developing an argument, which rests upon the diachronic changes in Goethe's intellectual biography or the chronology of his life. This has all been done before in order to specify, for example, definitive fault lines between the development of the "historical" and the "artistic" Goethe. Instead I am interested in looking at the ways in which the texts comprising *Reise I-II* and the diaries of the first two months (September-October 1786) bear witness to a common and largely constant, internal epistemological structure and how this structure bears on the relationship between mobility, transnationality, and subjectivity.

In both this chapter and the following chapter on Hegel and Heine, I will show how the travel narrative, by virtue of its narration of space and time—or, more precisely, by virtue of the way *the effect* of space and time is pro-duced—discloses concepts of subjectivity, nationality, and history, which are, in their epistemological and metaphorical structures, specific to, derived from, and justified by seafaring. I will call this structure the meta-epistemol-ogy of the ship in order to differentiate it from the meta-epistemology of the train and characterize the subject of German/Jewish modernity. Briefly, the meta-epistemology of the ship consists of the following: clear and stable distinctions are maintained between observer and observed, subject and object; the experiences of spectatorship are structured by the possibility of an ideal or transcendental perspective on the world "out there"; the space of the landscape can be mapped, translated, and reliably known in accord with a fixed topographical logic; and, finally, temporality, as experienced in both a given locality and conveyed over the course of the whole narrative, is structured in a continuous cycle, where experience and expectation are never broken apart and the ultimate potentiality of return, although not a mere repetition of the same, always determines the procession of the narration and the desire for nationality.

As Caren Kaplan has argued, building on the work of Michael Curry and E.H. Gombrich, the concept of the voyage is predicated on "the idea that travel produces the self, makes the subject through spectatorship and comparison with otherness. Thus, in this ideology of subjectivity, distance is the best perspective on and route toward knowledge of the self and others. Self-knowledge, standpoint, then requires a point of origin, a location that constitutes the subject as viewer and a world of objects that can be viewed or surveyed."[40] The voyage is linked with the production of knowledge, arrayed such that a knowing subject is simultaneously constituted as the objects being surveyed. It is thus not insignificant that the beginnings of German modernity and its various figurations of subjectivity, nationality, and history are invested in ship travel as both the material embodiment of mobility and a conceptual field for German/Jewish encounters.

As James Clifford and others have pointed out, the writing of a travel narrative and the genre of travel literature itself are always ideological not only because mobility and knowledge are historical and technological possibilities (or impossibilities) for some people but also because movement gains a valuation depending on who undertakes it and what its direction, goals, and reasons are. In developing a comparative methodology for studying cultural transit—what he terms "traveling-in-dwelling, dwelling-in-traveling"[41]—Clifford argues for the need to think comparatively about travel as both transnational and translational: such a project of comparative cultural studies as mobility studies "would have to grapple with the evident fact that travelers move about under strong cultural, political, and economic compulsions and that certain travelers are materially privileged, others oppressed. These specific circumstances are crucial determinations of the travel at issue—movements in specific colonial, neocolonial, postcolonial circuits, different diasporas, borderlands, exiles, detours, and returns."[42] Travel literature, then, is a particular kind of expression, whose material, social, linguistic, political, and economic conditions of possibility must be precisely articulated within the contours of comparative cultural criticism.

As we will see, travel narratives are fundamentally connected to the production of certain ideas of historicity, nationality, and subjectivity. The *Italienische Reise* is a particularly good text for showing how embodied mobility, namely ship travel, stages specific forms of spectatorship and facilitates certain forms of subjectivity because the composition of *Reise I–II* occurred precisely during the so-called *Sattelzeit* of 1780–1820. This means that we can use the emplotment of time and space in Goethe's text as a kind of possible witness to the oft-remarked epistemic shift of modernity: That is, we can ask, does the *Italienische Reise* evidence a shift away from an eschatological predetermination of temporality to an "open future" and "acceleration of time," as Reinhart Koselleck has argued?[43] Or, to use the terms of Friedrich Kittler, does the *Italienische Reise* bear witness to the creation of a new "discourse network," or *Aufschreibesystem* (system of writing down), which marks a whole set of practices of subjectivization that are unique to this epistemic moment?[44]

Thus the first task before us is to articulate, in the most precise terms possible, what these spatial and temporal structures are, how they inform Goethe's *Italienische Reise*, and how the narration of a form of mobility stemming from seafaring contributes to a specific form of subjectivity, knowledge, and spectatorship. After detailing Goethe's "meta-epistemology of the ship" and its ideological consequences for both subject formation and Goethe's unique practice of "translating" nationality, I will turn to an analysis of what I call Kafka's "meta-epistemology of the railway system." Taking Kafka's own observations about Goethe's travel writings as my starting point, I will argue that the emergence of a modernist Jewish subject in Kafka must be historicized with respect to Goethe's German subject and that both projects can be productively evaluated within a deterritorialized, transnational conceptual space in which German and Jewish come together to form a constellated image, a dialectic at a standstill.

The sea voyage or travel by ship is not only a classical mode of transportation, it is also one of the greatest, most persistent and specific metaphors of existence in the Western cultural tradition.[45] Among the countless examples, one need only bring to mind Odysseus and Aeneas, Columbus and Magellan, or Robinson Crusoe and Ahab, to begin to recognize its scope. Indeed, the ship journey, as both an actuality and an image, calls up a long history stretching back to antiquity and, in various permutations and valuations, stretching up through the present.[46] To see the dialectical complexity of the seafaring topos, one need only think of historical events such as colonial "voyages of discovery" and the horror of the middle passage, side by side with stock metaphors of self-discovery, progress, enlightenment, education, and shipwreck.[47] In its sheer cultural redundancy, the voyage, particularly the journey by sea, is vitally connected to Western culture's greatest and most horrific enterprises, institutions, and concepts.[48]

As Hans Blumenberg has argued in his brilliant overview of the seafaring paradigm, *Shipwreck with Spectator*, in antiquity seafaring was conceived as a transgression of natural boundaries but was considered by the Enlightenment to be the price and necessary risk of progress.[49] As historical events and as literary representations, sea voyages yield a wealth of metaphors for human potentialities, discoveries, and growth. In addition to tracing the metaphors generated by the sea voyage (a repertory that includes a vast array of nautical metaphors ranging from high seas to safe coasts, navigation to storms), Blumenberg also draws our attention to a persistent epistemological configuration stemming from ship travel: the ability to be a spectator.[50] Originating in Lucretius's *De Rerum Natura* and spanning the literature from Quintilian's ship of state (*navem pro republica*) to Goethe's own account of his near shipwreck in the *Italienische Reise,* and including even Heine's vitriolic, imaginary encounter with Ludwig Börne on a sinking ship, Blumenberg demonstrates what he calls the "emphatic configuration in which shipwreck at sea is set beside the uninvolved spectator on dry land."[51] This configuration of shipwreck (object) with spectator (subject) characterizes a fundamental epistemological stance, one that originates with and is specific to ship travel: the desire to observe movement from solid ground. In other words, Blumenberg shows how the valuation and cultural understanding of the seafaring metaphor changes, while its epistemological structure of spectatorship remains almost entirely constant.

Blumenberg argues that the shipwreck with spectator configuration has less to do with a distinction between those who suffer and those who do not and much more "to do with the relationship between philosophers and reality, [namely,] ... the possession of an inviolable, solid ground for one's view of the world."[52] The observation of a shipwreck or even the very fact of setting sail into the unknown is thus important because the certainty of solid land is set across from the uncertainty of seafaring. The clear distinction between terra firma and the sea (a distinction that is never sublated) is temporarily mediated but ultimately secured by the very fact that dry land is left behind and then returned to after the tumult of a (successful) sea voyage. In both the return to dry land and the possibility of a shipwreck at sea, the essential point is that solid ground is linked with subjectivity or spectatorship and that the ship or shipwreck is linked with objecthood. With this we have arrived at our first meta-epistemological point: Travel by ship, especially the uncertainty of the sea and the chance of a shipwreck, underscores the solid ground from which the belief in world spectatorship became possible. Expanding on the pattern of spectatorship derived from the ship's mediation, but ultimate guarantee, of the distinction between land and sea, the shipwreck with spectator configuration can be broadened to include the production of a reliable distinction between subject and object, observer and observed. The pattern of viewing the world "out there" as an object and securing a stable subject position to do so is thus fundamental to the epistemology of the ship-spectator configuration. This is, of course, also another way of approaching the Cartesian dichotomy between *res cognitans* and *res extensa*, mind and object, respectively. We can now turn to Goethe in order to see how both the seafaring metaphor and this meta-epistemology operate within the *Italienische Reise*.

As is evident from Goethe's writings on his trip to Italy and as numerous scholars have argued regarding the significance of the trip for his own development, Goethe's journey was essentially a voyage of self-discovery. It is no coincidence that Goethe's fact-in-fiction *Italienische Reise* approaches, and sometimes even intersects with, the educational journey undertaken by Wilhelm Meister.[53] As he says in the October 2, 1787, entry (written from the perspective of 1829, after having already written *Wilhelm Meister* in 1795–1796), "I have had the opportunity to reflect a great deal about myself and others, about the world and history, and, in my fashion, I shall tell you many good things, even though they are not new. Eventually, everything will be contained and included in *Wilhelm*" (330). Whether actually imagined as such in 1786/87 or conceived this way retrospectively is, however, of no consequence for us. What matters is that Goethe represented his own journey as a voyage of self discovery and, as we will now see, employed an extended seafaring metaphor to describe its critical progress.

In responding to a letter probably received from Charlotte von Stein, Goethe writes, just before heading to Naples, that contradictions in his letters and prose are inherent to his educational journey, which is nevertheless still goal directed. To illustrate this, Goethe tells the story of a boatman overtaken by a storm at sea. The boatman's son asks why the lighthouse is sometimes above the boat and at other times below the boat. The father explains that the sea rocked the boat up and down but the lighthouse still illuminated the way home. In the same vein, Goethe reflects on his own journey: "I too am steering to port on a tempestuous sea, and I just keep a close watch on the glow of the lighthouse; even if it seems to change its position, nevertheless I shall at last arrive safely on shore" (143–44). In this passage Goethe encapsulates both the metaphor of seafaring and the epistemology of the shipwreck-spectator configuration. The implied ship, Goethe's mode of transportation, is always already heading back to port, having survived the capricious sea.[54] His tumultuous journey will conclude safely, and, like all educational journeys of struggle and triumph, he will be better off for it. Moreover, the basic structural distinctions between sea and shore, alien and home furnish the basis for the production of a stable subject position: Goethe, as an observing subject having already arrived on terra firma, can retrospectively and safely perceive himself as an object thrashing about on a ship at sea. Here the epistemology of the ship-spectator configuration provides precisely the ground for the historical subject to observe himself as an object.

This narration of spectatorship on the world "out there" from the perspective of safe ground is the first component of the meta-epistemology of the ship. In more general terms, I would submit that the perceptual clarity of the subject/object division structures virtually all of Goethe's observations here, not only those that reflect back upon the constitution of his own transnational subjectivity but also those that enable him to characterize the national distinctiveness of Italy. Although the latter is foremost a geographic distinction (an experience of what is Italian versus an experience of what is German), Goethe is also concerned with showing how this spatial difference is confirmed by a temporality that is unique to Italy. In this respect, the sea voyage not only contributes to the formation of a subject position, but it also represents the conceptualization and evaluation of nationality.

Indeed, the single most important component of the subject/object division for Goethe's observations is the irreducible fact of the division itself: the distance separating subject and object, observer and observed, German and Italian, native and foreign, land and sea is never forsaken, and it is precisely the epistemological configuration of the ship-spectator that secures the integrity of these distinctions. The subject's observations are never confused, and Goethe accumulates knowledge and gains a perspective of world spectatorship through the experience of mobility. Upon the return voyage from Sicily, even as his ship nearly drifts onto the rocks and founders west of the bay of Naples, Goethe's totalizing, transcendental view of the world is never compromised:

> At sunset we enjoyed the most superb view given us on the whole voyage. Capo Minerva and the mountains adjacent to it lay before our eyes, enhanced by the most glowing colors, while the rocks extending down toward the south had already taken on a bluish tone. The whole illuminated coast stretched from the cape to Sorrento. We could see Vesuvius, over it a towering cloud of smoke, from which a long strip drew far eastwards, so that we could assume there had been a very strong eruption. Capri lay to the left, rising steeply; we could distinguish the outlines of its rocky walls perfectly through the transparent bluish haze. Beneath a completely clear, cloudless sky sparkled the quiet, scarcely stirring sea.   (251)

Goethe's spectatorship, made from the perspective of a returning ship at sea, is carefully organized in its bird's eye description and precise geography. As an object to be surveyed, the landscape is an orderly and encompassable panorama able to be observed, structured, and known as a totality. Even when the landscape is moving, for example, when his boat back to Naples nearly founders or when he watches the eruptions of Vesuvius, his embodied subject position is never compromised because his observations are always systematically oriented in a mappable space and emplotted, as we will see, in a cyclical time.

These ideal, transcendental perspectives on the world at large are not only specific to the instances of seafaring in Goethe's *Italienische Reise*, but they also contribute to the meta-epistemology of his project as a whole. In fact, Goethe consistently observes objects in the world from only the safest and most secure subject positions that afford him such views. His observations, replete with detail and descriptive charm, are often made from either the highest perspective he can find (atop a tower, a mountain, or an edifice) or from the slow and methodical accumulation of details on the ground. In both cases, his synthesizing vision allows a mastery of objects in the world. I would like to give a few salient examples of his techniques for such mastery. In Venice, after studying a map of the city, Goethe reports that he "climbed the tower of St. Mark's, where a unique spectacle meets the eye. It was noon and the sunshine was bright, so that I could clearly recognize places near and far without a telescope" (60–61). The high perspective over the city allowed Goethe's unaided eye to make the clear spatial distinctions necessary for an informed orientation.[55] This is even more apparent in Bologna, where he climbed the Torre degli Asinelli, a tower built between 1109 and 1119:

> The view is splendid! In the north I saw the Paduan mountains, then the Swiss, Tyrolean, and Friulian Alps, in short, the whole northern chain, now covered by mist. Toward the west a limitless horizon, broken only by the towers of Modena. Toward the east a similar plain, up to the Adriatic sea, which can be glimpsed at sunrise. Toward the south the foothills of the Apennines, cultivated up to their summits and covered with growth, studded with churches, palaces, garden houses, like the Vicenzian hills.   (87)

The geographic totality is organized by the visual clarity of the cardinal directions, mapped according to geography, and oriented according to his body in the center of the space. A couple of months later in Rome, Goethe likens his educational journey to that of an architect learning how to lay solid foundations for building towers (123).

Both times that he is in Naples, the first time after coming from Rome and the second time after returning from Sicily, Goethe is enchanted by the danger of Vesuvius. On at least three separate occasions he climbs the mountain and walks around near the precarious crater, observing the smoke-filled atmosphere and the gushing lava. But far from undermining his subject position, his close encounters with the volcano actually contribute to and even guarantee its strength. The might of the volcano certainly brings to mind both Kant and Burke's description of the sublime, and both of them illustrate the sublime by examples that will also figure prominently in Goethe's journey to Italy. Kant tells us, for example, to "consider bold, overhanging, and, as it were, threatening rocks, thunderclouds piling up in the sky and moving about accompanied by lightning and thunderclaps, volcanoes with all their destructive power . . . the boundless ocean heaved up" as examples of the sublime in nature.[56] Although Kant at first suggests that the sublime appears to betray the limits of subjectivity and reason because it cannot be readily thought or taken in (*fassen*), in the section "On the Dynamically Sublime in Nature" he proposes that the properly enlightened subject's relationship to the sublime is not based on passive respect or the inadequacy of intellect but rather on the subject's fortitude and superiority over nature. Kant writes, "we cannot pass judgment at all on the sublime in nature if we are afraid . . . we [find] in our mind a superiority over nature itself in its immensity" and, hence, must find an appropriately "safe" spot from which to take in and dominate nature (Kant 120–21).

Throughout the "Analytic of the Sublime" Kant underscores the importance of the body's physical relationship to that which is sublime or exhibits qualities of the sublime. Like Goethe, the body must assume the correct viewing distance "to get the full emotional effect" (108) of objects, such as the pyramids or St. Peter's Basilica; and the spectator's body must be careful not to "get too close" when encountering massive natural phenomena such as ravines, volcanoes, and raging streams ("General Comment"). More than once, Kant insists upon the importance of the spectator's "safety" in encountering the sublime: Any spectator on the edge of nature "is seized by *amazement* bordering on terror, by horror and a sacred thrill; . . . [but] since he knows he is *safe*, this is not actual fear. . . . We may feel that very power's might and connect the mental agitation with the mind's state of rest. In this way we feel our superiority to nature" (129; my emphasis). In a passage that strikes of Kant's safe sublime, Burke, too, writes: "Terror is a passion which always produces delight when it does not press too close."[57] Again, the physical encounter with the sublime, whether the Kantian nature or the Burkean titillation, is always predicated upon a zone of corporeal safety, a critical distance allowing a safe space for self-preservation.

For Goethe, just as with Kant and Burke, the encounter with Vesuvius and survival on the tempestuous sea do not undermine his subject position but rather strengthen it. Although close to danger, the spectator's body is preserved in the face of the sublime because the crucial distance between subject and object is never overcome. In arguably one of the most overdetermined statements he ever made about the relationship between the safe spectator and the sublime shipwreck, Goethe, reflecting on his distant spectatorship of the Battle of Jena with historian Heinrich Luden, said that he was "like a man who looks down from a solid cliff onto the raging sea and cannot help the shipwrecked men below but also cannot be reached by the breakers, and, according to some ancient [Lucretius, Luden interpolates], this is even supposed to be a comfortable feeling.... *Thus I stood there, safe and sound, and let the furious tumult pass by me.*[58] In other words, not only does Goethe's privileged subject position afford him a view of the battle, he remains inviolable because of his transcendental safety. And, once again, the metaphor of the ship and its attendant epistemology of solid ground for observation structure Goethe's remarks. His subject position is thus consolidated by sublime objects—whether historically decisive battles, erupting volcanoes, or tumultuous shipwrecks—that are observed at a safe distance from terra firma.

The last time that Goethe observes Vesuvius, the volcano is at its most dangerous, but Goethe's privileged distance is also at its greatest. He is invited to visit the palace of Giuliana, belonging to a certain Duchess of Giovane di Girasole. Standing at the window in the upper story of her palace, he observes an erupting Vesuvius:

> The sun had set long ago, and so the flames from the descending lava glowed distinctly and were beginning to gild the attendant smoke. The mountain roared violently, above it was an enormous stationary cloud of smoke whose various masses, at every eruption, were illuminated in separate sections as though by lightning.... *To survey all this at one glance*, and to see this most wonderful picture completed by the full moon, as it rose behind the mountain ridge, could hardly fail to cause astonishment. *From this vantage point my eye could take in everything at once, and although it could not scrutinize individual objects, it never lost the impression of the whole great scene.* (272; my emphasis).

Goethe's encounter with the sublime volcano is framed by a window (indeed, one of the oldest metaphors of picture making), which allows him a transcendental view of the whole object before his eyes. He surveys the volcano in a single glance, taking in the entire scene in one spectacular moment of visual mastery. Goethe's optical "voyage" of discovery thus culminates in the creation of a subject of the Enlightenment, pushed up to the edge of danger but never overcome by it. His knowing eye simply takes it in all at once.

Goethe's narrative of spectatorship is thus indebted to a subject/object configuration, which, in its articulation of the stability of solid ground for observation, owes its very formulation to what I have termed the meta-epistemology of ship travel. I have also indicated the ways in which Goethe's synthesizing perception of the world "out there" is structured by the maintenance of a strong subject who is positioned above or outside the world he observes. Again, this transcendental perspective on the world is predicated on the ability to both depart from and return to the security of terra firma. So far, however, I have spoken primarily about the epistemological stakes of Goethe's narrative of mobility. I now want to examine the specific ways in which Goethe determines nationality and national differences through the marking of space and the measurement of time. Although Goethe travels as a German subject without a nation, he introduces a specific concept of "transnational translation," to use Homi Bhabha's words, to determine and explain national differences.

In addition to the clear linguistic and geographic differences that Italy presents, Goethe is also convinced that national differences can be specified according to temporality. He believes that there exists both a "German" and an "Italian" way of marking the passage of time. That is to say, not only are German words able to be translated into their "equivalents" in Italian (and vice versa), Goethe also believes that German time can be translated into Italian time (and vice versa). Through the travel narrative, the recording of mobility becomes Goethe's own record of nationalizing subjectivity through language, space, and time. He does not seek to overcome nationality or render nationality hybrid through his journeys between two languages, two places, and two times; rather, through the realism of the travel narrative, he attempts to solidify the specificity of national differences and thereby endow the German subject without a nation with a form of nationality.

Let me begin with Goethe's articulation of the distinctiveness of marking national time. In Verona, just two weeks into his trip, Goethe observes that Italians, unlike Germans, orient their lives around "the time of day" (such as morning or evening), not the hour indicated by the clock. In characterizing the uniqueness of the Italian relationship to time, Goethe writes:

> In a land where people enjoy the day, but especially delight in the evening, nightfall is most significant. . . . When night falls here the day, which consisted of evening and morning, is definitely past, twenty-four hours have been lived, a new account begins, the bells ring, the rosary is said, the maid enters one's room with a burning lamp and says: 'Felicissima notte!' The cycle changes with every season, and the person who lives a lively life here cannot become confused because every joy of his existence is related not to the hour, but to the time of day. If a German

clock were forced on this people they would become confused, for their clock is most intimately connected with their nature. (42)

Goethe even wonders whether the German fixation on "clock time" has to do with the "eternal fog and gloom" that "we Cimmerians" (42) have to endure.[59] In a somewhat stereotypical fashion, Goethe writes that Germans have scarcely any time "to stroll and divert [themselves] beneath an open sky" (42), unlike Italians who apparently do so all day long.

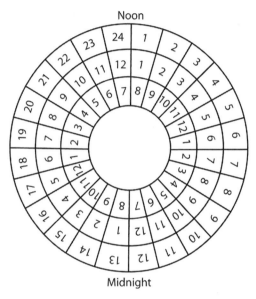

3.5 Goethe's comparison chart for the Italian and German clocks. *Author's drawing. Adapted from Johann Wolfgang von Goethe, Italian Journey, trans. Robert R. Heitner (New York: Suhrkamp, 1989), 44*

As a matter of convenience for himself, Goethe invents a "device" for translating between German and Italian time. According to Goethe, the inner circle represents the German twenty-four hours, in two cycles of twelve hours. The middle circle represents Italian time, indicated by "how the bells chime here" (43). And the outer circle represents "how in daily life one counts to twenty-four" (43). While the first hour of the day in Verona is simply indicated by one bell chime, the German clock would indicate "eight o'clock in the morning." Similarly, the last hour of the Italian day is indicated by twelve bell chimes or, translating to German time, seven o'clock in the evening. The whole cycle begins again with one bell chime (at eight o'clock German time), indicating that night has arrived. In essence, Italian time consists of two structuring blocks of time, day and night, each twelve hours long, with time beginning for both at one and ending at twelve. Although, Goethe observes, Germans and Italians tell and value time differently according to their national characteristics and patterns of life, these national temporalities can nevertheless be "translated" through the narration of mobility. In this way, as Bhabha mentions in his brief analysis of the *Italienische Reise* in his study of the time and space of the nation, Goethe's "realist narrative produces a national-historical time that makes visible a specifically Italian day in the detail of its passing time."[60]

But what Goethe seems to have really discovered in his translation of national time is the simultaneity of multiple, incommensurate, local times. Even though a "German clock" ostensibly still measured the passage of time in the same manner regardless of locale, virtually every (German or Italian) city in the late eighteenth and early nineteenth century maintained its own time, according to seasonal cycles and agricultural rhythms. The push for a uniform, nationwide and later worldwide standard time did not come about until the development of the railway system and the need to coordinate the arrival and departure times of trains as precisely as possible. This is probably attributable to the fact that, before the railway, transportation speeds were finitely fixed by horse-drawn carriages or largely uncontrollable because of their determination by the winds at sea. With the national and international spread of railways, the unprecedented acceleration of movement necessitated the abolition of locally determined and maintained times in favor of synchronized schedules and coordinated time zones.[61] However, in the life-world before railways, local times could still be "translated" since they exhibited local, if not national, particularities. In other words, despite his belief otherwise, Goethe's transnational translation of time is less specific to articulating nationality and more a consequence of locality: He was not translating the German clock into the Italian day, but simply the locality of time in one place into the locality of time in another. By the end of the nineteenth century, Weimar and Verona would be placed in the same time zone, and, hence, his translation of temporality would be superfluous (although national differences, seemingly paradoxically, would become all the more rigid).

Goethe, however, never gave up the belief that the way in which time is measured and experienced is an indication of national particularity. After all, one of the goals of writing a realist travel narrative is to convey the uniqueness of "Italian" measurements of time, or at least the impression or effect of this time, while consolidating his own—German—subjectivity through difference. This is especially the case in his characterization of the "Italian day," and, as Bakhtin has elegantly shown, it also figures prominently in his representation of *The Roman Carnival,* a short, illustrated picture book published by Goethe in 1789/90.[62] The description of the Roman carnival is shown to be specific to the locality of the Italians, evoked in all its unique color and dynamic presence, ranging from the promenade in the Corso to the spectacles of horse racing. Here, the realist travel narrative also reveals a certain anthropological practice of history: Goethe seeks to endow a space with its temporality or, in other words, link the specific geography of a place with the complexity of its patterns for marking time. In this respect, the Italian day has both a unique temporality and a specific space.

It is here that the realist organization of the travel narrative is most clearly betrayed as an ideological form of subject formation. While in Rome, for the first time on November 1, 1786, Goethe attempts to convey the impression of the uniqueness of the city's layered topography and its nonsimultaneous history. But since "the capital of the world," as he calls it, is essentially the telos of his voyage, he can think of nothing more to wish for after having arrived in Rome than simply to return home:

> What shall I ever wish for afterwards? Nothing more that I can think of, except to land safely at home in my pleasant boat.... Now ... [that I have arrived] my friends and fatherland truly become dear to me again. Now I look forward to my return, indeed all the more so because I feel very certain that I shall not be bringing all these treasures back just for my own possession and private use, but so that they may serve both me and others as guidance and encouragement for an entire lifetime.   (102–3)

Goethe considers his arrival in Rome as a "second natal day, a true rebirth" (121), one that serves both his own voyage of self-discovery and fosters new directions and relationships with his friends and homeland. He has not only accumulated objects of knowledge throughout the voyage but has also become a knowing subject; however, the journey can only be completed upon his return home. After all, these newfound treasures of knowledge and a strong, nationally distinctive subjectivity can finally only be articulated upon his return to Weimar. Otherness secures the self—but only upon returning home.

For this reason the realist travel narrative is not simply a chronology of transnational mobility but, just as important, a cycle of return. As he delves more deeply into the city, Goethe realizes that it is harder and harder to write about it. Using another seafaring metaphor, he says: "For just as the sea is found to be ever deeper, the farther one goes into it, so it is with me in my inspection of this city. The present cannot be understood without the past, and comparison of the two requires more time and leisure" (135). For him, as Bakhtin has also pointed out, past, present, and future are all bound together in "a ring of necessity."[63] He encounters the ruins of Roman history, in the specificity of the local present, for the sake of his own future. There is no rupture between past experience and future expectations, only a cyclical continuity uniting them together, as if "the whole world is just a simple wheel" (172) or, as Goethe says in another context, as if "you are enclosed in a magic circle."[64]

Indeed, Goethe's narrative of his journey is suffused with cycles of return. First of all, although he believes that Italian and German modes of measuring local time differ according to national characteristics, time runs in a reliable, seasonal cycle in both places. That is to say, even though Goethe argues that Italian time differs from the "German clock," a cyclical temporality, whereby experience and expectation are linked together in the present, is nevertheless still fundamental to both the north and the south. Second, Goethe's experiences of Roman antiquity are always closely linked with his present and the realization of his already fulfilled future. And finally, the voyage itself, derived from both an extended metaphor of ship travel and the actuality of two voyages by sea, is structured by and predicated on the desire to ultimately return home. It is no coincidence that one of the first things Goethe does upon landing on the island of Sicily is to rush out and buy a copy of Homer's *Odyssey* (195). He dutifully reads his daily portion while using "this living environment [as] . . . the best possible commentary" he could have for his readings and, eventually, for the production of the idea for his own *Odyssey* (238). With its newly resonant, descriptive detail of the sea voyage—particularly, Odysseus's encounters with foreignness, his ultimately safe return home, and, most of all, the retelling of the tale—Goethe reflects on his own journey. "Only now," he writes to Herder on May 17, 1787, does "the *Odyssey* become a living word for me" (256). With its structuring encounters with and observations of foreignness, coupled with its cycle of return and formation of a national subject without a nation, the *Italienische Reise* is essentially Goethe's *Odyssey*. In sum, then, the travel narrative—as both the realization of a form of subjectivity and the articulation of an idea of nationality and national difference—is an ideological form narrated according to cycles of foreignness, discovery, individuality, and return.

We can elaborate on the formation of the German subject without a nation by briefly comparing the structures discussed above with his paradigmatic novel of education, *Wilhelm Meister*, a novel largely written after Goethe returned from his trip to Italy. Although the protagonist, Wilhelm, never takes a trip on a ship, his education is certainly a temporal voyage of discovery, both metaphorically and literally, wherein the narration of the tale follows the logic of the meta-epistemology of the ship in terms of its telos of producing a socialized, autonomous, and nationally grounded subject. As Benedict Anderson astutely observed with regard to the temporal organization of the European novel, something that certainly applies to the bildungsroman: "The idea of a sociological organism moving calendrically through homogeneous, empty time is a precise analogue of the idea of the nation, which is also conceived as a solid community moving steadily down (or up) history."[65] Goethe and Wilhelm Meister develop socially as they move though the empty, homogeneous time of the calendar in which experience and expectation are reliably connected to one another. Their movements and growth are not only analogues for the nation but, through their repetition, are precisely how the nation emerges as a desired or imagined community.

Both the *Italienische Reise* and *Wilhelm Meister* are travel narratives that are structured by a linear temporal development (a series of formative educational encounters that build upon one another) and a cyclical return to the beginning: Like Goethe, Wilhelm returns home at the end of the novel to rediscover his past, accept his inheritance, and recognize the guiding hand of the perennial authority of the so-called Tower Society. Wilhelm's journey begins with him leaving home in order to join and later direct the "migratory empire" of a traveling theater.[66] Over the course of his journey, he meets many people, some of whom offer advice and guidance, others of whom seem to distract from his education. After completing his "apprenticeship" years and finally announcing his intention to renounce the theater, Wilhelm is initiated into the Tower Society, a secret society, which, it turns out, has been covertly guiding his educational journey from the very start. At the end, Wilhelm not only receives an ideal body ("deep-set" eyes, a "delicate" nose and mouth), but also gains "the feeling of fatherhood" and "all the virtues of a citizen" (*Gefühl des Vaters . . . alle Tugenden eines Bürgers*) who participates in civil society.[67] Having mastered the necessary skills and completed the educational journey, Wilhelm is integrated into the authority of the Tower Society and its architecture of timeless power. The novel of education concludes by coming full circle: In the end, Wilhelm is reunited with both his son Felix and the objects of art from his family's inheritance. He then gets married to a woman, Natalie, whom he has known all along. The end not only connects back to the beginning but was preprogrammed from the start. In this sense, at the end of the journey, Wilhelm goes home as a father and a productive German citizen precisely because he is fortunate enough to have always already been a father and a productive German citizen. The circularity is mutually reinforcing.

In *Wilhelm Meister* as well as Goethe's fictionalization of his travels in the *Italienische Reise* both characters leave home, explore foreign lands, learn about different customs, and, finally, get to return home having accumulated knowledge and social experience. On their respective journeys they both receive guidance and direction by virtue of their political privilege and prior familial positions: Goethe, knowing that his all-access freedom rests entirely on his political status in Germany, repeatedly mentions how fortunate he is that he can travel "incognito" and still benefit from elite social and political contacts. Similarly, Wilhelm can leave home and be guided "by some kindly hand" out of middle-class life[68] precisely because the noble authority of the Tower Society quietly directs his social and intellectual formation. Despite near misses, potential failures, and possible shipwrecks, neither character is undermined, weakened, or rendered impotent on his respective journey because a zone of corporeal and specular safety governs his observations and encounters with the external world. And, finally, although both Goethe and Wilhelm journey far from their homes, they never surrender their familial, cultural, linguistic, and social ties. The circularity of the bildungsroman ensures these bonds and always returns the protagonists home as better, stronger, and more socialized subjects than when they left. In this respect, the bildungsroman is a "voyage" of self-discovery, individualization, subject formation, and national mooring. In both its metaphorical capacity and its epistemological configuration travel by ship provides the basis for the generic integrity and narrative structure of the bildungsroman and its structures of subject formation.

Moreover, because the voyage by sea is, more or less, reliable and repeatable—that is, future expectations derive from and match up with past experiences—the novel of education can be, more or less, universalized and held together by structures of power that thrive on such reliability and repeatability. These structures of power, in play throughout both Goethe's texts, include the rules of inheritance and patriarchal authority, sexual and familial norms, the class-based stratification of society, the world of commodities and exchange, and, finally, the legitimacy of the weight of the past, represented primarily by museum objects, art and book collections, and relics from antiquity.[69] Both Wilhelm and Goethe benefit personally by them and even become socially integrated, educated, and responsible subjects precisely because their bodies and histories fit comfortably within these structures of power. When taken together, these structures also form the basis of an enlightened, civil society. The seafaring topos, with its characteristic journey of education, growth, and self-discovery, thus functions and gains legitimacy by repeatedly linking *Bildung* with *Besitz* (property) such that the individual subject, formed within such structures of power, also participates in the repetition, extension, and conservation of society.[70]

The goal then is not just the Bildung of the individual but also the production and enforcement of a broader, power-laden social ideal. As Jarno, one of the highest-ranking members of the Tower Society enthusiastically declares at the end of *Wilhelm Meister*, the pedagogy of the Tower Society should be "[extended] into every corner of the globe, and people from all over the world will be allowed to join it." His reason, however, is not worldwide altruism but rather strategic self-preservation: "We will cooperate in safeguarding our means of existence, in case some political revolution should displace one of our members from the land he owns."[71] The Tower Society's theory of education, with Wilhelm as its model student, not only desires to maintain its architecture of power ("the hall of the past") and its panoptic system of control in German-speaking regions, it also wants worldwide influence. In effect, the Tower Society—in its institutional, economic, patriarchal, and architectural authority—is both the product of the systematic connection between experience and expectation and also an ideological power realized and exerted through the cyclical organization of the travel narrative itself. Only Friedrich, the society's sole critic, disparages its self-serving pedagogy and Enlightenment-colonial goals, calling them nothing but a bunch of "young colonists."[72] The Tower Society, however, is already preparing to send its missionaries off "to Russia and the United States" to secure its future and spread the gospel of Enlightenment and Bildung. Indeed, this colonization by sea is crucial not only to spread the Enlightenment idea of subject formation and the attendant concept of nationality but, as we will see in chapter 4 on Hegel and Heine, also critical to the way in which the progress of world history was conceived. It is not until Adorno that this achievement would be most trenchantly assessed: the "fully enlightened earth radiates disaster triumphant."[73]

With this we can sum up the meta-epistemology of the ship and the life-world that it discloses. First of all, ship travel and the possibility of shipwreck initiates a long-standing epistemological configuration in which subjectivity and nationality are secured precisely by the insoluble difference between the sea and solid ground. This difference, as we have seen, is the basis of the desire for and the possibility of a transcendental perspective on the world as well as the production of the desire for a nationally grounded subject. Moreover, it is also the basis for the maintenance of a Cartesian subject/object dichotomy for observation and the steady accumulation of knowledge. Through this process of collecting knowledge and characterizing nationality through linguistic, spatial, and temporal difference, Goethe's realist travel narrative betrays its ideological edge. "Voyages of discovery" and cycles of return not only shore up individuality but also solidify the Enlightenment ideal of Bildung achieved through the exclusivity of structures of power in preserving and expanding the missionary reach of civil society. This is the narrative enactment of the "dialectic of Enlightenment."

We can now provide some answers to the questions I posed at the start of this chapter about the "acceleration of time" and the possible break with an eschatological predetermination of temporality. What we do not see in Goethe's *Italienische Reise*, contrary to Koselleck's determination of "new time," is the rupture between the space of experience and the horizon of expectation. Even David Wellbery's recent detection of "an acceleration of time" in Goethe's early work, particularly in Goethe's poem "An Schwager Kronos" (October 10, 1774), indicates only the *desire* for the acceleration of time.[74] After all, a passenger riding in a mail coach tells Cronos to go ever faster, despite the obvious physical limitations of the horses pulling the carriage. Wellbery argues that the figure of the absolute in Goethe—the moment (*Augenblick*) of excitement, death, or crash—is a harbinger of the acceleration, even annihilation, of time. But, what is yet to happen is the paradigmatic rupture between past and future, or the phenomenological experience of an acceleration of time. The latter does not occur until the birth of the railway.

In fact, the first two parts, *Reise I–II* (conceived in 1786 but written and published in final form in 1816–17), testify to the exact opposite: Temporality is experienced as a cycle of continuity, with the expectation of safe return structuring the procession of the journey.[75] In this respect, the narrative form of the *Italienische Reise* is essentially a *nostos*, one of the most antique of storytelling structures.[76] The narrative proceeds linearly insofar as days come and go in succession, but the end is always already determined from the start. Experience and expectation are linked together in a reliable framework whereby knowledge accumulates in an organized and repeatable fashion. Finally, although not a simplistic repetition of the same, the end returns to the beginning, completing the circle of development with a kind of inheritance of the past. Once again, the journey—a literal, metaphorical, and epistemological voyage—is always back home to the nation that does not yet exist. The "modernity" of both these travel narratives (the *Italienische Reise* and *Wilhelm Meister*) comes less from the narration and experience of time and space and more from the subject's obsessive desire to secure terra firma for his totalizing, systematic, and transcendental perspective on the world "out there." In much the same way that Cronos desires to go ever faster but cannot exceed the period's technological limitations on mobility, Goethe desires to return home to the nation, even though that possibility, too, does not yet exist, save the desire. As Goethe predicted in the last years of his life, not ships and seafaring would unify the German nation but the construction of the railway system and the narration of mobility in accordance with a phenomenologically new experience of space and time: "I have no fear about the unity of Germany: Our good roads and future railways will do their part,"[77] he remarked in 1828. But Goethe did not live long enough to ride a German train: He died three years before the first segment of the future German railway system opened between Nuremberg and Fürth. Space and time would soon be "killed," but national differences, as Goethe predicted, would be far from overcome.

KAFKA, SHOLEM ALEICHEM, AND THE (JEWISH) IMMIGRANT MASS OBJECT

In 1835 two ostensibly unrelated events occurred: the first German railway line, a six-kilometer track between Nuremberg and Fürth, began operation and, in Russia, Nicholas I established the Pale of Settlement, restricting Jews to a zone in Western Russia bordering Germany and Austria-Hungary. Jews from Fürth, a predominantly Jewish town, could take the train to work in Nuremberg during the day but were not allowed to stay overnight. As in many other German cities and provinces, mobility was permitted, but settlement was not. And, within the Pale, Jews could move between designated provinces; however, if they left the Pale, reentry could be denied and Russian citizenship revoked. Settlement was granted, but mobility was strictly regulated. "German modernity" might be seen as the story in which these two historically distinct events became ever more intensely connected through the creation of transnational spaces of encounter between Germans and Jews. At the same time, "Jewish modernity" might be seen as a story of settlement and mobility wherein the construction and spread of the railway became the means of both facilitating mass migration and checking emancipation. Because they conditioned one another, it only makes sense to speak of them as inseparably linked, as German/Jewish modernity.

The industrialization of Germany and most of Western and Eastern Europe in the nineteenth century was largely achieved by building new and efficient means for mobility and exchange. In the span of a few decades, isolated railway segments formed industrial railway nodes, and, by the 1870s, turned into a supranational railway system. Within Germanic regions railways were invested with a kind of salvific power since they quickly became regarded as the means and the symbol of unity for a modern, industrialized nation. As Goethe and Friedrich List had predicted before the first railway even began running in Germany, the scattered Germanic people and isolated Germanic states would be brought together and unified by the construction of a railway network. Indeed, they were not wrong. Railways advanced both national unification and massive economic changes for a modernizing Germany: railway growth and the accompanying industrial expansion (coal and iron production, exportation, the formation of infrastructure and capital) formed a greater part of Germany's total domestic production during the nineteenth century than that of any other country.[78] As Friedrich Harkort enthusiastically declared about the modernization achieved by way of the railway: "The locomotive is the hearse on which absolutism and feudalism will be carried to the graveyard."[79] And, as Wilhelm Raabe declared with regard to the German nation: "The German Empire was founded with the first railway line."

But both Harkort and Raabe forgot the Jews in German modernity. After all, as we will see in more detail in chapter 5, Jews played an important role in German industrialization and railway financing as well as comprised not a small part of the passenger list on the first German railway between Nuremberg and Fürth.[80] Moreover, during the last decades of the nineteenth and first part of the twentieth century, Jews were ubiquitous on trains, with hundreds of thousands of migrating Eastern Jews traveling through Germany to escape economic and political hardships in the Pale of Settlement. We might say more correctly that "the locomotive of traveling Jews is the hearse on which absolutism and feudalism will be carried to the graveyard" and that "the German Empire was founded with Jews traveling on the first railway line."

The construction of a network of trains connecting Germany to Eastern Europe and Russia thus wrought tremendous demographic and socioeconomic changes in the ways that national spaces were configured and monitored as well as in the ways that Germans encountered Jews and dealt with transmigration. National borders became simultaneously more porous and more stringently regulated. And, during the last quarter of the nineteenth century, Jews began to emigrate from the Pale of Settlement in historically unprecedented numbers. Not only did Jews play disproportionate roles in railway financing, but largely poor, Hasidic Eastern Jews also began to migrate west in disproportionate numbers through the major railway hubs in Berlin, Prague, and Vienna in order to find economic opportunity and escape pogroms. Nearly half a million Jews migrated from Galicia, Bohemia, Moravia, and Romania through Austria-Hungary and/ or Germany between 1870 and the end of the First World War, and over three million Jews from Russia and the Polish sectors passed through Germany—the vast majority through Berlin—during the same period.[81] In his study of the perception of Eastern-European Jews in Germany, Steven Aschheim likens this sudden surge in Jewish migration to "the floodgates [being] unleashed."[82]

Because of Germany's unique geographic position between the West, the Pale of Settlement, the czarist Russian Empire, and the Austro-Hungarian Empire, the German states formulated extensive and often contradictory administrative policies for regulating the immigration and transmigration of Jews. Unlike other European countries or the United States, Germany never enacted a national policy regarding Jewish immigration; instead individual states evaluated Jews based on economic utility, often facilitating transmigration to England or the "New World" from German ports but generally refusing citizenship to Eastern Jews and deporting tens of thousands who wanted to settle in the Reich.[83]

It is in this regard that the railway began to manifest a dialectical history: trains facilitated an unprecedented mobility and mass migration, but, at the same time, they also enabled people to be denied citizenship and deported en masse. This historical precedent was already established in its most basic form in 1835 when Jews began traveling by train to Nuremberg but were forced to dwell in Fürth. As Walter Benjamin remarked about the significance of the railway in his material history of the nineteenth century, trains contributed to the formation of mobile masses of people: "The historical signature of the railroad may be found in the fact that it represents the first means of transport—and, until the big ocean liners, no doubt also the last—to form masses. The stagecoach, the automobile, the airplane carry passengers in small groups only."[84] The dialectical complexity of the railway emerges precisely from the bidirectional movement of the Jewish masses: First, from East to West and, later, from West to East. In both cases, Jews are figured as mobile masses: Mass migration and mass deportation.

Sholem Aleichem's *Railroad Stories: Tales of a Commercial Traveler* address the dialectics of mobility against the historical background of the waves of mass migrations of Jews out of the Russian Empire.[85] For Sholem Aleichem the modernity of the railway system not only facilitated mass mobility but also prevented it because trains both enabled emancipation and unleashed terror. Jews who were previously isolated in small towns could now travel with comparatively greater freedom; but, at the same time, Cossacks could also travel to Jewish settlements, and Jews could be more efficaciously expelled from their land.[86] As we will see, Sholem Aleichem's trains are populated with gregarious, Yiddish-speaking Jews who are moving within a massive, transnational network embodying both the hopes and catastrophes of the dialectic of modernity. Not unlike Kafka's protagonist Karl Rossmann in his immigration story, *Der Verschollene*, the Jews in Sholem Aleichem's *Railroad Stories* comprise part of a mobile mass dissociated from the individualized privilege granted to "national subjects" who have a geographic, political, and linguistic mooring. Whereas Kafka's Karl is a figure of disposability who has either lost or is denied everything that might contribute to the creation of an identity or subject position, including any religious or cultural ties to Judaism, the

Jews in Sholem Aleichem's stories create a vibrant "diasporic conscious-ness" through their cultural and linguistic mobility as well as their chance encounters with others—Jews and non-Jews—on the train.[87] Karl, on the other hand, is never allowed the space to develop such a diasporic con-sciousness; instead he is buffeted about as the unfortunate byproduct of the forces of modernity, becoming nothing more than an anonymous, mass object of modernization.

Kafka's 1912 novel of transmigration, *Der Verschollene*, clumsily translat-ed as "the man who went missing" but better known by the title Max Brod gave the text, *Amerika*, is the story of the first few months of Karl Ross-mann's new life in America.[88] At the novel's start, Karl, a seventeen-year-old boy from Prague, arrives on the Hamburg-America line in the port of New York. The novel ends with Karl joining a traveling theater troupe sup-posedly based in Oklahoma and traveling with his new colleagues for days and nights by train over great bridges and through treacherous mountains into the unknown. From his arrival by ship to his departure by train, Karl is a figure of disposability, trapped in a world of unmasterable mobility wherein everything is connected together, but the linkages and networks betray precious little logic, openness, or necessity. In trying to navigate these linkages and networks, Karl is unrelentingly bombarded by nonstop movement, while his body is constantly cramped into tiny places where he has virtually no control over his own mobility: He is shipped off to Amer-ica on a giant ocean liner by his family in Prague but becomes stuck in a steerage cabin too small for two people; he is given a penthouse room in his American uncle's six-story home but becomes trapped and disoriented on the forbidden balcony; he is driven by car through New York to a fam-ily friend's country home but has no idea how he got there nor how much time expired since he left, and, upon entering the house, he becomes lost in its endless corridors; he lands a job as a lift boy in a gargantuan hotel but is forced to work twelve-hour shifts; he tries to escape the hotel by foot but becomes ensnared by an unbroken, unending stream of cars; finally, he decides to join the Theater of Oklahoma but is abruptly forced into a train compartment without any luggage and driven off to an uncertain destination.

Unlike Goethe who moves deliberately through the Italian landscape, accumulating knowledge by the methodical inspection of topography and the comparative measurement of temporality, Karl neither masters the American landscape nor gains an iota of knowledge about its geography or history. Whereas the *Italienische Reise* is carefully organized by Goethe's arrivals at and departures from precise places on specific dates—so much so that he even learns to "translate" between Italian time and German time—Karl never learns what it might mean to be an "American" and never even knows where he is, apart from the very first line of the novel, which places him in New York City.[89] Like so many of Kafka's other protagonists—Josef K., Gregor Samsa, K., Josephine—Karl Rossmann is a radically ahistorical character, severed by the force of circumstance from his past, with no constitutive hopes or expectations for the future. He is plucked down into an unplaceable geography of the present and buffeted about by constantly shifting, bewildering, and inexplicable contingencies.

Far from offering liberty and justice, Karl's America is a modernist nightmare presided over by the Statue of Liberty carrying a sword in her outstretched arm. Unlike the landscapes that Goethe so relaxingly surveys on his journey of education, every place that Karl perceives is not only unwelcoming but also lacks topographical stability, history, and meaning. For this reason he cannot orient himself according to geography, temporality, or language. In fact, the possibility of finding terra firma is foreclosed the very first time that Karl gets a broad view of the American harbor from the window of the stoker's tiny room:

> Great ships crossed each other's courses in either direction, yielding to the assault of the waves only as far as their weight permitted them. If one squinted one's eyes, these ships seemed to be swaying under their own weight. . . . Probably from some battleship there could be heard salvoes, fired in salute; the gun-barrels of one ship that passed at no great distance gleamed with the reflection of the sunlight on steel, as it seemed to be nursed along by the sure, smooth motion, although not on an even keel. Only a distant view of the smaller ships and boats could be had, at least from the door, as they darted about in swarms through the gaps between the great ships. And behind them all rose New York, and its skyscrapers stared at Karl with their hundred thousand windows.   (G 19–20/E 11–12; translation altered)

Not only does the view out the window preclude a systematic spectatorship on the external world, but the cacophony of mobility prevents Karl from finding any stable ground or any encompassing view to organize the entirety of the scene.[90] Unlike Goethe's specular mastery of Vesuvius from the window of the duchess's palace, Karl finds the undomesticated objects under visual inspection looking back at him. The windows of the skyscrapers function like undomesticated eyes, returning his gaze one hundred thousand times over.[91] Observer and observed have switched places. Kafka's America, in its adamant refusal and constant mocking of the possibility of securing a reliable subject position for any view on the world, is a very different landscape than Goethe's Roman Campagna.

As we have seen, Goethe's travel narratives are structured by what I termed the meta-epistemology of the ship, an epistemological configuration in which the subject/object division is never destabilized and Goethe's individualistic, systematic, and transcendental view of the world "out there" is made possible by the security of terra firma. The generic basis for the bildungsroman is encompassed by the realism of the spectator's persistent search for and successful voyage towards solid ground from which to observe and know the world. It is marked by a temporal structure of preordained development and cyclical return. As a counterconcept, then, the structure of Kafka's Der Verschollene might be productively termed the meta-epistemology of the railway system, a configuration characterized by the dissolution of the very possibility of solid ground, the utter destruction of a knowing subject with a transcendental perspective on the world, the relativity and contingency of all temporal and spatial frames of reference, and, finally, the articulation of an interconnected world of mass mobility. Far from an autonomous, knowing subject, the kind of subjectivity that emerges is a "desubjectified" mass object of migration.

Of course, the range and nature of the metaphors generated by railway travel are also quite different from those generated by the sea voyage. For one, although the train is often considered metaphorically as well as literally to "stitch together" the body politic of the nation (as we will see in chapter 5), the train is never a metaphor for the nation, unlike the Staatsschiff, the "ship of state." When it is given metaphorical form, the train is often linked with theology, as Heine perceptively noted in 1843: the invention of the railway is a "providential event." On the one hand, the train is the devil or the destroyer of nature and, on the other hand, the symbol for the faith in progress.[92] At no point, however, are metaphors of train travel likened to voyages of discovery, education, or growth, and, hence, as I argued earlier, the technological conditions of possibility for the genre of the bildungsroman were to be found in the prerailway life-world of carriages and ships.

From the moment he arrives in New York's harbor through the last time he looks out the train window on his way to Oklahoma, Karl is a figure of loss and rejection—"the one who went missing"—who is funneled through and finally ejected from inscrutable systems of power and unknowable topographies of displacement. Besides a single suitcase, umbrella, and photograph of his parents (all of which he will lose as he wanders through America), Karl has no possessions, no citizenship, no religion, and no home. According to his uncle, who rejects him and kicks him out of his house, Karl lacks a proper socialization, has an inadequate formal education, and can barely speak English. In other words, Karl has neither Besitz nor Bildung, the two constitutive components of subject formation in the traditional bildungsroman. He never becomes a subject because he never knows or produces anything. As Karl is moved through the novel, he becomes ever more ahistorical, losing all connections he once had to the past, learning nothing from his experiences in the present, and hoping for nothing particular in the future. He is always confined to the dislocation of a given moment, without direction, orientation, history, or expectation.

Whereas Goethe's *Wilhelm Meister* begins with the "uselessness" of the theater and ends with four marriages and the legitimacy of sexual reproduction, Kafka's *Der Verschollene* begins with the illegitimacy of sexual reproduction and ends with Karl joining a traveling theater. This reversal is not insignificant, for Kafka is quite deliberately subverting the genre of the bildungsroman, not only in its inevitable teleology of socialization and recitable subject formation but also in the latter's meta-epistemological structure of voyage, self-discovery, and return. In contrast to Goethe's Wilhelm Meister, seventeen-year-old Karl, after being seduced by his family's thirty-five-year-old maid and fathering a child, is expelled from his home and country. He never gains the social status of "father" or the political privilege of "citizen," and, over the course of his wanderings, is always an outsider who is in no way assimilated into American society.[93] Even in the few seemingly propitious moments in which Karl might gain status, he is promptly ejected from participation in or benefit from any system of power. He has no access to sexual, economic, social, political, or material privilege, and the associated structures of power consistently forbid him entry. On the contrary, Goethe's Wilhelm is always already admitted into the Tower Society's structure of power. He is named *Meister* (master) from the very start, and his travels record his development into a virtuous, productive, and autonomous citizen.

While Goethe's systematic and transcendental observations on the world "out there" were made from solid ground (both the narrative representation of a stable position for viewing and the historical stability accorded to his retrospective writing of the *Italienische Reise*), Karl's observations are consistently confused because neither his position for observation nor the objects in his world is ever stable. Not only do observer and observed unpredictably switch places in Kafka's narrative, the seemingly safe perspective from above offers none of the security or mastery that Goethe was accustomed to experiencing. Objects "escaped his eyes" (G 144/E 112); new vantage points do not contribute to knowledge or facilitate mastery (G 154/E 119); the highest or broadest views, for example, those from atop his uncle's sixth floor balcony, are instead the most disconcerting:

> But what would have been the highest vantage point in his hometown allowed him here little more than a view of one street, which ran perfectly straight between two rows of squarely chopped buildings and therefore seemed to be fleeing into the distance, where the outlines of a cathedral loomed in the dense haze. And in morning as well as evening and far into the dreaming night that street was the channel for a constant stream of traffic which, seen from above, looked like an inexplicable confusion, for ever newly improvised, of foreshortened human figures and of roofs of all kinds of vehicles, sending into the upper air another confusion, more riotous and complicated, of noises, dust, and smells, all of it enveloped and penetrated by a flood of light which the multitudinous objects in the street scattered, carried off and again busily brought back, with an effect as palpable to the beguiled eye as if a glass roof stretched over the street were being violently smashed into fragments at every moment.
>
> (G 55/E 38–39, translation slightly modified)

In this extraordinary passage, the possibility of a transcendental perspective on "America" is foreclosed to Karl. The objects before him are in a constant, inexplicable motion, and "the beguiled eye" can do nothing more than surrender to the simultaneous violence. Karl can neither orient his body in the space observed, nor discern any organizing logic inherent to the geography. He is neither the master nor the center of the coordinate system. Moreover, the view has no history and cannot be placed in a narrative of before and after, "no longer" and "not yet," because it has no temporal extension: it is pure event. Everything occurs simultaneously, from morning to evening, and repeats itself indefinitely, like a "glass roof . . . violently smashed into fragments at every moment."[94]

This description stands in marked contrast to Goethe's narration of travel in which chronological time, national spaces, and transcendental spectatorship are distinct, reliable, predictable, and absolutely determinable domains. In the *Italienische Reise* dates and places are strung together by the definitive connection between experience and expectation, whereby comings and goings by carriage and ship are always already contained in a continuous cycle of narrative return. Linear, historical time runs forward from day to day and repeats itself in seasonal cycles of return; the Cartesian spaces of national differences, filled with objects of beauty for contemplation, are amenable to the regularity of a coordinate system with clear borders and a mappable topography; and, finally, Goethe, as a mobile subject, can systematically observe the world "out there" from the most privileged positions and stable points of view that transcendental spectatorship will permit. However, in Kafka's travel narrative, time, space, and observation fold together, even unpredictably warping as a function of one another.[95] As Albert Einstein first demonstrated, an objective or transcendental perspective on the world from a stable subject position on terra firma does not exist; the experience and measurement of time is rather a function of the mobility, speed, and the relative position of an observer to what he or she is observing.[96] In Kafka's description of travel, characters and events do not develop against the procession of linear time or within an evenly coordinated, national landscape. Space and time are no longer absolute categories from which to demarcate events, actions, or plots—let alone secure the space of the "nation" or the time of "history"—but are rather a relative function of an observer's mobility from within an ever more densely linked and, at least for Karl, oppressive system of power.

One of the most salient examples of such a system of power comes early in the novel, soon after Karl meets his long-lost uncle Edward Jacob, a wealthy businessman and senator from New York who proudly tells Karl, "I am an American citizen from my very heart" (G 38/E 25).[97] Uncle Jacob, we are told, came over from Europe more than thirty years ago to start a successful business in New York and is now the living realization of the American dream. The business, "a sort of commission and dispatch agency," handles all the transfer of goods and raw materials between manufacturers and hence relies on an immense amount of coordination and transportation, maintained by "the most exact, uninterrupted telephone and telegraph connection" (G 65–66/E 47). By way of an "inhuman regularity and speed," diligent workers move goods all over the country from a building so large that "it took many days to traverse in its entirety" (G 66–67/E 47–48). In other words, his uncle's business is essentially a highly structured transportation and communication system, not unlike a third-order railway system in its linked complexity, temporal coordination, and relative simultaneity. Its unencompassable largeness and precise coordination between experience and expectation overwhelm Karl, who stands in awe but can hardly master a single part:

> Through the hall there was a perpetual traffic [*Verkehr*] of people rushing hither and thither. Nobody said good day, greetings were omitted, each man fell into step behind anyone who was going the same way, keeping his eyes on the floor, over which he was set on advancing as quickly as he could, or giving a hurried glance at a word or figure here and there on the papers he held in his hand, which fluttered with the wind of his forward movement.   (G 67/E 48)

The workers are nothing but perfectly coordinated parts in an elaborately linked, perpetual motion machine, which might be called industrial modernity.

Karl cannot "systematically" observe the operation of the business, although he discerns the existence of a complex, horizontally differentiated system in which every activity is somehow linked together. Once he is denied a position of informed spectatorship, the massive structures of power disallow his participation and, finally, expel him from their very operation. When Karl decides, against his uncle's wishes, to spend an evening in the New York countryside with a family friend, Uncle Jacob angrily writes Karl a letter, instructing him never to visit or be in touch with him again (G 122–23/E 94–95). Karl is forbidden from the one possibility he has of gaining social, political, and economic status. In fact, as Karl wanders through the American landscape, never again will he be this close to gaining admission to the structures of economic power and social legitimacy. He won't even be able to recall where his uncle's agency is geographically located.

Throughout the novel, Karl is repeatedly set up against inscrutable systems of power, which consistently disenfranchise him by forcing him to remain outside as their object or refuse. It is in precisely this way, for example, that we can read the operation of the law enforcement system, whose suburban police hound Karl for his identification papers, or the operation of the Hotel Occidental, whose diffuse job responsibilities and power structures Karl never learns, or the decision-making body of the Theater of Oklahoma, with its disarmingly panoptic control of its employees. For Karl, although he resides in "America," the national space is experienced as a network of intricately and inexplicably linked systems of power, which function ever more intensely to prevent his "citizenship." Even when Karl seemingly gains admission to the American geography, he never gains admission to the ideals of nationality, the formalities of the English language, or the virtues of citizenship.[98] Not only is Karl's identity completely divorced from nationality, language, and citizenship, he can never become a subject since his "voyage" yields no progress, knowledge, or concept of belonging. Instead he is turned into an object, the byproduct of modernity's mass mobility.

Kafka's travel narrative is, therefore, not organized according to the procession of time (such as a realist, progressive chronology) or the marking of geography covered (such as Goethe's "translation" of nationality). Instead Kafka has created a narrative effect of contingency and *terra infirma* in which subjecthood is forever displaced and dissolved. Precise temporal indicators, for example, are rare in Kafka's novel because Karl is not a character who develops over time. Such indicators show up either unpredictably as asides, or, just as unpredictably, as structures of power that Karl cannot penetrate. In the first two chapters of the novel time is intimated by vague, unmeasurable phrases ("one day" or "a relatively long time"), and we only find out retrospectively how much time Karl spent at his uncle's home when Karl befriends Delamarche and Robinson on the way to Butterford: "They could not understand how Karl could stay for more than two months in New York and yet had hardly seen anything of the city but one street" (G 145/E 112). Not only is a temporal quantity disclosed after the fact and in passing, but Karl's enormously feeble spectatorship on the space of the external world (one street in two months) is also underscored.

In the one instance that a precise time does enter into the narrative, it is arbitrarily handed down from above: Uncle Jacob's rejection letter is to be delivered to Karl at exactly midnight, no earlier and no later, in accordance with the unalterable strictures of world standard time. There is no undergirding reason why the letter is to be delivered only at midnight; nevertheless Karl must wait patiently until the proper time has arrived so that he can be told formally that he cannot go "home." He is both disoriented by and willfully subjected to the enforcement of time, but at no point does Karl become a temporal character. Only those in positions of privilege and power have the ability to master time. Quite unlike Goethe's *Italienische Reise*, time does not run in an inevitable direction or at a constant rate; it cannot be "translated," because it is not an objective quality that flows evenly over the course of the story. There are no small, equally long, repeatable units, such as sequentially ordered days succeeding one another in a regular, harmonious, and expected fashion. In the modernist narrative, Kafka produces an effect in which time appears to speed up and slow down as an unpredictable function of where Karl is, what circumstances he finds himself in, and which systems of power he runs up against.

Kafka's travelogue is thus neither "pastoral" nor "easy to follow." Perhaps partly owing to Kafka's unfamiliarity with American geography and partly appropriate to Karl's radical dislocation, space is profoundly difficult to map and impossible to predict. Similarly, time is profoundly difficult to anticipate and impossible to quantify, unless we are told outright how much time "went by." As Karl walks to Butterford with his newfound acquaintances, for example, he observes a decidedly strange panorama of New York geography: "The bridge connecting New York with Boston hung delicately over the Hudson, and if one squinted one's eyes it seemed to tremble" (G 144/E 111; translation corrected).[99] Of course, no such bridge exists. Several pages after, New York City and Boston are long gone, and Karl has arrived later that day, by foot, in a giant, unplaceable city called Ramses. We have no inkling why it takes less time to get from the outskirts of New York City to Ramses (a day by foot) than it takes to cross the length of the single building housing Uncle Jacob's business. Just like Karl, we have no knowledge about the geographic location of Ramses, nor do we know how close or how far New York City lies from it. The space through which Karl moves, just like the space of the narrative itself, does not obey the rules of Cartesian geography because it cannot be plotted on a systematic coordinate system. Instead both space and time are experienced as if parts of a warped, acentric, and nonlinear system. The spatial and temporal relationship between one place and another, just like the narrative relationship between one chapter and another, is not determined by an external necessity, such as geographic mimesis or cumulative development, as in generic form of the bildungsroman. Rather, both the description of travel and the narrative structure of the text itself are suffused with an unmasterable contingency.[100]

To elucidate this point, let's look briefly at how Kafka narrates the order of Karl's journey. The story begins on the Hamburg-America ocean liner with Karl's arrival in New York's harbor; Karl is rowed to shore from the liner and the next chapter takes place at his Uncle Jacob's house; after a period of about two months, Karl leaves his house in a car for Pollunder's country home; Karl stays in the home for a few hours, desires to leave by train, and, after being rejected by his uncle, finally sets off after midnight in a chance direction by foot; Karl arrives at an inn and leaves the next day with two strangers, Robinson and Delamarche, bound for the town of Butterford; they pass close to New York City and end up at a hotel in the town of Ramses; Karl stays in the hotel and works in an elevator for one and a half months; after being fired from his job, he flees in a taxi to the "suburbs" with his drunken acquaintance, Robinson; there, he stays briefly at Brunelda's house and quickly leaves by train to Clayton to apply for a job in Oklahoma's traveling theater; finally, bound for Oklahoma, he leaves Clayton by train and travels for two days and nights before the story breaks off.

Unlike the reliable and repeatable processes of subject formation in the travel journeys of the bildungsroman, Karl is never "formed" into a subject; instead, through the narration of mobility, he is radically denied subjectivity, agency, citizenship, and nationality. Events, places, and people come together by an inexplicable contingency of connection: After receiving the rejection letter from his uncle, Karl leaves the country house where he had been visiting but "could not tell with certainty in which direction New York lay. . . . Finally he told himself that he need not of necessity go to New York, where nobody expected him and one man certainly did not expect him. So he chose a chance direction and set on his way" (G 127/E 98). Karl discovers a small inn, finds two travel companions, tries to get back to New York City, but ends up at giant hotel in the unplaceable city of Ramses. Nothing necessary or external strings these random events and places together; they are placed side by side by the sheer and irreducible fact that they are placed side by side. Karl encounters systems of power in which everything is linked together for the sake of the system's preservation and for the sake of keeping him out, but nothing in this world is linked together to form him into a subject and nothing about the story can be elucidated by the logic of realism. Kafka has essentially given narrative form to what Luhmann, at the end of the twentieth century, would argue is "modern society's defining attribute," namely, contingency[101]: Without a controlling order, necessity, or teleology, Kafka's modernist travel narrative, like the social systems out of which it takes form and of which it is a symptom, disallows any kind of rational growth, evolutionary development, and social education by desubjectifying its subject into an object.

In this regard, the modernist space—whether Kafka's text or the geography of the railway system—is predicated on the idea that everything is not only linked together in a complex system but that it could also be otherwise. Unlike the *Italienische Reise* or even *Wilhelm Meister*, Kafka could have organized the narrative differently: Karl could have wound up first at the hotel in Ramses, later met Robinson and Delamarche, and perhaps later come back to New York to stay with his uncle. The order does not matter. Karl is not a character who develops over time, and, similarly, the narrative structure itself is not a linear or determinate development through history. In Karl Rossmann Kafka has produced a character who is not "in" space or time but rather subjected to systems of power that organize and effectively manipulate space and time. He is nothing but a mass object of modernity. The story has direction only insofar as Karl sets off in a given direction at a certain moment, and the novel has direction only insofar as Kafka contiguously links one action, event, sentence, or chapter with the next.[102]

The railway system and *Der Verschollene* thus share overlapping epistemological conditions of possibility and partake in the same structural logic of modernity. That is to say, they are both products of horizontally differentiated systems in which linked complexity and contingency—with all their social consequences—are modernity's defining attributes. In the same way that Kafka himself could essentially go from train to train and railway line to railway line within an always moving system, the modernist narrative is also a relative system of possibilities, impossibilities, and contingencies. The point is that once Karl is dropped down in New York City, virtually anything could happen, and the story we have is just one possibility. As Robert Musil would later reflect, this is because the direction of the modernist narrative does not follow the singularity of a thread but rather proceeds according to the contingency of a space.[103] Without a definitive teleology, a continuous cycle of return, or a ground for systematic observations, the meta-epistemology of the railway system results in the desubjectification of the protagonist who is merely buffeted about by the contingent logic of an indefinite and infinitely mobile system of connectivity.

In the final fragments of the novel, Karl, perhaps recognizing for the first time that he will never be assimilated into American society, decides to join a traveling theater after reading a sign, which purports that "everyone is welcome!" (G 388/E 273). He renames himself Negro (G 402/E 286) and is introduced to the troupe as doubly foreign: "Negro, a European intermediate pupil" (G 405/E 288). In calling himself Negro, he assumes the function of the slave and recognizes the incontestable power of the ubiquitous but unspecified master in preventing his formation into an autonomous, free subject.[104] Karl can never become the "citizen" and "father" that Wilhelm becomes upon his induction into the Tower Society because no external authorities or structures of power guide Karl's journey. He undergoes no sort of cumulative growth or education and never arrives at a destination because the novel, like the processes of desubjectification, is not guided by the strictures of teleology or voyages of return.[105]

The last sentence that Kafka penned for the novel underscores this modernist process of desubjectification by bringing it together with the meta-epistemology of the railway system. Karl sits in a moving train, bound for an uncertain Oklahoma, and observes the landscape from the framed window, not unlike the way in which one might experience the continuous discontinuities of a film sequence:

> Masses of blue-black rock rose in sharp wedges up to the railway line, even if one bent down to look out the window, one searched in vain for their summits; dark, gloomy, jagged valleys opened up, one tried to follow with a pointing finger the direction in which they lost themselves; broad mountain streams appeared, rolling in great waves down onto the foothills and drawing with them a thousand foaming wavelets, plunging underneath the bridges over which the train rushed, and they were so near that the breath of coldness rising from them chilled the skin of one's face.   (G 418–19/E 297–298; translation slightly modified)

Not only does Karl fail to observe the entirety of the pulsating landscape, he cannot find an orientation or point of stability in this world of the sublime. Quite unlike Kant or Goethe, this vision of the natural sublime is unencompassable, unsafe, and in no way contributes to the founding or strengthening of subjectivity. Even the syntax of Kafka's final sentence captures the geographic instability, historical dislocation, and relativity of any frame of reference. Here the narrative breaks off, but not for any reason or necessity. It just ends, because endings, like middles and beginnings, no longer matter or provide direction when realist narration is replaced by the relativity of observation and narrative contiguity is replaced by the contingency of experience. Exactly unlike the bildungsroman, then, no external structure of necessity, no historical order of continuity, and no spatial configuration of understandability characterize Kafka's modernism. The novel offers a bleak vision of modernity as the connected contingency of systems of power from start to finish, from decision to decision, from chapter to chapter, from arrival to departure. Karl Rossmann is its refuse.

In the last years of his life, Kafka had a number of conversations about his stories with an aspiring Czech poet by the name of Gustav Janouch. In one Janouch proposes, perhaps naively, that Kafka must have been "very young and happy" when he wrote "The Stoker"[106] because "there is so much sunshine and high spirits" in the youthful figure of Karl Rossmann.[107] Kafka then responds rather opaquely: "One speaks best about what is strange to one. One sees it more clearly. 'The Stoker' is the remembrance of a dream, of something that perhaps never really existed. Karl Rossmann is not a Jew. But we Jews are born old."[108] If we work backward through this curious passage, Kafka seems to be saying that if Karl was "old," he might be a Jew; however, in the story as it stands, Karl is the non-Jewish, youthful subject of a dream. Kafka then implies that he speaks best about what is foreign to him (namely, youthful non-Jews). In this respect, Karl, not hampered by Judaism precisely because he is not old and Jewish, might be interpreted as a figure for a kind of utopian freedom within a new American space of seemingly infinite and liberating possibilities.

Depending on one's inclination to believe what Kafka supposedly said about his "lost" subject, Karl Rossmann may or may not be Jewish. In the novel there are, indeed, no overt references to Judaism, although it is tempting to interpret Karl's Uncle Jacob as a supremely successful Jewish businessman, with a decidedly Jewish name. It is also tempting to interpret Karl Rossmann as an "allegorical" Jew, given his exile from his homeland, his non-national wanderings, and his perpetual outsider status.[109] In what follows, I will proceed from the assumption that Karl—as a mass object—has "lost" his Jewishness, just like he lost every other fixture that might have furnished him with an identity or might have ground the possibility of his development into an autonomous subject. Perhaps, then, Kafka declared Karl not to be Jewish precisely in order to offer a Jewish critique of the social consequences of modernity: Desubjectification also means de-Jewification. In other words, the new world in which Karl Rossmann finds himself precludes the establishment of any form of subjectivity or identity, whether national, linguistic, cultural, or religious. Rossmann is not a Jew precisely because he is reduced to an object of modernity's mass mobility.

From his letters and writings, we know that Kafka had Goethe's travel narratives and their particular form of subject formation in mind when he imagined the desubjectification and de-Jewification of Karl Rossmann.[110] But he also knew the broad tradition of Jewish mobility and travel writing, particularly the long-standing association of Jews in the diaspora with the history of wandering, movement, and exile.[111] To more fully appreciate the formation of the modernist German/Jewish subject, Kafka's Karl Rossmann must not only be set against Goethe and Wilhelm Meister but also placed within a context that includes the burgeoning of the modern, Jewish travel narrative in Yiddish. Here Sholem Aleichem's *Railroad Stories* are perhaps the most important contemporary literary expressions of the meta-epistemology of the railway system vis-à-vis the formation of modern Jewish subjectivity.

Although it is unclear whether Kafka encountered Sholem Aleichem's *Railroad Stories*, he did hear humorous sketches by Sholem Aleichem read aloud by members of the traveling Yiddish theater in 1911 and even included a small bibliographic blurb on Sholem Aleichem in his overview of Yiddish literature outlined in his diaries in 1912.[112] And numerous reasons have been given by critics for comparing and contrasting Kafka and Sholem Aleicheim, ranging from their interest in Yiddish and Yiddish literature to their stark representations of images of an "old Europe" and the New World.[113] My interest here is motivated by what I have termed the dialectic of German/Jewish modernity, a dialectic that assumed a new level of intensity in Germanic regions with the construction of the first railway line connecting Nuremberg and Fürth. At the end of the nineteenth century, it is Yiddish-speaking, Eastern Jews who, in trying to escape political, religious, and economic oppression in the Pale of Settlement, began to migrate westward en masse through Germany on trains. Just like Kafka's novel, Sholem Aleichem's stories bear witness to the historical condensation of these two forces of cultural transformation: the construction of the railway system and Jewish mass migration out of the Pale of Settlement. I will focus on the organizational structure of Sholem Aleichem's modernist travel narrative—its meta-epistemology of the railway system—and the

formation of the modern German/Jewish subject within the deterritorialized geography of Germany.

Let me begin with a brief overview of the *Railroad Stories: Tales of a
Commericial Traveler*. The twenty train stories, prefaced by a short note to
the reader by Sholem Aleichem's fictional narrator of the same name, were
composed between 1902 and 1910 and first published in Yiddish in 1911. Although not continuous in either composition or in thematic development,
the stories take place, for the most part, inside a third-class railway compartment populated primarily by Jews of all walks of life. They are essentially vignettes about Jewish life in the Pale, the politics of settlement and
migration, and the forces of modernization, represented paradigmatically
by the moving train itself. Thematically speaking, the stories cover a wide
range of contemporary subjects: Jewish poverty, the 1905 Russian Revolution, white slavery, military service, suicide, police raids, draft exemptions,
the vestiges of shtetl life, religious practices, and many other subjects, big
and small, that might arise in conversations among strangers on a train.

Although my discussion will only touch upon a few of Sholem Aleichem's
stories, what is particular about them all is that they are narrated on a train.
The railway compartment frames the narratives, and the stories themselves
are written as if told in the time between the train's departure and its arrival at a given destination. Jews on a moving train in an enclosed railway
compartment provide the conditions of possibility for what Walter Benjamin, in another context, would call "the ability to exchange experiences."[114]
For Benjamin, modernization put a rapid end to storytelling, and, in this
respect, Sholem Aleichem's stories might be seen as a testament to the passing of an oral tradition. In this turn-of-the-century world, Jews (and some
non-Jews) board and sit together in a third-class train compartment; when
the train begins to move, the Jews begin to talk. The *Railroad Stories* are
the written records of this transient but decidedly modern form of communication. Because of the oppressive social conditions under which most
of these Jews lived and traveled—ranging from extreme poverty and institutional anti-Semitism to pogroms, expulsions, and massacres—David
Roskies has even suggested that "storytelling on board a train became for
Sholem Aleichem the last frontier of hope because this vehicle made a
mockery of everything salvific. The chunk of moving metal was as far removed from Kasrilveke, from the community of the faithful, as a Jew could
go."[115] In themselves trains, of course, were not "salvific," let alone "Jewish."
But because the moving refuge gave rise to the possibility of storytelling

and the creation, if only for few fleeting moments, of a community, there was still an irreducible element of hope.

As the material products of modernization and the figurative embodiments of modernity, trains had occurred earlier in modern Yiddish fiction, since Yiddish travel literature has, in one way or another, always been concerned with the political and social articulation of Jewish mobility. In 1906, for example, I. M Weissenberg published a novella entitled "A Shtetl" in which Proletariat-Jewish revolutionaries arrived in the formerly secluded shtetl by way of the railway. In effect, the isolation of the Jewish religious community and the traditional authority of the rabbis were displaced by the revolutionary, "new time" forces of modernity. In 1909 David Bergelson published "At the Depot," a somber story about unfulfilled dreams and human yearning in which Jews wait for obscenely long times at the railway station for the arrival of a kind of salvation that never comes in any certain terms.[116]

It would probably not be an exaggeration to say that Yiddish literature and Yiddish stories, at least since S.Y. Abramovitsh (1836–1917), were written down precisely to give a comparatively secure cultural expression to the instability, mobility, and transformations of what Wisse has called the modern "Jewish experience."[117] In what its often considered to be the first modern Yiddish novel, Abramovitsh, who wrote under the pen name Mendele Moykher-Sforim (Mendele the Book Peddler), published *The Travels of Benjamin the Third* in 1878, a novel that is both a parodic and nostalgic tale roughly based on Don Quixote and the expansionist triumphs of Alexander the Great.[118] In Abramovitsh's parody of the "travel novel," his Jewish protagonists explore backwater Jewish shtetls in the unplaceable geography of the Russian Pale of Settlement but return home—quite unlike the characters in the bildungsroman or the imperialist conquests of great leaders—having learning nothing and, not only that, having forgotten where they were, why they went, and what they discovered. The Jewish travel novel is also a record of *not* being able to travel, of *not* being a citizen, of *not* being a nationally grounded subject, and, as in the case of Karl Rossmann, of *not* (or no longer) being Jewish. This is the basis of its critical, political edge.

But quite unlike any of his Yiddish literary predecessors, Sholem Aleichem produced a kind of travel narrative in which trains are not simply "represented" as antithetical forces disrupting the traditions of Jewish shtetl life. Instead the *Railroad Stories* are a description of travel informed by the modernity of the railway system as the basis for both his political criticism and the conditions of possibility of modernist narrative. That is to say, the stories conveyed, the narrative itself, and, hence, the very conditions of storytelling are all structured by the modernist logic shared by the meta-epistemology of the railway system. This is particularly evident in the ways in which the impression of time and space is conveyed in the *Railroad Stories* through the practice of storytelling.

"Baranovich Station" (1909), for example, is a vignette about storytelling on the train. In it a Jew from Kaminka claims that he has a story about Jewish bribery to tell that is far more exciting than the stories of other passengers. He recounts the story of a Jew named Kivke, whose death was faked by the leader of the local Jewish community, Nissl Shapiro, the grandfather of the storyteller, in order to protect Kivke from running the gauntlet. As the storyteller speaks, he interrupts the narrative by asking the stationmaster how much time is left before the train arrives at his transfer destination. After receiving a satisfactory answer, he resumes the story and tells how Kivke was forced to relocate to a German-speaking land. Because Kivke could not make ends meet there, he decides to bribe the Jewish community in Kaminka by threatening to "miraculously" return and tell the Russian authorities about their little secret. At that point, the traveling storyteller arrives at the Baranovich station and the story breaks off. The story ends with the fictitious narrator interjecting, "I wouldn't mind if Baranovich station burned to the ground!"[119] evidently a wish that the storyteller might be able to finish the story had the train not arrived at the station.

Although "Baranovich Station" shares many of the broad thematic concerns (particularly the struggles for Jewish political recognition) with the nineteen other stories in Sholem Aleichem's *Railroad Stories*, this story, just like each of the others, is remarkably discontinuous—in terms of the specific content, plot, and characters—with the stories that came before and the ones that come after it. The only continuity is the fictional persona of Sholem Aleichem, the commercial traveler, who supposedly hears, writes down, and conveys these "transient forms" called stories. Just like Karl Rossmann, Sholem Aleichem, the traveling narrator, does not move from place to place, chapter to chapter, story to story according to any kind of external logic or threads of necessity. The content of the stories, like the structure of the modernist narrative and the meta-epistemology of the railway system, is determined by the contingency of connectivity. That is to say, not only are the specific stories written *as if* determined by the comings and goings, arrivals and departures of the train, but the entire collection of *Railroad Stories* is also organized by the possibility of linkages within an always moving system. In the same way that Karl proceeds from place to place and chapter to chapter, the commercial traveler, too, moves from station to station, story to story within an open system of possibilities. At no point, however, is the entire system visible, knowable, or masterable because it can never be observed from a transcendental position of external spectatorship. Instead observers, narrators, storytellers, and listeners are all implicated within a relative, moving, and contingent system. The modernist narrative is the textual instantiation of the "new time" and acentric space of the railway system.

The *Railroad Stories* and *Der Verschollene* thus share overlapping epistemological conditions of possibility: They both describe and are structured by the conditions of modernity, that is to say, horizontally differentiated systems of geography and power defined by linked complexity and contingency. This can be seen in both the frame of a specific story, such as "Baranovich Station" or "The Man from Buenos Aires," in which Sholem Aleichem created a story both determined and cut off by the departure and arrival of the train. And it can be seen in the contingent structure of the text as a whole, in which chapters and stories are in no way necessarily connected together as demanded by the "developmental" structure of the traditional travel narrative as a variation of the bildungsroman. In fact, with the exception of "The Slowpoke Express" and "The Miracle of Hoshana Rabbah," none of the chapters is thematically connected; instead Sholem Aleichem produces the effect of a contingent railway linkage between the places encountered and the stories described.

Calling up the economic history of railway expansion into even the most distant regions of the Pale of Settlement, Sholem Aleichem relays the story of a train, the so-called Slowpoke Express, as a kind of neutralization of both the myth of modernity's "acceleration of time" and the myth of modernization's economic progress for everyone. In this story rural Jews are ecstatic that a railway line is going to be built through their little towns, Teplik, Golte, and Heysen. Not only do the poor Jews believe they will finally become "modern," but they also believe they will become rich through savvy railway investments. Of course, neither really happens, at least not as anticipated. Once the railway line finally does open, the train running on it is so slow that Sholem Aleichem's narrator tells us, in jest, that one resident apparently left on it "for his grandson's circumcision in Khashchevate and arrived just in time for the bar mitzvah."[120] Far from modernity's supposed primacy placed on speed and new accessibility to distant cities, the "slowpoke express" runs nowhere quickly. The slowpoke express can be seen as a critical instantiation of the dialectic of modernity: its neutralization of both speed and the expectations of modernization.[121]

Another story, "The Miracle of Hoshana Rabbah," relays the story of a runaway, slowpoke locomotive with a Jew from Sobolivke and a Russian priest from Golovonyevsk on board. After fighting about how to stop the runaway train, the Jew resigns himself to the fact that the day is Hoshana Rabbah, "the day in which the fate of every one of us is sealed in the Book of Life for the year—and not only who lives and who dies, but who dies what sort of death."[122] According to the Jew, God's decision about whether he will live or die is set on that day, and there is nothing he can do about it. Miraculously, the train runs out of coal, and thus both the Jew and the priest get to live. Once again the short story offers a description of the paradoxical forces and demands of modernity: In this case the train's time, which normally runs according to a predetermined railway schedule based on the strictures of world standard time, is described in accordance with a Jewish holiday and the cycles of the Jewish calendar. As Roskies writes, "Train time is linear time, historical time. Jewish time is cyclical, and mythic."[123] But here they switch places in Sholem Aleichem's critical take on the forces of modernization. Jewish storytelling and religious ritual intersect, in unpredictable ways, with the modernity of the railway system. It is these sorts of tensions—between Jew and Christian, religious and secular, shtetl and city, home and exile, particular and world-historical, Jewish time and train time—that Sholem Aleichem's stories bring to the foreground. In both their thematic and narrative tensions they are descriptions of modernity as a dialectical process of both celebrating and lamenting, enabling and preventing mobility.

Sholem Aleichem thus extends and transforms the generic tradition of travel literature by turning the Jewish travel narrative, in both its narrative structure and political criticism, into a record of the dialectic of modernity. Indeed, both Kafka and Sholem Aleichem offer complementary critiques of this dialectic, which bear directly upon the formation of Jewish subjectivity: Kafka's migratory fantasy of the New World is characterized by the proliferation of interconnected and inscrutable systems of power in which Karl is batted around as a desubjectified object and then expelled as its trash; Sholem Aleichem's cultural history of the Old World is characterized by the transformation—but also the uncanny persistence—of places for telling stories and exchanging experiences within the systems of modernization. In both an observer cannot "get outside" the system, occupy a position of terra firma, or safely observe and narrate the passage of time and space. There is no geographic or national mooring from which subject formation can be reliably derived or to which it can be affixed. The train, like the travel narrative itself, is always moving in both directions at once: emancipation and destruction.

Like Kafka, Sholem Aleichem examines this dialectic against the background of the historical reality of mass migrations; however, unlike the de-subjectified, de-Jewified figure of Karl Rossmann, Sholem Aleichem's traveling Jews, through their encounters with others on the train, create a kind of subjectivity, which might be called a "diasporized consciousness."[124] Reflecting on how to describe a Jewish political subject dissociated from land and independent of national space, Daniel and Jonathan Boyarin proposed the notion of a disaggregated identity or "diasporic consciousness." In their words, it represents "a Jewish subject-position founded on generational connection and its attendant anamnestic responsibilities and pleasures [in order to afford] the possibility of a flexible and nonhermetic critical Jewish identity."[125] To articulate this subject, they sought to describe Jewish identity outside the strict and highly aggregated dualities of belonging inherent to nationality and claims of autochthony. Inside and outside, subject and object, self and other, and, we might add, German and Jewish, are shown to overlap and mix together—not only as a possibility for a future identity but also in the past as a (nearly lost) conceptualization of Jewishness. "Jewishness," they write, "disrupts the very categories of identity because it is not national, not genealogical, not religious, but all of these in dialectical tension with one another."[126] In other words, the Jewish subject is a dialectical and disaggregated—"diasporized"—form of identity that maintains both difference and connection without appeals to territoriality or nationality.

The Jews in Sholem Aleichem's railroad stories are diasporized in this sense: Jewish identity is the product of mobility, displacement, connection, and contingent encounters with others, and, in this regard, is dialectically related to the German tradition of travel, subject formation, and movement. In the hybrid space of the railway car, the migratory Jews develop, to use James Clifford's words, a kind of "positive transnationalism,"[127] one that stretches from the Pale of Settlement to Germany and beyond. The *Railroad Stories* forge, in this respect, transient cultural geographies of the mobile, modern subject without a nation.

The subject of German/Jewish modernity thus emerges through the constellation of transhistorical, transnational encounters between Goethe,

Kafka, and Sholem Aleichem. The space of "Germany" stretches between Sicily, the Pale of Settlement, and America, and this space is connected together, however briefly and contingently, by experiences and narratives of mobility. The German language, like the national referent itself, is deterritorialized through the mobility of German-speaking Germans without a nation (such as Goethe), Yiddish-speaking Eastern Jews (such as Sholem Aleichem), and non-national German-speaking Jews (such as Kafka). In this transnational, conceptual-historical triangulation of Goethe, Kafka, and Sholem Aleichem, a new dialectical space of encounter becomes visible. This space came into existence and was radically transformed over the course of the nineteenth and early part of the twentieth century with the physical construction of the transcontinental railway system, rendering nationality, subjectivity, and language a function of the possibilities and pitfalls of mobility. The cultural geography of German/Jewish modernity begins to emerge through the mapping of these deterritorialized, dialectical spaces of connection, encounter, and exchange.

4. THE NORTH SEA

Jews on Ships

Or, How Heine's *Reisebilder* Deconstruct Hegel's Philosophy of World History

4.1 Emil Hundrieser, plaster model of *Weltverkehr* (1880).

DESIGNED IN 1880 by Emil Hundrieser and cast in zinc shortly thereafter by Friedrich Peters, a sculptural group known as *Der Weltverkehr* (World transportation) crowned the entrance hall to the newly reopened Anhalter Bahnhof. The sculpture was composed of an angelic female figure flanked by two youths, one of whom guided a locomotive with his arms. Installed at the highest point of the station, the sculpture stood for the dream of an interconnected world of mobility. The station represented its material instantiation, the dream made real. Even while the Anhalter Bahnhof epitomized the triumph of secular progress, it still needed a guardian angel at its apex to acknowledge a debt to the theological. Hence *Der Weltverkehr* celebrated material progress in both secular and theological dimensions: Speed was connected with transcendence.

In the nineteenth century railway construction was consistently likened to theology: Heine considered the opening of new railway lines to be
"providential events" and Benjamin would later describe the religious zeal
of Saint-Simon side by side with the secular deification of progress.[1] With
spatial progress linking cities and peoples together, railways were wed to a
concept of infinite historical development; progress itself was deified, both
in its material form and as an abstract ideal for societal evolution.[2] Religion
and railways became ways of binding or, essentially, covenants to progress. In
his material history of nineteenth-century Paris, Benjamin quotes the Saint-
Simonian Michel Chevalier on the relationship between religion and the
building of railway lines: "One can compare the zeal and the ardor displayed
by the civilized nations of today in their establishment of railroads with that
which, several centuries ago, went into the building of cathedrals."[3] Building railways was essentially the religion of modernity. In *One-Way Street*,
Benjamin even mentions a specific church that achieved precisely this union
between technology and religion in the space of its interior architecture: the
Marseilles Cathedral transformed itself into the "Marseilles religion station"
at the end of the nineteenth century. When the refurbished church building
was completed in 1893, it was the apotheosis of a "gigantic railway station . . .
[complete with e]xtracts from the railway traffic regulations in the form of
pastoral letters [hanging] on the walls, tariffs for the discount on special trips
in Satan's luxury train . . . [with] sleeping cars to eternity [departing] from
here at Mass times."[4] Religious dreams condensed into the reality of progress
such that the modernity of the railways could rapidly transcend any distance,
worldly or otherworldly. In Germany the name Anhalter became legendary
along precisely these theological lines, as both an allegory for and the material proof of the belief in progress.

This deification of progress and its secular triumph was not, of course,
without its dialectical counterpoint: The angel of "world transportation"
adorning the Anhalter station might also be seen as the other side of Benjamin's famed angel of history. While the railway ushered in a newly interconnected world of mass mobility and material exchange, it also ushered in the
conditions of possibility for this world's self-destruction. Railway tracks,
after all, are bidirectional, and railway cars were not always in the service of
the salvific. Benjamin imagines the "angel of history" propelled backward
into the future, while the "storm" of progress "keeps piling wreckage upon
wreckage" at his feet.[5] In Klee's original rendition of the *Angelus Novus* the
angel is a gaunt, terrified figure, with a head that is vastly disproportionate

to his feeble body. In Benjamin's words: "His eyes are staring, his mouth is open, his wings are spread."[6] He has limited agency and is unable to "make whole what has been smashed."[7]

The angel of "world transportation," however, is a voluptuous figure of determination: Her right breast is exposed; she has a purposeful look in her face; her wings are spread; and she carries a staff in her hand. The two youth who turn their sinewy bodies to face her are emblems of virility. It is not coincidental that the German word for "transportation," *Verkehr*, also connotes sexual intercourse. The profound sexuality of this scene is something that is completely absent in Benjamin's angel. And while the angel of history stares with his open mouth at the catastrophe called progress, the angel of world transportation has her back to progress: The trains departing the Anhalter Bahnhof left from behind her and sped southward, out of Berlin. She only looked forward, with her wings spread open, and saw no wreckage. Even after the station was bombed during World War II, the angel of world transportation remained ensconced high above the ruins. We might consider the angels to be kindred spirits, poised back-to-back, at a standstill, looking upon the same railway tracks and, hence, upon the same dialectic of modernity.

"The great tragedy of the Jewish people is no Greek tragedy."[8]

At first sight it would make sense to situate Heinrich Heine's *Reisebilder* within the well-defined generic tradition of travel literature as self-discovery and *Bildung*.[9] After all, not only are the *Reisebilder* full of references to Goethe's travel writings, particularly his *Italienische Reise* and paradigmatic novel of education, *Wilhelm Meister*; Heine planned the first of his journeys through the Harz Mountains in 1824 to include a meeting with the aged luminary in Weimar and later even retraces many of Goethe's footsteps through northern Italy. Both men were working in the already established generic form of the travel narrative, combining elements of a rich historical tradition of discovery with their subjective experiences of mobility on foot and by ship. And accounts of journeys to Italy were often produced by affluent men and women of letters, including Adam Smith, David Hume, J. J. Winckelmann, Laurence Sterne, and Karl Philipp Moritz, in the eighteenth century, and Germaine de Staël, Stendhal, and Chateaubriand in the first third of the nineteenth, when both Goethe and Heine penned their accounts of Italy.

Given this tradition, it is striking that Heine abruptly declares midway through the second book of his journey to Italy, *The Baths of Lucca*, how absurd it is to read and write travel literature about Italy:

> There is nothing more boring on the face of the earth as reading a description of travels to Italy—unless it is to write one—and the only way in which its author can make it in any degree tolerable is to say as little in it as possible about Italy. Although I have made use of this trick of the trade, I cannot promise you, dear reader, anything very captivating in the next chapter. If you become bored by the stupid stuff in it, console yourself by thinking of what a dreary time I must have had writing it! I would recommend that once in a while you skip several pages—for in that way, you will arrive much sooner at the end. Oh! How I wish I could do the same thing.   (*Sämtliche Schriften* 2:426)

Unlike Goethe, with his methodical observations and patient accumulation of detail, Heine interrupts his account and urges his readers to skip ahead to finish the story sooner. The task of reading and writing about a trip to Italy is anything but the opportunity for self-discovery and Bildung. Yet, to claim that the genre of travel writing is basically useless, Heine places himself in the paradoxical position of composing a book of travels in order to reject the legitimacy of the very genre.

Whereas for Goethe the specific journey to Italy is important as a voyage—Italy represents his connection to antiquity, the sea voyage to and back from Sicily completes his personal growth, the encounter with foreignness shores up his German subjectivity—for Heine the journey is background for another task, namely, the idea of writing a critical history of his present. He uses the form of the travel narrative not in order to convey the "history of his trip to Italy" or to map out the pathway leading to a strong, nationally grounded subject, but rather to question the presuppositions behind any such claims and critique the attendant ideas of national legitimacy and historical inevitability. His target is not so much Goethe as Hegel and the early practitioners of the so-called *Wissenschaft des Judentums* (Science of Judaism). As I will argue, Heine mocks the genre of the great travel narrative and the genre of the great historical narrative, mimicking them with a Jewish difference to ultimately expose their built-in claims about historicity and national belonging.[10] The *Reisebilder* deconstruct the so-called progress of Spirit and the eschatology of world history by taking the very ghosts that

Hegel supposedly exorcised or consigned to oblivion and pressing them back into history. He does this not by creating a "countersystem" to Hegel's world history but rather by creating a mobile space for particularity—especially Jewish particularity—in the form of the travel narrative.

Heine personally knew Hegel and attended his lectures during part of the four semesters the poet spent studying in Berlin. Although Hegel lectured on a range of subjects, including metaphysics, logic, the philosophy of religion, the philosophy of right, and the philosophy of world history, it is only known for certain that Heine attended the lectures on the philosophy of world history, delivered by Hegel during the winter semester of 1822–23.[11] About the same time, Heine became an active member in the Verein für Cultur und Wissenschaft der Juden (Society for Culture and Science of the Jews), first conceived by its founders, Leopold Zunz and Eduard Gans, in 1819 and formed into a society in November of 1821.[12] Heine joined the Verein on August 4, 1822, and began regularly attending meetings upon returning from Poland on September 29 of that year. Although its early philosophy and justification were imagined by Zunz in a manifesto that first appeared in Berlin in May 1818, "Etwas über die rabbinische Literatur," Gans quickly became the leader of the Verein and delivered three important lectures on its role in propagating the idea of Wissenschaft des Judentums. Gans, certainly the most committed Hegelian in the group, believed that Jewish particularity could be overcome by the Verein such that Jews could be productively reintegrated into the totality of European history.[13] The young Heine encountered Hegel's philosophy of history directly in the lectures that the philosopher himself delivered and from Hegel's most ardent Jewish disciple, Gans.

Despite Heine's sustained and intense encounters with contemporary notions of the philosophy of history, his ideas about historicity and his reception of Hegel have been almost completely ignored in his early writings such as the *Reisebilder*. In the wake of Georg Lukács's seminal attempt to position Heine definitively as an intermediary between Hegel and Marx, the scholarship on Heine's relation to Hegelian philosophy has tended to follow Lukács's periodization and focus almost exclusively on works produced after Heine went into exile in France.[14] The tendency has been to elucidate Heine's relation to Hegelianism by examining the more obviously philosophical-historical texts written after 1831, particularly his extended essays "On the History of Religion and Philosophy in Germany" (1834–35) and "The Romantic School" (1833), as well as the various on-again/off-again remarks and reflections Heine made about Hegel in his correspondences and confessions.[15] In "The History of Religion and Philosophy in Germany," certainly Heine's most important attempt to write a kind of revolutionary history of *Geistesgeschichte*, he begins with the Christianization of Germany, moves quickly from Luther to Mendelssohn and Lessing, dispenses with Kant and Fichte, and ends up with Hegel, who, he argues, concluded the German philosophical revolution. The idea, as Harold Mah points out, was to "[continue] Hegel's project of aligning Germany with France" by showing how revolutions in German intellectual history corresponded with the revolutions in French political history, thereby bringing Germany into the European ranks of "modernity."[16]

In a book-length study of the Heine-Hegel relationship, Eduard Krüger structures his argument by dividing Heine's work into a pre- and post-1831 Hegelianism, giving comparatively scant attention to the *Reisebilder* (save a few pages on *Ideen. Das Buch Le Grand*); instead, he focuses his attention on the later works that he believes illuminate Heine's Hegelian conception of *Geschichtsphilosophie*.[17] In so doing, he does not fundamentally reject Lukács's argument in explaining "Heine's ideological position between Hegel and Marx" but rather seeks to articulate the exact nature of the Heine-Marx collaboration during the critical years of 1843–44, when Marx wrote and published his "Introduction to the Critique of Hegel's Philosophy of Right" and "National Economy and Philosophy."[18] Although I have no reason to question Krüger's argument, I do not think that the relationship between Hegel's philosophy of world history and Heine's ideas about historicity can be adequately confined to his later "Hegelian" collaboration with Marx in Paris.[19]

Only recently has the scholarship on Heine and Hegel begun to rethink this periodization, particularly Klaus Briegleb, who has tried to articulate Heine's Jewish conception of history.[20] Briegleb has argued, with respect to the constellations of Heine's "Jewish historical consciousness," that, for Heine, "poetry is the true writing of history" and that his "entire work . . . is saturated with a structure of historical recollection."[21] Briegleb moves elegantly between some of the earliest poems and the lyrical cycles in *The North Sea* (*Reisebilder II*) to the later "Romanzero" (1851) in order to demonstrate how "Heine's Jewish consciousness of history gains its genuine philosophical quality from a de-ideologization of Hegel's positive dialectic *and* from the power of irony."[22] Here Briegleb's intervention is clearly recognizable: Heine's "consciousness of history," far from restricted to his essays on German intellectual history and his influence on Marx's critique of Hegel, can be seen throughout his "literary" writings, particularly his poetry, as a persistently "Jewish" alternative to the triumph of Hegel's "Christian" World Spirit.

In consonance with Briegleb's argument, I want to argue that Heine's *Reisebilder*, conceived, written, and published between 1824 and 1831, incisively critique Hegel's all-consuming philosophy of world history and that in these caustic, ironic, nonsystematic, and contradictory "pictures of travel" Heine's decidedly Jewish conception of historicity emerges. My argument has two main parts. First, through an analysis of the lectures on the philosophy of world history given by Hegel in 1822–23, I propose that Hegel's conception of the movement of Spirit (*Geist*) from East to West, from ancient times to the German nineteenth century, is a travel narrative, a nautical voyage of discovery. To make this claim, I will focus on how Hegel conceives of the movement and direction of Spirit as well as on how he relies on the specificity of a particular mode of transportation—ship travel—to characterize the uniqueness of world-historical peoples and the importance of mobility for colonialism and, hence, for the strength of the European nation. Travel by sea—something Jews supposedly do not engage in—turns out to be the prerequisite of nationality and the birth of Christian civil society. The second part of my argument will focus on the emergence of a Jewish conception of historicity in Heine's *Reisebilder*. I read Heine's travel narratives as a philosophy of history, and it is precisely here, in this shared space between Hegel and Heine—between a philosophy of history and a travel narrative, between a travel narrative and a philosophy of history—that my argument operates. Heine draws out a world of particularity—that other history, which Hegel's Spirit domesticated and consumed along the way to the universal—by reworking the Greek trope of seafaring and allowing Jewish "spirits" to haunt his conception of historicity.

THE TRAVELS OF WORLD SPIRIT

The lectures that Heine heard Hegel deliver in 1822–23 were the first systematic presentation of the philosopher's conception of world history.[23] The quadripartite structure and basic philosophical idea were articulated several years earlier, in 1819–20, at the end of his lectures on the philosophy of right.[24] For this reason it makes sense to look briefly at the *Philosophy of Right*. Here, Hegel introduces the idea that "world history" is a kind of court of judgment. Because world history is teleological and its end represents Spirit's last stage of development into the universal of absolute knowledge, this court represents a final place of adjudication. As Hegel says in the lectures on the philosophy of right, "World history is precisely the court [*Gericht*] of the universal Spirit, under which the particular [is subsumed]."[25] Although he does not develop this notion any further in these lectures, it reappears in a slightly, but significantly, altered form at the conclusion to the *Philosophy of Right*: "Weltgeschichte, als [. . .] Weltgerichte"[26] The famous formulation is difficult to translate because *Weltgericht* not only means the "court of the world" but also the "judgment of the world," particularly in the theological dimensions of the Last Judgment. In other words, world history is the place where the trial ("the court of the world") as well as the sentencing occurs ("the judgment of the world"). Neither this trial nor this judgment can be appealed because "world history is the Last Judgment." Hegel's juridical formulation of the progress of world history is thus eschatological: The end is always predetermined, and the process betrays a doctrine of Christian judgment.

What is important in Hegel's view of world history is that the specific end—a final determination of judgment—is also contained in and the basis of every prior stage of history. I suggested earlier that Hegel's philosophy of world history can be read as a travel narrative, and I now want to back up this claim by looking at the precise forms of historical movement that Hegel attributes to the development of *Weltgeist* and the specific kinds of metaphors that structure his account of mobility. What we will see is that they fall into two types: first, the dialectical movement of Geist, which is actually described by an appeal to a natural cycle, and, second, the concrete, historical fact of ship travel, particularly voyages of discovery, which facilitate the outward spread of the universal from its home port of Europe. Together, both describe the movement of world history.

The movement of Geist is not a simple repetition, as one finds in natural cycles, such as the orbits of the planets or the succession of seasons, but rather a progressive, dialectical stepping forth (*fortschreiten*; *Rechts* 198). This dialectical process also informs his lectures on world history, where he differentiates Spirit's progressive development from a mere cyclical motion: "Every successive stage [of Spirit] presupposes the others, is produced as a new, higher principle, through the elevation [*das Aufheben*], the reworking, and the destruction of the previous stages" (*Weltgeschichte* 39). This kind of movement contrasts with "the repetition of the same . . . in nature, wherein nothing new comes forth [and] everything just goes in circles" (*Weltgeschichte* 38). Corresponding to this dialectical process of universal sublation is a world historical process in which "the different stages through which World Spirit goes are characterized by different peoples and states. Every people expresses a specific moment of spiritual development" (*Rechts* 198–99). Thus each historical stage is a unique level of development that remains telos directed by the forces of historical necessity and moves forward through a dialectical process of elevation, reworking, and destruction.

World history is divided into four stages based on geography: the "Oriental world," the "Greek world," the "Roman world," and the "Germanic world." The last corresponds to the highest development of the family, civil society, and the state, having emerged, in successively progressive stages, from abstract rights and mere law-based morality (*Rechts* 202–6). This quadripartite formulation also provides the geographical basis of the direction and movement of *Weltgeist* in the lectures on the philosophy of world history. The movement, in accord with these stages of development, is in a singular direction, toward a specific, predetermined goal: World Spirit proceeds "from east to west, from southeast to northwest, from sunrise to sunset" until universal knowledge is attained (*Weltgeschichte* 106). And later, in discussing the transitions from the "Oriental world" to Europe, Hegel explains that world history follows a decidedly natural course: "The sun follows a course from east to west, and so we go from Asia to Europe, to the West" (*Weltgeschichte* 317). This mobility is rendered even more explicit in the standard edition of the lectures: "In the geographic overview the course of the world's history has been marked out in its general features. The sun—the light—rises in the East. . . . The history of the world goes from East to West, for Europe is absolutely the end of history, Asia the beginning" (*Werke* 12:133–34). World history has begun to emerge as a travel narrative.

This justification for the movement of World Spirit is striking for its dubious reasoning. First of all, it is a false analogy: why should the rising and setting of the sun correspond to anything historical? Second, in terms of astronomy, it is patently false: the sun does not move from East to West. Finally, it contradicts Hegel's earlier point about the particular movement of history: if Geist moves dialectically, why should Hegel make recourse to a natural cycle characterized by a repetition of the same? But I do not want to harp on these issues. The second type of movement—travel by ship—is more significant for our inquiry because it is here that Hegel provides the justification for the movement of world history by appealing to a specific material history of transportation.

Hegel's most important geographic observation about the production of world-historical people concerns their relation to the sea. World-historical people, Hegel argues, have a connection to seafaring and ship travel, whereas nonhistorical people are basically landlocked and condemned to wander on the ground. In his discussion of the history of the Greek and Roman worlds of antiquity, Hegel shows how the Mediterranean Sea played a critical role in the spiritual development of these civilizations by facilitating the emergence of a national identity and civil society and, more expansively, by spreading the universal outward. In his words, "The middle point of the ancient world is the Mediterranean Sea. . . . If the middle of the ancient world were not the sea, world history would be impotent. . . . Just as Rome and Athens would be unimaginable without forums and streets, the ancient world would be nothing without the sea" (*Weltgeschichte* 106). As the first stage in the development of Spirit, the Oriental world—where Hegel places the Jews—is overcome because "the sea has no meaning for Asia; quite the opposite: the Asian peoples have closed themselves off from the sea." By contrast, "the relation to the sea in Europe is important . . . [because] only through a connection to the sea can a European state become great" (*Weltgeschichte* 111).

Although the sea ostensibly separates nations from one another, Hegel argues that through seafaring and voyages of discovery "people became bound [*verbindet*] to one another" (*Weltgeschichte* 111). In other words, the geographic and material prerequisites of colonialism and imperialism— closeness to the sea and ships—are crucial for the direction of world history and the universal expansion of Geist. In fact, nations only become powerful and, hence, world-historical by their relation to the sea. Africa, for instance, dispensed by Hegel in a couple of pages, is not even a part of the history of the world because it does not have a colonial relation to the sea.[27] In the standard edition of the lectures on world history, Hegel explains that Africa has "remained impenetrable," "enveloped in the dark color of night," and filled with "the most thoughtless inhumanity and disgusting barbarism" (*Werke* 12:120–21). Not only do Africans not undertake voyages of discovery but the Europeans "have scarcely [been able to penetrate] into the interior of Africa and Asia because travel by land is much more difficult than travel

by water" (*Werke* 12:118). The African people, Hegel concludes, are "no historical part of the World" and, hence, are not a part of the narrative procession of world history (*Werke* 12:129).

World-historical nations, in contrast, are characterized by their power to
master the expansiveness of the sea and by their ability to undertake voyages of conquest. As Hegel writes, "The sea is not only a means for satisfy-
ing one's needs; it also puts property and life at risk . . . something brave
and noble. . . . Bravery is at the core of a sea journey [and] the ship, this
swan, so graceful in its movement, is an instrument that brings the boldness
of reason to the highest level" (*Weltgeschichte* 112). Hegel places colonial
expeditions and "voyages of discovery" (*Entdeckungsreisen*) in a lineage of
pivotal historical moments, including the invention of book printing and
gunpowder. Europe emerges as the telos of world history because it is here
that World Spirit has reached the highest level of outward development
(*Weltgeschichte* 487–89). The Germanic world—by which Hegel seems to
mean "Western Europe," including England[28]—is thus the culmination of
world history, the product of all the dialectical movements of Spirit from
East to West, and itself the fount of an outwardly realized, civilizing, colonial mission (*Werke* 12:490–91).

Through a process of ever increasing glorification and purification, the
crumbling of the Oriental world gave rise to the possibility of the Greek
world; the destruction of the Greek world gave rise to the Roman world;
the ruination of the Roman world, around the middle of the fifteenth century, set in motion the worldwide spread of Christianity and the advent of
the Germanic world. However, the rise of the Germanic world is "entirely
different from that sustained by the Greeks and Romans. For the Christian
world is the world of completion [*die Welt der Vollendung*]; the grand principle of being is realized, consequently, the end of days is fully come" (*Werke*
12:414). In other words, the Germanic world will not go to ruin because it
represents "the world of completion," one without temporal extension or
historicity. It is essentially nondialecticizable. Unlike the other worlds, the
three periods of the Germanic world do not correspond to the narrative
categories of beginning, middle, and end or birth, rise, and decline; instead,
they correspond, in his terminology, to the "Kingdoms of the Father, the
Son, and the Spirit" (*Werke* 12:417). In effect, Hegel's progressive narrative
of world history ends in overcoming narrativity itself by the eschatological
logic of Christianity. Here we also notice a decided tension in Hegel's story:
on the one hand, the "modernity" of the narrative underscores the progress

of history and the acceleration of time through the dialectical procession of Spirit; on the other hand, the narrative is fundamentally eschatological insofar as it announces the arrival of the end time, the Germanic world of the nineteenth century as the telos of history. What we are left with at the end of Hegel's narrative of modernity is pure space—a Germanic empire that extends outward in all directions, something that also explains the primacy Hegel gave to geography in his conceptualization of the advancement of World Spirit.

Hegel considers the "Germanic world" to exhibit the highest level of development in world history not only because Geist radiates outward from Europe to "bind" distant people to the universal but also because the state is founded on the Christian concept of love and freedom. In this world all particular wills and contingencies have been overcome in the name of the universal, ethical state. With "this urging of Spirit *outward*" (*dieses* Hinaus *des Geistes*)—through "the maritime heroes of Portugal and Spain who found a new way to the East Indies and discovered America," through the spread of Christianity to the New World, and through the discovery of a passage to India by the Cape—the Germanic stage emerges as the universal (*Werke* 12:490). World history thus has a direction and finality, culminating in the universality and absoluteness of the imperial European state.

Hegel's philosophy of history is a colonial travel narrative, in which past civilizations are dialectically overcome until we arrive at the end, the modern European state, at which point the truth of the European state radiates back outward. The ruins of past empires merely confirm the progress of Spirit and propel its march forward in a seascape that moves from overcoming the temporality of destruction and ruin to the permanent spatiality of a Christian empire spread the world over. As a part of a grand narrative that unfolds geographically, the non-European is simply accorded a place outside world history (as in the case of Africa) or else treated as a colonial space reachable by ship and thus to be subsumed into the progress of civilization and the expansion of empire. After all, as Hegel indicated in his earlier discussion of the English in India, "it is the necessary fate of Asiatic empires to be subjugated by the Europeans" (*Werke* 12:179). In its essential form *The Philosophy of World History* is a geographic narrative of the imperial imaginary and the subjugation of the non-European other.

As Hegel sums up the project of the philosophy of world history at the end of his lectures: "The point was this: to show that the entire course [of world history] follows the logic of Spirit and that all history is nothing more than the realization of Spirit, which the states carry out, and that the state is the same as this worldly realization" (*Weltgeschichte* 521). Spirit thus proceeds from the African threshold, making its way from the first world-historical peoples in the East toward the West, from where voyages of discovery and colonial expansion facilitate the spread of the European idea of the Christian state to the rest of the world. In this dialectical movement of Spirit, the particular and the contingent are domesticated and overcome in the wake of the universal. World history has a direction and finality, which, at its telos, is also the last judgment of the world. For Hegel the end of history is the truth of the European, Christian state.

Although Hegel spends little space detailing the significance of the Jews in world history, his terse remarks are nevertheless telling and are in complete accordance with his anti-Semitic description of Judaism in "The Spirit of Christianity and its Fate" (1798–1800). In the philosophy of world history Jews are quietly placed in the "Oriental world," where the sun supposedly rises, as an insignificant part of the first stage in the movement of World Spirit. Jews do not exhibit any freedom and are, instead, rigidly bound to laws but without the productivity of a state: "The [Jewish] subject never realizes freedom for himself . . . [and] the state is not consonant with Jewish principles and is alien to the legislation of Moses" (*Werke* 12:243).[29] Jewish ideas are affiliated with "particularity" (*Weltgeschichte* 500) and "locality," not in the sense of being bound to a place but in contrast to the universality of Christianity (*Weltgeschichte* 268). As Hegel makes clear in "The Spirit of Christianity," the first Jewish act was a "severance" [*Trennung*], in which Abraham, the progenitor of a nation, "completely tore himself from his family . . . severing the bonds of community and love" (*Werke* 1:277). Unlike Kierkegaard who praises Abraham as a knight of faith who transcended the universal laws of the ethical, Hegel sees Abraham as a selfish stranger who refused to enter into familial ties and, instead, tore himself away from the rootedness of place. In Hegel's words, "Abraham wandered here and there over a boundless territory, without bringing any parts of it nearer to him by cultivating or improving them. . . . He was a stranger on earth, a stranger to the soil and men alike" (*Werke* 1:278). Even though the notion was not conceived until the fifteenth century, Hegel anachronistically suggests that Abraham was always already the first wandering Jew.

According to Hegel, because Abraham, as the leader of the Israelites, refused to enter into any kind of familial, property, or national ties, Jews are condemned to "their original fate," namely, to remain forever at the first stage of world history, "in the mean, abject, wretched circumstances in which they still are today" (*Werke* 1:292). Here, Hegel considers Abraham's "original" severance (as an Israelite) to be a transgenerational, Jewish trait that explains the state of Jews in Hegel's Europe. The Jew is a perpetually negative moment in the progress of world history because the "Jewish spirit" is characterized by a "severance," which contradicts the formation of a civil society, polis, community of reason, or political subjectivity. By contrast, "Christian spirit" is characterized by a "union" of familial love and freedom wherein the slavish laws of Jewish morality have been "sublated . . . by something higher than obedience to law," the love of Jesus and the ethical community (Werke 1:324).[30] This manifestation of *Sittlichkeit* (ethics) is the culmination of a movement that began with the Greek polis, moved to the Roman ideal of citizenship, and ended in Europe with the development of civil society, from where the Christian ideal of the universal radiated outward. The few words that Hegel accords to Judaism are telling precisely because the Jew represents an undeveloped particularity, which was to be overcome in the first stages of world history. The telos of world history is a grand, dialectical synthesis, wherein the untruth of the Jewish particular has been sublated and, finally, forgotten by the totality of the Christian universal.

This is the version of the philosophy of world history that Heine encountered at Hegel's lectures in 1822–23 and in the Verein für Cultur und Wissenschaft der Juden. In the lectures Jews were considered barely world historical people because of their self-severance from any form of incipient nationality or communal belonging; in the Verein the particularity of Judaism could be productively overcome when Jews were absorbed into European world history. In both world history was a European domain, and Jews, because they had neither a homeland nor a nation, were to be either overcome by or assimilated into the progress of history. In no case, however, could Jews continue to subsist in their difference as Jews.

Among the members of the Verein, Gans was the most articulate and passionate advocate of the necessity of Jewish reintegration. Because he, often in parodic connection with Hegel, shows up with such frequency in Heine's *Reisebilder* and letters, it is important to briefly explicate the nature of his Jewish-Hegelian conception of history and the role he envisioned for the Verein in realizing it. Although Gans's radical "Hegelianism" may not have been representative of all his colleagues in the Verein, he was arguably the most outspoken and influential member of the Verein, playing a critical, public role in the wider dissemination of the organization's ideas. Gans not only gave the organization its name but also assumed its presidency in 1821 and, in his series of semiannual reports, publicly delivered the clearest statements of the Verein's political goals. *Wissenschaft des Judentums* not only meant that the "scientific study" was to be undertaken by Jews but that Jews were also to be the objects of such study precisely in order to achieve a "synthesis" into the totality of European history and culture.[31]

As evidenced by the first speech that he gave at the Verein on October 28, 1821, Gans's outlook on history was clearly Hegelian: "Just as the individual rises up into the genus in nature until it is lost in the all, the task of human civilization is for the particular to be ever raised up into the universal, in which the hoped for perfectibility of humanity would be the end point and final stage."[32] Just like Hegel, Gans considers world history to start in the "childlike particularity . . . [of] the East" and to move westward, like the sun.[33] Gans does not want Jews to "stand in the way . . . of the development of nature and history" but rather to assume their rightful place in history, as "citizens" (*Bürger*) who both participate in the "education establishment" (*Bildungsanstaltung*) and celebrate their love of the "fatherland" (*Vaterland*).[34]

Unlike Hegel, however, Gans still believed that Jews could be "world-historical" people, participating in the totality of European history once they overcame their strange particularity. The goal of the Verein was to expedite this process. In his second speech to the Verein, delivered on April 28, 1822, Gans appeals to the Hegelian quadripartite organization of history, not in order to place Jews in the Oriental first stage, but to argue that Jews, as inhabitants of Europe, have a claim to be world-historical people in "today's Europe."[35] For this to happen, however, Jewish particularity cannot continue to subsist "parallel to world history"—Jews must become "completely assimilated" (*ganz einverleiben*) into Europe.[36] Gans describes the nature of this process of assimilation: "to absorb" (*aufgehen*) is not the same as "to destroy" (*untergehen*). He continues: "The consoling teaching of history correctly understood is that everything passes by without passing away, and that everything remains, even when it is considered long past. Therefore, Jews cannot be destroyed, nor can Judaism dissolve away; but in the great movement of the whole it will appear to be destroyed and nevertheless live on, as a current lives on in the ocean."[37] In this extraordinary passage, highlighted by a sea metaphor, Gans desires a Judaism that is no longer Jewish in its particularity; he wants a people who have been assimilated into the "ocean" of Europe and are as historically indistinguishable from other people as one "current" is from another. In other words, the specificity of

Judaism and Jewish history is to be absorbed into the totality of European world history to survive not as Jewish but as European.

As Gans argues in his less philosophical and more pragmatic third speech, delivered on May 4, 1823, the "scientific" study of Judaism within Europe undertaken by members of the Verein will help accelerate "Jewish Bildung" and this process of reintegration. He tells the Verein that they are continuing to realize the production of a "better culture" and universal history: "The bad mixture [*Mischung*] of a half-Oriental, half-medieval life has been broken apart. In place of a completely alien culture [*Bildung*] came the dawn of a better upbringing [*Erziehung*] that moved toward the universal.... On this ground our Verein was formed."[38] Under the leadership of Gans, the Verein thus sought to overcome Jewish particularity for the sake of Judaism's absorption into the universal current of Europe.[39]

GERMAN/JEWISH GHOST STORIES

I now turn to what I earlier called Heine's "Jewish conception of historicity" and will show how Heine's *Reisebilder*, when read as a philosophy of history, offer a different take on Hegel's concept of world history and on this process of Jewish absorption into the totality of Europe. I will begin by showing how Heine mocked and rejected Hegel's systematic philosophy of history and its Jewish reception in the Verein.[40] Instead of chronologically going through Heine's *Reisebilder* to demonstrate these claims, however, I will focus on "places" where we can best see the emergence of Heine's conception of history and his deconstruction of Hegel's system: namely, in his reworking of Hegel's systematic voyage of Weltgeist into a ghostly, nautical, Jewish travel narrative.

As S. S. Prawer has shown in a meticulous study of the representation of Jewish characters in Heine's oeuvre, caricatures of Eduard Gans and his Hegelian commitments first appeared in *Briefe aus Berlin* (1822) and became frequent in the four volumes comprising the *Reisebilder*.[41] Heine ridicules Gans's Judaism, his baptism (which took place several months after Heine's), his pedantic scholarship, his profession (Gans was a law professor at the University of Berlin), and, most of all, his decidedly political commitment to a Hegelian philosophy of world history.[42] This mockery of Gans and Hegel receives one of its most critical formulations in the two cycles of North Sea poems (*Sämtliche Schriften* 2:167–205) originally published as parts of *Reisebilder I* and *Reisebilder II*. The immediate inspirations for the poems were Heine's vacations to the North Sea in 1825 and three sea voyages to the island of Norderney in 1826.[43] I will briefly summarize the cycles and then show how Heine uses the topos of seafaring and ship travel to rework Goethe's journey to Italy as well as Hegel's and Gans's reliance on the history of seafaring for the spread of the universal World Spirit. In both cases Heine takes up the "Greek" paradigm of seafaring to critically deconstruct the ways in which mobility contributes to a restrictive concept of nationality and world history.

The first cycle begins with a voyager gazing out into the unbounded ocean as he prepares to sever personal ties and leave behind his family and homeland. Having embarked on his journey, he encounters the spirits of Odysseus and Poseidon, the latter of whom tells him not to fear the tumult of the sea. The voyager survives a terrible storm, but, after the waves have calmed down, he has to be saved by the captain from falling off the side of the vessel while beguiled by a "sea phantom" deep beneath the waters (*Sämtliche Schriften* 2:182–84). The cycle concludes with a poem entitled "Peace," which ends with a tribute to the voyager's ultimate savior, Jesus Christ (*Sämtliche Schriften* 2:185–87).[44] The second cycle of poems begins with the voyager leaving the island and setting sail, as we later find out, back to "my German fatherland" (*Sämtliche Schriften* 2:202). Once again, the sailor braves a storm and a shipwreck, but he begins to question the worth of the journey in its mythological, historical, and personal valences. He yearns for "the German coastline" but can only discern water. The voyager then makes a wish for his homeland, Germany: "May, for all time, your lovely ground be covered / With madness, hussars, and wretched verses / . . . And may they tally votes every day / On whether cheese maggots belong to the cheese; / And deliberate for long periods of time / How one can ennoble Egyptian sheep / By improving their wool / . . . Oh Germany! / I still long for thee, / For at least you are still solid ground" ("Seaksickness," *Sämtliche Schriften* 2:202). In the penultimate poem, "In Port," the voyager has arrived in Germany and finds himself in a rathskeller in Bremen, reflecting on the direction and movement of world history. The cycle concludes with a short poem, "Epilogue," on artistic production.

As Jeffrey Sammons has pointed out, the North Sea cycles are not only original in Heine's oeuvre but also in German poetry: Heine was "the first German to write a body of major poetry about the sea."[45] Thematically speaking, German literature about seafaring goes back to the end of the fifteenth century with Sebastian Brant's *Narrenschiff* (Ship of Fools), the first German work, according to Fritz Strich, "to have reached the status of world literature" (since it was translated into multiple languages).[46] But what makes Heine's cycles particularly original and relevant here is that the poet critically replicates the antique journey of seafaring and return, as it was inherited and used by Goethe and Hegel, but with a *Jewish* difference: Heine has consciously taken up the most canonical and recognizably Greek of themes—the sea voyage—and made it into a satirical, semiautobiographical travel narrative of a baptized German-Jew, torn between land and sea. After all, not only is the grand sea voyage to the island of Norderney anything but grand (on a clear day the island is visible from the German coast across shallow mud flats), but onboard the great ship Heine's voyager desires the safety and solid ground of the German nation yet scorns the Germans' petty discussions about the improvement of the Jews: the "Egyptian sheep." In other words, Jews are no longer condemned to wander on land; they also set sail, like Heine, like Germans, like Goethe and Hegel, if only to cross a tame strait. In effect, if Jews engage in seafaring, they have a claim to be both nationally grounded subjects (the round-trip by sea shores up subjectivity and nationality, as Goethe suggested) and world-historical (the journey by sea is the condition of possibility for the spread of the universal World Spirit). This is Heine's first deconstructive claim.

To better understand how Heine achieves this deconstruction in the poem "Im Hafen" (In port), we should pay particular attention to his reformulation of Hegelian world history (*Sämtliche Schriften* 2:203–4).[47] The poem is roughly based on Heine's return from his travels to the North Sea during the fall of 1826, when he made a short stay in the port city of Bremen. It begins with a man who has returned to port after having weathered storms on the open sea. He thinks about the dialectical history of the world and the movement of "World Spirit," which he sees reflected in his glass of wine:

> Wie doch die Welt so traulich und lieblich
> Im Römerglas sich widerspiegelt,
> Und wie der wogende Mikrokosmus
> Sonnnig hinabfließt ins durstige Herz!
> Alles erblick ich im Glas,
> Alte und neue Völkergeschichte,
> Türken und Griechen, Hegel und Gans,

Zitronwälder und Wachtparaden,
Berlin und Schilda und Tunis und Hamburg,
. . .
Hallelujah! Wie lieblich umwehn mich
Die Palmen von Beth El!
Wie duften die Myrrhen von Hebron!
Wie rauscht der Jordan und taumelt vor Freude,
Auch meine unsterbliche Seele taumelt
Und ich taumle mit ihr und taumelnd
Bringt mich die Treppe hinauf, ans Tagslicht,
Der brave Ratskellermeister von Bremen.

Du braver Ratskellermeister von Bremen!
Siehst du, auf den Dächern der Häuser sitzen
Die Engel und sind betrunken und singen;
Die glühende Sonne droben am Himmel
Ist nur die rote betrunkene Nase,
Die der Weltgeist hinaussteckt,
Und um die rote Weltgeistnase
Dreht sich die ganze betrunkene Welt.

[Oh, how the world, so intimately and sweetly, / is reflected in the wine glass / and how the surging microcosmos / sunnily flows through the thirsty heart! / I see everything in the glass, / the history of ancient and modern peoples, / Turks and Greeks, Hegel and Gans, / Citron forests and parading guards, / Berlin and Gotham and Tunis and Hamburg [. . .] Hallelujah! How sweetly around me wave / The palm trees of Bethel! / How the myrrh from Hebron breathes! / How the Jordan ripples and tumbles with glee, / Just as my immortal soul tumbles, / And I tumble with it and, tumbling, / Am brought up the stairs, into daylight, / By the good rathskeller owner from Bremen. / You, good rathskeller owner from Bremen! / Do you see, sitting on the roofs of the houses, / angels, drunk and singing; / The radiant sun there above in the sky / Is only the red drunken nose, / which the World Spirit sticks out; / And around the red-nosed World Spirit / Revolves the whole, drunken world.]

Heine is unequivocally mocking the central concept of Hegelian history, the Weltgeist, which no longer deliberately and reasonably guides the development of history through successively higher stages but instead pulls the world in a drunken orbit according to the direction of its red nose. This is not the progressive movement of Geist articulated by Hegel in his philosophy of world history. But, more than that, Heine's voyager imagines the totality of history coming together not in the Germanic world but in a magical glass of wine after a sea voyage.[48] Here he perceives an array of apparently antithetical pairs—ancient and modern history, Turks and Greeks, Hegel and Gans, and so forth—which we might seek to sublate into a higher term if they are, in fact, opposing. But Heine does not do this. Instead, he critically juxtaposes them, as if dialectically at a standstill. Indeed, the only way that Hegel could be seen to be the antithesis of Gans would be by virtue of Hegel's Christianity and Gans's Judaism, which by 1826 Gans had given up through baptism. What emerges from these critical constellations is a new image, one that, because of its inherent tensions, bursts forth like a flash. The result, as Benjamin would later articulate, is the production of a revolutionary effect upon consciousness and historical practice. In this regard, Heine's *Reisebilder*—in their critical juxtapositions of images—can be seen to be the methodological antecedents to Benjamin's theory of the *dialektische Bild* (dialectical image). Both Heine and Benjamin rework Hegel's systematic philosophy of history, with its concept of strict development, teleology, and continuity, by attempting to salvage the very particularity that was lost in the triumphal spread of Weltgeist.

The particularity of Judaism is thus the critical subtext in Heine's poem and, as I already suggested, in the cycle as a whole: before being pulled outside by the owner, the voyager mistakes the stairs of the rathskeller for the steps of Jacob's ladder. Bethel, where Jacob dreamed of the ladder to heaven, is replaced by Bremen. In effect, Bremen, a port city leading to and away from Germany, leads, on some other journey, to a Jewish topography: to Bethel, Hebron, and the Jordan River. In these unresolved juxtapositions, from Hegel and Gans to Bremen and Bethel, and in his co-opting of the seafaring topos, Heine creates not only a new poetic space but also a new transhistorical and transnational space, which might be productively called Jewgreek or German/Jewish. In blending these seeming oppositions and holding them together in a moment saturated with tension, a new German-Greco-Jewish space emerges.

In the conclusion to an essay on the work of Emmanuel Levinas, Derrida asks what can "account for the historical *coupling* of Judaism and Hellenism? And what is the legitimacy, what is the meaning of the *copula* in this proposition from perhaps the most Hegelian of modern novelists [James

Joyce]: 'Jewgreek is greekjew. Extremes meet'?"[49] Although he does not propose to answer this question, the relationship between Greek and Jewish, like German and Jewish, cannot be reduced to a simple binary opposition. Instead, Hegel and Gans, Bremen and Bethel, and, for that matter, Hegel and Heine must be seen in a dialectical tension, as a kind of German/Jewish constellation that allows us to assess the very modernity from which these thinkers, images, and figures emerged.

Heine thus achieves two things in the poem that are crucial to the way he deconstructs the Hegelian consumption of particularity throughout the *Reisebilder*: First, he parodies the universal spread of Weltgeist by turning the deliberateness of seafaring into a Jewish voyage such that the ship and the journey by sea no longer represent the progress of World Spirit or the material and geographic preconditions of its (Greek, Christian) triumph. Second, he juxtaposes classification types and mixes genres but without resolving them into a higher form. Heine essentially presents the *Mischung*— the mixed form—without the Hegelian *Aufhebung* in order to tarry with the particular rather than subsume, integrate, or overcome it. The terms in the poem (*Turks* and *Greeks, Hegel* and *Gans, Tunis* and *Hamburg,* and, we might add, *Jew* and *Greek* as well as *Jew* and *German*) are readable, then, not merely as opposites—especially not if they are waiting to be sublated into something higher, as Hegel and Gans would have it—but as dialectical terms at a critical standstill.

Not surprisingly, this is also the way Heine conceives of the task of writing history. In the "Journey from Munich to Genoa" Heine rejects the historicist notion that the past can be faithfully represented as it was and the classic Aristotelian distinction between history and poetry in favor of a "mixed" form of representation: "[A people] desire their history from the hand of a poet and not from the hand of a historian. They do not desire the faithful reporting of bare facts but rather desire every fact to be dissolved again into the original poetry from which it sprang. The poets know this, and, not without secret gloating, they arbitrarily remodel the memories of a people, perhaps to the mockery of historiographers proud of their dryness and state archivists with their pieces of parchment" (*Sämtliche Schriften* 2:330). He later writes in a letter praising Jules Michelet's historical methodology in 1834: "You are a true historian because you are, at the same time, a philosopher and a great artist."[50] In this way we can already see the first results of Heine's conception of history: Not only does he reject the eschatology of the Hegelian journey of Weltgeist, he is also skeptical of the idea that the past can be purely and fully recuperated. Instead, Heine produces a critically poetic and parodic history of his present by mixing traditionally separated genres, such as literature and history, art and philosophy, not into some higher, purer form but into the most volatile, ironic, and bastardized forms he can imagine. The task of the *Reisebilder* is to present the travel narrative as a politically charged philosophy of history.

To underscore this methodological innovation, it is useful to recall briefly the definition made by Aristotle in chapter 8 of his *Poetics*: "The poet's function is to describe, not the thing that has happened, but a kind of thing that might happen, i.e., what is possible . . . the historian describes the thing that has been and [the poet] a kind of thing that might be."[51] In short, historians occupy themselves with reality, with what was, and poets are concerned with possibility, what might be. When history became a positivist discipline in the nineteenth century, it was precisely Aristotle's distinction, translated over and over again as one between fact and fiction, that turned the work of a historian into the work of a scientist. Histories could be tested, proved, and disproved by evidence and archival material such that eventually, over time, with careful and methodical accumulation, the reality of the past could be written, reconstructed, and finally filled in. The historian does "not judge the past" but, to use Ranke's famous words, merely shows "how it really was [*wie es eigentlich gewesen*]."[52] Cold facts and scientific objectivity would lead to the reality of what happened; the past was "out there."

Heine wants no part in this. Heine's *Reisebilder* are not histories in the strict sense of the Aristotelian or Rankean definition, nor are they philosophies of history in the strict sense of a Hegelian system of teleological movement and historical development. Moreover, they are not stories of return as in Goethe's *Italienische Reise*, with its self-certain investment in the antique paradigm of *nostos*. Through his unfettered mobility, Goethe's narrator boasts a remarkably total spectatorship on the world, and it is the narration of his transnational accumulation of knowledge that contributes to the construction of a stable, nationally grounded subject. The *Reisebilder* reject both Hegel's world history as the nautical expansion of the universal and Goethe's self-discovery of nationality by deconstructing their overlapping investments in the absolutism and teleology of mobility.

To do so, Heine invents a bastard form, which is not quite literature and not quite history, not quite art and not quite philosophy, not quite Jewish and not quite Greek. The *Reisebilder* occupy a middle space between temporal, spatial, national, and identity registers that all remain "out of joint."[53] He unpredictably mixes the narration of past, present, and future; he confounds the narration of geographic space by mixing near and far, shallow and deep; he plays with identity categories by mixing Jewish, German, Greek, and Christian; he blends reality (what happened) with possibility (what might have happened) and with falsehood (what did not happen), such that none of these distinctions is tenable; and, finally, he combines "dreams" and "ghosts" with waking images of the supposed clarity of the past. In effect, spirits—particularly Jewish ghosts and Hegelian spirits— move through and haunt his world of simultaneous particularity.

As critics have pointed out, *Die Harzreise* (1824), just like the other narrative journeys, is only vaguely organized as a travelogue, for neither the narration of geography nor temporality conforms to the expectations of national or relational coherence, whether linear or circular.[54] *Die Harzreise* begins with the specificity of a place, namely, Göttingen, and ends in a fragment, in an unspecified place, on the first of May. In between this journey from place to time, Heine's narrator climbs mountains and descends into mineshafts, talks about the past and reimagines the future, dreams of the dead and is haunted by spirits. On many occasions he ridicules the very notion of systematic thought. The narrator does not travel through space or in time to realize a preordained voyage of self-discovery, national identity, or universal history but rather to critically juxtapose volatile images from his present.

Of these images, unsettling dreams and disruptive spirits persistently undermine narrative coherence achieved through cumulative self-discovery and thwart systematic conceptions of the progress of world history. Not only does Heine use dreams and ghost stories as historical sources in the tradition of Herodotus and Artemidorus, the unsystematic narration of these dreams and ghost stories also allows Heine to elude censorship and still stage trenchant political criticism.[55] This is particularly evident in *Die Harzreise*, when he is visited, for example, by the "Jewish" ghost of the recently deceased rationalist, Saul Ascher (*Sämtliche Schriften* 2:126–29), or when he narrates a dream of his law student days in Göttingen:

> I stood in the corner of the Hall of Jurisprudence, turning over old dissertations, and lost myself in reading. . . . The bell of the neighboring church struck twelve, the hall doors slowly opened, and there entered a proud, gigantic woman, reverentially accompanied by the members of

the law faculty. . . . The goddess cried out and rivulets of tears sprang from her eyes; the entire assembly howled as if in the agonies of death; the ceiling of the hall burst asunder, the books tumbled down from their shelves. . . . I found refuge from this bedlam in the Hall of History, near that gracious spot where the holy images of the Apollo Belvedere and the Venus de Medici stand next to one another, and I knelt at the feet of the goddess of beauty. . . . My eyes drank in with intoxication the symmetry and immortal loveliness of her infinitely blessed corporeal form; Hellenic calm swept through my soul.

(Sämtliche Schriften 2:108–10)

As an ironic "historical source" (Heine supposedly dreamed it while staying at an inn in Osterode), the dream mocks the idea of history as salvation. The weight of the Greek past—as cultural treasures and historical artifacts—offers a temporary respite from the juridical chaos. But Heine—a baptized Jew—can only partake in this glorious salvation and enjoy such perfect forms in a dream. For his waking vision, as he later remarks in the *North Sea III*, is nothing like that of Goethe's, who "sees all things with his clear Greek eyes . . . in the true outlines and true colors in which God clothed them" (*Sämtliche Schriften* 2:221). Heine is stuck with his "sickly, torn [*zerrissene*] romantic feelings" (*Sämtliche Schriften* 2:221). His waking world—that is, the world of a wandering, baptized yet eternal, seafaring Jew—is far from the dreamed forms of Greek perfection, Hegel's European universal or Goethe's Greco-German spectatorship.

Although Heine sometimes even followed Goethe's footsteps through northern Italy, particularly from Verona through the Tyrol, he never experiences or is able to convey the perfection of Goethe's worldly and historical spectatorship. As Heine says of the *Italienische Reise*: "Everywhere in it we find the actual comprehension and the calm repose of nature. Goethe holds a mirror up to—or, to speak more accurately, is himself the mirror of—nature. Nature wished to know how she looked, and therefore she created Goethe" (*Sämtliche Schriften* 2:367). Heine's "Jewish" perspective on the world appears to preclude such mastery of nature—he might as well say that nature would never ask a Jew how she looked. Telling of his daydream in the amphitheater of Verona, Heine, as a Jew, can only fancy his way into the beauty, grandeur, and safety of Greco-Roman antiquity, unlike Goethe who convincingly sees himself as a direct descendent and surviving spirit of antiquity:

I walked for a long time on the upper benches of the amphitheater, pondering my way back to the past. As all buildings reveal their inner spirit [Geist] most clearly at twilight, so did these walls speak to me. . . . They spoke of the men of old Rome, and I was there, as if seeing the Romans wander around as white shadows in the darkened circus. I seemed to see the Gracchi with their inspired martyr eyes! "Tiberius Sempronius!" I cried aloud. "I will vote with you for the Agrarian Law." . . . Then suddenly the heavy tones of the vesper bell sounded and the horrible drumming of the evening roll call. The proud Roman spirits [Geister] disappeared, and *I found myself once more in the Austrian Christian present age.*

(*Sämtliche Schriften* 2:365; my emphasis)

On awaking from his daydream, Heine inevitably returns as a Jew, in the here and now of his untimely Christian present. He can only dream himself into the harmony of this other place, with its glorious power and historical prestige, by temporarily imagining himself among such mythical, antique spirits.[56] No matter how deeply he believed his German roots to run, Heine was still left wandering—in his present—as an eternal Jew. As he famously wrote to his friend Moses Moser in October 1826 while traveling to the North Sea, "It is very clear to me that I am most longingly forced to say good-bye to the German fatherland. Less the desire to wander and more the torture of my personal circumstances (that is, the Jew that can never be washed away [*die nie abzuwaschende Jude*]) drives me away. . . . For how deeply rooted is the myth of the eternal Jew! [*der Mythos des ewigen Juden*]."[57] Not even baptism, seafaring, or Hegel can "wash away" the Jew. In this respect, Heine's Judaism is a personal specter and a spirit to be eternally tarried with.

Neither exorcised nor forgotten, Jewish ghosts unmistakably haunt Heine's travels through Europe. While a psychobiographical argument about Heine's "torn" identity is not irrelevant here,[58] I want to underscore the way in which Heine subtly deconstructs Hegel's world history, wherein Jews are circumscribed in the first stage of world history and condemned to be overcome, in a negative moment, and never mentioned again. In this way Heine's poetry reveals the violent consequences of Hegel's totalizing philosophy of world history.

To do so, Heine carefully reads the Hegelian system—world history as a systematic, geographically driven Greek voyage or travel narrative of Spirit—

in order to mimic it with a Jewish difference. Hegel wants to exorcise the Jewish ghost unequivocally in favor of the Christian Geist, but he can only keep the Jewish specter at bay by cutting it out. In effect, Hegel must enact a severance (*Trennung*) not unlike the one he accuses Abraham of enacting with the Jewish people: Hegel cuts the Jews out of his system, by not only ignoring Jesus's Judaism but also the contemporary Jews of the "Germanic world," in order to accelerate the end of history and the universality of Christian spirit. But, in so doing, Hegel, by this logic, performs a Jewish act. For precisely this reason and perhaps also because he cannot do otherwise, Heine lets the Jewish spirits back in. Not only do Jewish ghosts haunt his travelogues, in dreams and on waking, Jewish ghosts also haunt the supposed totality of Europe as a world-historical achievement. Far from Gans's desires for Jewish absorption into the ocean of Europe, Heine's Jews haunt his European travels persistently, as ghosts, in dreams, on ships, and in everyday encounters. These range from the stereotypical to the uniquely cultural-historical: Jews are rationalist thinkers, as in the caricature of Saul Ascher, and are also bankers, as in the caricature of Christian Gumpel with a big nose and hungry pocketbook; as cosmopolitan figures, Jews are historically some 5,588 years old and, in this sense, are hardly suspended in the first stage of world history. Heine does not cut the Jews out, nor does he systematize their belonging to a particular place in history; rather he creates a mobile space for their appearance. In short, he writes Jewish ghost stories of a Christian ghost story.[59]

If Heine had simply offered the positive image of the Jew as an antidote to Hegel's anti-Semitic image of the Jew or proposed the singularity of the Jewish ghost as a counter to the Christian Geist, he would still have been operating in the terms and logic of the Hegelian system. Instead Heine mimics the travelogue with an ironic difference in order to deconstruct its built-in claims about nationality, self-discovery, total spectatorship, and, most of all, historicity. For Heine Jewish particularity cannot be systematized or contained in the absolute logic of a developmental structure because this would inevitably domesticate Jewish difference and endow it with an ontological stability or, worse, a final, historical resting place. The travel narrative as a philosophy of history is always on the move, slipping away into paradoxes and irony, mixing genres and types, playfully contradicting itself, and, sometimes, outright lying. This political *Mischung*, this nonspace for particularity, is Heine's "Jewgreek," German/Jewish conception of historicity.

In this way Heine reclaims *Geistesgeschichte* (intellectual history) from its Enlightenment-rationalist stronghold: Heine's "ghosts" disrupt the sys-

tematic and national exclusivity of the Greco-German historical-philo-
sophical tradition. On the Harz journey, for example, in the town of Goslar,
Heine is visited by the ghost of the recently deceased Dr. Saul Ascher, one of
several visits by various Jewish ghosts and religious spirits throughout the
Reisebilder. Ascher was the rationalist, Jewish author of an antinationalist
book called *Germanomanie* (1815), which was famously burned by patriotic
German youths at the Wartburg Festival of 1817 as they proclaimed, "Woe
upon the Jews that cleave to their Judaism and defame our German nationhood [*unser Volkstum und Deutschtum*]."[60] Heine relates the otherworldly
visit of Ascher's ghost, who, true to nature, proceeds to espouse the tenets
of rationalism and proclaim the mighty principles of reason to ironically
prove that he is not a ghost:

> At last the door opened, and the late Doctor Saul Ascher slowly entered.
> A cold fever trickled through my marrow and veins—I trembled like
> an ivy leaf, and I scarcely dared to gaze upon the ghost [*Gespenst*]. He
> appeared as usual, with the same transcendental gray coat, the same
> abstract legs, and the same mathematical face; only it was a little yel-
> lower than usual, and the mouth, which used to form two angles of 22.5
> degrees, was pinched together. . . . "Don't be scared, nor believe that I
> am a ghost. It is a deception of your imagination, if you believe I am a
> ghost. What is a ghost? Give me a definition. Deduce for me the condi-
> tions of possibility of a ghost. In what reasonable connection does such
> an apparition coincide with reason itself? Reason, I say, reason!" And
> now the ghost proceeded to analyze reason, cited from Kant's *Critique
> of Pure Reason*, part 2, section 1 of the second book, chapter 3, the dis-
> tinction between phenomena and noumena, then constructed a hypo-
> thetical problematic for the belief in ghosts, placed one syllogism on
> another, and concluded with the logical proof that there are absolutely
> no ghosts.   (*Sämtliche Schriften* 2:128)

Ascher's ghost appeals to the most systematic, law-based principles of reason in order to prove the nonexistence of ghosts. Satirizing enlightened rationalism, Jewish ghosts both exist and do not exist; they haunt the integrity
of a philosophical system and, at the same time, use the system ironically to
rationalize themselves away.

But, most significantly, throughout all the *Reisebilder*, there is the
Hegelian ghost of universal history. The Hegelian ghost is nothing but the

progressive movement of Christian Geist in which Jews are circumscribed in the first stage of world history and condemned to be overcome through the progress of world history. It is here that Heine's *Reisebilder* betray the violent consequences of the Hegelian project and offer a deconstruction of its totalizing view of history: Jewish ghosts, rather than exorcised and forgotten, haunt his travel narratives to make space for another conception of historicity, namely, the promise or futurity of Jewish difference.

Ideen. Das Buch Le Grand, often considered the most successful work of his pre-Paris period, is arguably the best place to see the results of this volatile, political *Mischung*. The travelogue, structured as a contradictory, monologic conversation with an unidentified woman, enacts this generic blurring by moving between historical references and autobiographical reflections, social commentaries and allegorical reflections, history and literature, past and present, Jewish and Christian, German and Jewish, factual and counterfactual, the said and the unsaid:

> Please do not complain of my digressions. In every foregoing chapter, there is not a single line that does not belong to the business at hand. I am coerced to write; I avoid all superfluity; I often pass over what is necessary; for example, I have not once quoted with any regularity—I do not mean spirits [*Geister*], but, on the contrary, I mean writers. . . . In case of an emergency, I can get a loan of quotations from my learned friends. My friend G. [Gans] in Berlin is, so to speak, a little Rothschild in quotations and will gladly lend me a few million, and if he does not have them, he can easily find some cosmopolitan spiritual bankers [*kosmopolitische Geistesbankier*] who do. . . . Everywhere I discover opportunities to display my pedantry. If I happen to mention eating, I at once remark in a note that the Greeks, Romans, and Hebrews also ate—I quote all the costly dishes. . . . Soup is my favorite dish. Madame, I have thought of going to London next year, but if it is really true, that no soup is to be had there, a deep longing will soon drive me back to the soup flesh-pots of the fatherland. . . . I might also allege the refined manner in which many Berlin intellectuals have expressed themselves relative to Jewish eating, which would lead me to the other excellences and preeminences of the Jews, to whom we are all indebted, for inventions such as bills of exchange and Christianity.
>
> (*Sämtliche Schriften* 2:284–85)

The seemingly maniacal, uninhibited play of free associations is, however, anything but apolitical. This ludic mixture of genres, identities, and types not only mocks the idea of a systematic and necessary organization of experience into a dialectical history of the progression of Weltgeist, but it is also a strategy of defiance that enables Heine to avoid suppression by the German censors. The reader need only recall that the previous chapter as well as the chapter just quoted are both written *as if* partially censored. Save four words, the former is simply represented by empty dashes: "Die deutschen Zensoren———————————————— ... Dummköpfe——————— ..." (*Sämtliche Schriften* 2:283). We can apply Seeba's argument in his study of Heine's *Briefe aus Berlin* to Heine's political criticism and history writing: Heine avoids a systematic method in order to produce an uncensored nonspace for the emergence of particularity.[61] He says one thing, then immediately contradicts himself; he reveals his identity, then suppresses it; he blends historical fact with fiction, and both are blended again with the counterfactual, that is, what might have or could have happened. There is no resolution, absorption, purification, or sublation: Heine's history not only differs from Hegel's in its refusal of systematics but also defers the absolute eschatology and the insistent finality of the movement of Spirit in Hegel by creating open spaces for the emergence of another history. This mobile space of paradox and irony, contradiction and *Mischung*, is Heine's Jewish historicity.[62]

We can see this even more clearly in Heine's extension of the earlier dialectical constellations of Turks and Greeks, Hegel and Gans. The poet concludes the chapter from *Ideen. Das Buch Le Grand* quoted above by listing exiles and ironically imposing a system of thought. The people in the list are "great" because they had to "run away" at a significant time in their lives. They have nothing in common but self-imposed or forced exile: "If we go through history, Madame, we find that all great men have been obliged to run away once in their lives: Lot, Tarquin, Moses, Jupiter, Madame de Staël, Nebuchadnezzar, Benjowsky, Muhammad, the whole Prussian army, Gregory VII, Rabbi Isaac Abrabanel, Rousseau—to which I could add very many other names, as for instance those whose names appear on the 'Black Board' of the stock exchange" (*Sämtliche Schriften* 2:287). The heterogeneous list ranges from Moses's leading the Jews out of Egypt to Germaine de Staël's exile in Switzerland to avoid the guillotine, from Muhammad's hegira to the Prussian army's retreat from the French after double defeats by Napoleon in 1806, from Isaac ben Judah Abrabanel's forced exile in 1482 to Castile.[63] We might also add Heine's exile as a "wandering Jew" and the traveling tales of his Jewish narrator to this list. What they all have in common is travel, or, more precisely, fleeing. History turns out to be pictures of travel, exile, and escape.

He concludes the chapter with an ironic embrace of *Systematie*: "So, Madame, you see that I am not wanting in well-grounded erudition and profundity. Only in systematology am I a little behind. . . . I shall, therefore, proceed to speak: I. Of ideas. A. Of ideas in general. 1. Of reasonable ideas. 2. Of unreasonable ideas. a. Of ordinary ideas. b. Of ideas covered in green leather" (*Sämtliche Schriften* 2:287). Once again Heine has targeted the systematic thought of Hegel. The "idea," a manifold concept in the Hegelian lexicon, refers to the absolute movement of Geist as an already completed historical process anterior to reality. For Heine the Hegelian concept is complicit with violence because the enclosed logic of any system forces some people into exile, if it does not kill them straight out. Heine's *Reisebilder* are, therefore, acts of freedom, defiant and decidedly political acts creating cracks for the survival of a little bit of Jewish alterity.

Unlike Hegel's philosophy of world history, inexorable in its movement and inviolable in its systematization, Heine's *Reisebilder* produce a space for the survival of particularity. To use the critical words of Adorno, Hegel's systematic philosophy consumes every trace of difference in its "paranoid zeal to tolerate nothing else" but a total synthesis of identity and nonidentity.[64] Universal history, then, becomes nothing but an "insatiable identity principle that perpetuates antagonism by suppressing contradiction" until all particularity is subsumed into the universal.[65] Glossing Schiller's famous dictum that concludes Hegel's *Philosophy of Right*, Adorno points out: "The fact that history has rolled over certain positions will be respected as a verdict on their truth content only by those who agree with Schiller that 'world history is the world tribunal.'"[66] In other words, in the Hegelian system, world history, as the final court of judgment, determines the truth or untruth of certain people and positions and thereby either raises them up into the universal or condemns them to oblivion. The "untruth" of the particular or the heteronomous is simply "rolled over" by that process of carrying out verdicts and final judgments: world history.

As that other history, Heine's *Reisebilder* are particular, mixed, and utopian both temporally and spatially: In terms of time, they call forth a future, a kind of messianic promise, and, in terms of space, they are ultimately located in no real topographically or nationally delimited place and are, hence, u-topian. This is not the geographic and national determinism of Hegel's concept of world history. We might even say that Heine has broken the spell of Spirit.[67]

Toward the end of his "Journey from Munich to Genoa," Heine articulates this "utopian" hope to allow a little bit of Jewish difference and alterity to survive:

> It seems . . . as if world history is no longer a robber legend but rather a ghost story [*Geistesgeschichte*]. The grand lever that ambitious and avaricious princes are so eager to employ for their own ends, namely, nationality, with all its vanity and hatred, is now musty and used up; day by day foolish national prejudices are disappearing; all harsh peculiarities are disappearing into the universality of European civilization; now there are no longer nations in Europe but parties. . . . What is this great task of our time? It is emancipation. Not only the emancipation of the Irish, the Greeks, the Frankfurt Jews, the West Indian blacks, and other oppressed people, but the emancipation of the whole world, indeed of Europe, which has attained maturity and is now tearing itself free from the iron shackles of the privileged aristocracy.
>
> (*Sämtliche Schriften* 2:375–76)

Here Heine considers universal or world history as a "history of spirit" in order to imagine the end of both nationality and race-based prejudices. Although upon a cursory reading this passage may sound Hegelian vis-à-vis the disappearance of racial particularities, Heine's philosophy of world history is moving in an entirely different space: Rather than prematurely declaring the arrival of the end time, as Hegel does, Heine recognizes its futurity, its emancipatory promise, and keeps open, to quote Benjamin, its "*weak* Messianic power."[68] In effect, Hegel's definitive messianism is nowhere to be found here because Heine is not rendering any final judgments or resting places for those forgotten, unliberated, or condemned spirits. This is a philosophy of world history that has never arrived and is always conscious of the space for preserving difference.

To conclude, Heine uses poetry to ultimately subvert the absolutism of philosophy by exposing the metaphors on which Hegel's geographically inflected conception of world history relies. Instead of immobilizing particularity or attempting to relocate it in a preordained system of universality (as

Gans does), Heine strives to create a crack, a conception of historicity that in its openness and playfulness is not lethal to the other, does not imprison the heteronomous, and does not domesticate the nonidentical. He cannot create another system antithetical to the Hegelian system because, if he did, the difference Heine seeks to liberate would be locked up again in a new ontological positivity. It is, indeed, a matter of thinking another historicity by creating a space for the narration of other "ghost stories." The narrative of his travels to the North Sea turns into a philosophy of world history, wherein the Christian movement of Geist is haunted and displaced by the hybrid German/Jewish/Greek ghosts so thoroughly exorcised by Hegel. By way of this work of deconstruction, Hegel and Heine—precisely like the German and Jewish ghosts of the *Reisebilder*—become locked together in a dialectic, permanently entangled in one another: Hegel cannot be understood without his "Jewish other" and, recursively, Heine cannot be understood without his "German other." Through Heine's transformation of the genre of travel literature and the philosophy of history, the narration of Jewish mobility thus becomes the basis of a new freedom by way of an awareness of this other history.

5. NUREMBERG-FÜRTH-PALESTINE

Some Assembly Required

Global Anxieties and Corporeal Fantasies of German/Jewish Nationality

5.1 Railway timetable of luxury trains leaving Berlin (1910).

AT THE START of the twentieth century, service from Anhalter Bahnhof fanned out all over Europe, with more than one hundred trains arriving and departing daily from Berlin. If we look at a timetable from January 1910, for example, we see that a number of luxury trains began their journeys from Berlin's Anhalter station, including, among others, the North-South Express (connecting Berlin to Munich, Verona, Genoa, and Cannes), the Egyptian Express (connecting Berlin to Rome and Naples and, from there, to Alexandria and Cairo by ship), and the Riviera Express (connecting Berlin to Amsterdam, Lyon, and Marseille). Other lines connected Berlin to Paris, Vienna, Prague, Athens, and Budapest. In 1912 the editor of the prominent cultural review, *Der Kunstwart*, wrote, somewhat stereotypically, that he heard "the luxury cars of the train from Berlin to the Riviera are nigh-exclusively occupied by Jews."[1]

Adding to its mythological proportions, a gigantic underground passageway connecting the train station to the luxurious Hotel Excelsior across the street was opened in 1928. Guests arriving at the Anhalter station could walk to a doorway at the end of the platform, take an elevator downstairs, stroll through the "longest hotel tunnel in the world," shop around the clock in the underground retail stores, and emerge 80 meters away in the lobby of the "largest hotel on the continent," the Excelsior.[2] Perhaps only Kafka's fantastic Hotel Occidental, with its thirty-one elevators, could compare.

5.2 Hotel Excelsior (ca. 1930). *Courtesy of Landesarchiv, Berlin*

The year before, Walter Ruttmann immortalized both the hotel and the train station in his film, *Berlin: Symphony of a Great City*: A roaring train speeds through the countryside before entering the city at daybreak with its arrival at the Anhalter Bahnhof. The camera then follows the luggage of a passenger as it makes its way up the elevator and into the Hotel Excelsior. At the film's end, fireworks explode over the wildly illuminated, technically pulsing city in a celebration of Berlin's modernity. It is the Anhalter Bahnhof that both embodies and gives us access to this modernity.

Analogous to the arcades of Paris in the nineteenth century, these twentieth century passageways—railway stations, underground tunnels, and gigantic hotels—became hubs of capitalist culture, dream places of modernity. The materiality of the arcade and the railway station were imbued with
a type of myth that simultaneously valued innovation—speed, size, beauty,
and efficiency—above all else yet, at the same time, were always vulnerable
to what would supersede it. In this respect, the Parisian arcades and Berlin's
Anhalter station are also material witnesses to the finitude and passage of
the very epoch that they inaugurated. What, after all, could be more transient than claims to permanence?

THE SEAFARING JEW AND THE MISSING GERMAN NATION

In 1902 Max Grunwald, a rabbi from Vienna sympathetic to the
incipient Zionist cause, published an essay called "Jews as Anchormen
and Seafarers" in the Jewish cultural periodical *Ost und West* in which
he insisted that Jews, despite popular opinion and ostensible historical
evidence to the contrary, are in fact a seafaring people.[3] Far from being
condemned to the first stage of world history, as Hegel would have it,
Jews actually have a long and rich tradition of setting sail and, hence, can
claim to be world-historical people in their own right. As we saw in the
previous chapter, it was Hegel who established one of the most enduring arguments for Jewish impotence by implying that Jews were a people
who constitutionally lack a great seafaring tradition. Citing the voyages of
Columbus, the discovery of a sea route to India, and the spread of Christianity across the world, world-historical people are characterized by their
power to master the expansiveness of the sea and their ability to undertake voyages of discovery and conquest. Jews, Hegel claims, know nothing
of this history.

Several decades before Hegel delivered his lectures on the philosophy
of world history, Johann Gottfried Herder published his magnum opus,
a multivolume book called *Ideen zu einer Philosophie der Geschichte der
Menschheit* (Reflections on a Philosophy of the History of Humankind,
1784–1791). In this book Herder set out to map the general direction of humankind by presenting the characteristics of various peoples in a manner

that anticipates many of Hegel's ideas for the organization of world history. As Hegel would later do, Herder starts his account of world history with the African peoples before moving from the Far East to the Western world, ending up in Europe with the Greek and Germanic peoples. Midway through this movement, he dedicates several chapters to the Near East, including one on the "Hebrew peoples." In this chapter he argues that one of their most prominent features is that they are not a seafaring people:

> Although they possessed for some time the ports of the Red Sea, and dwelt so near the shores of the Mediterranean, they never became a seafaring people. . . . Like the Egyptians, they dreaded the sea, and from times immemorial preferred to live among other nations, a feature of their national character against which Moses strenuously fought. In short, they are a people spoiled by their education, because they never attained political maturity on their own soil, and consequently never attained a genuine awareness of honor and freedom. . . . The people of God, whose country was once given to them by heaven itself, have been for thousands of years, yes, virtually from their inception, a parasitical plant upon the trunks of other nations; a tribe of cunning brokers throughout almost the whole world who, in spite of all oppression, nowhere long for their own honor and habitation, for a country of their own.[4]

In effect, the Jewish people are not a great seafaring people, and, more than that, they are merely a "parasitical" people who prefer to live stealthily among other peoples rather than seek "honor and freedom" on their own soil.[5]

Building off of Herder and Hegel's account of Jews in world history, Houston Stewart Chamberlain, in his *Foundations of the Nineteenth Century* (1899), a race-based, anti-Semitic philosophy of history, argued that not only are present-day Jews racially unfit for nation building, but Jews have, according to his version of history, always been so. After describing the physical, religious, and cultural deficiencies of the Jews in his chapter "On the Entrance of the Jews into Western History," Chamberlain looks back to the history of the Judeans to show how Jews, unlike Germans, have never been able to found a great nation:

> They were so unwarlike, such unreliable soldiers that their king had to trust his protection and the protection of their land to foreign troops; that *they were so unwilling to undertake any endeavors that just looking*

at the ocean . . . horrified them; that they were so slothful that for every task at hand one had to hire designers, production managers, and even handworkers for all the delicate work from neighboring countries; that they were so unfit for agriculture that (as it says in many places in the Bible and the Talmud) the Canaanites were not just their teachers but were the only ones up until the end who worked the land; yes, even in a purely political respect, they were such opponents of all stable, well-ordered conditions that no rational form of government could come about by them and they felt best from early on under the pressure of foreign rule, something that did not prevent them, however, from burrowing underneath of it.[6]

Through their scheming, their "materialistic worldview," and their "demonic genius" (1:455), the Jews have, despite (or perhaps because of) their laziness and other deficiencies, nevertheless managed to survive as a race under the rule of other nations; however, they remain nothing more than "a foreign element," as he quotes Herder with approbation (1:463). Because of these transhistorical racial qualities, Jews can never know the greatness of their own nation. By contrast, Germans, Chamberlain maintains as he expands on Hegel's quadripartite structuring of history, represented the pinnacle of "world history" because their cultural and national strength was the outgrowth of the great colonial empires of Greece and Rome. After all, reckoning with the ocean, traveling by ship, and cultivating the new land were world-historical achievements that, according to Herder, Hegel, and Chamberlain, assured national greatness.

Given the importance of seafaring for the great theoreticians of world history, it is not surprising that Grunwald crafts his essay on Jewish seafaring as a historically pointed rejoinder to their claims. Citing sources from the Talmud, antiquity, and the Middle Ages, Grunwald shows that Jews—far from simply averse to traveling by sea or somehow incapable of undertaking sea journeys—have always engaged in seafaring, including voyages of discovery, trade, adventure, and even conquest. Moreover, he argues, in the age of exploration, Jewish adventurers traveled right alongside their non-Jewish counterparts, sailing with Christopher Columbus, Vasco da Gama, and the East India Company. He tells his presumably astonished readership that there were even Jewish pirates, Jewish skippers, and Jewish sea captains at this time. In other words, Jews are and have always been a seafaring, world-historical people.

In so arguing, Grunwald tries to debunk the prevalent idea that Jews—due to certain historical, social, and political circumstances—are restricted to traveling, or more precisely, wandering on land. Jews are not simply condemned to wander the earth, but they also set sail, like great explorers and pioneers.[7] In Grunwald's revision of this history of the landlocked, wandering Jew, he shows that Jews have always participated in seafaring, arguably the greatest—and most horrific—enterprise and institution of Western civilization. After all, travel by ship is not only a classically Greek mode of transportation, it is also, as we have already seen, one of the most persistent and specific metaphors of existence in the Western cultural tradition, something that Grunwald certainly knew. As Georges Van Den Abbeele astutely writes: "The dearest notions of the West nearly all appeal to the motif of the voyage: progress, the quest for knowledge, freedom as freedom to move, self-awareness as an Odyssean enterprise, salvation as a destination to be attained by following a prescribed pathway (typically straight and narrow)."[8] In this respect, then, the history of Jewish seafaring is a testament to Jewish participation in and extension of both the noble and the dubious ideals of Western civilization: Discovery and conquest, knowledge and colonialism, progress and enslavement.

Indeed, he is anxious to write Jews back into colonial history. I quote Grunwald:

> In the voyages of discovery and conquest undertaken by the Portuguese, the Dutch, and the English, Jews played a not unimportant role as seamen and pilots. The ship's doctor on Christopher Columbus's expedition was a Jew, and it is said to have been a Jew that first discovered land; a Jew was the first to found a settlement on the newly discovered land. . . . Vasco da Gama made use of Jewish seafarers, and his constant companion, Alfonsos d'Albuquerque, was a Jew. In 1334, Jayme IV, the last King of Mallorca, testified that the Jew, Juceff Faquin of Barcelona, had sailed around what was then the known world. There were many Jews on the Portuguese expedition of 1415 which accepted Mauritanians. A linguistically gifted Jew accompanied Captain James Lancaster on the first enterprise of the East-India Company in 1601 and was in charge of the negotiations with Sultan von Atschin of Sumatra.   (JR 482)

The list of examples cited by Grunwald goes on and on. His point is that Jews have always engaged in seafaring and, for better or for worse, thus have an incontestable, historically substantiated claim to be a world-historical, colonial people. But what makes his essay so important for our purposes here is that Grunwald sought to legitimize the incipient national-colonial fantasies of Zionism by grounding them in a revisionist history which emerged directly from the tensions of German/Jewish modernity. Jewish seafaring is important to the Zionist idea of nation building because Jews, like Germans, are a colonial, world-historical people.[9] After all, it was the great theoreticians of history—Herder, Hegel, and, most recently, Chamberlain—who had claimed that Jews, by definition, are not a seafaring people and, hence, are nothing but inconsequential for the progress of world history. Grunwald was attempting to turn this claim on its head. Without any embarrassment, criticism, or irony, Grunwald argued that Jews not only engaged in seafaring but—like the great powers of Europe—also engaged in conquest and colonization. Zionists would simply be continuing this tradition by journeying to and resettling in Palestine. In so doing, Grunwald not only buys into this conception of world history but also creates an uncomfortably close alliance between the Zionist ideals and those of the great apologists for empire and expansion. Informed by the meta-epistemology of the ship, it is not coincidental that Herzl published his bildungsroman, *Altneuland*, in the same year. Inspired by the German tradition, the seafaring paradigm legitimized the Jewish state and created a strong, nationally grounded Jewish subject.

Nearly a century before Grunwald and Herzl articulated their ideas of Jewish nationality by calling upon the topos of seafaring, the philosopher Johann Gottlieb Fichte, reflected on the *insignificance* of seafaring for the German nation in his *Reden an die deutsche Nation* (Addresses to the German nation, 1807–1808).[10] In these addresses, delivered the year after Napoleon's victorious campaign against Prussia and the fall of Berlin in October of 1806, Fichte turned to German history to legitimize the future-directed project of national unification. Unlike Grunwald, however, Fichte did not seek to reclaim a mighty seafaring and colonial history, something that would have entailed an outward expansion of the German spirit. Rather, he maintained that German national unification would come by looking inward and cultivating an autocentric development of German originality and strength while combating all threats of foreignness and external corruption. A decade before Hegel declared that seafaring was critical to the spread of World Spirit and the touchstone of world-historical nations, Fichte—perhaps prematurely—repudiated its necessity for the German nation, which, for its part, needed only to concentrate on its inward self-sufficiency and strength:

> Foreign to the German is the freedom of the seas, which is so frequently
> preached in our days. . . . Throughout the course of the centuries, while
> all other nations were in rivalry, the German showed little desire to par-
> ticipate in this freedom [of seafaring] to any great extent, and he will
> never do so. Moreover, he is not in need of it. The abundant supplies
> of his own land, together with his own diligence, afford him all that is
> needed in the life of a civilized man; nor does he lack skill in the art of
> making his resources serve that purpose. As for acquiring the only true
> advantage that world-trade brings, namely, the increase in scientific
> knowledge of the earth and its inhabitants, his own scientific spirit will
> not let him lack a means of exchange.
>
> (*Addresses* 230; translation modified)

According to Fichte, Germans have never participated in seafaring "to any great extent," and they do not need to in order to reap its advantages of exchange and knowledge. Remarkably, in rejecting seafaring, what Fichte is attempting to do is to provide a radically different framework for thinking about nationality: Rather than derive the idea of German nationality from outwardly directed fantasies of colonial expansionism, something that, as Susanne Zantop has shown, was actually quite common during this period,[11] Fichte sought to demarcate nationality through a rhetoric of inward originality, purity, and self-sufficiency. The problem, Fichte argued, was that German national purity had been corrupted by foreignness, something that had subsequently pitted the German states against one another. Therefore, Germans must turn inward, not outward, to unify the fragmented nation.

To do so, Fichte posited that the German people, despite their present fragmentation, were actually "a single body" (*Addresses* 96) and "a single nation" (*Addresses* 3)—that an underlying unity already existed. This is because Germans shared a common cultural tradition, a common language, a common history, and a common rootedness in place. But more than this, the Germans were an "original people . . . without admixture of, or corrup-tion by, any alien element" (*Addresses* 135–36). The uncertainty that Ger-many is currently living through is not the fault of the Germans themselves, Fichte assures his audience, but rather the result of "foreign countries . . . ar-tificially [destroying] German unity" (*Addresses* 227-28). Of course, Fichte, in barely veiled terms, is alluding to the fact that Prussia, as one of the last German states to fall to Napoleon, was now occupied by the French who had taken over Berlin. In effect, the French were responsible for Germany's downfall and division.

Several years before delivering these addresses, Fichte had already spelled-out the fundamentals of his plan for German autarky in *Der geschloßne Handelsstaat* (The closed commercial state, 1800), a political-economic treatise in which he advocated for an internally directed, autocentric development for Germany: German borders were to be largely closed to foreign trade and disconnected from the rest of the world such that Germany could catch up.[12] His theory was that the German states should internally produce, process, and trade their own raw materials and goods between themselves by nationalizing the work force. This would free the German states from economic dependence on "stronger" nations like England and ultimately facilitate unification and the formation of a strong sense of national identity. As Fichte wrote, when "the members of a closed nation depend only on themselves and have as little contact as possible with foreigners . . . a higher degree of national pride and a sharply defined national character will emerge very quickly . . . an entirely new nation will come about."[13] He then rails against the "world" system of capital, what he calls *Weltgeld* (world gold), and its dominance over Germany. As he says in the *Addresses*: "Oh! That we might at last see that all those swindling theories about world-trade and manufacturing for the world market, though they suit the foreigner and form part of the weapons with which he has always made war on us, have no application to the Germans" (231). Seafaring, colonial expansion, and world trade would only exacerbate the "German" problem. For this reason Fichte called for Germans to turn inward and disconnect from the emerging world system.

Indeed, he was not alone in this regard. Germany's foremost railway pioneer, Friedrich List, also argued passionately against what he termed the "cosmopolitan world system" of capitalism precisely because it would continue to be detrimental to "backward" or divided countries like Germany.[14] Before Germans could seriously embrace "cosmopolitanism" and the global economy, they had to first create internal strategies for unifying the developing nation. As List wrote in 1837:

We regard ourselves as cosmopolitans [*Kosmopoliten*], but our cosmopolitanism rests on the solid ground of nationality [*Nationalität*]. We

hope to be at a point where the system of free trade for a nation is pref-
erable to a restrictive trading policy ... but we are citizens of the state
[*Staatsbürger*] before we are citizens of the world [*Weltbürger*]. We devote our energies and efforts to the culture, welfare, glory, and security
of our nation ... [this is because] we owe our culture, our language, our
way of life, our spiritual values in general to the nation.[15]

Because the nations of the world have developed unevenly in terms of economic output, free trade and open borders will only hinder developing
nations until they are able to elevate themselves to the level of developed
nations. In so arguing, both List and Fichte suggest that global anxieties,
particularly the emergence of a world system of capital, cosmopolitanism,
and cultural hybridity, necessitate and—at least for Germany—even entail
a heightened consciousness of nationality and resurgence of nationalism.

Using the ideas of Fichte and Grunwald as my two theoretical starting
points, the purpose of this chapter is to articulate a peculiar aspect of the
German/Jewish dialectic of modernity, namely, how German fantasies of
nationality responded to "globality" by turning inward and, later, how Jewish fantasies of nationality, derived from the model of German nationality,
reconfigured Jewish history as outwardly expansive. I focus on two discursive periods, which are paradigmatically represented by the ideas of Friedrich List and Theodor Herzl, respectively: the period around 1835 for German fantasies of nationality and the period around 1900 for Jewish fantasies
of nationality. I am interested in how the development of inwardly directed
fantasies of German nationality was dependent upon the encoding of the
Jew as "global," and how the subsequent development of outwardly directed
fantasies of Jewish nationality was dependent upon the inward history of
German unification. The German/Jewish dialectic comes to a standstill by
way of the productive tension governing the discursive formation of these
fantasies of nationality. In both cases, the national fantasy needs its "other"
for self-legitimization.

While proponents of German nationality argued that unity would come
by looking inward and connecting together the scattered Germanic people
through railway technologies, proponents of Jewish nationality sought to
reconfigure Jewish history to reflect the world-historical status of the Jewish people. They did this, first, by writing Jews into the expansive history of
seafaring, nationality, and colonialism, with a particular focus on the model
of German unity as achieved under Bismarck, and, second, by configuring

Jewish national identity as the end of exile or as a kind of voyage home. In both cases, seafaring negated claims that Jews are constitutionally unfit for nation building. Not without irony, it was precisely this notion of seafaring that had been rejected by German nationalists such as Fichte, List, and, to a certain extent, Bismarck, even while it formed a staple of both philosophical and popular critiques of the emergence of Jewish national identity.

During the first half of the nineteenth century, I will argue, this dialectic of German/Jewish nationality is structured by an inverted relationship between the national and the global imaginary: Succinctly put, the hopes and anxieties of the global solidify the national. As I will show, these hopes and anxieties can be detected in a wide range of cultural forms. Beyond Fichte and List, for example, the hope that the German nation would emerge from the global is the central issue in Ludwig Klüber's theoretical reflections on the expansion of the postal system in Germany; it is the raison d'être for the sudden eruption of a surfeit of "national literary histories" during the 1830s and 1840s; it is the basis of Wolfgang Menzel's anti-Semitic anxieties over the spread of "unpatriotic" literature and the emergence of the "Young Germany" controversy in 1835; and it is the primary concern of List's analysis of the political economy and his unbridled enthusiasm for the salvific power of railway technologies. The expansiveness of the global—especially as a threat—gives rise to the inwardness of the national.

Significantly, this anxiety of the global, far from fuzzy or abstract, was always localized on the body and, for this reason, a persistent figure emerges throughout the nineteenth century to imagine "Germany" and search for practical ways to unify the divided German states through various technological or cultural-historical means: the unification of the German nation becomes tantamount to the resurrection and redemption of a broken body. Yet at the same time that the nation is connected together as a body might be reassembled, the fear of too much connectivity—seen in the fears of foreignness, globality, and hybridity—increases in like measure. Jewish bodies, in particular, because of their cosmopolitan, non-national heritage and ties to international finance, provide both the justification for German nationalism and boundaries for delimiting the developing body politic of Germany. In other words, the global—world literature, world capital, world trade, and world religion—becomes coded as Jewish, and this threat is precisely what grounds, unifies, and strengthens the German national body.

In the second part of this chapter, I show how German fantasies about national unification and anxieties over globalization during the first half of

the nineteenth century impacted the conceptualization of Jewish nationality in the second half of the nineteenth century. Here I focus on the ideas
of Theodor Herzl, giving particular attention to the ways in which the concept of Jewish nationality emerges as a politics of mobility. As we will see,
Herzl imagined Zionism as a kind of modern "movement" in which the
Jewish people would not only be relocated out of Europe but would also
be regenerated—very much like a body that has been resurrected. Drawing
on the rhetoric of unity used by Bismarck and Fichte, Herzl's conception
of Jewish nationality sought to elevate Jews into world-historical people
with a unique difference, namely, that they would travel by sea to Palestine.
In his last major work, the travel novel, *Altneuland* (*Old-New Land*, 1902),
Herzl does just this by creating an imaginative fantasy for the realization
of the Jewish state. Using the basic form of the bildungsroman, a narrative structure that, as we have seen with Goethe, is intimately connected to
the paradigm of the sea voyage in its quest for knowledge, maturity, and
subjectivity, Herzl wrote Zionism's first colonial novel. Told as a seafaring
journey through space and time, the novel represents the rationale for and
the fulfillment of the Zionist colonial dream: Exodus out of Europe—by
ship—would mean arrival in Palestine. Jews—like Germans—could become modern, world-historical, national subjects.

GERMAN/JEWISH BODIES: HOW GLOBAL
ANXIETIES CONDITIONED NATIONAL FANTASIES

Claims about the contemporary consequences of globalization for
the nation-state are familiar: With the rapidity and volume of information
and material exchange across national borders, with the interconnection
of the world through telecommunication networks, with the dominance
of transnational financial aggregates, the old, territorial concept of the nation has been superseded and even made irrelevant by global demands. Although there are simply too many such claims to enumerate, let me provide
a few salient examples: in conceptualizing what he terms the "new global
condition," Barrie Axford, like so many others, argues that the "core of the
idea is that the world is undergoing a process of ever-intensifying inter-
connectedness and interdependence, so that it is becoming less relevant to
speak of separate national economies, or separate national jurisdictions
founded on principles like the sovereignty of the territorial nation-state."[16]

Of course, he is not wrong: contemporary networks of communication and economic interdependence certainly characterize the globalization of production, finance, trade, and technology, rendering the borders of the geographically defined nation-state porous and seemingly obsolete. But there is no mention of the fact that the "sovereignty of the territorial nation-state" was threatened before the Internet, MTV, and Nike by the world postal institute, railway transportation, and world banking magnates; yet the nation-state somehow managed to survive, if not thrive. Does this historical fact not necessitate further investigation of the relationship between globalization and nationality?

Indeed, there are many contemporary studies on globalization that focus on the imminent demise of the nation-state.[17] The argument is deceptively convincing: because globalization, by definition, exceeds the geographic or territorial borders of the nation, the nation as a unit of political and economic analysis is no longer (or very soon will no longer be) relevant. Cultural commentators point out that "never before" has the nation—with its outmoded Cartesian spatial and temporal coordinates—been so threatened by global structures that transcend its borders as it is today. As the inflated rhetoric of recent book titles like *The Death of Distance* or *Collapsing Space and Time* posit,[18] the demise of the geographically defined nation-state is largely seen through the optimistic lenses of a postnational identity politic or welcomed as the positive product of a hybridized "global community."[19] In the wildly sanguine words of Nicholas Negroponte on the birth of the "digital age":

> The nation-state itself is subject to tremendous change and globalization. . . . The harmonizing effect of being digital is already apparent as previously partitioned disciplines and enterprises find themselves collaborating, not competing. . . . Like a mothball, which goes from solid to gas directly, I expect the nation-state to evaporate. . . . Without question, the role of the nation-state will change dramatically and there will be no more room for nationalism than there is for smallpox.[20]

But why should humanity, "bonded together by the invisible strands of global communications" with the rise of the Internet and other telecommunication technologies, "find that peace and prosperity are fostered by the death of distance"?[21] Indeed, the very same optimism and rhetoric—ultimately unredeemed—also came along with other ostensibly "global" developments. Among other things, railways were supposed to end world hunger, bind together humanity into one, and make war impossible. Of course, this is not quite what happened.

As Jürgen Habermas has rightly argued, there is no reason to see the rise and renewal of "world citizenship," "cosmopolitanism," or "global" technologies as somehow divorced from or opposed to the continuing historical reality of xenophobia, racism, nationalism, and forms of class-based social stratification.[22] In other words, celebrating the transcendence or demise of the nation with the birth of new, "global" technologies and "cosmopolitan" ideals might actually neglect the very fundamental ways in which nationality contributes to, if not determines, our thinking about and responses to the history of globalization.

Although writing in a very different political and geographic context some 170 years ago, Friedrich List—Germany's most indefatigable advocate of the beneficial effects of railways during the 1820s and 1830s—once echoed precisely Negroponte's unbridled enthusiasm for the "digital age" in his conviction that new railway and steam technologies would eventually bring about global understanding and the unification of the countries of the world:

> Through the new means of transportation, man will become an infinitely happy, wealthy, perfect being.... National prejudices, national hatred, and national self-interest [will disappear] when the individuals of different nations are bound to one another through the ties of science and art, trade and industry, friendship and family. How will it even be possible for cultivated nations to wage war with one another[?].[23]

Unimpeded by borders, List stalwartly, if not naively, believed that worldwide communication networks—ranging from mail deliveries to railways and stream transportation—would bring the "effects and benefits of these gifts from God ... to the interests of all of humankind."[24] Although List did not believe the nation would "evaporate," to use Negroponte's term, he shared much of the same enthusiasm and expectations for new, global technologies, but with one noteworthy difference: He historicized the forces of globalization by placing them within the conceptual, political, and economic histories of nationality. As List recognized, the relationship between nationality and globalization is more complicated than the latter simply phasing out the former. In this regard, we might look to the nineteenth century not in order to "model" the world of today or derive facile analogies but rather to see why these same kinds of prognoses and expected consequences, saturated with both hopes and anxieties, failed to pan out.

Declarations about the death of distance and borders, the end of the nation-state, the rise of the interconnected world, the primacy of speed and material transport, the acceleration of time, the dominance of transnational financial aggregates, the celebration of cosmopolitanism (or, conversely, the horror of hybridity) all had historical, technological, and prognostic precedents at the beginning of the nineteenth century, precedents that were also the conditions of possibility for the very diagnoses of globalization made today. These precedents range from the technological to the economic, cultural, and social. They include the conceptualization of a worldwide postal system and a world postal institute (1811); the building and spread of passenger trains across the European continent (the first of which was in 1825); the development and refinement of the electric telegraph (1836); the first delivery of mail by train (1838); the conceptualization and the first stages of implementation of an international network of trains linking newly opened canals and ports in the Netherlands and along the Rhine to France, to the unified Germanic states, and eventually to Russia (beginning in 1835); the systematization of a world time (*Weltzeit*), first imagined and implemented in England between 1840–1842 to coordinate railways and postal deliveries; the realization of the idea of world literature (*Weltliteratur*), a term coined by Goethe in 1828 to describe the increasing speed of cultural exchange (by which he meant translations, journalism, and book trade); the increasing industrialization and spread of capitalism at the expense of the proletariat (in Marx's analysis, both capital and the proletariat transcended national borders); the worldwide ascendancy of international bankers, such as the Rothschild family; and, finally, the simultaneous embrace and fear of hybridization, cosmopolitanism, and transnationalism vis-à-vis identity, linguistic, religious, and cultural politics.

My contention is that, in order to understand how the specific concept of nationality emerged in Germany during the first half of the nineteenth century, we have to, seemingly paradoxically, examine the idea of globalization. This focus on globalization will turn out to be far from paradoxical: The invention of German nationality in the historical, cultural, and technological imaginary was, I will argue, a function of the hopes and anxieties over this diffuse group of changes, which I will collectively term *globalization*. I think that the use of the concept globalization to describe these transformations in the early nineteenth century, far from being anachronistic, is both historically justified and conceptually necessary to elucidate the way in which the idea of nationality was imagined before "Germany" existed. Rather than opposing concepts or successive stages, then, nationalism and globalization were mutually reinforcing in Germany such that the emergence of a global system of dominance created the desire to delink from it by turning inward to a heightened awareness of national identity, nationality, and, ultimately, nationalism.

One of the earliest formulations of this seemingly paradoxical dialectic between nationality and globalization came not from railway rhetoric but rather from a German advocate for the founding of a "world postal institute" named Johann Ludwig Klüber. In 1811 Klüber, a cabinet and privy councilor to Karl Friedrich of Baden,[25] published a 225-page treatise entitled *Das Postwesen in Teutschland, Wie es war, ist, und seyn könnte* (The postal system in Germany: How it was, is, and could be), in which he argued that the creation of a "world institute" (*Weltanstalt*) for the delivery of mail, unimpeded by local, state, and national borders, would not only unify Germany but bring about universal happiness.[26] Because postal deliveries crossed borders and fostered communication on a worldwide scale, the postal system is inherently "universal in nature" and its "perfection rests on *unity, commonality, expansion* (universality to a large area), *coherence, freedom, security, speed and affordability*" (PT 225, 217). At the time Klüber formulated these ideas, there were "no less than forty-three different territorial postal systems" throughout the German states, and, hence, due to transit fees charged by each territorial ruler, postage had increased markedly since 1806.[27] For a package to go from Berlin to Frankfurt am Main, for example, it had to go through nine different territorial postal agencies, accruing taxes, tariffs, and other costs along the way (PT 121). The internal division of the German states not only impeded written communication (something Klüber believed would hinder German Bildung, cultural refinement, and modernization) but also militated against the potential unity, commonality, universality, freedom, security, and speed that a world postal institute could bring about.

What Klüber essentially argued was that a "global" communications system would benefit the nation by overcoming the internal divisions plaguing "Germany" and fostering a spirit of "unity." As Klüber buoyantly wrote, "How infinitely redeeming [*heilbringend*] the postal system could be if it were treated universally as a world institute [*Weltanstalt*]. . . . Its nature and purpose do not tolerate competition, rivalry, or postal divisions; it offers unity and universality" (PT 129, 207). By eliminating the taxes and tariffs on and internal divisions around mail, Klüber believed that a world postal system could really "save" Germany: "If anyone doubts the hope that I have that the main ideas of this treatise can be put into practice in our fatherland, I ask them to consider the fact that it is already stopping things from getting worse" (PT iv).

Although he was probably a little overenthusiastic about its beneficial consequences, Klüber was convinced that the postal system would create the "practical linkages" (*Verbindungen*) between people necessary for the "cultivation of humanity" (PT 4, 5). In his most hyperbolic moments he even argued that "mail is indispensable for every kind of trade and exchange, for arts and sciences, for the study of countries and peoples, for the boundless field of the natural sciences, for the most sublime of all sciences, astronomy, the first, greatest, and most astonishingly important of all revelations from God!" (PT 4–5). In effect, the creation of a world postal institute would not only "redeem" Germany by creating a cultivated nation, but educated Germans could better know God when humanity was "connected" together by efficient and cheap mail.

Klüber imagined that Germany, newly unified by postal deliveries, would also play an important role in helping the world become "a cosmopolitan whole" (*weltbürgerliche Ganze;* PT 222). Because of its strategic geographic location in the middle of Europe, Germany could function like a thoroughfare for the transportation of letters: "All of northern Europe corresponds with southern Europe and vice versa through Germany. . . . Letters from England and Holland to Switzerland, Italy, Austria, Hungary, Bohemia, Poland, Russia, and the majority of Denmark and Sweden travel through Germany. . . . No other country has so many varied and important postal communication lines [*PostCommunicationsLinien*] to offer" (PT 221–22). The postal system would essentially create a spatial revolution: nation-states would become both unified and connected by a "global" communications system, while the German nation—not paradoxically—became stronger and, more important, poised to lead the way.[28]

Although probably only matched in his optimism and zeal for new "global" technologies by List, Klüber was certainly not alone in his hope that new, global communication technologies could unify Germany and bring "universal" benefits to humankind. In fact, the year before he published his first treatise on the postal system, Heinrich von Kleist published a short, half-satirical, half-serious proposal for "a cannonball postal system."[29] Kleist suggested that, to expedite worldwide communication, mail could literally be "shot" from place to place, like a projectile, from strategically located stations across the globe until it reached its final destination. Kleist considered his invention to be an "advancement in the art of long-distance communication . . . across the four corners of the globe" and placed the cannonball postal system within a historical context that included the electric telegraph.[30] He ended his short proposal by describing the immense benefits of the technology: compared with mail delivered by horse-drawn carriages, the cannonball method would be ten times faster, save money, accelerate commerce and communication, and unite distance places. "One could write or reply from Berlin to Stettin or Breslau within half a day's time . . . [it has] the same effect as if a magic wand were to move that place ten times closer to the city of Berlin."[31] In effect, the cannonball postal system would potentially unify Germany by flinging letters through the air; it would also shrink space, or at least have the effect that space was smaller. Not only does the "collapse of time and space" or "the death of distance" thus predate contemporary diagnoses of globalization, it also predates Wolfgang Schivelbusch's famous analysis of railway technologies causing "temporal and spatial shrinkage."[32] Both of these inventions—the world postal institute and the cannonball postal system—shared a common desire: Their inventors hoped that the creation of a global communication network would unify Germany and, at the same time, result in tangible benefits for all of humankind.

In order to explicate how globalization in the nineteenth century was the condition of possibility for imagining the German nation, I would like to turn to three synchronic developments—each articulated as fantasies—around the year 1835: first, the idea of the *Kulturnation,* a product of the shared cultural and literary achievements of the German people, paradigmatically represented by the birth of *Germanistik* and the publication of scores of literary histories during the mid 1830s; second, the emergence of the Young Germany controversy in 1835–36, galvanized by Wolfgang Menzel's anxiety over "unpatriotic" literature produced by cosmopolitan thinkers, particularly Jews; last, List's conception of a network of railway lines connecting all of the German states together, inspired by the English invention of the railway in 1825 and the opening of the first German—or, more precisely, German/Jewish—railway line between Nuremberg and Fürth on December 7, 1835.

I will start with the idea of the *Kulturnation*. Commentators such as Michael Batts have argued that *Germanistik,* as a discipline of study and historical research, first arrived around 1835/36.[33] After all, in comparison with the relative paucity of histories of German literature before 1835, no fewer than ten major histories of German literary production were written and published between 1834 and 1836—and, if we look forward to 1848, we are talking about more than a hundred largely redundant such histories. Ludwig Wachler's seminal lectures and history of German national literature, although reissued and expanded in 1834, originated in 1818/19 and would have to be seen as a lone harbinger.[34] Most of these works published around 1835 came from a number of already well-established literary scholars, authors, and schoolteachers, ranging from Gotthard Marbach to Johann Wilhelm Schaefer, Karl Gutzkow to Wolfgang Menzel and Georg Gervinus. All of the authors attempted to write a history of the German people by diachronically organizing their written culture—the poetry and literature—into an accessible, coherent, and necessarily connected record.

Judging from the titles, most of these histories were meant to be accessible to a broader public interested in Germanics: *Outline, Handbook, Overview, Introduction, Guide, Encyclopedia* were the terms they used. Schaefer provides the reason for writing such a history in the introduction to his *Grundriß der Geschichte der deutschen Literatur*: "In the sequence of available intellectual works in the German language from the oldest time of national formation [*nationale Bildung*] to our own days, the history of German literature demonstrates the shape of the literary life of the German people, showing how national literature, under the right conditions and with the right interactions, quickly flourishes . . . and quickly shines forth with its particular national characteristics."[35] The point of writing a history of German literature is to chart the growth and development of a national culture until the particularity of its people emerges. The story he tells, like the other literary histories of this period, emphasizes the continuity of "national formation," with special attention to its internal unity and liberation from foreign influences. According to Schaefer, German literature has emerged by severing the "chains of imitation" and by combating the external corruption of German "morality" (*Sittlichkeit*).[36]

Of these literary histories from around 1835, by far the most influential were those published by Gervinus, *Neuere Geschichte der poetischen National-Literatur der Deutschen* (the first volume came out in 1835, followed by four additional volumes by 1842, under the more general title, *Geschichte der deutschen Dichtung*), and those published by Wolfgang Menzel, *Die deutsche Literatur*.[37] Parts of Menzel's three-volume history were published in 1828; the revised and significantly expanded final version appeared in 1836. Later in this chapter I will give special attention to Menzel's *German Literature* because I think it best represents the anxieties over cosmopolitanism, hybridity, and globalization that were rife during this period. Moreover, Menzel was arguably one of the best-known "public" intellectuals of the period thanks to his often acerbic reviews in his journal *Literaturblatt*, his single-handed instigation of the Young Germany controversy, and his love-hate relationship with Germany's foremost railway pioneer, Friedrich List.

But 1835 was not only an extraordinary year for the sheer number of literary histories written and subsequently published, but also because of the politically charged controversy over suppressing "unmoral" and "unpatriotic" literature represented by the so-called *Junges Deutschland* (Young Germany). With the exception of Wolfgang Menzel's influential and critical condemnations of Young Germany and the discourse around defining national literature, I will not discuss the individual works cited in the controversy here.[38] Suffice it to say that the controversy, sparked by an article Menzel published on October 26, 1835, in his *Literaturblatt*, "Unmoralische Literatur," resulted in a Federal German ban, inspired by and laced with anti-Semitic justifications, on the works of Heinrich Heine, Karl Gutzkow, Ludwig Wienbarg, Theodor Mundt, and Heinrich Laube beginning in December of that year.[39] With respect to Karl Gutzkow's so-called Jewish novel, *Wally, die Zweiflerin*, which provided the fodder for Menzel's charge of *Unsittlichkeit* and the absence of *Vaterlandsliebe*,[40] Jeffrey Sammons has written that, "as an outcry of pain and bewilderment at the alienation of the individual and the erosion of sustaining values in society, [the novel] is a symptomatic event of this turbulent year of 1835."[41] As I will argue here, much of this turbulence has to do with the way in which the nonexistent German nation was imagined as a unified body, purged of its foreign or cosmopolitan—especially, Jewish—parts.

And, finally, defining the imaginary German nation was not only the domain of critics like Menzel, it was also that of Friedrich List, by far the most important and tireless advocate of the beneficial industrial, cultural, economic, and political consequences of the railway. As early as the mid-1820s, List had already foreseen the practical ways in which railways could contribute to national unification by facilitating open communication and

increased trade between the German states. In 1833, two years before the first
railway began operation in Bavaria, he published the first of his imaginary
"national" maps for a unified Germany, and called it the "German railway
system."[42] List's map was published in a pamphlet addressed to the people
of Saxony and outlined the economic reasons why a railway should be constructed between Leipzig and Dresden, one segment of what was clearly
intended to be a proposal for a national project of unity. As List imagined
it, the completed railway system would connect together thirty-seven cities, with major nodes in Leipzig, Berlin, and Hanover. Railway connections
would extend as far east as West Prussia, to Danzig and Thorn, as far west as
Cologne, and as far south as Basel and Lindau. Tracks also extended slightly
into Habsburg territory (represented by the Dresden-Prague line), but List
quite obviously left two major Habsburg cities off the map entirely: Only a
large blank space on the bottom right intimates where Vienna and Budapest are, and not even the Danube flows on this map.

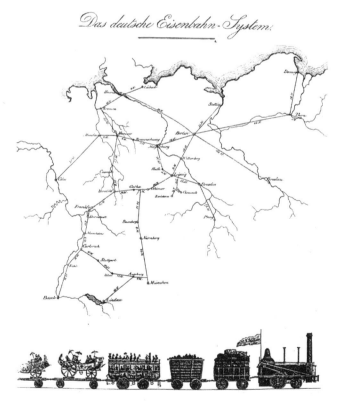

5.3 Friedrich List, *The German Railway System* (1833).

List's exclusion of Austria-Hungary from the German railway system was an overtly political decision, probably based on his desire to secure autonomy for Germany and his antagonism with Vienna's Chancellor Clemens von Metternich.[43] Metternich famously regarded List as "one of the most active, shiftiest, and influential German revolutionaries" and persistently worked to block List from receiving any consular or political appointments in the German Confederation (List 9:73). Metternich considered List's proposals for a unified Germany dangerous to Austria-Hungary's dominance in central Europe, and, in response, List left Austria-Hungary entirely out of the "German railway system."

Along the bottom of his 1833 map he placed a train running eastward, presumably from Leipzig to Dresden, carrying packages, coal, and passengers (in both open railway compartments and on stagecoaches, now securely tied to flat railway beds). As if to show how a single train can be multiplied into many for the sake of unification, the train that runs along the bottom of List's map also runs the whole length of his representation of Germany itself. The train bears the name of three cities (Leipzig, Dresden, Berlin), not connected in that order, but as possible routes from Leipzig on the new "K Sachsen" line. The first part of the Leipzig-Dresden line actually opened in 1838, and by 1843 it was indeed possible to take a train from Leipzig to either Berlin or Dresden.[44] By connecting together each of the thirty-eight German states (represented by either a railway in a major city or by a railway segment that ran through the state) without indicating the names or borders of any of them individually, List presented the public with a plan for the unification of Germany by way of new railway technologies.

In the March 7, 1835, edition of List's *Pfennig-Magazin,* a weekly journal that he founded alongside his *Eisenbahnjournal* (April 1835) to advocate for the development of the railway in Germany, List published a slightly revised version of the 1833 "railway system." In the new version Danzig is gone, but three new cities are added: Perleberg, Saarbrück, and Fürth. In addition, a couple of new railway segments are also added and the Danube is penciled in along the right-hand, bottom region of the map. Again, there was no need to indicate much about the Habsburg Empire: both these journals would be banned in Austria by 1837.[45] Fürth would be important, as List knew, less because of its location as a significant economic node and more because of its symbolic significance as the terminus for the first German railway.

As List spelled out his intentions in a series of articles published a few years later under the same name, "The German Railway System": The railway was a "means of connection" (*Verbindungsmittel*), a remedy for overcoming "the malady of small-statehood" (*Kleinstädterei*) (List 3.1:348). Moving seamlessly between the railway as a means of connection and the German nation as a fragmented body, List writes: "Stripped of almost all attributes of nationality because of early disunity [*Zerrissenheit*], no other nation requires the internal connection of its limbs [*Glieder*] as much [as Germany]" (List 3.1:348). According to List, the railway system even functions as "the nervous system of a shared spirit [*das Nervensystem des Gemeingeistes*]" (List 3.1:348). In this respect, we are well advised to see the imaginary nation not only connected together by way of the technology of railways—List's hopes for unity, internal coherence, national strength, and border-free trade—but also to see the nation as a healthy body, reinvigorated and newly stitched together. List's maps, then, are both programs for unity and depictions of the already unified body politic. Just as Fichte

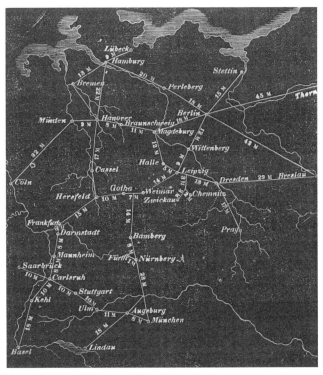

5.4 Friedrich List, *The German Railway System* (1835).

believed Germany already to be a single, unified body, List essentially performed a vivisection of the dormant nation to reveal its guiding nerves; he takes these nerves and lays them down like tracks across the ground. Not unlike medical diagrams of the opened (but healthy) body, his maps both call upon and reveal the essence of a central German nervous system.

In so arguing, List introduces an important metaphor for thinking about the nation, namely, the newly reassembled body. As List probably knew, this metaphor had received one of its fullest articulations in Fichte's *Addresses to the German Nation*, wherein the philosopher posited that the German people needed to stop "weeping over [their] own corpse" and realize that the body of the nation is already being reassembled, resurrected, and given new life (*Addresses* 18).[46] Juxtaposing a telling passage from Ezekiel on corporeal regeneration with his own belief in the resurrection of the German nation, Fichte argued: in the same way that God breathed new life into dead bones, laying them with muscles, flesh, and skin such that they "stood upon their feet, [as] an exceeding great army," the scattered "bones" of the German nation would soon have new life breathed into them, such that "the quickening breath of the spiritual world . . . will take hold, too, of the dead bones of our national body [*Nationalkörper*], and join them together, that they may stand glorious in new radiant life" (*Addresses* 51). In other words, the dead bones of the German people will be resurrected—muscles and all—such that the new Germany will be strong enough to exact revenge on France.[47] As Hinrich Seeba has cogently argued in his analysis of Fichte's rhetoric, this linkage of "nation" and "body" is not only tied to Fichte's belief in the Christian concept of resurrection, it also represents "the founding eschatological metaphor of German nationalism."[48] This is because the German national body was analogous to a "real" body, able to be broken, die, and, ultimately, be resurrected. A couple of decades later, List would simply apply this metaphor in a new way: the body of the nation would now be reassembled and resurrected by railway tracks.

In the same way that List imagined the railway as a *Verbindungsmittel* for the body of the nation, one that would essentially rebuild or regenerate the latent nerves already binding the German people together as one, Gervinus saw the task of the historian of literature in much the same light: Rather than connect the nation together by resuscitating its shared cultural and linguistic geography (as List wanted to do), Gervinus sought to "regenerate" the German nation by way of connecting together its common cultural and linguistic history. In other words, List sought to unify the space of the body politic (its geography) and Gervinus, among other contemporary literary historians, sought to unify the time of the body politic (its history). In the methodological preambles to his *Geschichte der poetischen National-Literatur der Deutschen* (first published between 1835 and 1842), Gervinus clearly lays out both the need for and the goals of this history: In comparison with other countries in Europe, particularly France and England, "We have in Germany, up until now, no history, no state, no politic; but we do have literature, science, and art . . . [yet] still no literary history."[49] Because "we only have the ruins of an actual and strongly native and national poetry" (G 1:11), Gervinus wants to write a history that allows "one to have a successful overview of the whole" (G 1:10). His method of writing this history is not to render "aesthetic judgments" but merely to present the entire history of German literature from its beginnings to the present day: "*bloß eine Geschichte der Dichtung* [*zu schreiben*]" (G 1:12, 14). As he further indicates, his book "is quite different from all those literary handbooks and histories [which make aesthetic judgments]": his "is nothing but history [*nichts als Geschichte*]" (G 1:12). "I am not writing for the specialist and the scholar of literature, nor for a particular class of readers, but rather, if I am successful, for the nation [*für die Nation*]" (G 1:12–13).

Although Gervinus certainly appears to share some of the dubious goals of a historicism that desires to recuperate the past "as it really was," his literary history is far from objective, written for the nation with a decidedly liberal political bent. Gervinus was among the "Göttingen Sieben" who lost his faculty post in 1833 for protesting against the English monarchy's refusal to honor Hanover's commitment to a constitutional government.[50] In this respect, his literary history is also a call for the formation of a state organized by, and historically grounded in, the rule of law and subject to the regulations of a nationally adopted constitution. He even dedicates the fourth volume of his history to his ousted Göttingen colleague, Friedrich Dahlmann, one of the most outspoken critics of the king: "I fight for the immortal king, the legal will of the government, when—with legal weapons—I resist what the mortal king does in violation of existing laws."[51] For Gervinus, writing such a literary history—binding together the "old" literature with the "new"—is "at the same time the ability to connect [*verbinden*] the state" in order to move it in the direction of a nationally secured constitutional government (G 4:vii). He intimates this link in his fourth volume by drawing on the familiar state as body metaphor: "Our beautiful literature has become a stagnant swamp, filled with poisonous little pieces; since up until now no German government wisdom has come to see that a body politic [*Staatskörper*] needs both physical and pedagogic movement, one would have to wish for a storm from the outside to come in . . . to cast a new spirit" (G 4:vii). It is no big surprise, then, that Gervinus, not unlike Fichte in his *Addresses to the German Nation*, began the very next part of his literary history with the corporeal title: *Regeneration der Poesie*. In other words, he fashioned history writing into a storm for achieving both national unification and the historical legitimacy for his politics.

Both List and Gervinus shared a common faith in the future viability of the German nation and worked, in their respective ways, to bring about its regeneration. Both made the imaginary nation a conceptual category for their political criticism and had a common anxiety that their ideas, taken to an extreme, could potentially sublate the nation rather than re-suscitate it. Although neither List nor Gervinus went so far as Fichte had several decades earlier in advocating for a "closed commercial state" with internal unity achieved by way of impermeable external borders, both feared what they perceived to be the logical progression of their ideas: the emergence of a global or cosmopolitan, not national, consciousness. List needed only to look to the ideology of Saint-Simon in France to see how industrialization fed an embrace of the supranational or the zeal of in-ternational financiers to fund German railway construction. After all, the technological achievements of globalization (a European or international railway system, the telegraph, the world postal institute, the worldwide expansion of capitalism) appeared to potentially eradicate the stability, and even relevance, of national borders. This, however, was never List's goal, judging from his extensive writings on the concept of nationality as an economic and industrial imperative—and it's also not what happened. And analogously, for Gervinus, it was Goethe's concept of *Weltliteratur* that appeared to "globalize" and threaten the relevance of the nation he was working to "regenerate." Gervinus critiqued the idea of *Weltliteratur*, as he understood it, as "incomprehensible . . . [for its] chimerical hopes" and scorned the "unification of all literatures . . . and the prophecy of their elevation into a world-language [*Weltsprache*]" (G 5:579). Instead, he maintained, the identity and recognition of German literature abroad would only happen "when we preserve our national resolution [*nationale Festigkeit*] more and more . . . and hold firm to the ground of the father-land" (G 5:579).

Although seemingly logical (German literature needs to be grounded in national particularity), Gervinus's belief that "world literature" was the opposite (*Gegenkonzept*) of "national literature" was both a misunderstanding of Goethe's idea and historically inaccurate. Goethe never prophesied or advocated for a "world language" or thought that the cultural specificity of the nation-state would dissolve into a single unity with "globalization." Instead he imagined the emergence of a world literature, side by side with national literatures, precisely because technological developments on the global level fostered the accelerated interaction and translation of each nation's culture. Goethe's examples and reasons come from the world of commerce and exchange, namely, the increasing rate of global intercourse, the acceleration of everyday life, and the ease of worldwide communication due to steamship, postal, and railway services: World literature would continue to encourage "close . . . intercourse [*Verkehr*] among the French, English, and Germans"[52] because of the "ever increasing acceleration of traffic [*Verkehr*]" between countries.[53] World literature is not the death knell of the nation-state but rather the means by which "nations will be able to become stronger, by more quickly benefiting by each other's advantages."[54] Interpreting Goethe's concept in this way, Karl Gutzkow wrote in 1836: "World literature does not seek to suppress nationality . . . on the contrary, world literature is the guarantee of nationality."[55]

Not only did Goethe see the concept of "world literature" as compatible with, if not derivable from, nationality, he also sought the unity of Germany (not its sublation) in the same technology and for the same reasons as List, namely, railways for the health of the body politic. In an 1828 conversation with Eckermann, a full seven years before the first railway began running in Bavaria, Goethe said: "I have no fear about the unity of Germany: our good roads and future railways will do their part." He then extols the benefits of unity: "May Germany be one, so that German dollars and groschen may be of equal value throughout the whole empire! One, so that my traveling chest may pass unopened through all thirty-six states! . . . May there be no more talk about inland and outland among German states! In fine, may Germany be one in weight and measure, in trade and commerce, and a hundred similar things."[56]

Indeed, the first steps toward the implementation of a German customs union were taken the same year, in 1828, when Bavaria and Württemberg signed a bilateral customs agreement, but it was not until 1834, two years after Goethe's death, that eighteen German states merged together to form the *Zollverein*, significantly lowering taxes, tariffs, and other economic boundaries for intra-German trade.[57] As early as 1819 Friedrich List had petitioned the German Diet to "remove all customs duties and tolls in the interior of Germany . . . [because] thirty-eight customs boundaries cripple inland trade, and produce much the same effect as ligatures that prevent the free circulation of the blood."[58] This body of state metaphor also returns in Goethe in the same conversation he had with Eckermann about railways, free movement, and unification: "A state has been justly compared to a living body with many limbs; and the capital may be compared to the heart, from which life and prosperity flow to the individual members, near and far. But if the members be very distant from the heart, the life that flows to them will become weaker and weaker."[59] Railways—as internally realized technologies of national unification—stitch together the fragmented body politic.

Whether welcomed or feared, whether real or imagined, the effects and consequences of globalization—ranging from the conceptualization of a "world literature" and a "world postal institute" to the worldwide spread of capital and the financing and construction of railways—played a decisive role in the formation of a German national consciousness before a unified German nation existed. Even in cases where the benefits of "globalization" and "cosmopolitanism" are openly embraced, as in Goethe's concept of world literature or Klüber's advocacy of a world postal system, the primacy placed on securing nationality is never forsaken. But more often globalization is perceived to be a threat to nationality, and, hence, the necessity of turning inward or separating from the emerging world system is emphasized, in various degrees of extremity, from Gervinus and List to Fichte and Menzel.

I now want to look at how the greatest anxieties over globalization also spawned an inwardly directed nationalism, which, in its most virulently anti-Semitic forms, sought to "purify" the space and the populace of the imaginary German nation. This is because all these "global" hopes—the desire for unification, the reduction of distance, the freedom of exchange and mobility—shared a dialectical counterpart, namely, the anxiety over the potential sublation of nationality, the breakdown of the distinction between foreign and domestic, and the loss of German identity through a hybridization of people, languages, and customs. The locus of these anxieties was, once again, the body, but, this time, it was the body of the foreigner, often coded as the Jew, corrupting the German body politic.

Let me first be clear where this anti-Semitism did and did not come from. In the literary domain, it did not come from Goethe or Gervinus; in the domain of railway politics there is scarcely an anti-Semitic comment in List's ten volumes of writings, letters, and strategies. But if we broaden our scope slightly, we encounter the anti-Semitic anxieties over Young Germany in 1835, ignited by, but hardly limited to, Wolfgang Menzel's *Literaturblatt* and his three-volume history, *German Literature*. Jews, especially Jews in France such as Heinrich Heine and Ludwig Börne, are to blame for creating a hybrid German-Jewish, German-French identity that is unfaithful to Germany's geographically grounded cultural history.[60] We also encounter a persistent fear of foreign capital, manifested most obviously in the state-by-state refusal to allow the Rothschild family and other Jewish bankers to finance German railways during the first decade of their construction.[61] Although List once proclaimed that "Rothschild was the pride of Israel, the mighty lender and master of all coined and uncoined silver and gold in the Old World, before whose money box kings and emperors humbly bow," the Rothschild family, despite its Frankfurt origins, and Jewish banking families in general, played no significant role in German railway financing until after 1848.[62] In Germany the first railways were almost all financed by local state governments and private regional funders. This is in striking contrast to France, for instance, where the Rothschild family invested 84.6 million francs between 1835 and 1846 in railway capital formation, or 38 percent of the total.[63]

Two interrelated reasons explain this difference: first, local German states were wary of infusions of foreign, Jewish capital and, second, Jewish financiers, like the Rothschilds, had to seek cooperation from multiple governments for constructing railway lines that crossed state borders.[64] Both of these facts explain why international Jewish financiers played such a modest role in early German railway construction. During this period of initial railway projects, two German caricatures from around 1840 can be seen as illustrative of the fear of Jews financing the German railway system or, in other words, German national unity stemming from international Jewish investments. In both the body of the corpulent, crooked-nosed Jew holding moneybags and power is staged in the foreground. The first depicts the rush by potential Jewish investors to buy railway stocks (*Aktien*), knocking over their fellow citizens in their haste to buy thousands of shares. At the top, three Jews point the way: the first gives direction to the crowd, the second points to the people, and the third points to the Jewish justification, the Ten Commandments. On the right-hand side, we see a Star of David next to the exhaust shoot of a locomotive, what is certainly the critical message of the

5.5 "Shareholder's stampede" (ca. 1840).

entire caricature. In the other caricature we see a grotesquely distorted Jew (probably a composite of the five Rothschild brothers) standing in a moneybag and labeled a "general pump" or "general lender." This complicated caricature is particularly interesting for our argument here because the Jew's body is literally depicted as the "global body" and, by virtue of international finance, has seized control of the body politic of the individual nation. On Rothschild's bloated belly we see a globe, with the axis of the earth running straight through the Jew's navel and marked by a gold coin, a Louis d'or. National boundaries are irrelevant because the Jew, as a "general lender," knows no borders and wears his financial conquests as a diadem: loans to the Danish, the Neapolitans, the Russians, the Austrians, the Prussians, and the Portuguese. We are meant to see that the Jew's financial empire has not only transcended the borders of these nations but, by virtue of his ever expanding tendrils, could soon invade any small German state too. The little town on the left-hand bottom struggles to keep the financial foot of the Jew out: the German sign reads "imports forbidden," what we might interpret as a final attempt to keep foreign, Jewish capital at bay.

5.6 "The General Lender"—caricature of the Rothschild family (ca. 1840).

Using many of the same rationales and arguments, Menzel took it upon himself in his journalism and literary histories to protect the future unity of the German nation from Jewish corruption. He believed that the German language and culture had lost much of its "purity" (M 1:39) because of an imitation of and mixture with foreign literatures and a shortsighted adoption of a "cosmopolitan" worldview (M 1:57). He critically laments that "our nationality consists in wishing to have none" (M 1:57), and blames Goethe—who he later calls the "new Messiah of the Jews" (M 3:267)—and the so-called Young Germans, particularly Heine and Ludwig Börne, for their cosmopolitan, unpatriotic writings. Menzel feared that the "fantastic mixtures" of literatures and languages would obstruct the possibility of a national unity by producing a weakened, "hybrid" culture with no national grounding. Goethe—as the champion of "world literature"—is condemned for his "Jewish" cosmopolitanism, having "mixed the most heterogeneous manners . . . antique and romantic, northern and southern, eastern and western, Christian and pagan, Greek and Indian, old German and French" (M 3:51). Germany must not continue to eradicate national differences and distances through such "monstrous mixtures" but rather must seek to secure its borders through a unified, internal coherence true to itself. With the growth of "global" cultures and "cosmopolitan" ideologies, Menzel feared these kinds of mixtures would become ever more prevalent, causing national specificity to become more porous and less pure.

For Menzel, even worse than a German-French mixture was a German-Jewish mixture, because for Jews "patriotism was only an animal impulse of the blood" (M 3:335). Jews looked to world literature, he thought, because it was not connected with a nation, instead coming from and espousing an ideology of the cosmopolitan and the hybrid. He writes: "The coterie called itself 'Young Germany,' but only as an emanation of 'young Europe;' for they expressly declared . . . that we must devote ourselves not to one nation but to the whole human race (which, however, is to be derived from France), and therefore the hitherto national literature must be annihilated and a literature of the world substituted for it" (M 3:335). As Menzel knew, sentiments not unlike these had, indeed, been expressed by Börne—second only to Heine as Germany's most famous baptized Jew living in exile in France—in his political *Letters from Paris* of 1834: "The nationality of Jews has been in a beautiful and enviable way destroyed. . . . The Jews are the teachers of cosmopolitanism [*Kosmopolitismus*], and the whole world is their school. And because they are the teachers of cosmopolitanism, they are also the apostles of freedom. No freedom is possible as long as there are nations."[65] Since Jews had no fatherland—no cultural or linguistic boundaries determined by nationality—their literature, Börne suggested, was always already inherently free, both hybrid and cosmopolitan, two things that Menzel believed would thwart German national unity. In his most anti-Semitic tirade against "Young Germany" in the *Literaturblatt*, Menzel argued that Jews both "disturb and poison . . . our inner nationality" because Jews, by their very definition, "revoke the nation [*entnationalisiren*]."[66] He even offers a reason: "Without [their own] fatherland, love of the fatherland must be a folly to them."[67] Jews and the supporters of Young Germany espouse a "doctrine of humanity that universalizes and annihilates every nationality," in turn "suppressing our national literature . . . [in the name of] a world literature."[68]

Menzel's greatest fears thus concern the corruption and disappearance of national distinctiveness. He sees the permeability of borders, the mixing of traits, and the breakdown of distinctions and distances between peoples as dangerous to the future of German nationality. In order to unify the cultural traditions of Germany, the nation must preserve its original purity. In the final pages of his literary history, he calls for a "concentric" nationality, not unlike the "autocentric" doctrines of Fichte, where all the interests of the nation are pulled inward. And, not fortuitously, just like List and Goethe, he cites the "customs union" (*Zollverein*) and "the railways" as two possible ways to do just that (M 3:358).

Although List never gave up the category of the nation or the benefits of nationality, Börne did notice how "the significance of List's ideas" potentially rendered the nation permeable and hybrid by collapsing the distance between foreign lands and Germany—precisely what Menzel feared. In fact, Menzel even wrote a scathing critique of List in his *Literaturblatt* of 1832 because the latter had written an encyclopedia article in French about how railways could economically and commercially help France.[69] List may have exploited the category of the nation, but he was, Menzel feared, not exclusively a German nationalist, and, more than that, railways were not exclusively a German domain. As Börne realized the implications of List's ideas: he could take a train from Paris to Strasbourg, and from there to Frankfurt, all in just eighteen hours. "Heine thinks it's a horrible thought to be in Germany in twelve hours. For me and List, these railways are our fantasy because of their unbelievable political consequences" (List 9:190). In other words, the cosmopolitan freedom of the Jew might become the built reality of the railway system once national distances and differences are overcome. Börne, swept up by List's enthusiasm for new railway technologies, welcomed the eradication of the distance and the difference between France and Germany. But this is, of course, not what happened—and it is also what Menzel worked to prevent. The nation-state became ever more entrenched, not sublated, and new, "global" technologies of communication and transportation, far from simply "saving" humanity and bringing forth a happy cosmopolitanism, played a decisive role in securing nationality and making possible the rise of nationalism.

ZIONIST FANTASIES OF THE JEWISH NATIONAL BODY

If we shift our attention from the fantasies of German nationality that emerged during the discursive period around 1835 to the reality of railway construction projects and the unification of the German states, it becomes clear that the development of the railway system in

Germany, compared to its development in France or England, betrays a striking feature about national unity: Especially in France, but also to a certain extent in England, the construction of primary railway lines fanned out from the nation's capital because national unity preceded railway technologies. Such unity did not exist in Germany. During the 1840s in France, for example, legislation was passed for the construction of the five great railway lines radiating from Paris and extending to the nation's main ports: the *Nord* was to extend to the Channel, the *Ouest* to Nantes, the *Sud-ouest* to Bordeaux, the *P.L.M.* to Marseille, and the *Est* to Strasbourg and the Rhine.[70] If we look at French railway construction in the 1850s and 1860s, the centralized star pattern extending from Paris (although strategically unsound for military reasons) is quite unlike the acentric network that developed in Germany during the same period. As is evident from an 1862 military map published by M. Charié-Marsaines, the inspector general of bridges and roads in France, in a pamphlet titled "Mémoire sur les chemins de fer considérés au point de vue militaire," France was already a centralized nation, whose defense would fan out from Paris to its land borders and, from there, to its colonies by way of the expansiveness of the sea.[71] As military leaders such as Charié-Marsaines argued, railways "fundamentally changed social relations" by shrinking distances and facilitating the deployment of military troops.[72] He terms the "converging" and "concentric lines" critical "for the defense of France" and concludes by recognizing that railways have "profoundly changed the conditions of war."[73]

In contrast to the development of the French or English railway systems, regardless of when one examines the history of German railways, an analogous system of centralization characterized by "concentric" railway lines that extend to the sea is never discernable because a centralized, colonial nation with a single capital barely existed. Although this fact cannot be ignored in assessing the role of the railway in the history of German national unification,[74] my purpose is not to give another example of Germany's so-called backwardness, belatedness, or special path to modernity, as the political, historical, and even technological limits of such lines of argumentation have been well established and well trodden.[75] Instead I am interested in how the conceptualization and construction of the German railway system modeled a process of nation formation (a process in which the scattered parts of the nation's body were reassembled), which was, to a large extent, studied and imitated by Zionists at the end of the nineteenth century. Particularly for Theodor Herzl, it was Bismarck's plan to unify the German states and nationalize the railways that gave form to Herzl's fantasies for Jewish nationality. As we will see, the Zionist conception of the Jewish state derived both its model and legitimacy from the newly unified German nation.

In the most famous speech that he ever gave before the Budget Committee of the Diet on September 30, 1862, Bismarck brought together the rhetoric of national unity with the new technological capacities of modernization:

> Germany does not pay attention to Prussian liberalism, but rather to its strength. . . . Prussia must bring together and hold together its power in an opportune moment, which it has already missed many times. Under the treaties of Vienna, Prussia's borders are not favorable for the healthy existence of the state; the great questions of the day will not be decided through speeches and majority votes—that was the great mistake in 1848 and 1849—but rather through iron and blood.[76]

As evidenced by the extensive use of railways for troop deployment in the three wars that immediately preceded German unification in 1871—the war with Denmark in 1864, the war with Austria in 1866, and the Franco-Prussian War of 1870–71—Bismarck was not speaking metaphorically about iron and blood. It was quite clear that unification meant an aggressive Prussian expansionism abetted by modern means of communication and rail transportation throughout the German federation and beyond.

As early as the 1848 revolution, Prussia had recognized the military benefits of railways (as well as its own unpreparedness) when revolutionaries began moving through the German states on train. This became even clearer in 1850 when the Austrian army deployed more than seventy-five thousand men and eight thousand horses to the Silesian frontier—all moved by rail—in order to force Prussian submission at the "Punctuation of Olmütz."[77] It was not until 1866 that Prussia had the internal rail capacity to effectively move the necessary troops to its contested borders: Nearly two hundred thousand troops and fifty-five thousand horses were moved by rail in the first three weeks of the Prussian campaign against Austria. Railway transportation would both create and defend national space.

But just as important as the clear military benefits that railways offered for troop mobility and deployment was the fact that Prussian strength— hence German nationality—depended on the control, use, and ownership of the railways. From the construction of the first lines in Prussia in 1838 up until the year after the 1848 revolution, every railway line built in Prussia was privately financed, owned, and operated. It was not until 1850 that the first state-owned railway lines even opened under Prussian direction, a 77.77 kilometer line licensed between Paderborn and Hamm.[78] By 1866, the Prussian state owned 2,803.27 kilometers of track, whereas private companies and regional shareholders owned 3,841.44 kilometers.[79] Bismarck realized the significant problems that private ownership of the railways potentially presented to both effective military mobilization and the consolidation of German nationality. In fact, after Prussia absorbed some 1,200 kilometers of state-owned rail from Hesse and Hanover with its 1866 expansion, Bismarck proposed the nationalization of all railways throughout the German federation.[80] His goal of nationalizing the railways, however, would not be finally realized until after German unification, in December 1879 with the passage of the Reichseisenbahngesetz.[81]

Although the "nationalization" of the privately owned railways was itself not a strict prerequisite of German unification, the mobility and communication afforded by rail transportation certainly was: Railways played a critical role in generating both the German concept of nationality and practically enabling the expansion, unity, and defense of the states in the German federation after 1850. The relationship between German unification and the railroads thus had less to do with specific ownership and more, as Friedrich List predicted decades earlier, to do with the future "stitching together" and defense of the German body politic. As Benjamin pointed out in his cultural study of the Saint-Simon imaginary in France, railways transmogrified the fantasies of modernity—nationality, progress, rationality, speed—into a religious zeal to "rally the scattered populations."[82]

Bismarck was quite prescient in realizing the great potential for unity and nationhood by turning the regional and privately held railways into a uniform, state-run, national railway system. Together with a plan to generate more taxes for the Reich through internally directed industry reforms and externally mandated tariffs, Bismarck's dream was finally realized with the help of a speech given by General Helmuth von Moltke on December 17, 1879:

It cannot be doubted that the conversion of the most important railways of the country into State lines is, in a military sense, most desirable. Railways have in our time become one of the most important factors in war. The transportation of large masses of troops to given points constitutes a task of the most complicated and comprehensive kind, which must be continuously kept up to date. Each new connecting line necessitates new work. . . . It is clear that there would be a substantial simplification if, instead of having to deal with forty-nine authorities, we had practically to deal with only one. Gentlemen, I do not by any means wish to ignore the debt we owe to private railways for the work done by them at critical periods, but I am convinced that a still greater success is achievable.[83]

The law requiring German railways to be sold to and operated by the state was passed shortly thereafter. At the beginning of 1879, the state owned a little more than six thousand kilometers of track; by 1890 it owned close to twenty thousand kilometers. As Fritz Stern wrote about "Bismarck's scheme": "There were hardly any private lines left [in 1890]; the state operated a model system, efficient, reliable, and economical. The power of the state was greatly enhanced by running what became the largest enterprise in Prussia."[84] But, more than this, the nationalization of the railways helped to stabilize and "refound the Reich" by indirectly applying the protectionist theories of Fichte and List: the nation was now internally unified, connected together by uniformly running railways, and protected from foreign competition by newly enacted tariffs on virtually all imports. In effect, Bismarck had ensured that Germany was linked together for the nation to now, more or less, delink—or, in von Moltke's words, to achieve "still greater success" through a new nationalism.

In what Stern calls a "bafflingly candid account of his plans" to create this protectionist state by nationalizing the railway system and enacting such tariffs, Bismarck laid out his plan in detail to the French ambassador St. Vallier in January of 1879. Knowing that he will have to weather storms in uncharted waters as the leader of the newly unified body politic, Bismarck describes his leadership by appealing to an extraordinary "seafaring" metaphor: "I shall act like a navigator who has set his course and encounters adverse winds; he more or less modifies his route; he uses more or less coal; he avails himself of the sails more or less, following the caprice of the storm, but as for the end of the voyage, he never changes. I shall act like him, and now you know my aim; as for the means of reaching it, I reserve my choice, depending on the game of the adversaries and the liveliness of the battle."[85]

Here Bismarck effectively employs a metaphorical language, which was virtually absent until the last quarter of the nineteenth century: The nation, physically unified by rail and decree, was now a ship—as in a *Staatsschiff* or "ship of state"—with a solitary captain responsible for its future direction. Indeed, only after railways and Prussian political expansionism "stitched together" the fragmented body of the German nation could ship of state metaphors return to describe nationality, hence explaining why such metaphors were entirely absent from previous German discourses about nationality.[86] And, beginning in the mid-1880s, under Bismarck's newly adopted colonial policy, Germany secured a rapidly expanding colonial empire in Africa and the South Pacific.[87] German nationality had finally realized Hegel's injunction that world-historical people have a colonial relationship to the sea. With this we can now turn to fantasies of Jewish nationality.

In June of 1895 Theodor Herzl confidently proclaimed that he had solved the recalcitrant, age-old "Jewish question." Since this was no small announcement, he decided to present his solution to found a "Jewish state" to Vienna's Rabbi Güdemann to gain support among the Jewish community and to the wealthy Jewish patron Baron Moritz von Hirsch to gain financial backing for the realization of his plan. But both Güdemann and Hirsch ignored him, believing Herzl to be "cracked"; his plan to "nationalize" the Jews in their own state is impossibly absurd. So Herzl decided to look elsewhere for support: "I'm turning to Bismarck. He is big enough to understand me, or cure me."[88]

Herzl crafted a long-winded letter to Bismarck in which he solicited the German leader's support and remarks that only someone like Bismarck— who had himself united a scattered people—could judge the true viability of his plan: "Only the man who so wonderfully stitched together a torn Germany with his iron needle such that it does not even look patched together—only he is big enough to tell me once and for all whether my plan is really the solution or a perceptive fantasy" (T 2:144). Clearly alluding to Bismarck's "iron and blood" policies stretching from the construction and later the nationalization of the railways to the so-called Wars of Unification, Herzl desired the support of "the greatest living empire builder [*Staatskünstler*]" (T 2:145) for his own plan to collect, transport, and nationalize Europe's Jews outside of Europe. He waited several days for a response, but none was forthcoming. Herzl then began to wonder if perhaps Bismarck

would not understand the solution and the relationship to its German an-
tecedent. Already intimating a connection between Zionism and a modern
mode of transportation, Herzl wrote: "Napoleon did not understand the
steamboat—and he was younger [than Bismarck] and thus more accessible
to new ideas" (T 2:152). Perhaps Bismarck would not understand Zionism.
Just over a week later, Herzl became regrettably convinced that he would
have to pursue his solution without the help of the German leader. In effect,
Herzl would have to become the Jewish Bismarck.

Although Bismarck never responded to his letter, Herzl had, in fact, already learned more than enough from the German leader about nationhood. He had studied the policies, rhetoric, and especially the technologies
of modern state formation side by side with the rabid anti-Semitic sentiment in Europe as the Paris correspondent for Vienna's daily, the *Neue Freie
Presse*. His solution emerged after having covered the Panama scandal, the
start of the Dreyfus affair, and the victory of the anti-Semitic Christian Social Party in municipal elections in Vienna.[89] Herzl insisted that his solution
is a "plan," which he likened to that other plan called the "Unification of
Germany," because it "represents the actual details of the future" (T 2:245).
Herzl offers an elaborate description of how his "plan" for Jewish nationality will be implemented with a view back to the German precedent:

> And out of what was [German] unification created? Out of ribbons,
> flags, songs, speeches, and, finally, out of singular struggles. Do not
> underestimate Bismarck! He saw that the people and the princes
> would not even make small sacrifices for the objects of those songs
> and speeches. So he exacted great sacrifices from them, forced them to
> wage wars. . . . A people drowsy in peacetime jubilantly hailed unifica-
> tion in wartime. It is not necessary to attempt a rational explanation.
> It is fact!   (T 2:246)

Herzl essentially realized what Benedict Anderson and Homi Bhabha have
argued about the formation of nationality and the rise of nationalism:
Namely, that nations come into being through the ways in which communities imagine, narrate, and disseminate fantasies and projections for national
identity.[90] As Hinrich Seeba argued in his analysis of the making of German
national identity in the nineteenth century, cultural expressions such as patriotic poems about the German Rhine, the *Lied der Deutschen,* the myth
of the Nibelungen, and the myth of Barbarossa all functioned as "*aesthetic*

concepts for rather than *historical reflections of* national identity."[91] The ribbons, flags, songs, speeches, and struggles that Herzl observes in Germany are precisely these kinds of cultural expressions for nationality.

Herzl continues his reflections by presenting an analogy between Bismarck's unification of Germany in a time of great apprehension and his own rise to leadership in a time of great Jewish suffering and need. His plan for the creation of a Jewish state does not need a rational grounding or explanation to legitimize it, he says, rather only a force to drive it forward and guide it: "My plan calls for the utilization of a driving force that already exists in nature. What is this force? The suffering of the Jews! . . . I say that this force is strong enough to run a great machine and transport human beings. The machine may look however one wants" (T 2:247).[92] Inspired by German unification and constructed out of modern technologies of transportation, the machine will be called Zionism, and Herzl will be its conductor. He had already begun to conceive of Zionism as a politics of transportation.

In his program for the creation of the Jewish state, *Der Judenstaat,* he begins by positioning his solution within an array of other "problems" modernity has solved: Electricity and lightbulbs remedied darkness; trains and steamships mastered distance; the telegraph facilitated rapid, worldwide communication; and the Jewish state, he maintained, could resolve both anti-Semitism and the "medieval" problem of Jewish nonbelonging (J 24–25). Herzl believed that the Jewish people—despite internal linguistic, monetary, educational, religious, and geographic differences—were indeed one people who needed one nation. Although he did not know where this national space would be, he argued that true emancipation, and, hence, the real solution to the Jewish question, would only come when the Jews were gathered up, transplanted, and "stitched together" in their own sovereign state. According to his assessment in 1896, possible places for wealthy Jews to buy enough land for the benefit of world Jewry included Palestine, Argentina, and Uganda; but Herzl would leave the decision to Jewish public opinion. What he was certain of was that Jews must be "carefully lifted up and transplanted to a better ground" such that the "homeless nation" could be geographically grounded and united (J 72). In this respect, the Zionist idea of nationality and colonization rested upon a modern politics of transportation.

Herzl even lays out the logistics of the travel plans: the relocation will be carried out by two Jewish agencies, called in English (a choice that was hardly fortuitous given Britain's colonial history), "The Society of Jews" and the "Jewish Company." The former would take care of scientific and political matters; the latter would deal with the practical and financial side of organizing the economy of the new state (J 42–43). He imagines that the poorest will go first "to construct streets, bridges, railways, and telegraph communications" (J 43). The Jewish Company would buy the necessary land, handle all the financing of the infrastructure, and help convert the assets of the departing Jews into funds to support the transmigration (J 48). He imagines the implementation of a standard seven-hour working day, the creation of large-scale housing projects, welfare agencies and systems of social support, and democratic governance by a constitution. The full-scale relocation of the Jews would take place over a period of several decades until Europe was finally left behind.

Shortly after *Der Judenstaat* was published, Herzl produced a series of further reflections on the relationship between mobility and the creation of the Jewish state. As he wrote in a tellingly philosophical diary entry on the rationale behind the Zionist politics of transportation:

> Great things do not need a solid foundation. One has to put an apple on the table so that it does not fall down. The earth hovers in mid-air. In the same way, I can perhaps found and support the Jewish state without out a sure foundation. The secret lies in the movement [*Bewegung*]. (In this, I believe that somewhere a guidable airship [*das lenkbare Luftschiff*] will be invented. Weight overcome by movement, and not the ship but rather its movement is to be steered.) (T 2:341)

The secret of his movement was precisely the fact that it was a literal movement and, for this reason, not only differed from those fantastic utopias that Herzl dismissed but was also an undertaking of the masses and thus differed physically and structurally from the movement of a single individual.[93]

Although not unanimously well received by every Jewish group, the publication of *Der Judenstaat* was immensely successful and secured Herzl as the leader of the burgeoning Zionist movement. It was immediately translated into multiple languages and, in the words of Herzl's biographer, Alex Bein, the tract "broke like the effect of a thunderbolt."[94] Even though Russian censorship kept the book out of much of the Pale of Settlement, his ideas and name were widely known and enthusiastic responses came from all over Western and Eastern Europe, many crowning Herzl "the genius like Moses to lead us" back to the Promised Land.[95] In the short span of a few months in 1896, he managed to secure the backing of the grand duke of Baden, various Turkish statesmen, and the Bulgarian minister, Natchevitch; he traveled to Paris, London, Sofia, and Constantinople, garnering support and adulation from both politicians and Jews who met him in cheering masses at the railway stations. He was likened to the Jewish messianic leader Sabbatai Zevi, Christopher Columbus, Moses, and, of course, Bismarck.[96]

As Carl Schorske indicates in his analysis of Herzl's meteoric rise to become the leader of the Jewish masses, Herzl tapped the latent energies and sufferings of the Jews by combining "archaic and futuristic elements in the same way as Schönerer and Lueger. . . . All three connected 'forward' and 'backward,' memory and hope in their ideologies."[97] For his part, Herzl sought to reclaim the prediaspora kingdom of Israel by using the modern technologies of transportation to return the Jews, by way of an allegorized airship, to the Holy Land. On multiple occasions in his diaries, Herzl even notes that the founder of Zionism will have to become a kind of hypnotic leader, likened to that of Sabbatai Zevi (T 2:316). As early as June of 1896, Herzl writes about leading the Jewish masses: "People crowded into every corner. A stage served as the platform from which I spoke. . . . Succeeding speakers eulogized me. One of them, Ish-Kishor, compared me to Moses, Columbus, etc. . . . Great jubilation, hat waving, cries of hurrah that followed me out into the street. Now it really depends on me whether I shall become the leader of the masses" (T 2:403).

Although Herzl never produced a systematic theory or psychology of the masses like Gustav LeBon, he certainly called upon some of the same energies and experiences that both he and LeBon had observed in Paris during the early 1890s, namely, mob demonstrations and mass politics stemming from the Panama scandal and the Dreyfus affair.[98] Believing that he lived in the "era of crowds," LeBon attempted to show how the unconscious activity of the crowd is a decidedly modern phenomenon.[99] The psychology of the crowd demanded a leader—as in a hero or God—above all else in order to arouse its passions and guide its activities. Herzl, in fashioning himself into a modern-day Sabbatai Zevi, certainly tapped precisely these energies as the leader of the Jewish masses. As one of the Zionist delegates described their modern leader at the First Zionist Congress in 1897:

Before us rose a marvelous and exalted figure, kingly in bearing and stature, with deep eyes in which could be read quiet majesty and unut-

tered sorrow. It is no longer the elegant Dr. Herzl of Vienna; it is a royal
scion of the House of David, risen from among the dead, clothed in
legend and fantasy and beauty. Everyone sat breathless, as if in the presence of a miracle. And in truth, was it not a miracle that we beheld? And
then wild applause broke out; for fifteen minutes the delegates clapped,
shouted, and waved their handkerchiefs. The dream of two thousand
years was on the point of realization; it was as if the Messiah, son of
David, confronted us.[100]

Zionism's modernity was clearly a politics of both moving and guiding the
Jewish masses, not unlike the psychology of the crowd analyzed by LeBon.[101]

Even though the mother tongue of the Jewish masses was Yiddish, Herzl
always maintained a profound attachment to the German language. This
manifested itself most clearly in his deeply ambivalent relationship to Hebrew and his outright dismissal of Yiddish.[102] In *Der Judenstaat*, for example, he imagines a "federation of tongues," but not including the "stunted
and crumpled jargons of those Ghetto languages" (J 94). Yiddish, always
already a non-national language, would not be given any space in Herzl's
state, for it was nothing "but the stealthy tongue of prisoners" (J 94). The
founding of the Jewish nation needed the linguistic authority of national
languages like English, French, or German, which were geographically attached to the unified, territorial concept of the modern European nation. In
this respect, the idea of the Jewish nation was, once again, to derive its sense
of nationality from the German model.

Indeed, Herzl never hid his dislike and distrust of Yiddish. Elaborating on
his ideas about linguistic nationality, Herzl wrote a scathing article, "Mauschel," about a month and a half after the First Zionist Congress, in which he
argued that *Mauschel* (speaking Yiddish or speaking German with a Yiddish
accent) was "anti-Zionist."[103] In this article he clearly equates the nationalistic goals of Zionism with national language traditions: "The Germans are
a nation of poets and thinkers because they have produced Goethe, Schiller,
and Kant. The French are brave and brilliant because they have brought
forth Baynard, Duguesclin, Montaigne, Voltaire, and Rousseau. We are a nation of hagglers and crooks because *Mauschel* practices usury and speculates
on the stock exchange. . . . *Mauschel* is the curse of the Jews!"[104] Here Herzl
conflates the speech with the person speaking. Since national languages have
great cultural traditions, Zionism was conceived—in Herzl's German—as
the origin of Jewish cultural and national greatness. It sought to transform

the Jew speaking Mauschel in the Eastern European ghetto and living off the expanding world system of capital into the culturally refined Jew speaking German in a new and modern, sovereign nation-state. In Herzl's words, "a national consciousness . . . is alien to Mauschel" because his identity is based upon the economic benefits of international commerce and transnationality: "Mauschel has his eye on distant places—not on Zion, but on some country where he might slip in with some other nation."[105] The furtive non-nationality of Mauschel's world of commerce and the stock exchange was to be replaced by the "German" dream of Jewish nationality.

Arguably co-opting some of the nationalist and anti-Semitic rhetoric prevalent in contemporary right-wing political ideologies of pan-Germanism, Herzl even suggests that Mauschel and "the Jew" are of two "different races."[106] Zionism then became a task of trying to separate them, a separation enacted in terms of language and on bodies. If Mauschel could somehow be severed from Jews—through racial sophistry and assertion or linguistic, corporeal, and national regeneration—the Jewish state would be one step closer to realization. In perhaps the most violent, nationalist image he ever gave to the "movement," he ends his article on Mauschel with an admonition that Zionism "could act like [Wilhelm] Tell": "When Tell got ready to shoot the apple from the head of his son, he had a second arrow in waiting. If the first missed, the second was to serve as revenge. Friends, the second arrow of Zionism is meant for the chest of Mauschel."[107] Schiller's legendary play, *Wilhelm Tell*, to which Herzl was undoubtedly alluding, is a call for nation formation, motivated by the recurring mantra "Wir sind ein Volk, und einig wollen wir handeln [We are one people, and as one we will act]."[108] In Herzl's modern incarnation, the Zionists, should they fail, would seek revenge by scapegoating the backward, Yiddish-speaking, ghetto Jews. In effect, Herzl's Jewish nationality not only derived its technological inspiration from the German model but also—at least in part—an exclusionary, nationalist legitimacy.

By 1899 Herzl declared—somewhat more compassionately—that Zionism was "a kind of new Jewish care for the sick," quoting its justification from a poem by Heine, "Das neue Israelitische Hospital zu Hamburg," in which Jews suffer from "das tausendjährige Familienübel [that thousand-year-old family affliction]."[109] As Herzl says, "We have stepped in as volunteer nurses, and we want to cure patients—the poor, sick Jewish people—by means of a healthful way of life on our own ancestral soil." He even conceived of his work as a kind of mitzvah: "People should never forget that the cause which we have championed was once the most hopeless, the most lost, the most despised thing in the world."[110] In a word, Zionism was configured as both a preventive and a potential cure for Jewish national, racial, and linguistic sickness. Zionism was thus a nationalist movement of the healthy body in the German language.

The Zionist idea of the healthy Jewish body living in the modern nation-state, however, did not derive just from Herzl's nationalist commitments but was also given a theoretical justification by Max Nordau's conception of Jewish regeneration. Herzl first met Nordau in Paris in 1895, and both worked closely together in the formulation of the Zionist movement until Herzl's death in 1904. Nordau's claim to fame was a cultural diagnosis written and published in German in 1892–93: *Entartung* (Degeneration). In the unwieldy, five hundred pages of contemporary cultural criticism, Nordau argues that humans have become sick, pathological, weak, and degenerate because of their failure to adapt to the modern pace of society. The only way that degeneracy could be overcome, Nordau argues, was for the nervous and weak to perish and the healthy and strong to become "true moderns" in the face of modernity's new challenges.[111]

Of all the sources of degeneracy that Nordau identifies in modern society—and they range from tainted corn and alcohol consumption to sexually transmitted diseases and urban density—the most manifest and hence the most worrisome source of degeneration is the speed of modern life, represented paradigmatically by technologies of movement, particularly railways. Nordau writes:

In 1840 there were 3,000 kilometers of railway in Europe; in 1891, there were 218,000 kilometers. In Germany, France, and England, the number of travelers in 1840 amounted to 2.5 million; in 1891, it was 614 million. In Germany in 1840, every inhabitant received 85 letters; in 1888, 200 letters. . . . All these activities, however, even the simplest, involve an effort of the nervous system and a wearing of tissue. Every line we read or write, every human face we see, every conversation we carry on, every scene we perceive through the window of the flying express, sets our sensory nerves and our brain centers in motion. Even the little shocks of railway traveling that are not perceived by the consciousness, the perpetual noises, the various sights in the streets of a large town, our suspense before the progression of events, the constant expectation of the newspaper, of the postman, of visitors—all cost our brains wear and tear.[112]

When Nordau penned these words in 1892, railway lines not only connected together all of the major cities throughout Europe in an intricate
network, but the connections themselves looked like a complex nervous
system, as Friedrich List had imagined nearly fifty years earlier. Nordau's
solution to the degeneracy caused by the fast pace of modern life, however,
was not a return to the slower rhythms of the prerailway life-world; rather
he called for a Nietzschean-inflected, evolutionary adaptation to the pressures of modernity. He concludes by heralding the emergence of a race of
"true moderns" who are best adapted to this society and, in the most violent image of his book, for the members of the new humanity to prosper,
progress, and develop by "mercilessly [crushing] under [their] thumb the
anti-social vermin [*Ungeziefer*]."[113]

In his 1892–93 version of the history of degeneracy, Jews hardly play a role
at all, and his book is certainly not a critique of Eastern Jewish backwardness
or Mauschel. Instead Nordau, a Western-schooled Enlightenment Jew like
Herzl, who believed resolutely in the evolutionary progress of civilization
and the survival of the fittest, saw modern culture as degenerate because it
sanctioned, even desired, the biologistic, moral, and aesthetic achievements
of the "pathological." Only through the calm rationality of science and civil
society would humanity be able to regain its vital energy and recover from
this degeneracy. He intended his book to be a kind of therapeutic cultural exposé. It ends with an optimistic prognosis that the degeneracy of the
present age would soon come to an end: "People will recover from their
present fatigue. The feeble, the degenerate will perish; the strong will adapt
themselves to the acquisitions of civilizations, or will subordinate them to
their own organic capacity. . . . Is it possible to accelerate the recovery of the
cultivated classes from the present derangement of their nervous system? I
seriously believe so, and for that reason alone I undertook this work."[114]

In 1898, after Nordau became a Zionist, both he and Herzl urged Jews
to reform their bodies, and thereby reform their whole race, by becoming physically stronger, energetic, and vital. He imagined the creation of a
"new type" of Jew who is specially adapted to the colonial project of Zionism. Thus, in the same way that Herzl envisioned Zionism as a nationalistic
movement for curing the "sickness" of Eastern Jews by transporting them
out of Europe via modern technologies of transportation, Nordau imagined
the creation of a "new type" of Jew who is specially adapted to the stresses
and strains that modernity caused. The celebrated genus was, according to
Nordau, the German-speaking "muscle Jew." In his rally cry for a "muscular

Judaism" (*Muskeljudentum*), Nordau argued that Zionists are rejoining "our oldest traditions by becoming strong-chested, tautely-jointed, bold-looking men" (*tiefbrüstige, strammgliedrige, kühnblickende Männer*).[115] Nordau first provided the rationale for the muscle Jew at the Second Zionist Congress, and, a couple of years later, Herzl imagined the future Palestine to be populated with strong, regenerated muscle Jews in his colonial travel narrative, *Altneuland*. As I have argued elsewhere, while the concept of the muscle Jew represented a new paradigm of national regeneration for the Jewish people, Nordau's idea was not only consistent with his 1892 call for "true moderns" but also partook in a long history of attempting to redeem the individual body in order to strengthen the broader body politic.[116] In much the same way that Fichte imagined the resurrection of the German nation through regenerating and reassembling the bones and muscles of a fragmented body, Herzl and Nordau would now render this "German" conception of nationality into a Jewish corporeal politics of national regeneration.

The same year that Nordau called for the formation of a "muscle Jews" at the Second Zionist Congress, Herzl, alongside a small Zionist delegation from Germany, made a greatly publicized sea voyage to Palestine to meet the German kaiser, Wilhelm II, and enlist his support for establishing a Jewish state. He wanted to ask the kaiser to speak with the Turkish sultan about creating a "German protectorate" for world Jewry in Turkish-controlled Palestine. In a letter written to the kaiser on October 18, 1898, Herzl argues, "Even if his Majesty the Sultan does not immediately realize what aid the Zionists would bring to his impoverished, decaying state [*verarmte, verfallende Staate*], he will accept your Imperial Majesty's advice in a personal discussion as to how his administration and finances could be regenerated [*regeneriren*]" (T 2:655). Drawing on the rhetoric of national regeneration as used by German nationalists in the early nineteenth century, Zionism, Herzl argued, was a European form of civilization that would cultivate the "decaying" country and, as a universally regenerative project, could even "regenerate" the insolvent Turkish Empire. Its colonialism was not that of "conquering" the land and its inhabitants but rather that of "cultivating" and "regenerating" them, something that the Zionist Jews, Herzl maintained, knew quite well. He concludes his letter with a vaguely Hegelian description of world history: "God's secrets hover over us in these world-historical hours. There is nothing to fear, if he is with us" (T 2:655).

On the same day that he wrote his letter, Herzl was granted an audience with the kaiser, who, after their conversation, agreed to speak to the Turkish sultan about Herzl's plan. They decided to meet in Palestine as part of the kaiser's historic visit to the Holy Land. Accompanied by a small Zionist delegation, Herzl set sail aboard the steamship *Nicholas II* to Egypt and, from there, sailed aboard another ship, the *Russian,* to Palestine. He traveled via Smyrna, Piraeus, Alexandria, and Port Said before finally arriving in Jaffa seven days later. Not only was it Herzl's first (and only) visit to Palestine during his lifetime, it was also the first time that a German emperor had set foot in the Holy Land in 670 years. Wilhelm II arrived in the port of Haifa on October 25, 1898, and Herzl arrived in the port of Jaffa shortly thereafter. They met one another in the kaiser's imperial tent in Jerusalem on November 2, 1898. As Herzl justifiably wrote in his diary on that date: "This brief reception will be preserved forever in the history of the Jews" (T 2:688).

Although nothing concrete ultimately emerged from their negotiations, the overdetermined, symbolic significance of the German kaiser meeting with the Jewish founder of Zionism in Jerusalem is hard to overestimate. This historical convergence of German and Jewish nationality in 1898—the former already a reality, the latter still a fantasy—can perhaps best be seen in two photographs of seafaring, taken at roughly the same time: the first shows Herzl and the Zionist delegation aboard their ship *Nicholas II* and the second shows the German kaiser and top officers aboard their ship, the *Hohenzollern.* Both are on their way to Palestine. In the photograph of the Zionist delegation, Herzl (the third man from the left) wears a double-breasted jacket and a visor hat, maintaining a decidedly erect posture. He has the disposition of a leader embarking on a journey to lay claim to his people's land. Much like the German kaiser, clad in a double-breasted hussar uniform and a military hat with the insignia of the German empire, Herzl is undertaking a sea voyage to corroborate the claim that Jews are, in fact, a world-historical people. He recounts in his diary the first impression that he had of the German leader: "When I entered, the kaiser looked at me with his great sea-blue eyes. He really has imperial eyes. I have never seen such eyes. A remarkable, bold, inquisitive soul shows in them" (T 2:664). Herzl, it seems, desired to see with the imperial eyes of the German kaiser.

When Herzl finally arrives in Jaffa, he is disappointed by the "poverty and misery" (T 2:675) that he sees throughout the backward land and in its Arab inhabitants. In a brief exchange with the kaiser, who "flashed his imperial eyes" at him in Jerusalem on October 29, Herzl relays in his diaries that the kaiser himself considered the country "to have a future." Herzl

5.7 Theodor Herzl and the Zionist delegation traveling to Palestine (1898).

5.8 Kaiser Wilhelm II traveling to Palestine (1898).

responded: "At the moment it is still sick" (T 2:678). A couple of days later he describes the clean-up work that he envisions for Jerusalem:

> The musty deposits of two thousand years of inhumanity, intolerance, and uncleanliness lie in the foul-smelling streets. . . . If we ever get Jerusalem back and if I'm able to still do something, the first thing I would do is clean it up. I would get rid of everything that is not sacred, set up homes for workers outside the city, empty out and tear down the nests of filth, burn the secular ruins, and move the bazaars elsewhere. Then, retaining the old architecture as much as possible, I would build a comfortable, well-ventilated, well-organized, new city around the holy places.   (T 2:680–81)

Echoing the thoughts of a speech that he composed for the kaiser several days earlier, he argued that the Jewish people have the right to return to their ancient homeland in order to colonize, improve, and cultivate it. Even though "many generations have come and gone since this earth was Jewish," Herzl says:

> This is the land of our fathers, a land suitable for colonization and cultivation [*Colonisirung u. Cultivirung*]. Your Majesty has seen the country. It cries out for people to build it up. And we have among our brothers a frightful proletariat. These people cry out for a land to cultivate. . . . We are honestly convinced that the implementation of the Zionist plan must mean welfare for Turkey as well. Energies and material resources will be brought to the country; a magnificent fructification of desolate areas may easily be foreseen and, from this, more happiness and civility will flourish for all human beings. We plan to establish a Jewish Land Society for Syria and Palestine, which is to undertake this great work and request the protection of the German kaiser for this company. Our idea threatens no one's rights or religious feelings; it breathes a long-desired reconciliation. We understand and respect the devotion of all faiths on this soil, upon which the beliefs of our fathers also arose.
>   (T 2:657–68)

Although couched in terms that emphasize religious tolerance, Herzl's plan clearly involves a marginalization and displacement of the current population. The Zionists would cleanse the foul-smelling streets, tear down the secular buildings, and get rid of the means of sustenance for the Arab people, while "cultivating" and bringing "fructification" to the impoverished land. In its essence, Herzl imagined Zionist colonization as a project of cleansing, resettling, and cultivating, which would take the German model of Bildung as its historical justification.[117]

When Herzl finally met the German kaiser in Jerusalem, the kaiser's observations were essentially the same as Herzl's: "The settlements that I have seen, both the German ones and those of your people, can serve as a model for what one can make out of this country. There is room for everyone. Only provide water and trees. The work of the colonists will serve as a stimulating model for the native population. Your movement, which I know quite well, contains a healthy idea" (T 2:689). Jews, like Germans, could cultivate the land and the people, in turn improving them both. However, the kaiser hesitated to commit to do anything more to further the Zionist cause. In Herzl's words (written in French), which he relayed to the Zionist delegation, "Il n'a dit ni oui ni non [He did not say yes or no]" (T 2:690). The following day, the kaiser's flotilla departed Jaffa, and Herzl's Zionist delegation set sail back to Vienna via Egypt and Italy. The reality of German nationality and colonialism—from Bismarck to Wilhelm II—had already provided Herzl with a convincing model for realizing Zionist national fantasies.

These fantasies were no more explicit than in Herzl's *Altneuland*, a novel conceived immediately after his meeting with the German kaiser in 1898 and published four years later.[118] Generically, the novel is a work of travel literature depicting a journey through space and time: by way of a seafaring journey, the novel moves from the hopelessness of Herzl's contemporary Europe to the regeneration of Palestine in the year 1923. Using the basic form of the bildungsroman—a structure intimately connected to ship travel, education, subject formation, and return—Herzl imagines the transformation of Palestine from a barren wasteland into a fantastic, colonial wonderland modeled on the cosmopolitanism of the German universal. For Herzl and many of his Zionist contemporaries, the idea of return meant reclaiming the Holy Land and populating it with strong, cultivated, German-speaking muscle Jews and polite, clean, well-behaved, German-speaking Arabs, as he depicted in his novel. Through the processes of Bildung, not only would the decaying land be regenerated but both Jew and Arab would be raised up into the ranks of Europeans and thereby, in Hegel's formulation of world history, into the fourth—Germanic stage of world history.

I will briefly summarize a few of the salient features of the plot. The novel begins with a disillusioned Jewish man by the name of Friedrich Loewenberg in turn-of-the-century Vienna, a city deeply riven with anti-Semitism. Loewenberg meets a German-American misanthrope named Kingscourt who convinces him to permanently leave Europe and sail around the world to his personal island in the South Seas. Although Loewenberg (as a Jew) is "not familiar" with seafaring and "life on a yacht" (A 155), he nevertheless decides to accompany Kingscourt to his island and live in seclusion from the world with no one but their two servants, "a dumb Negro and a Tahitian" (A 156). Kingscourt explains to Loewenberg that he needs a "companion" so that he "does not unlearn human speech" (A 156) in this uncivilized, colonial territory. They depart from the Trieste harbor but, before heading to the South Seas, decide to make a stop in Palestine so that Loewenberg can see his "fatherland" (A 163). This is how the city looks:

> Jaffa made a very unpleasant impression on them. Although situated by the wonderful blue sea, everything was in a state of extreme decay. Landing in the miserable harbor was difficult. The alleys were filled with the worst possible stenches; everything was unsanitary, dilapidated, and draped with colorful Oriental misery. Impoverished Turks, dirty Arabs, and timid Jews lounged around—indolent, beggarly, and hopeless. . . . The train to Jerusalem revealed pictures of the deepest degeneracy. The flat land is almost all sand and swamp; the meager fields looked burned. The Arab towns were black; the inhabitants looked like bandits. Naked children played in the dirty alleys . . . with few traces of a present or former culture.   (A 166)

After witnessing such degeneration, they sail away together and spend the next twenty years on their colonial enclave in the South Seas.

The second chapter of the novel skips ahead to the year 1923, with Loewenberg and Kingscourt returning to the Red Sea on their yacht. Upon meeting other sailors, they quickly find out that shipping traffic between Europe and Asia no longer moves through the Suez Canal but now via Palestine; its port cities of Jaffa and Haifa have in the intervening twenty years become the centers of world trade: "A marvelous city had been built on the deep blue Mediterranean. Magnificent stone dams rested on the water and, at the same time, revealed what the wide harbor really was to the foreign gaze: the most convenient and safest harbor on the Mediterranean

Sea. Ships of all sizes, all kinds, and all nationalities docked in this sanctuary" (A 183). Noticing the inhabitants' clean, cosmopolitan wardrobes, Loewenberg and Kingscourt remark that the people "look more civilized [*zivilisierter*] than we do" (A 183). Although the city "seemed entirely European," it was actually "more modern and cleaner" (A 185–86). In the twenty years that they were away, Palestine had actually become more European than Europe.

On shore, Loewenberg is reunited with a young man named David Littwak whom he had known in Vienna as a poor, dirty, Yiddish-speaking beggar child from Galicia. He and his family immigrated to Palestine shortly after Loewenberg left on his voyage and, in the intervening twenty years, Littwak had become a well-respected, wealthy, German-speaking leader of the Zionist movement. He takes the two travelers on a tour of the new cities, showing them the impressive technology, culture, and social structures, which are all modeled on their European antecedents but are more refined, dignified, and, most of all, cosmopolitan. Loewenberg and Kingscourt are amazed by the immeasurable progress, diverse civilization, cleanliness, and efficiency of the new land: "The blue sky and the brilliantly colored sea was reminiscent of the Riviera. But the buildings were much more modern and cleaner, and the street traffic, although lively, caused little noise.... There were neither hoof beats from horses nor the crackling of whips nor the rumbling of tires. The pavement was as smooth as the sidewalks, and automobiles sped noiselessly by on rubber tires.... [Above them] hovered an electric train" (A 186). Now cleansed and cultivated, Palestine has become a testament to Jewish progress.

The Jews, Littwak says, have successfully migrated en masse to "civilize" Palestine and, in so doing, have built a modern nation based on the European model. They have thus become, in his words, both nationally strong and "physically fit," something that Jews achieved through gymnastics associations and rifle clubs (A 203). Both Jews and Arabs have given up their formerly "Oriental" qualities, evolving—in a mere twenty years—from the first stage of world history to the final stage. After countless paeans to technology, universal freedom, and socialist economics, the novel concludes with Loewenberg and Kingscourt deciding to become citizens of the "new society." Loewenberg marries Littwak's sister and Kingscourt becomes the caretaker of Littwak's son. As would be played out innumerable times over the course of the century, the Zionist seafaring voyage ends with the decision to dwell as citizens in the new state.[119] A celebration of all the things that made Zionism possible follows, as Littwak, who was just elected the president of Palestine, joins with a diverse group of people—Jewish and Christian, European and Arabic, old and young—in celebrating the "new and happy form of human society" (A 419). The novel ends with a brief afterword by the "editor" directed at the readers: "If you don't want it, all that I related to you is and will remain but a fairytale. I tried to write an instructive poem. . . . All the deeds of human beings were first dreams" (A 420).

As an "instructive poem" [*Lehrdichtung*], the novel is intended to give form to the possible, that is, to the imagined Jewish state of the future. Herzl insists that everything needed to realize the "dream" is already available and, for this reason, his answer to the Jewish question is a modern solution, derived from and making use of the technologies, social conditions, and politics of his present. In updating the conclusion of the Passover seder's call for "next year in Jerusalem," Herzl presents his readers with a modern seder, in Tiberias in 1923, that recounts how the mass movement of the Jews was based on the historical presuppositions of today:

> First we shall finish our seder in the manner of our forefathers. Then we will let the new era tell how it was born. Once again, there was enslavement in "Egypt" and, once again, there was a happy exodus. This time, of course, it happened with respect to the cultural conditions and technological means available at the beginning of the twentieth century. It could not have been otherwise. It could not have been earlier either. The industrial age had to have first arrived. The nations had to have grown mature enough for colonial politics. Instead of sailing ships, there had to be great steamboats, which could speed by sailing ships at twenty-two knots or more. In short, the whole inventory of the year 1900! We had to become new men and yet not be disloyal to our ancient heritage. And we had to win the support of other nations and rulers, or else the whole thing would have been impossible.   (A 313)

The conditions of possibility for Zionism are to be found, ready at hand, in early twentieth-century Europe: from technological, political, and financial support to the suffering of Jews, the will to leave, and, of course, charismatic writers and leaders like Herzl. Emphasizing that the colonial ideas do not need to remain mere fantasies, Herzl writes: "With the ideas, knowledge, and means that exist today, the 31st of December, 1902, humankind possesses everything needed to help itself. One does not need an oracle or a dirigible [*lenkbare Luftschiff*]. Everything needed is already at hand to make the world a better place. And do you know who, man, can show the way? You! The Jews! Because your situation is so bad. You have nothing to lose" (A 174).

In so doing, Herzl presents Zionism as an optimistic, colonial bildungsroman that moves almost effortlessly through space and time: It relocates the Jews in Palestine in the near future and reveals a perfectly rationalized, perfectly open, and perfectly efficient society of freedom, tolerance, and wealth. There is no dialectical underside to Herzl's society: War is nonexistent; degeneracy has been overcome; nations persist without nationalism; technology is salvational; imperialism has been squelched; colonialism is mutually profitable for both colonizer and colonized. As a smiling David Littwak tells Loewenberg from the post-Zionist perspective of 1923, "On the whole, it was a bloodless operation" (A 189). And, on the whole, what Herzl failed to see, or was unwilling to see, was that all the technological, social, political, and economic hopes that he harbored for Zionism's nationality could—and did—run in exactly the opposite direction. The immense railway network, for example, that Herzl imagines to link Jerusalem to all the cities of Western and Eastern Europe, was also the precondition of military expansionism and the reinvigoration of nationalisms. The happily global technologies and progressive cosmopolitanisms did not simply subvert or attenuate nationalism but rather justified its reassertion.

This is because the colonial project—no matter how open, progressive, or utopian—must nevertheless domesticate and in some way subjugate its other. In the case of Herzl's novel, this becomes evident in the ways in which he understands the processes of cultivation, both the cultivation of "Eastern" Jews and the "Oriental" population. As for the first, Herzl's novel is driven forward by overcoming the "weakness" of homosexuality and the reinstitution of the strong, reproductive, heterosexual familial unit. And, as for the second, the "dirty," uneducated Arabs Herzl first observed in Palestine when he visited the kaiser are precisely the people who most require cultivation and integration into the European ideal of civility. In Daniel Boyarin's critical words: "Herzlian Zionism is thus itself the civilizing mission, first and foremost directed by Jews at other Jews and then at whatever natives happen to be there, if indeed, they are noticed at all."[120]

Before Loewenberg makes the decision to bid farewell to Vienna and essentially elope with Kingscourt to the island, Kingscourt checks whether he is ready to spend the rest of his life with a man: "I want to take a companion [*Gesellschafter*] back with me . . . so that there may be someone by me when I die. Do you want to be that someone? . . . I must remind you that you are undertaking a life-long obligation. . . . If you come with me now, there will be no going back," Kingscourt warns him (A 156). But, after twenty years together, Loewenberg apparently begins to long for family, and so Kingscourt takes him on a trip to Palestine. Speaking to Friedrich Loewenberg in the diminutive, Kingscourt remarks, "You know Fritzchen that I can no longer live without you. Indeed, I arranged this whole trip for your sake, so that you would be patient with me a few years longer" (A 178). They then joke at the prospect that Loewenberg is being "dragged back to Europe" in order for Kingscourt "to marry him off" (A 178).

But, while in Palestine, Loewenberg develops feelings for David Littwak's sister, Miriam. She has matured into a beautiful, German-speaking woman who works as an English and French schoolteacher, teaching her students the languages of Western-European nationality. Loewenberg sadly explains to her that he cannot marry: "I am tied to someone else for life" (A 278). But upon realizing that homosexual relationships don't count (since they cannot populate colonial lands), Miriam's "face lit up" (A 278). It was only Kingscourt: "What if he were to release you from your promise to him?" (A 278), she asks. Indeed, heterosexuality was just around the corner. Loewenberg falls in love with Miriam and eventually marries her at the novel's conclusion. But Kingscourt is not left behind: He too is integrated into a family and willingly accepts child-rearing duties for David Littwak and his wife Sarah. Transferring his homosexual love of the older Fritzchen, Kingscourt develops a close bond with their infant son, who is, not fortuitously, also named Fritzchen. When the child becomes deathly ill at the end of the novel—something that threatens the reproduction of the family—Kingscourt steps in and miraculously saves the child. In the end, even homosexuals are integrated into the new society.

And in the same way that sexual fertility was linked to the fertility of the nation, Herzl always imagined the colonization of Palestine to be a process of "cultivating" the backward land and people. This becomes most disturbing in his portrayal of Reschid Bey, the single Arab character in the novel, who is unable to utter a critical word about Zionism. Bey, a chemist by training who received his doctorate in Berlin and speaks fluent German, can only express his unreserved gratitude to the Jews who regenerated and saved Palestine. While touring the Palestine of 1923, Kingscourt remarks that he must be in Europe, perhaps Italy, with all the lush foliage and modern means of agriculture. Not only did the Jews cultivate the soil, we are told, they also civilized this formerly backward land: "Jewish settlers who streamed into this country brought with them the experiences of the whole cultured world [i.e., Europe]" (A 251). Bey tells Loewenberg and Kingscourt what a sorry state Palestine was in before the Jews came to save the Arabs:

> Nothing could have been more poor and wretched [*jämmerlicher*] than an Arab village at the end of the nineteenth century. The peasants' clay hovels were unfit for animals. The children lay naked and neglected in the streets like dumb beasts. Now everything is different. . . . When the swamps were drained, the canals built, the eucalyptus trees planted . . . the ground became healthy. . . . The Jews have enriched us, why should we be angry with them? They dwell among us like brothers. Why should we not love them? (A 247–48)

Indeed, both Jew and Arab have been regenerated in the image of the European universal.

At the upshot of the Zionist bildungsroman, then, weak, Eastern, Yiddish-speaking Jews have become transformed into politically and physically strong, heterosexual, German-speaking Jews who reside in Palestine, the outpost of European civilization. And, at the same time, the unkempt, uncivilized "Orientals" have been transformed into polite, European-educated, German-speaking citizens of the "new society." Herzl's Zionism—as a colonial mission—touches everyone, forming them in the image of the European ideal of civilization.

With reference to Hegel, we might then organize Herzl's concept of world history into four stages that mark the Zionist idea of progressive regeneration: condemned to the first stage, we find Kingscourt's "dumb Negro" and Tahitian, neither of whom presumably have the capacity for human speech or culture; on the next stage we find the masses of "timid," Yiddish-speaking Jews in Eastern Europe and the hordes of "dirty Arabs" in Palestine before the arrival of the Zionist settlers; on the third stage we find Loewenberg and Kingscourt, who, by returning to Palestine, redeemed their original, Abrahamic *Trennung* by reconnecting with the "new" Europe; finally, in the Palestine of 1923, we find the highest development of the Jewish-European state, represented by the "new society" and the likes of David Littwak and Reschid Bey. As Herzl writes in the novel, this is because Jewish settlers who "brought the experiences of the whole cultured world [*Kulturvölker*]" (A 251). As a civilizing mission for all, Jews supposedly imported the universalizing education, culture, and political ideals of Europe without the divisive anti-Semitism, racism, classism, and colonialism associated with these ideals. In effect, Herzl's Zionist imaginary is a radically nondialectical vision of the "Germanic" stage of world history.

In conclusion, Herzl created a heroic fantasy of nationality inspired by the reality of German national unification in which seafaring Jews, as world-historical people, return to Palestine to claim their "old-new land" and regenerate its soil and inhabitants. As Moritz Goldstein would later reflect in an extraordinary essay on the need for Jewish national literature, the "effect of Herzl's ideas is to be found not with the technocrats but with the poets."[121] In other words, literature—like Herzl's *Altneuland*—was important for cultivating a "feeling of nationality" (20) and, hence, creating the conditions of possibility for a future nation. In this respect, Jews, Goldstein argues, would be well-advised to look to the German model: "As the Holy Roman Empire of the German nation was split into pieces at the beginning of the nineteenth century, a passionate call to rebuild was unleashed. . . . But where was the unity of the Germans to be found after it was apparently lost? In its shared writings. . . . Bismarck could never have created political unity had our classic authors not already established intellectual unity [*geistige Einheit*] beforehand" (19–20). He then insists that the Jews should learn from this: "The new Judah must be completed as an idea before it can exist in reality" (20). This ideational process must be the work of poets who would cultivate "a Jewish national literature" with "ideal Jewish heroes" (18). In this respect, Grunwald's history of Jewish seafaring and Herzl's novel not only represent the first testaments to the birth of a heroic Jewish national literature; they also represent the extent to which Jewish conceptions of nationality were dependent upon German literary and cultural history, German national unity, and German nationalism. Triangulated between Nuremberg, Fürth, and Palestine, we find another snapshot of the German/Jewish dialectic of modernity.

6. AUSCHWITZ

"The Fabrication of Corpses"

Heidegger, Arendt, and the Modernity of Mass Death

6.1 *Kindertransport* from the Anhalter Bahnhof (September 2, 1936). *Photograph by Herbert Sonnenfeld. Courtesy of Alfred Gottwaldt*

IN THE 1930s, the Anhalter Bahnhof became known as an "*Abschieds-bahnhof*" (farewell station) with a "platform of tears" because 3,262 Jewish children were sent out of Germany by their parents from this station.[1] On the *Kindertransport* of September 2, 1936, German-Jewish children from Berlin were sent to the French port city of Marseille, before traveling further by ship to Palestine. Norbert Wollheim tells about his work seeing the transports off:

> We had approximately twenty transports which left Berlin. It was my duty to see them all off. On the day the transports left, we assembled the people at the railway station. I had to rent a special room where everyone could gather. Then came the parents, and the brothers and

sisters, and the kids with their knapsacks. There was laughing, there were tears. . . . The children went with the hope that the parents will follow, or that one day they could come back and they would see them again. I did not realize, and I could never realize, that only a year-and-a-half later, from the same railway station, trains would go in the other direction to Hitler's slaughterhouses.[2]

After 1939, Jews still remaining in Berlin were unable to emigrate. Beginning on October 18, 1941, "special trains" began leaving Berlin, almost all from Anhalter Bahnhof and Grunewald Bahnhof, to gathering points in Germany and concentration camps in the East. More than 110 "elderly transports"—all consisting of Jews over 65 years of age—left Berlin from the Anhalter Bahnhof bound for the concentration camp of Theresienstadt.

In his book, *Meine liebste Mathilde: Die beste Freundin der Rosa Luxemburg*, Heinz Knobloch gives the names and places of residence of the elderly Jews collected on "transport list no. 30."[3] Many of the 101 people on this transport came from the Hansaviertel, a middle-class neighborhood north of Berlin's Tiergarten, where Rosa Luxemburg once lived. They were all sent to the town of Terezín, where an unknown number died in the concentration camp. Knobloch writes in disbelief: "In freight cars, a hundred elderly men and women were carried off. The train went to the Anhalter Bahnhof. . . . They were taken to Theresienstadt. With the German National Railway . . . The Berlin Jews left from the Anhalter train station on a regular D-train from the Berlin-Dresden line."[4]

The Anhalter Bahnhof became part of a journey of terror for Jews leaving Berlin, who earlier left begrudgingly with the rise of fascism, and who later were deported and killed in the name of fascism. In 1943, in the middle of the horror, the Anhalter Bahnhof was used to save more than seven hundred thousand non-Jews who were evacuated from Berlin after an order by Joseph Goebbels, who feared imminent air raid attacks on the city. Even after the intense aerial campaigns of February of 1945 and the collapse of the station's roof, the German citizens of Berlin were able to continue to flee the city up until April 17, 1945, the day the last such train left the Anhalter Bahnhof.

Unlike the brief encounters between Heidegger and Celan, the relationship between Heidegger and Arendt was marked by an intellectual and romantic intensity that spanned the better part of half a century. Indeed, much has been written about their relationship, ranging from voyeuristic accounts of their trysts and interpretations of Arendt's unrequited love for Heidegger to intellectual histories documenting the influence of Heidegger's ideas on the development of Arendt's thought.[5] Their "affair" has also generated much interest because it was between a German, who at one time was a card-carrying Nazi party member, and a Jewish intellectual forced to flee Nazi Germany. I will give only the barest rehearsal of the facts of their relationship here: Arendt was a student at the University of Marburg when she met Heidegger in the fall of 1924. They corresponded up until 1933, when Arendt left Germany, and they did not speak again until Arendt prepared to return to Germany for a visit in 1950. Their renewed, postwar relationship was marked by a kind of Heidegger hagiography in the later years and lasted until Arendt's death in 1975.

Although I am not interested in probing any part of the personal side of their relationship, I will situate my analysis of Heidegger and Arendt at a particularly significant juncture in their lives: the period of time immediately following World War II in which both thinkers attempted to articulate the significance of the Nazi death camps for philosophy. In 1949, Arendt finished the first edition of *The Origins of Totalitarianism*, a resolutely ambitious book in which she sought to explain the emergence of Nazism and Stalinism by analyzing the formation of the modern masses and the creation of superfluous human beings.[6] In the book's last sections, she discussed the "mass production of corpses" (OT 441) in the Nazi death camps, referring more than once to what she called the "insane mass manufacture of corpses" (OT 447). The same year, Heidegger gave two lectures in Bremen in which he referred to the "fabrication of corpses in gas chambers and death camps."[7] Although Heidegger never mentioned the specific fate of Jews in Nazi Germany, he wrote in a letter to Arendt in 1950 of the need for "a thinking that reflects on the extent to which history [*Geschichte*], imagined only historically [*historisch*], does not necessarily determine the essential being of humankind ... that man must learn another memory ... that the fate of the Jews and the Germans has its own truth which our historical calculation [*historisches Rechnen*] does not reach."[8] One of the things that makes this letter so extraordinary is its timing—that it comes just after he and Arendt have struggled to comprehend and explain the modernity of mass death. Moreover, the letter represents the only time Heidegger acknowledges, if only obliquely, the fate of Jews and Germans, namely that it cannot be encapsulated by "historical" approaches to the past or reached by conventional memories and "historical calculation." Heidegger, however, does not reveal anything more about the "truth" of the "fate of the Jews and the Germans" or the nature of this new "memory." Given his notorious silence with regard to the Holocaust, this letter might be interpreted as a kind of conclusion to, rather than an opening on, his thoughts on Jews and Germans during the Holocaust. In what follows, I will confine my own discussion of Arendt and Heidegger to this short period between the end of the Second World War and the resumption of their correspondence in 1950 in order to analyze how they each reflected—in both converging and diverging ways—on "the fabrication of corpses" and the modernity of mass death.

On December 1, 1949, Heidegger gave four lectures entitled "Einblick in das was ist" (A Look at that which is). They represent one of the clearest and earliest distillations of his reflections on the alienation of the modern world caused by the dominance of technology. In fact, the concepts that Heidegger introduces in the four lectures—*Das Ding* (the thing), *Das Gestell* (the en-framing), *Die Gefahr* (the danger), and *Die Kehre* (the turning)—anticipate much of his thinking after World War II with regard to technology destroying the essence of being. Nowadays, however, these Bremen lectures are primarily known because it is in the lectures on "Das Gestell" and "Die Gefahr" that Heidegger mentions, for the first and only time, the existence of "the gas chambers and death camps" (BV 27) and the fact that "hundreds of thousands . . . are discretely liquidated in death camps" (BV 56). He never mentions or alludes to the Holocaust again.

In these lectures, Heidegger does not name the perpetrators and victims; instead, he speaks of death strictly in the passive tense: "*Sie werden umgelegt. . . . Sie werden . . . liquidiert* [They are done in. . . . They are liquidated]" (BV 56). At no point does he say that German Nazis murdered Jews. Moreover, he does not indicate where these deaths occurred, when they happened, or the kind of ideology that justified them: He simply says that "hundreds of thousands" are killed, as if the Holocaust was somehow out of time, devoid of place, and without ideology. He avoids all facticities that might have endowed the Holocaust with a specific historicity. Indeed, as many commentators have argued, Heidegger's brief allusions to the Holocaust are scandalously insufficient, particularly for someone who, at least in his early years, openly supported the policies of the Nazi party and, even in his later years, never distanced himself unequivocally from anti-Semitism.[9]

As Jean-François Lyotard famously put it in his indictment of Heidegger: He "has lent to extermination not his hand and not even his thought but his silence and non-thought. That he 'forgot' the extermination."[10]

As in my earlier discussion of Heidegger and Celan, I am not interested in trying to convict or exonerate Heidegger on the charge of Nazism by undertaking a deep hermeneutics of his works or his silence vis-à-vis the Holocaust. This was, of course, the intent of Victor Farías's 1987 exposé, *Heidegger and National Socialism*, and it has been the subject of many extraordinary defenses and condemnations of the social and political affinities and consequences of Heidegger's thought.[11] Instead, I am much more interested in how his brief remarks on the gas chambers and death camps betray a consistent trajectory of thought concerning the concept of death, a trajectory that goes back to his 1926 magnum opus, *Being and Time*.[12] It is here that Heidegger articulates the importance and centrality of the paradigm of authenticity for conceptualizing the individuality of death, namely the fact that no one can "take away" my death because it is my "ownmost" and "uttermost" possibility (BT 294). Understood in its properly authentic-existential dimension, death is not an event at the end of one's life, something that will happen one day, but rather my "ownmost potentiality-for-Being" (BT 294), a possibility that is always and only mine. This is also the concept of death that informs the Bremen lectures of 1949. For Heidegger, the mass death in the gas chambers turns out not to be "death" at all because death is predicated on the principle of individuality, lived as a permanent possibility, and evaluated by its authenticity. However, as I will argue here, this fundamental structuring distinction between authentic and inauthentic dying is untenable, even thoughtless and absurd, in a sociality where anonymous mass death is its defining and ultimate purpose.

In what follows, I first explore Heidegger's early conceptualization of death in order to suggest how his thinking precludes the thought of "mass death."[13] In this regard, I am not simply arguing that Heidegger "forgot" the Holocaust as Lyotard does; rather, I am suggesting, somewhat more boldly, that Heidegger cannot think the Holocaust. With reference to the work of Giorgio Agamben and Edith Wyschogrod,[14] I argue that the existential concept of authentic death presupposes a life-world in which death is a singular, individualizing possibility and temporality is organized according to a tripartite schemata of past experiences, present possibilities, and future projects. This life-world is radically incommensurate with the death-world of the concentration camps, and, for this reason, the possibility of authentically "being-towards-death" reaches its limit with the reality of man-made mass death. Heidegger, however, never changed or surrendered the concept of authentic death; instead, he maintained that the victims of the Holocaust did not "die."[15]

Using Arendt's essay, "What Is Existential Philosophy?" (1946), I argue that her genealogy of totalitarianism begins with a critique of Heidegger's notion of authenticity, a notion that not only informed the individuality of death as Dasein's own-most possibility in *Being and Time* (1926), but also informed his characterization of the death-camps as places where "death" did not occur. Heidegger accords a very specific meaning to death as "the shelter of the truth of being," which differs significantly from Arendt's account of death in the last chapters of *The Origins of Totalitarianism*, even while she embraces his critique of modernity in its dimensions of technologization and atomization. Whereas Arendt attempted to understand the conditions of possibility of mass death and its significance for human nature, Heidegger treated mass death as a kind of negative proof of the paradigm of authenticity and the authority of the self. In her reflections on how totalitarian violence rendered human beings "superfluous," Arendt writes:

> What totalitarian ideologies therefore aim at is not the transformation of the outside world or the revolutionizing transmutation of society, but the transformation of human nature itself. The concentration camps are the laboratories where changes in human nature are tested, and their shamefulness therefore is not just the business of their inmates and those who run them according to strictly 'scientific' standards; it is the concern of all men. Suffering, of which there has always been too much on earth, is not the issue, nor is the number of victims. Human nature as such is at stake.   (OT 458–59)

Unlike Heidegger who refused to give up the paradigm of authenticity, Arendt is suggesting that it no longer makes sense to presuppose human nature, individuality, or death. All of these things changed with the advent of anonymous, state-sponsored mass death. Arendt is not interested in trying to reclaim a "lost" way of being or a "lost" conception of dying; rather, she is interested in the genealogy of totalitarian violence, something which she traces back to the rise of the modern masses, the creation of the "mass man" (OT 311), and the atomization of the individual. Although Arendt will adopt much of Heidegger's critique of modernity into her political theory, the critical phrase betraying the exterminatory possibilities of the dialectic of modernity—"the fabrication of corpses"—ultimately means quite different things to Heidegger and Arendt. As a snapshot of the German/Jewish dialectic, the purpose of this chapter is to probe this difference by considering how Heidegger and Arendt thought about the significance of mass death.

The Limits of Authenticity: Death in the Age of Mechanical Annihilation

The twentieth century can claim that it has mastered the execution of mass death, as both an absolutely efficient and absolutely anonymous event. Human beings are now able to kill each other faster and in greater numbers than ever before possible: Beginning in 1915, the Ottoman government collected, deported by train, and executed some 600,000 to 2,000,000 Armenian people in the span of several years. With World War I, it became possible for tens of thousands of soldiers to be killed and mutilated beyond recognition every month for four years, many only identified negatively as "unknown." Between 1942 and 1945, the Nazis systematically evacuated the Eastern European ghettos and transported by train millions of Jews as well as thousands upon thousands of Sinti and Roma, homosexuals, and so-called social or political 'misfits' to forced labor and death camps, where they were gassed or shot and their bodies incinerated or left to rot in mass graves. Between 1975 and 1979, approximately 1.6 million Cambodians were murdered or starved to death by Pol Pot's Khmer Rouge in his attempt to centralize dictatorial control and eradicate Buddhism and ethnic minorities from Cambodia. In less than ninety days between April 1994 and July 1994, members of the government-sponsored Hutu tribe slaughtered, primarily by machete, over 800,000 people, mostly minority Tutsis, in Rwanda.

The magnitude of the dead and the short span of time required to decimate these populations bespeak a mentality of reproducible annihilation of people deemed to be expendable or less than human. Although such a mentality was certainly realized and streamlined by the accepting employment of new technologies of mass transportation and new weapons (from machine guns to nerve gas agents, to railway transportation and Zyklon B), ultimately all that is needed is the single-minded will to designate people as expendable and reproduce mass death. That hundreds of thousands of Armenians cannot be accounted for in the most reliable statistics—as either killed or as, in fact, never existent—not only testifies to the anonymous nature of mass death but also to the targeted future reality of plausibly consummating nothingness. For the dead, it is possible that nothing but an uncertain number remains.

And within this thanatological litany, perhaps the most extreme manifestation of technological distancing and efficacious mass death occurred on August 6 and 9, 1945, the days a solitary United States B-29 bomber dropped atomic bombs on Hiroshima and Nagasaki. The U.S. Strategic Bombing Survey of 1946 placed the number of deaths in Hiroshima between seventy to eighty thousand and the number of deaths in Nagasaki between thirty-five and forty thousand. Many of the Japanese people were completely annihilated in the searing flash, reduced immediately to the nothingness of dust. Others were detectable only by a severed white shadow scorched on a wall near where they last were. These are the ones whose bodies were radically unidentifiable and utterly dematerialized in the instant of the flash. They remain among the forever more-or-less, the plus-or-minus ten thousand, who can never be finally checked, accounted for, or named. Every possible connecting trace of who they might have been (their bodies, their lives and personal histories, their relatives and friends, their records and private livelihoods) was simultaneously eradicated when they were atomized.

The Armenian genocide, two world wars, the Holocaust, Stalin's purges, Hiroshima, Nagasaki, Cambodia, Bosnia, Burundi, Sri Lanka, Nigeria, Sudan, Rwanda, Darfur—and the list goes on and on. In mentioning these man-made disasters, I am not trying to draw equations, nor am I attempting to level distinctions between these histories of mass death. This was, of course, the ostensible subject of the so-called *Historikerstreit* in 1986, namely whether the Holocaust was a unique genocide. I have no interest in participating in this debate or in using such terms. In speaking about the modernity of mass death, I am not trying to dispense with, minimize, or ignore each of the historically specific and historically unique circumstances, events, and justifications that led to and created these human disasters. My concerns lies elsewhere, with a philosophical question, which could be asked of any or all of these man-made disasters: Does the possibility of mass death—the factorylike production of anonymous death—constitute a new way of being in the world, a new way of living? And what does this mean for the modern subject, for German/Jewish modernity?

It used to be that humans could be conceptualized as finite beings in time, as simultaneously our past (experiences and futures past, how we used to imagine the future), our present (memories, activities, and projects), and our future (expectations and hopes alongside the contingency of the unknown).[16] It also used to be that humans died as individuals and were buried or otherwise commemorated as such. With the advent of the age of mass death, these temporal and corporeal facticities of being have been blasted apart: Experience and expectation, past and future no longer applied as a framework for orienting experience in the sociality of the "death-world" where human lives were reduced to the presence of an annihilating now-time and killed anonymously en masse. The production of an event (the disaster) or sociality (the death-world), where death is its defining and ultimate purpose, seems to necessitate a reconsideration of the inherited relationships between a conventional tripartite temporality and a singular death, what I will term an "authentic" and individualized Heideggerian death for short.

In her landmark study of Western philosophy and mass death, Edith Wyschogrod coined the term "death-world" as a counter-concept to Husserl's "life-world" in order to articulate the necessity of a new philosophical account of death and dying in the twentieth century.[17] The critical question that she posed was this: "[Does] the emergence of the death event, including war and related phenomena, as well as the death-world, affect present historical existence? . . . Is it possible that the existence of the death event constitutes a new historical a priori, a new grid that determines further experience?"[18] Her argument, which I will build on here, is that the creation of the death-world is a fundamentally new and unique form of social existence, in which vast populations of people are condemned to a meaningless death. Although I will not be comparing the political, social, or historical "reasons" or "contexts" for the genocides and mass deaths of the twentieth century, I think it can be said that they are all characterized by the attempt to kill, in the most efficient way possible, a targeted group of people, and that anonymous, mass death is thus their defining and ultimate purpose. As Wyschogrod and others have recently argued, the technological achievement of mass death necessitates a reconsideration of the ways in which philosophy describes the temporality of historical experience and conceptualizes the individuality of death: In the death-world, time is no longer experienced as a space of experience coupled to a horizon of possibilities but as an annihilating present; and similarly, death is no longer dying alone but the anonymous production of masses of corpses.[19]

The seemingly natural and inevitable division of human experiences into a tripartite schematic—in which the past is linked to a fictive point in the present, which, in turn, is linked to the possibility of an always arriving (and ultimately unknowable, although sometimes foreseeable) future—is a persistent topos for organizing and narrating human temporality.[20] As Husserl argued, our life-worlds—our experiences and expectations of the everyday—are imaginable and livable because of the existence of pregiven, familiar spatiotemporal structures for organizing our lives. As "the spatio-temporal world of things," the life-world is the ground of all our activities precisely because expectations can be, more or less, derived from and based upon experiences.[21] In Husserl's words: "The pregiven world is the horizon which includes all our goals, all our ends, whether fleeting or lasting, in a flowing and constant manner, just as an intentional horizon-conscious-ness 'encompasses' [umfaßt] everything in advance."[22] Expectations flow in a regular, world-founding manner, from the stock of experiences. To quote Husserl again: "The life-world . . . is always already there . . . the 'ground' of all praxis . . . [it] is always and necessarily pregiven as the universal field of all real [wirklich] and possible [möglich] praxis, as horizon."[23] The pos-sibility and perpetuation of the life-world—the more or less stable, certain, regular, given, intuitable, predictable and translatable spaces of experience and horizons of expectation—comprise the coherent sociality of being. The life-world is not an object of contemplation that persists outside human be-ings; it is synonymous with the temporality of being human.

In addition to this tripartite conceptualization of time, we also need to think about the traditional concept of death and what used to happened to corporeal remains, specifically how corpses and lives were valued, mourn-ed, and memorialized together. As Philippe Ariès has shown in his historical anthropology, the burial of the dead is connected—across place and time— to the perpetuation of community and the consolidation of a memory of the dead for the sake of generations yet to come.[24] Elaborate and precise funeral rites accompany burial: locating the appropriate grave site (inside or outside the city, a particular plot in a cemetery or monastery), marking the tomb by an identificatory epitaph (often the name of the deceased, the years of birth and death, but sometimes also the profession, last words, so-cial or political status), dressing the deceased and preparing the body (vari-ously embalmed, wrapped, covered, exhibited, or cremated), and mourning the passing of the dead (by saying eulogies or prayers, sitting Shivah, light-ing yearly remembrance candles, making pilgrimages, and participating in anniversary ceremonies and other rituals of memory). In every case, the singular individuality of the dead is mourned and memorialized.

Often the very hour of death could be anticipated, expected, and prepared for with the gathering of friends and family at the bedside of the
dying.[25] It is in this respect that deathbed confessions arose to purify sin and
settle accounts in this world before passing on. In the last hour, the entire
life was said to pass before the eyes of both the living and the dying, able to
be surveyed, evaluated, and possibly redeemed with a final urgency. Death
was not just the end of life but the substantive moment in understanding
and evaluating one's life. Over time, the hour of death became stretched
into longer and longer durations such that the art of living and the art of
dying became ever more closely joined to one another: 'To be blessed in
death, one must learn to live / To be blessed in life, one must learn to die.'
In this late-medieval conception of life in death and death in life, we might
see a prelude to the nineteenth and early twentieth century's obsession with
"authentic" dying and, later, Heidegger's "existential" conception of living
as always "being-towards-death." For Heidegger, an authentic relationship
to death—"the possibility which ends all other possibilities"—is not to be
prepared for merely in the final hour of one's life but is the "anticipation" or
"running-ahead" [*vorlaufen*] of death one's entire life long (BT, 306). Death
does not simply arrive at a certain hour but is a way of living: Death confers
individuality to life, and like life, it is what is truly one's own. In Heidegger's
words, "Death is Dasein's *ownmost* possibility. Being towards this possibility discloses to Dasein its *ownmost* potentiality-for-Being, in which its very
Being is the issue" (BT 307).

Although the survivors cannot, Heidegger argues, experience "the dying
of others," the dead are still "an object of 'concern' in the ways of funeral
rites, interment, and the cult of graves" (BT 282). Rituals of mourning and
commemoration are enacted as a kind of "Being-with the dead" (BT 282)
for the living, even if the death of the other is ultimately unknowable and
incomparable. The reason for this unknowability, Heidegger maintains, is
that "death is in every case mine" (BT 284). Not only can the other not take
my death away from me, the other cannot experience my death since it is
my ownmost possibility. Death cannot, by definition, be shared or transferred and is, therefore, characterized by Heidegger as "nonrelational" [*un-
bezüglich*] (BT 294).

Heidegger is adamant that the properly existential understanding of
death is not to conceive of it as a singular event, which happens at the end
of life. Death is not to be understood as something which has "not yet" arrived or is still outstanding, such as, to use his example, a piece of fruit in

the process of ripening (BT 286–88). At the same time, death is not to be interpreted as the ending of something, such as when the rain stops falling (BT 289). Instead, dying stands for a *"way of Being* in which Dasein *is towards* its death" (BT 291). It is here that Heidegger distinguishes between an authentic "being towards death" and an inauthentic "tranquillization" with regard to death (BT 298). In terms of the latter, he sees the everyday attitude of "the they"—the generalized public—as "fleeing in the face of death," something that manifests itself in fear, idle talk, and forms of evasion and concealment (BT 298). Heidegger cites Leo Tolstoy's short story, *The Death of Ivan Illich*, as an example of this fleeing from death: Ivan only confronts his death after becoming extremely ill, having always considered it as something which did "not yet" concern him.[26] Such an attitude toward death as an event in the future fails "to recognize Dasein's kind of Being and the Being-toward-death which belongs to Dasein" (BT 301).

By contrast, the authentic, properly existential conception of death conceives of Dasein as "constantly" and "factically" dying because death is Dasein's uttermost, nonrelational possibility (BT 303): "Authentic existence" is defined as the "anticipation" (literally, the "running ahead") of death, "the possibility of understanding one's *ownmost* and uttermost potentiality-for-Being" (BT 307). Death cannot be "actualized" because it represents the impossibility of being; instead, it is always a potentiality or possibility, which "individualizes Dasein down to itself" (BT 308). In sum, authentic death is defined as my ownmost, nonrelational possibility, which is constantly anticipated, in anxiety, by being-towards-death. For Heidegger, authenticity is thus the touchstone for evaluating Dasein's attitude toward death, and being-towards-death is what individualizes Dasein.

Although Heidegger does not cite Rainer Maria Rilke in *Being and Time* and does not even seriously write about his work until 1946, many of his ideas about authentic death—particularly the understanding of death as something that should be "one's own"—were clearly articulated in *The Notebooks of Malte Laurids Brigge* (1910).[27] In these notebooks, Paris—as the modern metropolis of alienation—represents the site for the loss of individual death: The modern hospital has 559 beds in which people die in a "factorylike" way (*fabrikmässig*). The result is that "with such an enormous production, each individual death is not very carefully considered, but that doesn't matter. It is the mass that matters [*die Masse macht es*]. Who today cares about a well worked-out death? No one. . . . The wish to have a death of one's own [*ein eigener Tod*] is ever more seldom."[28] By contrast to the masses dying anonymously in the city, Chamberlain Brigge, Malte's grand-father, still "had a death of one's own" (*einen eigenen Tod gehabt*), one that conferred and secured the individuality of the self.[29] This is an experience of death that should be privileged, perhaps even prized.

According to Blanchot, contempt for "anonymous death" goes back to the end of the nineteenth century and becomes a staple of critiques of mo-dernity from Nietzsche up through Rilke, Heidegger, and, we might add, Arendt.[30] Death is to be something that is unique, individually possessed, and properly experienced as meaningful as opposed to something anony-mously suffered and devoid of meaning: "He does not want to die like a fly in the hum of mindlessness and nullity; he wants to possess his own death and be named, be hailed by this unique death."[31] Rilke rejected the inauthenticity of anonymous mass death, and he strove, like Heidegger, to make death a part of the self, not something "foreign and incomprehen-sible." Rilke sought "to draw it into life, to make of it the other name, the other side of life."[32] The problem, which Rilke recognizes a few years later, is that the prayer of Chamberlain Brigge for his own death or for an indi-vidualized death that is drawn into life no longer makes sense after World War I, "in these days of monstrously intensified dying [*in diesen Tagen des ins Ungeheuere gesteigerten Sterbens*]."[33] Anonymous, factorylike death in the modern city had now been radically outstripped by the technical an-nihilation of the Great War.

Thus, more than a decade before *Being and Time* was published, the pos-sibility of death—as my ownmost, uttermost, individualizing potentiality—had already begun to fundamentally change in Europe with the experiences of the First World War. Death could no longer be authentically anticipated, let alone planned for in the inauthentic sense of considering it an "event." Moreover, it could not be made meaningful by burial services, mourning rituals, and traditional commemorative ceremonies that individualized the dead.[34] The deceased were often mutilated beyond recognition, their corpses radically unidentifiable, and their bodies swallowed-up anonymously by blood- and rain-soaked trenches.[35] Mass graves became the norm with the advent of technologies that facilitated an infinitely reproducible death. Dying was no longer a singular, individualizing possibility able to be anticipated as a way of being; rather, death was now suffered en masse as a nullifying ac-tuality. Death in the age of mechanical annihilation transformed the entire nature of dying and, I would submit, the very concept of being human. This, however, is not something Heidegger seriously explored. Perhaps the mass death of the First World War not only forms the "traumatic unconscious" for Heidegger and Rilke's reflections on death but also the negative condition of possibility for the philosopher's insistence on preserving the paradigm of authenticity.[36]

If the reliability of the relationship between experience and expectation created the modern life-world and the temporal concept of a human being who is not only the sum of his past, present, and future but also an individual who dies, then the death-world is the fundamental *unmaking* of this world and the destruction of this being. If we cast our gaze on how contemporary witnesses characterized this "unmaking" and destruction, we find that it is quite common, especially for those who experienced disasters first-hand, to use apocalyptic imagery that draws upon the revelation of an end-time to describe the disaster. Expressionist lyrics and landscapes are, of course, suffused with end-of-the-world images from World War I. It is also no coincidence that Thomas Mann decided to have Adrian Leverkühn perform his first work as a last work, "Apocalypsis cum figuris," in 1919. About it, Leverkühn says: "I felt that an epoch was ending, which had not only included the nineteenth century but gone far back to the end of the Middle Ages ... [to] the emancipation of the individual, the birth of freedom ... the epoch of bourgeois humanism."[37] *Doktor Faustus* is, indeed, a tale of the end-time, which finally ends in a lamentation where nothing "remains behind" [*übrigbleibt*] but "silence and night."[38] The modernity of the disaster, it might be said, severed all relation between experience and expectation, "our thousand-year history"[39] and a Germany "tomorrow."

In this respect, we can also understand Paul Valéry's own lament of 1919: "No one can say what will be living tomorrow and what will be dead, in literature, in philosophy, in aesthetics."[40] Or even more ominously, Benjamin on Brecht: "Tomorrow may bring disasters of such colossal dimensions that we can imagine ourselves separated from the texts ... of yesterday as though by centuries."[41] The fundamental temporal structuring principle of modernity—that experience and expectation are open yet also progressively linked, as von Moltke demanded or as Husserl articulated in the idea of the life-world—is also the condition of possibility for their rupture or disastrous undoing. In other words, armies and trains, bombs and broadcasts, had first to be coordinated in order to successfully destroy that very coordination. The disaster then is a kind of coordinated destruction that has been realized in, by, and through modernity; it could return at any time by radically severing past, present, and future.

Writing immediately after World War I, Paul Valéry in his letters of April and May 1919, "La Crise de l'esprit" ('the crisis of spirit,' as in *Geist* or intellectual spirit), tells us, as he realizes it himself, that human beings and knowledge, languages and histories, critics and critics of critics, civilizations, and even whole worlds are mortal: "Elam, Nineveh, Babylon were vague and splendid names; the total ruin of these worlds, for us, meant as little as did their existence. But France, England, Russia . . . now we see that the abyss of history is deep enough to bury all the world."[42] After World War I, the "European Hamlet," as Valéry imagines him, is standing in the marshes of the Somme, the mounds of Alsace, the plateaus of Champagne, "[staring] at millions of ghosts . . . Hamlet hardly knows what to do with all these skulls," he writes—they are the remains of broken lineages, ideas, bodies, histories, and civilizations.[43] Mass death is an achievement and product of modernity, and Valéry can only plaintively survey the remains of what amounts to its own destruction.

The disaster is thus the fundamental *making and unmaking* of the modern world, its coordinated possibility *and* self-destruction. This is chillingly apparent in the death-world of the concentration camps. Here, the spaces of experience (ideas about the past, histories, memories, recollections) and the horizon of expectations (ideas about the future, hopes, dreams, desires) were compressed into the tortuous eternity of a never-passing present. For its victims, the time of the concentration camp took the form of an annihilating now, a *Jetztzeit* from the other side. Primo Levi indicates the inhumanity of this time: "We had not only forgotten our country and our culture, but also our family, our past, the future we had imagined for ourselves, because, like animals, we were confined to the present moment."[44] According to the astute analysis of sociologist Wolfgang Sofsky in his book *The Order of Terror,* time in the concentration camp "locked people into an eternal present," eradicating all beginnings and all prospects of an end, save death.[45] Sofsky details what he calls "the destruction of time"[46] in the concentration camp by analyzing how first the prisoners' future (expectation of release, survival) was severed from them and then the past similarly obliterated. The result was the creation of a sociality in which "the future contracted, withered, and closed up, as did the past" leaving only "an eternal present, a constancy of uncertainty and horror."[47] Or, as Koselleck observed in an essay on dreams in the concentration camps: an inversion of temporal experience took place whereby "past, present, and future ceased to be a framework for orienting behavior."[48]

The concentration camp's utter unpredictability, contingency, and incomprehensible terror not only foreclosed a reliable relationship between the past and the future but also grounded the testimonial aporia of bearing witness to the death-world. Those who were vaporized, those who "touched bottom," as Primo Levi famously wrote of the Nazi genocide, "those who saw the Gorgon, have not returned to tell about it."[49] The survivors—the people who did not "touch bottom"—Levi says, do not comprise the rule but rather form an "anomalous minority" who by the fate of good fortune, prevarication, or sheer chance managed to survive. As Agamben recently argued in his reflections on Levi, the value of testimony from this anomalous minority "lies essentially in what it lacks; at its center it contains something that cannot be borne witness to and that discharges the survivors of authority."[50] The survivors "bear witness to a missing testimony," that of the nameless *Muselmänner* condemned to a meaningless, anonymous mass death.[51] Sofsky describes the *Muselmänner* as "persons destroyed, devastated, shattered wrecks strung between life and death. They are the victims of a stepwise annihilation of human beings."[52] As Levi wrote of the *Muselmänner* in the section on "the drowned and the saved" in *Survival in Auschwitz*:

> All the Musselmans who finished in the gas chambers have the same story, or more exactly, have no story; they followed the slope down to the bottom, like streams that run to the sea. . . . Their life is short, but their number is endless; they, the *Muselmänner*, the drowned, form the backbone of the camp, an anonymous mass, continually renewed and always identical, of non-men who march and labour in silence, the divine spark dead in them, already too empty to really suffer. One hesitates to call them living: one hesitates to call their death death, in the face of which they have no fear, as they are too tired to understand.[53]

Their stories are preserved as nonstories in the testimonies of the survivors: Stories that have not and cannot be told. Absolute annihilation—the complete destruction of body, place, and time without a trace, with no remains—would permit no testimony, no stories, and not even "nonstories" because it would evacuate any possible historical relationship to the present. Levi's testimony that there are countless nonstories indicates how close both his testimony and the nonstories of the *Muselmänner* are to absolute oblivion.

Death Without Dying

Shortly before *The Origins of Totalitarianism* was published, Arendt wrote a critical essay in 1946 entitled "What Is Existential Philosophy?" in which she traced the lineage of existential philosophy in the ideas of Kierkegaard, Heidegger, and Jaspers.[54] In this essay, she made the most incisive critique of Heidegger that she would ever make in her lifetime and even implies—opaquely, if not somewhat unfairly—that the origins of totalitarianism can be found in Heidegger's thought. She pinpoints the beginnings of modern existential philosophy with Kierkegaard's emphasis on the subjectivity of the individual.[55] The thought of death is what makes a person "subjective and separates himself from the world and everyday life with other men" (WEP 174). It is death that is "the guarantor of the *principium individuationis* because death, even though it is the most universal of all universals, nonetheless inevitably strikes me alone" (WEP 175). For Heidegger, as we have already seen, death is individualizing because it is my ownmost possibility, one which is radically nonrelational. No one can know, experience, share, or understand my death, and, more significantly, the anticipation of death is the only way in which the self is authentically and individually constituted. Being-towards-death establishes the self, and Arendt adds that it is "the guarantor that all that matters ultimately is myself" (WEP 181).

She considers "this absolute isolation . . . of the Self as the total opposite of man" (WEP 181), which is for her always a concept of relationality. Not unlike Celan's condemnation of the "Dulosigkeit" (you-lessness) of the philosopher of memory,[56] Arendt is suggesting that Heidegger's conception of existence leaves the individual "independent of humanity and representative of no one but himself" (WEP 181). Theodor Adorno offers a similar critique of Heidegger: "The loneliness of the individual in death, the fact that his 'non-relatedness singles out Dasein unto itself,' becomes the substratum of selfness. This attitude of total self-sufficiency becomes the extreme confirmation of the self; it becomes an Ur-image of defiance in self-abnegation. As a matter of fact, abstract selfness *in extremis* is that grinding of the teeth which says nothing but I, I, I."[57] She takes this conception of the self to its logical conclusion, namely a world filled with alienated, isolated individuals existing selfishly for their own ends, not unlike the masses of uprooted, superfluous men she traces in *The Origins of Totalitarianism*. As she scathingly writes of Heidegger's philosophy:

If it does not belong to the concept of man that he inhabits the earth together with others of his kind, then all that remains for him is a mechanical reconciliation by which the atomized Selves are provided with a common ground that is essentially alien to their nature. All that can result from that is the organization of these Selves intent only on themselves into an Over-self in order somehow to effect a transition from resolutely accepted guilt to action.   (WEP 181–82)

In effect, Arendt sees Heidegger's concept of man leading to the creation of "atomized Selves," who eventually organize themselves into an "Over-self," much like the lonely individuals of the masses who submit to totalitarian domination. Although this essay is unique in its harsh treatment of Heidegger, it gives us some insight into how she formulates her genealogy of totalitarianism. In much the same vein, Arendt argues that "the masses grew out of the fragments of a highly atomized society . . . totalitarian movements depended less on the structurelessness of a mass society than on the specific conditions of the atomized and individualized mass" (OT 317–18). In this analysis, what Nazism and Stalinism have in common historically is that they are both totalitarian movements predicated on the "mass organizations of atomized, isolated individuals" (OT 323). For Arendt, it is only a small step from mass society and mass leadership to mass liquidation and mass death.

In the penultimate chapter of *The Origins of Totalitarianism*, Arendt discusses how the concept of death changed in a sociality characterized by "total domination" in which "everything is possible" (OT 437). In the concentration and death camps, the victims are forced into a world where the significance of the very distinction between life and death is eradicated through death factories of anonymous, enforced oblivion. In the camps, people are "cut off from the world of the living" and reduced to nothing but "superfluous human material" (OT 443). The camps not only took away the individual's life but also their death and the memory of their death: Mourning, rituals of remembrance, and even grief are all forbidden. As Arendt writes with respect to the destruction of the meaning of death: "The concentration camps, by making death itself anonymous (making it impossible to find out whether a prisoner is dead or alive) robbed death of its meaning as the end of a fulfilled life. In a sense they took away the individual's own death, proving that henceforth nothing belonged to him and he belonged to no one. His death merely set a seal on the fact that he had never really existed" (OT 452).

Arendt does not, however, limit her reflections on death to the fate of the victims. She asks whether the actions of the perpetrators of mass death can be understood and judged within conventional grids of intelligibility: "What meaning has the concept of murder when we are confronted with the mass production of corpses?" (OT 441). That is to say, how can murder be adjudicated in the sociality of the death-world where mass death—the efficacious production of corpses—is its defining objective and ultimate purpose? Murder, after all, is a juridical notion, which, in addition to requiring the structures of a legal system for its adjudication also needs the structures of a life-world for understanding human agency. The life-world renders the concept of murder culturally, socially, and historically intelligible by endowing it with a particular significance within the realm of human experience. The camps, however, exist outside of the operation of all legal systems and life-worlds, and this is why Arendt sees "the killing of the juridical person" in man as the prerequisite of the complete destruction of his rights and his total domination (OT 451). The death-world of totalitarianism is a social order based on complete domination, arbitrary terror, and mass death as a way of life.

Both Arendt and Heidegger recognized the modernity of the factorylike production of mass death in the concentration camps and gas chambers. Heidegger, in fact, used the term *Fabrikation von Leichen* (fabrication of corpses) twice in his Bremen speeches of 1949 to refer to mass death (BV 27 and 56), while Arendt referred, on more than one occasion in *The Origins of Totalitarianism*, to "the insane mass manufacture of corpses" (OT 447).[58] Even though he will couch his analysis in much the same terms as Arendt, Heidegger is not interested in the juridical problem of murder vis-à-vis mass death. Instead, he will ask: What meaning has the concept of *death* when we are confronted with the mass production of corpses? In contrast to Arendt, he is not concerned with questions of agency, ethics, legality or the intelligibility of the life-world, all of which are implied by Arendt's question about the status of the concept of "murder." Heidegger is concerned about the status of the concept of death because this concept expresses the authenticity of being.

For the sake of clarity, I will quote the entire passage from Heidegger's Bremen speech so that we can more carefully understand his trajectory of thought and the significance of the phrase, "the fabrication of corpses:"[59]

Hundreds of thousands die in masses. Do they die? [*Sterben sie?*] They are killed. They are done in. Do they die? They become pieces of stock

in a reserve of the fabrication of corpses. Do they die? They are discretely liquidated in death camps. And also as such—millions now suffer
and perish in China due to hunger. However, to die means to bear death
in its essence. To be able to die means to be capable of this bearing. We
are capable of it only if our essence wants the essence of death. Indeed
in the midst of innumerable deaths, the essence of death remains obstructed. Death is neither empty nothingness nor is it the transition
from one kind of being to another. From the essence of being, death
belongs to the occurred Dasein of humankind. In this way, it conceals
the essence of being. Death is the highest shelter [*Gebirg*] of the truth of
being itself. . . . Death is the shelter of being in the poetry of the world.
To be capable of death in its essence means to be able to die. Those
who can die are foremost the mortal ones [*die Sterbliche*] in the decisive sense of the word. Everywhere there is massive misery of countless,
atrocious deaths that have not died [*ungestorbene Tode*]—and at the
same time, the essence of death is obstructed to men. Man is not yet the
mortal one [*der Sterbliche*].   (BV 56)

Unlike Arendt, he is not concerned with the phenomenon of mass death
as a challenge to traditional structures of legality or the death-world as the
achievement of a radically new kind of terror and domination. Moreover,
he is not interested in how the phenomenon of mass death is the culmination of the totalitarian mentality, something which Arendt traced back
historically to the pan-movements of imperialism and nationalism as well
as discerned in the widespread cultural legitimacy of anti-Semitism in
the nineteenth and early part of the twentieth century. For Heidegger, the
historical fact of "the fabrication of corpses" in the death camps and gas
chambers betrays the limits of being because death—understood authentically—is Dasein's insuperable possibility; it shelters and conceals the truth
of being. Thus, to be a mortal one [*der Sterbliche*] means to be able to die
and, hence, able to be in a certain way: that is to say, able to be as "an impas-
sioned freedom towards death," which "brings it face to face with the possibility of being itself" (BT, 311). This is the essence of authenticity.

As Heidegger indicates by his repetition of the question, "Do they die?"
[*Sterben sie?*] with reference to the mass production of corpses, the verb
"*sterben*" has a very specific meaning for him. It is distinguished strictly
from other seemingly synonymous terms such as "*umkommen*" (to be
killed), "*werden umgelegt*" (to be done in), or "*werden liquidiert*" (to be

liquidated). All of the latter are terms that presuppose the existence of an other, someone who kills me, does me in, or liquidates me. Although Heidegger uses these terms in the passive construction, they each necessitate an agent and an object on whom this agency is enacted. By contrast, "*sterben*" is a term reserved exclusively for something that is nonrelational: My death is entirely my own and, hence, "to die" is my ownmost, individual possibility. He asks three times whether the victims of mass death actually die in the sense of "*sterben*," and the answer he implied is that they do not. Something else happens to the victims of mass death: "They become pieces of stock in a reserve of the fabrication of corpses" (*Sie werden Bestandstücke eines Bestandes der Fabrikation von Leichen*).

To understand this strange phrase, we need to look back to Heidegger's second Bremen lecture, "*Das Ge-Stell*" (the En-framing), where he clarifies the concept of "*Bestandstücke*." In this lecture, he is concerned with how technology reduces the essence of being by turning it into something available, able to be used, stored, manipulated, and distributed at will. Modern technology—such as tractors, power plants, motorized vehicles, and, we might add, gas chambers—"en-frames" being by transforming it into an object to be tapped and, as necessary, kept in reserve or stock as a "*Bestand*." He explains:

> What the machine brings out piece for piece, it puts in the reserve of that which can be ordered. That which is brought out is a piece of stock [*Bestand-Stück*]. . . . The pieces of stock are the same piece for piece. Their piecemeal character demands this uniformity. As the same thing, the pieces are cut off from one another in the most extreme sense; in this way, they solidify and secure precisely their piecemeal character. . . . A piece of stock is replaceable by another. . . . Ordinarily, we imagine something lifeless when we think of the word "piece," although one can speak of a piece of cattle. The piece of stock is, however, bound to an order from which it is placed. Man also belongs, certainly in this regard, to this framing, be it that he works on a machine, be it that he constructed and built the machine within the order of the machinery. . . . Man is in this way a piece of stock [*Bestand-Stück*], in the strong sense of the words stock and piece. (BV 36–37)

In other words, technology has a leveling effect, producing objects over and over again that are, in their essential qualities, the same. These objects—as replaceable, uniform pieces—can be called up, used, and consumed.[60]

In the concentration camps and gas chambers, according to Heidegger, technology was used to turn human beings into "pieces of stock in a reserve of the fabrication of corpses." Their bodies became "uniform" pieces, "cut-off" from and "replaceable" by one another: The corpses in the death camps are "the same piece for piece." Human beings have been reduced, in Arendt's horribly accurate phrase, to "superfluous human material" (OT 443), which is, in its corporeal form, all the same. It is in this regard that Heidegger can argue, "agriculture is now a motorized food-industry, in essence the same thing as the fabrication of corpses in the gas chambers and death camps" (BV 27). Reserves of food, like reserves of corpses, are produced over and over again, in the same fashion, in the same units or pieces, with the same kind of machinery. In every case—whether the motorized food industry, the production of corpses in the gas chambers, or the starvation of millions in China—individuality is replaced by the mechanized, mass production of the same.

A few years later, in 1955, Heidegger will employ a truncated version of the same locution in his "Memorial Address" for the composer Conradin Kreutzer as well as in his essay "The Question Concerning Technology." In both, he writes that "agriculture is now the mechanized food industry."[61] But he stops short of mentioning the concentration camps and "the fabrication of corpses." Instead, he continues by explaining: "Air is now set upon to yield nitrogen, the earth to yield ore, ore to yield uranium, for example; uranium is set upon to yield atomic energy, which can be released either for destruction or for peaceful use."[62] In essence, the earth is turned into a "standing reserve" (*Bestand*) able to be tapped, exploited, and variously in-strumentalized. Significantly, it is not uranium but rather the mass murder of the Jews that functions as one of Heidegger's first examples of the leveling effect of modern technology; Jews are turned into the "reserve" or "piece of stock" par excellence. By virtue of the absence of any mention of the Holo-caust in his later lectures and essays, Jews and the Nazi concentration camps figure even more conspicuously—as an absent presence—in his philosophy than they would have figured had he continued to place the "fabrication of corpses" at the top of his list of the ills of modern technology.

Perhaps it should not be surprising that Arendt's treatment of technol-ogy and its atomizing effect largely follows Heidegger's critique in the wake of the *Origins of Totalitarianism*. This is perhaps nowhere more apparent than in her chapter on "world alienation" in *The Human Condition*. Here, she argues that three "great events stand at the threshold of the modern age and determine its character": The discovery of America and exploration of the whole earth, the Reformation, and the invention of the telescope.[63] Arendt argues that the mapping of the world—through voyages of discovery and human surveying capacity—contributed to an ever greater "closing-in process" and "shrinkage of the globe," which, in turn, "[put] a decisive distance between man and earth . . . alienating man from his immediate earthly surroundings."[64] This process of turning the world into an object to be surveyed and calculated had the effect of alienating human beings from the world. Although she does not mention Heidegger, Arendt's notion of world alienation accords precisely with Heidegger's critique of the modern age as that of "the world picture."[65] When "the world is conceived and grasped as a picture," Heidegger argues, human beings have turned it into an object to be surveyed and known from a distance, as something set up, en-framed, and exploited.[66] In essence, modern technology turns man into a subject and the world into an object, one which is able to be called up, tapped, and exploited. And most chillingly, this logic of instrumentalization could be turned against its beholders: Human beings turned Jews into pieces of stock and thereby "fabricated" corpses in the concentration camps.

We can now understand what Heidegger means when he maintains that the victims of the concentration camps and gas chambers did not die, that "everywhere there is massive misery of countless, atrocious deaths that have not died [ungestorbene Tode]." The victims may not be alive anymore, but they did not die either; instead, they were turned into pieces of corpses, reserves of human material. To become a "piece of stock in the reserve of the fabrication of corpses" is completely commensurate with Heidegger's critique of technology and, at the same time, radically incommensurate with his conception of death as "the shelter of the truth of being." I would like to dwell on the latter here. Although the inmates in the concentration camps existed every second of every day towards death as a permanent possibility, their death does not count as authentic because it conferred no individuality. Dying is a permanent potentiality for being, my ownmost, insuperable possibility, which individualizes the conduct of my life. In the final analysis, the victims of the Nazi death camps did not die and, hence, they have no "truth of being." Heidegger will not even name the victims as Jews because masses of corpses who did not die have no individual or group identities.

Unlike Arendt, Heidegger never attempted to understand the specificity or genealogy of the concentration camps; he considered them to be one instance of a long history of the loss of being caused by modern technology.

He refused to name, let alone describe, the victims and perpetrators or even speak about their actions in anything but the passive tense. And, at the same time, he never gave up the existential conception of authentic death, despite the fact that the distinction between inauthentic "fleeing" from death and authentic "being-towards-death" no longer made sense in a sociality designed exclusively for anonymous mass death. The very distinction between inauthenticity and authenticity is only tenable in a life-world where the possibility exists to either evade death by covering up the fact that it could come at any moment or live in such a way that death is always considered my ownmost possibility that no one can take away from me. In the death-world, one could neither flee in the face of death, nor could one become individualized by being-towards-death. The possibility of conceiving death authentically *and* inauthentically is foreclosed because the nature and presuppositions of death itself have changed: Mass death does not individualize but anonymize; death is no longer a possibility and individual potentiality for being but an absolute actuality, taken away from me and enforced by oblivion.

Nevertheless, perhaps it is tempting to be somewhat more charitable to Heidegger by recognizing how his remarks on the death camps betray a certain insight into the Nazi debasement of death and dying, even if he never mentioned the Holocaust or the victims by name. As Agamben wrote in his analysis of Heidegger: "Curiously enough, for Heidegger the 'fabrication of corpses' implied, just as it did for Levi, that it is not possible to speak of death in the case of extermination victims, that they did not truly die, but were rather only pieces produced in a process of an assembly line production."[67] After all, it was Levi, who suggested with reference to the anonymous masses of *Muselmänner* tottering on the edge of living and dying: "One hesitates to call their death death."[68] It would seem that both Heidegger and Levi recognized the way in which the sociality of the death-world and the phenomenon of mass death not only produced masses of "walking corpses" but also degraded dying itself. As Agamben writes, glossing both Heidegger and Arendt: "it is no longer possible truly to speak of death, that what took place in the camps was not death, but rather something infinitely worse, more appalling. In Auschwitz, people did not die; rather, corpses were produced. Corpses without death, non-humans whose decease is debased into a matter of serial production."[69]

However, I think Heidegger is ultimately saying something else. Although his recognition of the debasement of death may have accorded with Arendt and Levi's trajectory of thought, Heidegger is also making a distinction between those who are capable of dying in its essence and those who are not. This is a distinction made from a life-world in which deportations, arbitrary imprisonment, starvation, terror, gassing, and mass death are not the structuring features of being in the world. According to Heidegger, those who were killed en masse did not die because dying is reserved for those who are capable of conducting their lives in such a way that they can still bear death in its essence. This distinction, it seems to me, has the effect of tacitly elevating the perpetrators' mode of being in the world precisely because they can bear death in its essence. Even as a mass murderer, the Nazi officer could still "authentically" be towards his own, individualized death. This fundamental structuring distinction between authentic and in-authentic dying becomes absurd, if not thoughtless, in a sociality where anonymous mass death is its defining and ultimate purpose.

Why should the concentration camps function as nothing more than an example of the leveling power of technology? Why should mass death be evaluated under the limited rubric of authenticity, something that presupposes the singular nonrelationality of dying and the social structures of the life-world? When Arendt speaks about the serial production of corpses, she is referring to the absolute debasement of human life in the concentration camps, the fact that even the dignity of death is taken from the victims; she is not trying to reclaim a selfishly authentic mode of being. At the same time, Arendt is also showing how the perpetrators have changed the concepts of death and dying, and, hence, have altered human nature: Mass death is a possibility of being human, of existing in the modern world—of being subject to mass death and effecting mass death. This is what she traces in *The Origins of Totalitarianism*: Mass death as an achievement of humanity, the product of "uprootedness and superfluousness which have been the curse of modern masses" (OT 475). It is never a question of reclaiming a privileged mode of authentic being, as it is for Heidegger. To put it more boldly, Heidegger did not simply "forget" the Holocaust (à la Lyotard); instead, it seems that Heidegger cannot think the Holocaust, that his thinking—not just about death but also about memory—fundamentally precludes the thought of mass death.

Heidegger's remark about "the fabrication of corpses" misses something else, too: The perpetrators of mass death desired the consummation of nothingness such that future generations will not even know that there was a Holocaust. Not only are there no Jews, Armenians, Tutsis but there never were any; they did not exist. The most final and absolute annihilation aims to accomplish even more than killing every member of the targeted group; for it ultimately desires to annihilate all memory of that group, the very existence and being, the very traces, histories, and remains of a people. As Arendt characterized the difference between the traditional concept of murder and the Nazi attempt "to treat people as if they had never existed and to make them disappear in the literal sense of the word":

> The murderer who kills a man—a man who has to die anyway—still moves within the realm of life and death familiar to us; both have indeed a necessary connection on which the dialectic is founded, even if it is not always conscious of it. The murderer leaves a corpse behind and does not pretend that his victim never existed; if he wipes out any traces, they are those of his own identity, and not the memory and grief of the persons who loved his victim; he destroys life, but he does not destroy the fact of existence itself. (OT 442)

In the final act, in the last deed, an absolutely annihilating mass death destroys both life and death by eliminating all remains of existence. Heidegger does not recognize that "the fabrication of corpses" is essentially a trace of the perpetrators' failure to consummate their crimes. And this is why his decision to speak of the fabrication of corpses in a strictly passive construction that elides the German Nazis as agents and the Jews as victims is problematic: He essentially redeems the Nazi failure to consummate nothingness. This intention to consummate nothingness is nothing other than the intention to destroy the other absolutely. It is to end the German/Jewish dialectic by eradicating the other and stopping its movements forever.

To be sure, Heidegger and Arendt both offered similar critiques of modernity: Heidegger condemned the "rootlessness" caused by modern technology and the retreat into "calculative thought," while Arendt condemned the "worldlessness" and "uprootedness," which she saw to be the conditions of possibility of totalitarian terror. Arendt, however, actually thought about the phenomenon of mass death, the origins of the totalitarian mentality and its human consequences. She recognized precisely what Heidegger could never think: the potentiality of absolute annihilation without a trace. Totalitarianism not only exacted the "complete disappearance of its victims" but created the conditions of possibility for their oblivion, the fact that they "ceased ever to have lived" (OT 434). As Arendt chilling writes: "When no witnesses are left, there can be no testimony" (OT 451).

This is why, in *The Human Condition*, she considers "the task and potential greatness of mortals [to be] their ability to produce things—works and deeds and words—which would deserve to be and, at least to a degree, are at home in everlastingness. . . . By their capacity for the immortal deed, by their ability to leave nonperishable traces behind, men, their individual mortality notwithstanding, attain an immortality of their own and prove themselves to be of a 'divine' nature."[70] To be human is to leave behind traces, to testify, to have a story; it is precisely the opposite of the totalitarian idea, which was first to destroy human beings and then to destroy the very fact of their existence. As Primo Levi testified, there are countless non-stories from the disasters of the twentieth century, but because something remained behind—survivors, bodies, gas chambers, testimonies, diaries, poems, and stories—none of these disasters was absolute. This places most of us—those who, for now, have been fortunate enough to be "untouched" by disasters or the death-world, those of us who are historically "separated," "uninvolved," and still "lucky"—into a possible and present relationship with the remains of the disaster. And it is in this respect that the death-world presents a new historical a priori for the concept of being human in modernity: Mass death could return at any time in the form of genocide or nuclear war. To be a human being in modernity means not only to be a temporal being who individually dies but also the lived possibility of a radically atemporal instant of anonymous mass death. The potentiality of anonymous mass death is now a potentiality of being. We might even say that Being-towards-mass-death is Dasein's uttermost possibility. That is to say, our future, too, could be the disaster—and if it is not absolute, there might be some remains for someone in another life-world, like Arendt or Levi, to bear witness to the disaster. Perhaps this is what Arendt is ultimately doing in *The Origins of Totalitarianism*: first, bearing witness, in "the world of the living" (OT 444), to the past and future possibility of the death-world and, second, bearing witness, in "the world of the living" (OT 444), to the past and future possibility of a new life-world, of a new beginning.

7. VIENNA-ROME-PRAGUE-ANTWERP-PARIS
The Railway Ruins of Modernity
Freud and Sebald on the Narration of German/Jewish Remains

7.1 Ruins of the Anhalter Bahnhof, Berlin (1997). *Courtesy of the Granger Collection, New York*

ALTHOUGH THE iron and glass roof of the Anhalter Bahnhof collapsed during one of the last bombing raids of Berlin, the station was not completely destroyed, and, after the war, trains began running again as of August 1945. They continued to run until 1952 when the tracks were cut by the division of Berlin and later by the erection of the Wall. After much debate the ruined station was razed in 1961. Most of its remains were disposed of in the early 1960s, except for part of the front portal and the southbound railway tracks. These tracks were more or less left to the forces of nature since their last use on May 17, 1952. Weeds and even trees have grown over and between the tracks since then. As Sebald remarked, in reference to the firebombing of Hamburg, on what he called the natural history of destruction in his Zurich lectures: "In contrast to the effect of the catastrophes insidiously creeping up on us today, nature's ability to regenerate did not seem to have been impaired by the firestorms. In fact, many trees and bushes, particularly chestnuts and lilacs, had a second flowering. . . . If the Morgenthau Plan had ever been implemented, how long would it have taken for woodland to cover the mountain of ruins all over the country?"[1] Judging from the trees sprouting out of the remains of the railway tracks, the proposal for the "pastorification" of Germany was not a prerequisite for nature to begin—almost immediately—to cover over the material ruins.

7.2 Trees growing between the train tracks leaving the Anhalter Bahnhof, Berlin (ca. 1998). *Author's photograph*

When the station was razed in 1961, the *Frankfurter Allgemeine Zeitung* declared: "Now, the Anhalter Bahnhof finally belongs to the past."[2] With the station removed, a line could finally be drawn under this part of history. But "the past"—especially when it is the material embodiment of the hopes and horrors of an epoch—is never easily contained or exorcised as simply past. Just like the ground where the train station once stood and where the overgrown tracks still run, the immediate surrounding region remains today very much steeped in and haunted by ghosts, dreams, and nightmares: a several-story bunker from World War II, which was turned into a "museum of haunts" in the 1990s, stood intact beside the empty space of the station;

just across the street the ruins of the unearthed Gestapo headquarters comprise the so-called Topography of Terrors; in 1987 the land of the former Anhalter Bahnhof was used as the site of one of the most extensive 750th anniversary exhibitions to commemorate the founding of the city of Berlin;[3] along its northernmost border one of the last segments of the Berlin Wall ran until it was removed in 1998; and today a new structure stands on the empty grounds of the railway station: Tempodrom.

This layered materiality—from the mid-nineteenth century up until the present—testifies to the power of the *Gleichzeitigkeit des Ungleichzeitigen* (simultaneity of the nonsimultaneous), a felicitous concept that helps articulate the experience of simultaneously perceiving the remains of the Anhalter Bahnhof alongside the multiple, temporally distinct events contributing to its glorification, horror, ruin, and recent reclamation. More significant, the concept also betrays the failure of certain modes of historical practice that desire to assign stable "resting places" to particular times. The Anhalter Bahnhof does not finally belong to something called the past, as if the past was a kind of distant ontological unity. In fact, the stability or settledness of a temporal distinction marking "how far away" the past has become might be, at best, premature (given the fact that the ruins are also a part of the present) and, at worst, play into the service of "mastering the past" (*Vergangenheitsbewältigung*) in that it becomes forever consigned to a fictive dominion of the dead, long gone, and foreign. One could understand Christa Wolf's admonitory exasperation with respect to the impossibility of coming to grips with the Holocaust in such terms: "Who would dare to say at any particular time: we have come to grips with it?"[4] We might imagine the same question posed to German/Jewish modernity: who would dare to say at any particular time that we have come to grips with it?

Probing the Limits of Representation

It might be assumed that the blurring of generic fault lines between fact and fiction, history and literature, and reality and imagination has been adamantly rejected in accounts of the Holocaust. After all, the absoluteness of the Holocaust and the need to continually prove its absoluteness by securing the truth of its referent seem to be at loggerheads with any sort of postmodern relativism, be it historical, moral, juridical, linguistic, or generic.

The difference between fact and fiction must be maintained as positively clear-cut so as not to endanger or in any way impugn the reality of the Holocaust and the truthfulness of its historical representations.[5] In the now famous debate between Carlo Ginzburg and Hayden White, Ginzburg posits that the testimony of "just one witness" is sufficient to get us closer to the truth of the Holocaust.[6] To underscore his rejection of what he sees to be postmodernism's failure to secure the truth and stability of reality, Ginzburg cites Pierre Vidal-Naquet's argument to refute Robert Faurisson and other Holocaust deniers: "I was convinced that there was an ongoing discourse on the gas chambers; that everything should necessarily go through to a discourse; but beyond this, or before this, there was something irreducible which, for better or worse, I would still call reality. *Without this reality, how could we make a difference between fiction and history?*"[7] For Ginzburg it is reality that allows fiction to be distinguished from history and thereby neutralize the insidious claims of Holocaust deniers.

White, however, does not consider the blurring of fiction and history to open up the door to Holocaust deniers, nor is he interested in rebutting the charge of relativism: He openly asserts "that there is an inexpungeable relativity in every representation of historical phenomena."[8] Instead, he is concerned with arguing that nineteenth-century realist modes of representation, with their clear oppositions between fact and fiction, subject and object, agent and patient, literal and figural, may not be sufficient or even appropriate for representing "modernist" events such as the Holocaust. In his words, "the kind of anomalies, enigmas, and dead ends met with in discussions of the representation of the Holocaust are the result of a conception of discourse that owes too much to a realism that is inadequate to the representation of events, such as the Holocaust, which are themselves modernist in nature."[9]

In a later essay, "The Modernist Event," White augments his argument by showing how "certain 'holocaustal' events" of the twentieth century not only "bear little similarity to what earlier historians conventionally took as their objects of study" but that modernist events in general resist the "inherited categories and conventions for assigning meanings to events."[10] Events are no longer observed and observable, let alone scalable; agents are no longer singular and individually responsible; and representations can no longer be reduced to a single, authoritative story. The conclusion that he draws is that, in modernity, the event—with a traditional narrative structure of beginning, middle, and end, with a definitive inside and an outside, with a meaning that can be definitively adjudicated on a spectrum of true and false, fact and fiction, real and imaginary—has dissolved. And because of this he sees the kind of stories "produced by literary modernism [as] the only prospect for adequate representations of the kind of 'unnatural' events—including the Holocaust—that mark our era and distinguish it absolutely from all of the history that has come before it."[11] Modernist modes of emplotment—such as intransitive writing, the dissolution of objective narration, the embrace of contingency, and, most of all, the blurring of fact and fiction through narrative ruptures, levelings, and blockages—are needed for representing "modernist events."[12]

The stories of W. G. Sebald that deal with the representation of the Holocaust—*The Emigrants* and *Austerlitz*—might appear to compromise the reality of the Holocaust because they effectively blur the distinction between fact and fiction, history and literature, and thus potentially destabilize its reality and truth.[13] Although parts of the stories are invented, they correspond—in much of their biographical and autobiographical detail—to the experiences of real people, including Sebald himself. Told from the perspective of post-World War II, *The Emigrants* is the story of a narrator who tries to piece together the lives of four people who fled Europe over the course of the twentieth century. *Austerlitz* is the story of a German narrator who befriends a Jewish man named Austerlitz, who, as he discovers in the course of their meetings and journeys together, was sent by his parents to England on a *Kindertransport* before his family was murdered by the Nazis. Both novels are based upon real events—forced exiles—as well as upon real people: in the case of Austerlitz, Sebald says that the character is a composite of "two and a half" people, one of whom was an architecture historian in London and another of whom was a German-Jewish woman who was sent with her twin sister from Munich to England on a *Kindertransport*.[14] The books also include a substantial corpus of visual material, particularly scores of photographs, ranging from family pictures and portraits to snapshots of landscapes, train stations, libraries, and even concentration camps. The photograph of Austerlitz as a young boy, given to him by his nursery maid, Vera Ryšanová, upon returning to Prague more than fifty years later to search for his "true origins" (125), is, according to Sebald, "an authentic childhood picture of the London architecture historian."[15] All the photographs are, at least nominally, anchored in reality since they did have an actually existing referent at the time they were taken, a referent that Sebald does not necessarily retain. This is not to imply that photographs somehow mirror the truth of the world "out there" like a naive historicism,[16] nor is it to say that Sebald, in reconfiguring the photograph's original referent, is falsifying reality. However, it is to say that Sebald's novels, by virtue of their interweaving of photography and narrative, biography and autobiography, history and literature, cannot simply be classified as fiction or reduced to an incarnation of the "historical novel," which unconditionally preserves the distinction between fact and fiction.

Sebald's work is paradoxical: He writes history without appealing strictly to historical reality and, at the same time, he writes literature without creating a strictly fictional representation. An attempt to determine the value of Sebald's work by adjudicating its "historical truth"—its accuracy or lack thereof with respect to the historical record—fails to recognize the way in which his writing unlinks history from a literal reproduction of the past and, in so doing, forces us to imagine another kind of history, what I will term a history of the present. This history of the present takes the contingency of the remains of the past as its starting point but does not presume to "explain" them, write their "history," or in any way rehabilitate the fullness of the past. Instead, very much like Benjamin, Sebald's novels, bound to their own "time-kernel" (*Zeitkern*), produce a dialectical image between the remains of that which is past and "the now of a particular recognizability" (AP 463). As Benjamin writes, "It's not that what is past cast its light on what is present, or what is present its light on what is past; rather image is that wherein what has been comes together in a flash with the now to form a constellation. In other words, image is dialectics at a standstill" (AP 462). The images that emerge gain legibility and importance at a certain time, for historically specific reasons; and they also fade and become illegible at a certain time, for historically specific reasons. Sebald's novels function like Benjamin's dialectical images.

The precedent for this kind of thinking about historical truth and representation—particularly a thinking in which the representation of the past is separated from its literal reality—is not, however, Benjamin but rather Freud. As I will argue here, Sebald (not unlike Benjamin) shares an important conceptual connection with the early thought of Freud: after giving up the logocentric explanation of hysteria in 1896, Freud created a theory of representation in which mobility and contingency became the defining features of interpreting and narrating the past. Freud, as Sebald will later do, looks to the present in order to divorce the representation of the past from its literal reproduction.[17] Sebald's blurring of the fault lines between fact and fiction, history and literature, reality and imagination does not, in fact, endanger the truth of the Holocaust but has actually emerged—from its decidedly modernist roots in Freudian theory—as a powerful way of representing the reality of the past. For both Freud and Sebald the railway system is not only the figure par excellence of the dialectic of German/Jewish modernity—its emancipating freedom and its coordinated destruction—but it is also the material condition of possibility for conceiving of this modernist practice of representation and thereby reimagining both memory and history. It is in this respect that Freud and Sebald look to the German/Jewish railway system—as a conceptual structure and historical reality—to articulate the nexus between modernity and mobility.

MEMORY AND MOBILITY AGAIN

Certainly one way of discussing Sebald and Freud would be to perform a psychoanalytic reading of Sebald's novels. *Austerlitz,* for example, seems to lend itself almost effortlessly to an analysis using the Freudian concepts of trauma theory.[18] After all, the protagonist, Jacques Austerlitz, suffers from deeply repressed memories of his traumatic childhood that plague him, ever more intensely, in the present until he verges on collapse. As the novel progresses we learn the extent to which Austerlitz is driven by necessity to find out who he is and where these memories originate. Replicating the dynamic of patient and doctor, Austerlitz begins by recounting the torturous process of his self-discovery to the unnamed narrator:

> Since my childhood and youth ... I have never known who I really was. From where I stand now, of course, I can see that my name alone, and the fact that it was kept from me until my fifteenth year, ought to have put me on the track of my origins, but it has also become clear to me of late why an agency greater than or superior to my own capacity for thought, which circumspectly directs operations somewhere in my brain, has always preserved me from my own secret, systematically preventing me from drawing the obvious conclusions and embarking on the inquiries they would have suggested to me.   (44)

Austerlitz suggests that, perhaps in other circumstances, he might have been able to assemble the hints about his past into something intelligible since they were all preserved, in one way or another, within his psyche; however, due to the traumatic nature of the "secret," these memories remained, to use Freud and Breuer's assessment, "inadmissible to consciousness" (SE 2:225). In his early work Freud conceived of psychotherapy as a process of helping patients articulate such secrets: "by means of my psychical work I had to overcome a psychical force in the patients which was opposed to the pathogenic ideas becoming conscious (being remembered)" (SE 2:268). For Austerlitz the pathogenic idea, which was heretofore inadmissible to consciousness, was the fact that he was sent, at age four and a half, by his family on a *Kindertransport* from Prague to the country town of Bala, Wales, in the summer of 1939.

To shield himself from recollecting these traumatic memories and their associated history of horrors, Austerlitz says that he created "a kind of quarantine or immune system which, as I maintained my existence in a smaller and smaller space, protected me from anything that could be connected in any way, however distant, with my own early history" (140). Austerlitz protected himself from the past by quarantining and repressing his traumatic childhood memories.[19] As Freud wrote in one of his early formulations explaining the etiology of hysteria: "The actual traumatic moment, then, is the one at which the incompatibility forces itself upon the ego and at which the latter decides on the repudiation of the incompatible idea. That idea is not annihilated by a repudiation of this kind, but merely repressed into the unconscious" (SE 2:123). Of course, this is not without psychical consequence. As Austerlitz conveys to the narrator, "the self-censorship of my mind, the constant suppression of the memories surfacing in me . . . demanded ever greater efforts and finally, and unavoidably, led to the almost total destruction of my linguistic faculties, the destruction of all my notes and sketches, my endless nocturnal peregrinations through London, and my hallucinations which plagued me with increasing frequency up to the point of my nervous breakdown" (140). It was not until more than fifty years later, in the summer of 1992, upon hearing a radio broadcast of two women discussing what happened to them during the summer of 1939, when they, as children, were sent to England on a special transport, that Austerlitz realized that "these fragments of memory were part of my own life as well" (141). This is clearly a textbook case of the return of the repressed.

Indeed, the psychoanalytic interpretation of Austerlitz could be pushed further. For example, just before arriving at the decision to search for his "true origins" (125), Austerlitz, overwhelmed by implacable anxieties and thoughts of suicide, makes the following extraordinary confession to the narrator:

> The entire structure of language, the syntactical arrangement of parts of speech, punctuation, conjugations, and finally even the nouns denoting ordinary objects were all enveloped in impenetrable fog. I could not even understand what I myself had written in the past—perhaps I could understand that least of all. . . . *I could see no connections anymore*, the sentences resolved themselves into a series of separate words, the words into random sets of letters, the letters into disjointed signs, and those signs into a blue-gray trail gleaming silver here and there, excreted and left behind it by some crawling creature, and the sight of it increasingly filled me with feelings of horror and shame. One evening, said Austerlitz, I gathered up all my papers, bundled or loose, my notepads and exercise books, my files and lecture notes, anything with writing on it, and carried the entire collection out of the house to the far end of the garden where I threw it on the compost heap and buried it under layers of rotted leaves and spadefuls of earth   (124–25, my emphasis)

This, I would submit is, as good as any, a description of the Freudian death drive. As is well known, Freud introduced the notion of the death drive in his book-length essay, *Beyond the Pleasure Principle* (1920), to account for the compulsion, particularly in highly traumatized people, to repeat the unpleasure of the trauma. Freud wants to know why people who have survived "severe mechanical concussions, railway disasters and other accidents involving a risk to life [and] the terrible war which has just ended" (SE 18:12) are, in effect, "possessed by some 'daemonic' power" (SE 18:21), which compels them to repeat the trauma and ultimately aims at death and destruction. Indeed, Austerlitz will be compelled to repeat the trauma of the *Kindertransport* by taking a train, decades later, from Prague via Nuremberg and through the Rhine Valley: "Even today, Austerlitz continued, when I think of my Rhine journeys, the second of them hardly less terrifying than the first, everything becomes confused in my head: my experiences of that time, what I have read, memories surfacing and then sinking out of sight again, consecutive images and distressing blank spots where nothing at all is left" (226).

To explain the death drive, Freud calls upon an extended metaphor from cellular biology and posits that, as a counterconcept to the life instinct, there must exist a death instinct that desires an end to life and seeks to restore living organisms to their prior state, namely, inorganic, inanimate substance. The death drive originates in the need to "restore an earlier state of things" (SE 18:57). In the case of Austerlitz, the breakdown of language into its constitutive parts—until it became nothing but "a blue-gray trail gleaming silver here and there, excreted and left behind it by some crawling creature"—is analogous to the cellular processes of radical decomplexification that Freud describes.[20] This is because the death drive, in contrast to Eros, or the life drive, operates by way of dissociation or unbinding. As Freud succinctly puts it in "An Outline of Psycho-Analysis": "The aim of the first of these basic instincts [Eros] is to establish ever greater unities and to preserve them thus—in short, to bind together; the aim of the second [the death drive] is, on the contrary, to undo connections and so to destroy things. In the case of the destructive instinct we may suppose that its final aim is to lead what is living into an organic state" (SE 23:148). Because he "could see no more connections anymore," Austerlitz destroyed his life work, returning it, quite literally, to the organic rot from which it arose.

To be sure, this psychoanalytic reading of Sebald's *Austerlitz* could be productively carried further. However, my goal in bringing Sebald and Freud together in this chapter is not to produce a character analysis using the tools of psychoanalysis, nor is it to trace lines of influence. After all, this will only get us so far, although it does provide a preliminary justification. Instead, as I suggested in the introduction, I want to examine Freud along with Sebald because they are both trying to conceive of and imagine a modernist structure for investigating the presence of the past, one that frees the representation of the past from a literal reproduction of "what happened." Freud does this by articulating a theory of memory in which what is remembered does not necessarily correspond to what actually took place; and Sebald, building on Freud's conception of memory, articulates a theory of history in which what is represented does not necessarily correspond to what literally happened. To do so, both Freud and Sebald use the railway system—an extended metaphor, an epistemological configuration, and a particular material reality bound to the German/Jewish dialectic of modernity—as a conceptual tool and model for this practice of interpreting the presence of the past. For the post-1897 Freud, the railway system represents the seemingly infinite, mobile, and contingent processes of interpreting and narrating what remains of the past, while, for Sebald, the railway system represents the ruins of modernity, the starting and ending point for any meditation on the Holocaust.

I will begin with the background to the decisive shift in Freud's theory of memory. Before giving up the "seduction theory" as an explanatory mechanism for understanding the past, Freud believed that traumatic memories, although not yet "at the patients' disposal," would emerge, with the help of hypnosis or other forms of psychotherapy, "with the undiminished vividness of a recent event" (SE 2:9). It was the task of analysis to "clearly [bring] to light the memory of the event" (SE 2:6) so that it can "find a way out" (SE 2:17). He summarizes the process of psychotherapy as follows: "The pathogenic idea which has ostensibly been forgotten is always lying ready 'close at hand' and can be reached by associations that are easily accessible. It is merely a question of getting some obstacle out of the way" (SE 2:271). Freud recognizes that the pathogenic recollection does not emerge right away but rather through intermediate links and chains of associations that eventually lead to the event itself. In "The Aetiology of Hysteria" (1896), he endeavors to show that hysterical symptoms can be traced back—through such links and associations—to an originary trauma and that these symptoms can be removed through "the reproduction of the traumatic scene" (SE 3:193). What is critical is that the memory of the actual traumatic event that occurred in the past can and must be recovered, articulated, and reproduced in the present in order to determine the meaning of the hysteria and cure it.[21]

To explicate the physical expression of hysteria, Breuer and Freud describe how the actuality of the trauma is "converted into a somatic phenomenon" (SE 2:209) and account for its "intracerebral" transmission in terms of neurological theory (SE 2:192–203). Using metaphors that derive from the conduction of electricity and traffic, metaphors that Freud also employed in his neurophysiological *Project for a Scientific Psychology* (1895), Breuer posits that we ought to properly imagine the neurological pathways for conduction in the brain like "a widely-ramified electrical system for lighting and the transmission of motor power; what is expected of this system is that simple establishment of contact shall be able to set any lamp or machine in operation. To make this possible ... the dynamo engine must expend a given quantity of energy for this purpose" (SE 2:194). He continues by arguing that "hysterical conversion" takes place when excitations, which normally move throughout the "interconnected whole" of the nervous system, encounter points of tension or weakened resistances, resulting in "abnormal 'facilitation'" (*Bahnung*) and faulty discharge (SE 2:203). He then points out that some people, given the "abnormal" structure of their "sensory, vasomotor and visceral apparatuses," are innately predisposed toward hysteria because their "'facilitation of attention' in the sensory path of conduction concerned exceeds the normal amount" (SE 2:241). In other words, the neuropsychic apparatus is constructed according to the logic of a network, and hysteria arises when the facilitations (*Bahnungen*) within this network operate abnormally.

It is in these early works on the scientific study of hysteria that Freud and Breuer first explicate the psychic processes of memory by appealing to metaphors derived from transportation systems, electricity grids, and railway networks.[22] These metaphors are initially enlisted to model the psychic apparatus and explain the etiology of hysteria by way of a literalist conception of memory. Traumas are events that happened in the past, resulting in identifiable neurological excitations, mnemonic traces, and somatic expressions whose trajectories of meaning can be definitively deciphered through analysis. After 1897 these same metaphors will continue to appear; however, upon abandoning the seduction theory, Freud will also abandon the logocentrism of this preliminary theory and thereby open up the way for a conception of memory and interpretation characterized by the infinite possibility and unsurpassable contingency of an endless railway network. Here there is no originary, "master memory," only an intricate and open network of associations, interpretations, and further connections.

Arguably the most important concept within this intellectual transformation is that of *Bahnung,* translated in the standard edition as "facilitation." *Bahnung* is the nominalization of the German verb *bahnen,* to make or clear a path, opening, throughway, or road. The coinage calls upon a group of terms associated with transportation technology, such as *Eisenbahn* and *Ring-Bahn,* and, within psychoanalysis, the concept certainly accorded with, if not derived from, the traffic and network metaphors employed by Freud, Breuer, and Exner. The term not only refers to the process of "facilitating" a material connection (such as laying down iron tracks) but also refers to the creation of a connection through a kind of pathbreaking or breaching, something Freud directly attributes to the functioning of memory.[23] Drawing on the neurophysiological work of his teacher, Exner,[24] Freud makes the important claim in the *Project* that "memory is represented by the differences in the facilitations [*Bahnungen*] between the ψ-neurones," the so-called impermeable neurones, which Freud claims are "the vehicles of memory" (SE 1:300).

In this densely argued treatise, Freud sought, in Ernest Jones's words, to "combine neurone theory" with the idea that "neurophysiology—and consequently psychology—was governed by the same laws as those of chemistry and physics" and, therefore, "psychical processes [could be specified according to] quantitatively determinable states of material elements."[25] In his own words, Freud states that the critical driving force behind the *Project* is to support his belief that "a psychological theory deserving any consideration must furnish an explanation of 'memory'" (SE 1:299). By attempting to show how neurophysiology determines psychology, he sought to explain memory in terms of how the "nervous tissue" is "permanently altered by single occurrences" and yet able to receive "fresh excitations . . . with the same conditions of reception as . . . the earlier ones" (SE 1:299). Since he cannot yet imagine "an apparatus capable of such complicated functioning,"[26] Freud posits the existence of two sorts of neurones: impermeable neurones (ψ-neurones), which form the basis of mnemonic function because of their resistance and alteration, and permeable neurones (ϕ-neurones), which are always fresh because they retain nothing. "Facilitation" refers to the state or degree of conduction between the "contact barriers" of the ψ-neurones when a certain "quantity" passes through the neurone.

The extent to which Freud's neurophysiological theory of memory is essentially a model of transportation becomes clearer from his discussion of how the model functions. He claims that "a direct pathway leads from the interior of the body to ψ-neurones" (SE 1:315) and that between these neurones several different paths of connection and facilitation exist. Once he defines the ego as "the totality of the ψ cathexes"—that is to say, the totality of our memories—we find out that the neurological pathways both mirror and account for certain psychic processes such as repression, inhibition, and wishful attraction. Using a diagram "to picture the ego as a network of cathected neurones well facilitated in relation to one another" (das Ich als ein Netz besetzter, gegeneinander gut gebahnter Neuronen),[27] Freud writes:

> Let us suppose that *a* is a hostile mnemic image and *b* a key neurone to unpleasure. Then, if *a* is awakened, primarily unpleasure would be released, which would perhaps be pointless and is so in any case [if released] to its full amount. With an inhibitory action from α the release of unpleasure will turn out very slight and the nervous system will be spared the development and discharge of Q without any other damage. It is easy now to imagine how, with the help of a mechanism which draws the ego's attention to the imminent fresh cathexis of the hostile mnemic image, the ego can succeed in inhibiting the passage [of quantity] from a mnemic image to a release of unpleasure by a copious side-cathexis [a-α]   (SE 1:324)

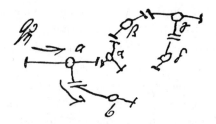

7.3 Sigmund Freud, diagram 14 from *The Project for a Scientific Psychology* (1895), in *The Stan-dard Edition of the Complete Psychological Works of Sigmund Freud*, trans. James Strachey, vol. 1, 324. *Sigmund Freud © copyrights the Institute of Psycho-Analysis* and *the Hogarth Press for permis-sion to reproduce the diagram. Reprinted by permission of the Random House Group Ltd.*

In effect, what Freud is proposing is a structural model of the psychic apparatus in which cathected ψ-neurones travel along certain determin-able paths, triggering certain mnemonic images that, in turn, result in the production of pleasure and, potentially, unpleasure. The unpleasure of a traumatic memory, for example, may not be directly facilitated or reawak-ened because of the mechanisms of inhibition and repression, but it can be reached through the correct path of verbal and neurological associations. This is because the various facilitations between cathected neurones and contact barriers follow a definitive movement within a fixed network. It is this logic—what I would suggest is a kind of metaphysics of presence—that informs Freud's early theories on the elucidation of hysterical symptoms. Meaning, like a neuronal pathway, is determinable according to the fixed, structuralist logic of a finite and reproducible network.

While Freud feverishly composed the *Project* in September of 1895 (the bulk of which happened to be written while traveling by train), he wrote to Breuer that only two things were still unresolved about it: first, he wanted "to test [the theory] against the individual facts of the new experimental psychology" and, second, "to adapt the theory to the general laws of mo-tion," something for which he looked to Breuer for help.[28] In the next ex-tant letter that Freud sent to Breuer, he makes the following remarkable statement on the neurophysiological application of the *Project*: "Just think: among other things I am on the scent of the following strict precondition for hysteria, namely, that a primary sexual experience (before puberty), ac-companied by revulsion and fright, must have taken place; for obsessional neurosis, that it must have happened, accompanied by *pleasure*."[29] If hyste-ria is "the consequence of a presexual sexual shock," its cause can be traced back to a definitive event, which is preserved by the ψ-neurones within the neurophysiological network. Freud could hardly contain his excitement at having figured out the operation of the system: "the barriers finally lifted, the veils dropped, and everything became transparent—from the details of the neuroses to the determinants of consciousness. . . . I had the impression that thing really was a machine that shortly would function on its own."[30] The meaning of hysteria had finally been pinned down.

What is important for our purposes here is not simply that Freud considered psychological processes to be determinable by underlying chemical and physical processes but that the neurological processes of memory followed the precise logic of a transportation system or network in which everything was conserved and could be traced back, according to the network's connected logic, to originary causes. The *Project*, composed just months after Freud and Breuer published their *Studies on Hysteria*, thus provided a neurophysiological basis for their account of the etiology, functioning, and treatment of hysteria: Everything is explicable by and accessible within the underlying logic of the network, wherein nothing is lost. As Freud wrote in the *Studies on Hysteria*: "The patient's ego had been approached by an idea which proved to be incompatible, which provoked on the part of the ego a repelling force of which the purpose was defense against this incompatible idea. The defense was in fact successful. The idea in question was forced out of consciousness and out of memory. The psychical trace of it was apparently lost to view. *Nevertheless the trace must be there*" (SE 2:269; my emphasis). The trace is always preserved because mnemonic images are never destroyed, only repressed and resisted. Once the pathogenic idea is recognized by the patient and finally turned into words, the hysteria abates and "the [pathogenic] picture vanishes, like a ghost that has been laid" (SE 2:281). In effect, Freud understands the reproduction of the pathogenic memory to be a task of exorcising ghosts. They can be conjured and driven out once and for all.[31]

By December of 1896 Freud's theory of memory began to undergo a radical transformation: memory was no longer conceived according to a logocentric logic of origins and, hence, hysteria could no longer be explained by reproducing and exorcising the "original" trauma. Memory became something that was both malleable and multiplicative, a function of a broad range of interpretative possibilities within a given present. As Freud indicated in a letter to Fliess on December 6, 1896, about this new conception of memory:

As you know, I'm working on the assumption that our psychic mechanism has come into being by a process of stratification: the material
present in the form of memory traces being subjected from time to
time to a rearrangement in accordance with fresh circumstances—to
a retranscription [*Umschrift*]. Thus what is essentially new about my
theory is the thesis that memory is present not once but several times
over, that it is laid down in various kinds of indications [*Zeichen*].[32]

Significantly, Freud is now suggesting that memory is not something that
is set down once and for all but is subject to "rearrangement" and "retranscription" as new situations ("fresh circumstances") present themselves.
While Derrida rightly emphasizes the writing metaphorics,[33] he fails to recognize that Freud's new theory of memory represents a decisive shift away
from reproducing origins and exorcising ghosts. It is not simply that Freud
consistently represents the structure of the psychic apparatus by a writing
machine, but that he reconceptualizes both memory and the task of interpretation according to the open-ended logic of a transportation system,
one that allows for a seemingly endless process of connection, mobility, and
contingency. This reconceptualization represents the decisive shift in which
Freud unlinks memory from a literalist reproduction of the past.

In the short essay "Screen Memories" (1899) Freud will do just that:
Childhood memories, he suggests, rarely originate in childhood but rather
are produced much later as fantasies put back into childhood. With respect
to a patient who amalgamated two fantasies from his late adolescence and
made a childhood memory of them, Freud states that these memories "are
almost like works of fiction" (SE 3:315); however, when his patient demurs
that "the scene is genuine," Freud responds: "There is no general guarantee
of the data produced by our memory. But I am ready to agree with you
that the scene is genuine" (SE 3:315). Significantly, Freud does not dispute
the authenticity of his patient's memories; these memories are real and
genuine. This is because Freud has divorced the evaluation of genuineness
from the faithful reproduction of the actuality of the past, yet without giving up the affective bind of the past. "Screen memories" are genuine not
because they replicate or approximate the reality of the past but because
they bring the present together with memories and fantasies of the past.
As Freud continues, "So the phantasy does not coincide completely with
the childhood scene. It is only based on it at certain points. That argues in
favour of the childhood memory being genuine" (SE 3:319). A "genuine"

memory need not (and perhaps cannot) agree with the literal reality of the past precisely because there is no master past to be recovered. The memory is almost—but not quite—fiction; at the same time, it is almost—but not quite—fact. Freud concludes his reflection on screen memories by stating: "And a number of motives, with no concern for historical accuracy, had a part in forming them [the childhood memories], as well as in the selection of the memories themselves" (SE 3:322). Neither historically true nor historically false, neither completely fictional nor completely factual, the screen memories are nevertheless "genuine" memories.

What Freud has arrived at, to quote Richard Terdiman, is "the extravagant mobility of psychic contents,"[34] in which memories, meanings, and interpretations are no longer evaluated by the faithfulness of their representation of the past, nor stabilized through their systemization. The past can no longer be called up or reassembled—as it really was—in order to bring the memory of a traumatic event to light through its reproduction. Pathways and facilitations do not finally converge, by way of a necessary chain of associations, at a "nodal point" that "infallibly" (SE 3:198–99) leads to a singular cause (namely, premature sexual experience); instead they extend into an open web of associations, further connections, and endless interpretations.[35] This new understanding of memory and interpretation finds its fullest expression in Freud's magnum opus, *The Interpretation of Dreams* (1899). Here mobility is not a function of preexisting, predetermined networks—whether neuronal conductions or interpretative pathways; instead mobility comes to define the interpretative work of psychoanalysis itself.

Having already dissociated memory from the factual reproduction of the past, Freud endeavors to show how the interpretation of dreams—what is essentially a problem of memory—necessitates an analogous methodological and conceptual move. Rather than interpreting dreams based upon their "manifest" meanings, Freud argues that we must begin to unpack their "latent content," where countless dream thoughts converge through the mechanisms of condensation and displacement. However, he is quick to point out that "it is in fact never possible to be sure that a dream has been completely interpreted. Even if the solution seems satisfactory and without gaps, the possibility always remains that the dream may have yet another meaning" (SE 4:279). This is because new "trains of thought" (*Gedankenverbindungen*) can always arise through further analysis, and these "new connections" are not really new but rather "loop-lines [*Nebenschliessungen*] or short-circuits made possible by the existence of other and deeper-lying connecting paths [*Verbindungswege*]" (SE 4:280).[36] Because the number of paths, loop-lines, and short-circuits can be almost infinitely proliferated through new combinations and connections, the process of analysis is essentially endless.

This becomes most explicit in the sections of the chapter on the dream work entitled "The Means of Representation" and "Considerations of Representability." Here Freud theorizes that the dream thought emerges "as the most intricate possible structure," often containing "more than one center, though having points of contact" (SE 4:312) among the different, often contradictory and seemingly incompatible parts. Although the aim of analysis is "the restoration of the connections which the dream-work has destroyed," it is not possible to fully restore the temporal and spatial complexity of the dream or translate it into a coherent and closed narrative structure because of the psychical modifications of the dream thought through the processes of condensation, displacement, and transvaluation. New "connecting points" can always be generated and, perhaps even more important, as Freud posits in a later chapter, a part of the dream thought exists that cannot be finally interpreted: "during the work of interpretation . . . there is a tangle of dream-thoughts which cannot be unraveled and which moreover adds nothing to our knowledge of the content of the dream. This is the dream's navel, the spot where it reaches down into the unknown." He then adds that the dream-thoughts have "no definite endings" but "branch out in every direction into the intricate network of our world of thought" (SE 5:525).

Significantly, this model of interpretative mobility is very different from the infallible singularity of meaning in Freud's earlier work. Freud will still describe the processes of memory and interpretation through the use of metaphors derived from traffic and transportation, particularly railway networks; however, now, unlike in the early works on the study of hysteria or the neurophysiological functioning of memory, he has completely given up the assumption of a logocentric network of meanings and meaning production. In *The Interpretation of Dreams* the acentric networks branch out in every possible direction, extending indefinitely through new chains of associations and linkages, without a claim that all the connections can finally be resolved into a coherent, meaningful whole. And, just as important, the connections do not inevitably lead to a singular place or nodal point (such as an originary trauma) but are mobile, contingent, and forever incomplete.

To see how this looks in practice, I would like to map one of Freud's most famous (Jewish) dreams, "My Son, the Myops."[37] In the expansive literature on Freud and Judaism, this dream has generated considerable scholarship because it represents, as a number of commentators have argued, "how deeply thoughts about anti-Semitism were embedded in his psyche."[38] The dream was apparently provoked, according to Freud, upon seeing Theodor Herzl's play, *Das neue Ghetto*, in January 1898. Herzl's play—a reflection on the erection of ever newer barriers for Jews in contemporary Vienna, which ends in the death of the Jewish protagonist— was written in 1894, shortly before his publication of *Der Judenstaat* and the crystallization of the Zionist idea of refounding a permanent Jewish state. As Freud tellingly writes about his dream: "The Jewish problem, concern about the future of one's children, to whom one cannot give a country [*Vaterland*] of their own, concern about educating them in such a way that they can move across frontiers [*freizügig*]—all of this was easily recognizable among the relevant dream-thoughts" (SE 5:442).[39] Indeed, given Freud's own acknowledgment of the direct influence of Herzl's play on the dream and his "concern" about the so-called Jewish problem in fin-de-siècle Vienna, it is certainly understandable that the dream has played a critical role in assessing Freud's relationship to his Judaism.[40] Peter Loewenberg, for example, extracts the dream's "hidden Zionist theme"[41] and, more recently, Ken Frieden argues that it "reflects Freud's concern with questions of national identity . . . [and his] associations recall . . . the exilic mourning for Zion."[42]

Rather than examining the dream by analyzing its manifest content and Freud's interpretation vis-à-vis his Jewish identity or, more broadly, the relationship between psychoanalysis and Judaism, something that has already been exhaustively done,[43] I first want to map Freud's analysis of the dream so that we can see how its interpretation follows the logic of an open, mobile, and contingent network. From there, building on an insight from Yerushalmi's *Freud's Moses*, I want to make the hypothesis that it is the interpretation's openness to the future—the fact that analysis can never finally be closed or contained within a logocentric network of stabilized meaning but is, instead, always mobile and slipping away—that betrays its Jewish subtext.

For the sake of convenience, let me start by quoting Freud's entire dream report:

On account of certain events which had occurred in the city of Rome, it had become necessary to remove the children to safety, and this was done. The scene was then in front of a gateway, double doors in the ancient style (the "Porta Romana" at Siena, as I was aware during the dream itself). I was sitting on the edge of a fountain and was greatly depressed and almost in tears. A female figure—an attendant or nun— brought two boys out and handed them over to their father, who was not myself. The elder of the two was clearly my eldest son; I did not see the other one's face. The woman who brought out the boy asked him to kiss her good-bye. She was noticeable for having a red nose. The boy refused to kiss her, but, holding out his hand in farewell, said "AUF GE-SERES" to her, and then "AUF UNGESERES" to the two of us (or to one of us). I had a notion that this last phrase denoted a preference.

(SE 5:441–42)

Within the scholarship on Freud, the standard interpretation of this dream rightly places it within the context of Freud's "Rome neurosis," that is, his wish—conveyed in several other dreams—to enter Rome like Hannibal, his "favorite hero of [his] later school days" (SE 4:196). After all, it was in a previously narrated dream about traveling to Rome and fighting on behalf of Jewry that Freud recalls being ashamed, as a child, of his father's "unheroic conduct"[44] in the face of anti-Semitism (SE 4:197). Moreover, although Freud claims not to have known what the word *Geseres* means before consulting "philologists" (SE 4:442),[45] Yerushalmi, like Frieden and others, points out that "*Geseres* was commonly known, even among assimilated Jews, to mean anti-Jewish decrees and persecution."[46] In summing up his analysis of the Jewish subtexts in the dream, Frieden eloquently argues:

> Freud's Passover dream represents and responds to the uneasy position of assimilated Jews in turn-of-the-century Vienna. Confronted by anti-Semitic policies such as those of Karl Lueger, the post-Enlightenment version of ancient and medieval gezeres [edicts], Freud's dream work sought a solution. At the same time, repressed Yiddish and Hebrew signifiers remained present, awaiting expression. Because it was impossible to escape "the new ghetto," as Herzl's play showed dramatically, Freud's dream found a linguistic compromise. In the dream, his son employs an "absurd" expression that posits continuity with the Jewish condition and ritual, and which casts him as an opponent of persecution. This act and its consequences differentiates Freud's son from Freud's father, whose public humiliation Freud never forgot.[47]

Although I do not think there is anything to contest in this astute interpretative analysis, I want to propose a different way of analyzing Freud's dream and the question of Jewishness. To do so, I will first map its manifest content, given by Freud as a linear narrative, and then map Freud's network of interpretative connections onto it. In what follows I do not claim to have exhausted the connections Freud articulates, nor do I claim that this map represents the only way Freud's dream could be analyzed: It is a *possible* mapping—as in the sense of mobile modernity—and should be seen as one among others. If we begin with the dream content—what Freud remembers of his dream—we could organize the narrative he tells into nine connected "stations," which might proceed from left to right. These stations would be Rome; remove the children to safety; a gateway with double doors (the Porta Romana at Siena); Freud sitting by a fountain, greatly depressed; a female attendant with two boys; Freud's recognition of his elder son; the children's leave-taking and notice of the woman's red nose; the son's refusal to kiss good-bye and his utterance of "Auf Geseres"; the son's utterance of "Auf Ungeseres" as a preference. Two of these "stations" should be additionally connected together because Freud draws the link in his dream content: Rome is connected to Siena, a place Freud actually visited where he saw the Porta Romana; and the boy's utterance of "Auf Ungeseres" is connected to Freud himself since the phrase was uttered "to the two of us (or to one of us)" (SE 5:442). To use Freud's terms, we might consider these nine stations to be nodal points because, as we will see, "a great number of dream-thoughts converged" at them and "because they had several meanings in connection with the interpretation of the dream" (SE 4:283).

At this point, Freud begins the analysis by explicating the "connecting paths" and possible meanings, which I have drawn out together with the nodal points. He first mentions Herzl's play, which is not immediately or directly connected to one of these stations. He relates it to "the Jewish problem" and his "concern about the future of one's children" (SE 5:442), thereby connecting his concern to the female attendant accompanying the two boys in the dream. Next, he mentions Psalm 137:1, "By the waters of Babylon we sat down and wept," an allusion that connects directly to Freud sitting by the fountain "almost in tears" (SE 5:442). Rome, like Siena, is famous for its fountains (this pathway is already established), and Freud draws another connecting pathway here to his memory of the Manicomio in Siena, an insane asylum, where a Jewish colleague was forced to resign his position due to anti-Semitism. This pathway connects directly to the theme of Herzl's play.

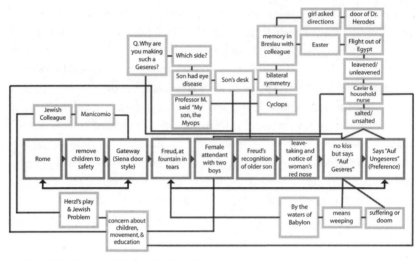

7.4 Map of Freud's dream "My Son, the Myops." *Author's drawing*

Freud then spends a fair amount of time drawing possible associations
with the phrases *Auf Geseres* and *Auf Ungeseres.* He begins by mentioning the fact that *Geseres* is "a genuine Hebrew word derived from a verb
'goiser,'" which can be translated as "imposed sufferings or doom" and
that, in slang, connotes "weeping and wailing" (SE 5:442), something that
connects to both Freud in tears and the psalm. From there he remarks
that the two phrases, one the negation of the other, call up analogous
relations such as "salted" and "unsalted" or "leavened" and "unleavened,"
in which the latter term is the preferred one. Unsalted caviar, for example,
is "esteemed more highly than salted," something that provokes Freud to
remember his own household nurse, who he had hoped would "look after
my children in the future" and was "portrayed in the female attendant or
nun in the dream" (SE 5:442–43). He decides to pursue the other verbal
association further—namely, leavened and unleavened bread. This association, of course, calls upon the holiday of Passover and the commemoration of "the flight out of Egypt" (SE 5:443). He connects this to Easter
and then pursues a complicated group of associations arising from the
memory of a conversation that he had with a colleague in Breslau during
one Easter holiday.

This memory represents another "nodal point" within Freud's interpretation: one path connects back to Easter, while another connects to the topic
of their discussion, "bilateral symmetry," while still another connects to a

pathway that dead-ends with a girl who happened to approach Freud for directions and his memory of a doorplate for a certain "Dr. Herodes." He does not push the latter association any further, although more connecting paths could presumably be created. Instead, he remembers his colleague starting a sentence with the words, "If we had an eye in the middle of our foreheads like a Cyclops" (SE 5:443), which reminds him of Professor M.'s son who, while sitting at his school desk, had suffered from an eye disease. According to the professor, had the disease stayed in just one eye, it would have been no cause for concern, but "if it passed to the other eye it would be a serious matter" (SE 5:443). However, when the one eye got better and the other became infected, the doctor who treated the son said to the mother, "Why are you making such a Geseres? . . . If one side has got well, so will the other" (SE 5:443). This explained the term *Geseres* in his dream. The desk, according to Freud, was to prevent the son from becoming "short-sighted" and "one-sided," hence the phrase, "My son, the Myops," referring to the son's myopia and lack of bilaterally symmetrical vision: "It could refer not only to physical one-sidedness but also to one-sidedness of intellectual development" (SE 5:444), something that connects back to his initial concern for the children and their education.

Upon connecting all of these interpretations together, what emerges is an acentric network or a kind of railway map. The map has neither a beginning nor an ending, neither a center nor a periphery. Nodal points connect to as few as two and as many as six other interpretative thoughts (as in the Auf Geseres station), facilitating multiple connections that cannot be resolved into a linear framework. Everything is connected, but without converging at or diverging from a single point. It is, in Freud's words, a branching "meshwork" or "intricate network" without "any definite endings" (SE 5:525). As such, this mobile mapping of the interpretative process eludes the logocentrism of truth claims because it refuses to pin down meaning by appealing to origins, ontology, or any sort of metaphysics of presence. Meaning—like memory—emerges through mobility, through the possible associations and connections within the network itself. The interpretation of the dream could be continued indefinitely with the production of new linkages and connections. At the same time, there is no transcendental perspective or point of exteriority, which would ground meaning by stopping and deciding the free play of associative links. The associations Freud gives thus represent one possible network of associations, not the only network or the singular truth of the dream.

In this respect, Freud's theory of interpretation functions according to the logic of contingency, namely, that which is neither impossible nor necessary. The connections emerge in this in-between space as possibilities, which, as the interpretation proceeds, turn into a complex, horizontally differentiated, third-order network. With the proliferation of interpretations, every link is connected to every other link, though not in a linear or direct fashion. Indeed, this is also how the systems theorist, Niklas Luhmann, defines modernity: Modern society is composed of complex, horizontally differentiated systems where contingency and connectivity are the defining features.[48] A system of organized complexity means, to recall Luhmann's definition, that "it is no longer possible at any moment to connect every element with every other element,"[49] even though, within the interpretative network or railway system, every "station" may eventually be reached by way of a series of linked connections.

If we compare the mapping of Freud's interpretation of his "My Son, the Myops" dream to a railway network at the end of the nineteenth century, the so-called German Empire, what becomes clear is that in both there are multiple nodal points, connected throughout the system, without a center, a beginning, an ending, or even borders.[50] A virtually infinite number of possible routes exists to traverse a given distance—for example, the distance between Berlin and Vienna—because not every city is directly connected to

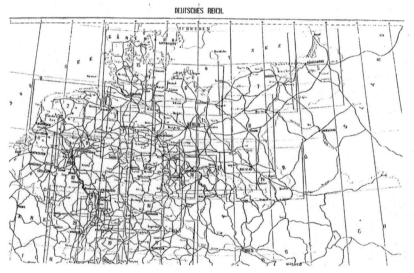

7.5 The German Empire (ca. 1892).

every other city, yet any place within the complex network can be reached by virtue of the *Bahnungen* between them. The connections emerge as a space of possibilities within a complex, horizontally differentiated, third-order network. Complexity, contingency, horizontal differentiation, and endless connectivity are thus the defining features of the modernity of both the railway network and of Freud's theory of interpretation. The linearity of a logocentric, realistic narrative is transformed into a modernist space of mobility and endless interpretation. And it is precisely this space of mobility—exemplified by the modernity of the railway system—that allows Freud to divorce the representation of the past from its literal reproduction. It might even be said that the railway system is the conceptual condition of possibility of psychoanalysis itself.

This does not mean, as Freud points out, that anything goes or that the connections are simply arbitrary associations generated by the "free play of ideas" (SE 5:529). Freud explains: "No connection was too loose, no joke too bad, to serve as a bridge from one thought to another. . . . Whenever one psychical element is linked with another by an objectionable or superficial association, there is also a legitimate and deeper link between them which is subjected to the resistance of the censorship" (SE 5:530). This is because censorship "makes the normal connecting paths impassable" ("dieses normale Verbindungswege ungangbar macht"; SE 5:530).[51] Psychoanalysis thus operates in this space between the unconscious and the conscious, between the necessary and the impossible, between the past and present memories of the past.

At the same time that psychoanalysis occupies itself with the endless mobility of memory and the infinite connectivity of interpretations, Freud never gave up his belief that everything from the past was completely preserved—although not accessible—in the unconscious. "In the unconscious nothing can be brought to an end, nothing is past or forgotten," he famously writes in *The Interpretation of Dreams* (SE 5:577). The unconscious is timeless, or, more precisely, exists outside time, because it functions as total storage, complete archivization, such that nothing is lost or destroyed. Freud explains: "A humiliation that was experienced thirty years ago acts exactly like a fresh one throughout the thirty years, as soon as it has obtained access to the unconscious sources of emotion. As soon as the memory of it is touched, it springs into life again" (SE 5:578). This is because events stored in the unconscious are not subject to attenuation, change, or destruction—all of which represent temporal processes: "The processes of the system *Ucs*.

are *timeless*, i.e., they are not ordered temporally, are not altered by the passage of time; they have no reference to time at all (SE 14:187).

Throughout his career, Freud consistently adduced archaeological metaphors to underscore how the unconscious and psychic processes preserve the totality of the past.[52] In *Civilization and Its Discontents*, for example, Freud compares the "psychic entity" to the city of Rome, "in which nothing that has once come into existence will have passed away and all the earlier stages of development continue to exist alongside the latest one." He emphasizes that this does not mean a succession of developments but rather the existence of the simultaneity of all pasts: "On the Piazza of the Pantheon we should find not only the Pantheon of today, as it was bequeathed to us by Hadrian, but, on the same site, the original edifice erected by Agrippa; indeed, the same piece of ground would be supporting the church of Santa Maria sopra Minerva and the ancient temple over which it was built" (SE 21:70). In other words, the unconscious processes not only preserve our own memories and experiences of the past but the species memory as well.[53] Everything exists as it once was and nothing is destroyed in this cultural geography of historical simultaneity.

With this conceptualization of the unconscious, Terdiman argues that Freud "unexpectedly revives something that functions very much like the positivist model of the past—a paradigm of data unerringly and permanently recorded."[54] After all, in positing that the unconscious stores everything—in all its literalism—Freud certainly seems to be allying himself with the naive historicist fantasy that the past can be recovered as it really was, something that ostensibly contradicts his dissociation of memory from the literal reproduction of the past. However, there is a critical difference between the historicist fantasy and Freud's notion of the unconscious, one that, as we will see in the next section, will bear directly on my assessment of Sebald. The historicist takes the past as gone and presumes that it can be reconstituted and represented (as in made present again) through certain historical practices and narrative strategies that aim to fill in gaps and, finally, fix it in place. Freud, on the other hand, does not take the past as gone, only as inaccessible. Psychoanalysis exists precisely because the unconscious cannot be directly accessed. The work of interpretation cannot and does not reconstitute or represent the past in its literalness because this would be to endow it with an atemporality possessed only by the unconscious. Unlike the historicist who believes there is a direct, correlative link between the practices of representation and what happened in the past, there is, for Freud, no such link between the representation of the past and the unconscious. All we have consciously are interpretations and memories of the past, both of which are temporal processes open to the future because of their incompleteness, tentativeness, and contingency.

Therefore, since the origins of unconscious drives and dreams can never be determined, known, and represented, the meaning of a dream or a memory is never finally secured, nailed down, or settled. Instead its meaning is shifting, deferred, reinscribed, and open toward the future. It is this openness to the future—the contingency and mobility of a virtually endless interpretation—that, in my opinion, presents Freud at his most Jewish. After all, it was Yerushalmi who, in another context, accused Freud of being "most un-Jewish" when he rejected religion as "the great illusion, [which] has no future" in his famous treatise, *The Future of an Illusion*.[55] Following Yerushalmi's logic, then, Jewishness can be understood, in its irreducible essence as an openness to the future. In Derrida's words, which gloss Yerushalmi's argument, "What would be the least Jewish, the most 'un-Jewish,' the most heterogeneous to Jewishness, would not be a lack of Judaism ... but the nonbelief in the future. . . . The being-Jewish and the being-open-toward-the-future would be the same thing."[56] It is this openness to the future in Freud's dream interpretation, not the specific dream content, that shows him to be most Jewish.

Of course, Freud's Jewishness can be interpreted by pushing on certain psychoanalytic concepts and elisions, biographical details and historical conditions, such as his avowed atheism, his hidden Zionism, his Rome neurosis, or his famous dithering with respect to whether psychoanalysis is or is not a "Jewish science." It is this latter question that Yerushalmi wants to know the answer to and where he ends his "monologue with Freud": "Professor Freud, at this point I find it futile to ask whether, genetically or structurally, psychoanalysis is really a Jewish science; that we shall know, if it is at all knowable, only when much future work has been done. . . . I want only to know whether *you* ultimately came to believe it to be so. . . . Please tell me, Professor. I promise I won't reveal your answer to anyone."[57] Although Yerushalmi does not answer the question or provide the last word on the matter, it seems, as Derrida rightly points out, that "it is as if he wanted the last word, the last will, the ultimate signature ('ultimately') of a dying father."[58] He wants to know the "answer" right now, presumably before "much future work has been done" that may or may not yield an answer. More than that, he promises to selfishly guard the secret from anyone else.

But there is, of course, a significant difference between the desire for a last word, the wish for a final interpretation, the longing to know a secret, and the declaration of a last word, the ascription of a final interpretation, and the knowledge of a secret. Despite what Derrida perceives to be his "archive fever"—namely, his will to know by calling upon the archive as an originary repository of the truth of the past—Yerushalmi still leaves open a space of indeterminacy, a future that has not yet been told.[59] He calls on the specter of Freud to speak, but he knows full well—as a historian—that the dead can never speak and offer up answers.[60] Once again, we are left with the desires, wishes, hopes, and anxieties of the present, desires that, like interpretations, are forever unfulfilled, open, contingent, and mobile. If Jewishness, then, is about being open to the future, Freud's unlinking of memory from the literal reproduction of the past in favor of the openness of interpretation can be seen as an eminently Jewish act. Perhaps Yerushalmi's inclination was right: psychoanalysis is a Jewish science, even if we will never know that from Freud himself.

A HISTORY OF THE PRESENT

While Freud divorced memory from a literal reproduction of the past, his theories of how memory functioned emerged from patients who had, to various degrees, direct experiences of what they were recollecting. Although he no longer insisted on an univocal origin (such as an act of childhood molestation explaining hysteria), actually experienced events, through composites of present wishes and ideas about the past, comprise memory. In his studies on trauma and war neuroses, for example, Freud sought to explain the compulsion among war veterans to repeat the unpleasure of their trauma or loss even while the direct memory of the event or experience remained repressed. As he wrote in *Beyond the Pleasure Principle*, the patient "is obliged to *repeat* the repressed material as a contemporary experience instead of, as the physician would prefer to see, *remembering* it as something belonging to the past" (SE 18: 18). Even though the traumatic experiences are no longer completely accessible in their originary content and cannot be remembered or represented as such, the patient's successful therapy is dependent upon remembering—reconfiguring more than reconstituting—these traumatic experiences as "genuine" memories of the past. Indeed, these genuine memories, as he argues in his essay "Screen Memo-

ries," are not literal replications of what actually happened but multilayered, mobile amalgamations of the past and the present, shot through—not
unlike Benjamin's dialectical images—with desires and wishes stemming
from the present. Childhood memories are genuine not because they were
formed during childhood but because they emerged later, as present fantasies that correspond "at certain points" with the reality of the past. Similarly,
for a war veteran, memories of World War I may not have been formed
during the war itself but may, in fact, have only emerged later, as a function
of present anxieties mixing with layered recollections of the past. Memory,
like interpretation, is genuine not for its fidelity to the past but for its relationships to and rewritings in the present.

Like Freud, Sebald divorces memory from the literal reproduction of
what happened; however, unlike Freud, his reflections on memory and history involve not only people who were directly affected by certain traumatic
events but also people who were born without direct perceptions and experiences of the events they are encountering, remembering, and describing.
Both *The Emigrants* and *Austerlitz* begin with a narrator who was born in
roughly the last year of World War II, like Sebald himself, without memories formed from personal experiences of the brutality of the war and the
Nazi genocide. Far from embodying what Helmut Kohl once called "the
grace of late birth" (*die Gnade der späten Geburt*)—that is to say, one of
those people supposedly fortunate enough to be born free of direct memories of the Nazi period—Sebald, who was born in May of 1944, explains that
he was deeply and personally connected to the "catastrophe then unfolding
in the German Reich."[61] Although he "remained almost untouched by [it]"
since he was born in an isolated village in the Allgäu Alps during the last
year of the war, the "catastrophe had nevertheless left traces in my memory"
(*Spuren in meinem Gedächtnis hinterlassen*)."[62]

In reflecting on the reaction to his Zurich lectures, *Luftkrieg und Literatur*, on the repression of the devastation caused by the aerial war in Germany, Sebald makes the following autobiographical remark: "At the end of
the war I was just one year old, so I can hardly have any impressions of that
period of destruction based on personal experience. Yet to this day, when I
see photographs or documentary films dating from the war I feel as if I were
its child, so to speak, as if the horrors I did not experience cast a shadow
over me, and one from which I shall never entirely emerge" (*Destruction* 71).
He continues, looking at a photograph published in a 1963 on the history
of the small German town of Sonthofen, where Sebald moved at age eight:

"Before my eyes pictures of paths through the fields, river meadows, and mountain pastures blur together with images of destruction, and it is the latter, perversely, and not the entirely unreal idylls of my early childhood, which evoke a feeling of coming home [*Heimatsgefühl*], perhaps because they represent the more powerful and dominant reality of my first years of life" (*Destruction* 71).[63] In effect, Sebald's memories of the air war and the German catastrophe are not based upon direct and personal experiences but upon shadows cast by retrospectively encountered images that were contemporaneous with the beginnings of his own life. These images blur, like Freudian screen memories, with his own idyllic experiences of childhood, and, remarkably, it is these images of destruction that evoke "a feeling of coming home."

Unlike Pierre Nora who argues that history takes over when memory—always connected to eyewitness testimony and direct experience—dies away,[64] Sebald is suggesting that memory may not be tied, exclusively, to actual and direct experiences. Memory then is not only, as Freud argued, a function of the mobility and contingency of interpretation in which later experiences influence and shape earlier ones—so much so that childhood memories are often first formed years later and retrospectively inscribed into childhood—but memory might also be derived imaginatively from representations of events that entirely preceded one's direct perceptions and experiences. Building on an observation of J. J. Long,[65] Sebald's second-generation memory, mediated and formed by representations of earlier events that he did not personally experience, might be characterized, to use Marianne Hirsch's fraught concept, as *postmemory*. Having developed this notion while working with children of Holocaust survivors, Hirsch explains:

> Postmemory is distinguished from memory by generational distance and from history by deep personal connection. Postmemory is a powerful and very particular form of memory precisely because its connection to its object or source is mediated not through recollection but through an imaginative investment and creation. This is not to say that memory itself is unmediated, but that it is more directly connected to the past. Postmemory characterizes the experience of those who grow up dominated by narratives that preceded their birth, whose own belated stories are evacuated by the stories of the previous generations shaped by traumatic events that can neither be understood nor recreated.[66]

Although I have reservations about the predicate *post* since, despite Hirsch's reassurances, it nevertheless calls up clean temporal breaks, I think that her articulation of the concept usefully draws our attention to the crux of Sebald's thought: How can the artificial, the fictional, the contingent, and the imaginative contribute to the extension of both memory and historical knowledge without in any way impugning survivors' memories and historical truth? Or, to pose the question differently using Hayden White's language on the possibility of representing the "modernist event": Does "literary modernism," of which Sebald's prose is one prominent example, "offer the only prospect for adequate representations of the kind of 'unnatural' events—including the Holocaust—that mark our era and distinguish it absolutely from all of the history that has come before it?"[67]

With respect to the aerial bombardment of Germany, Sebald argues that the eyewitness accounts produced by people who directly experienced the destruction, such as Friedrich Reck or even Victor Klemperer, are "somehow untrue" (*irgendwie Unwahre*) because of their employment of everyday language, marked by clichés, to describe the extremity and incomprehensibility of the total destruction.[68] The result of such stereotypical language is "to cover up and neutralize experiences beyond our ability to comprehend" (*Destruction* 25). Sebald suggests that

> the apparently unimpaired ability—shown in most of the eyewitness reports—of everyday language to go on functioning as usual raises doubts of the authenticity of the experiences they record. The death by fire within a few hours of an entire city, with all its buildings and its trees, its inhabitants, its domestic pets, its fixtures and fittings of every kind, must inevitably have led to overload, to paralysis of the capacity to think and feel in those who succeeded in escaping. The accounts of individual eyewitnesses, therefore, are of only qualified value, and need to be supplemented by what a synoptic and artificial [*synoptische, künstliche*] view opens up.
>
> (*Destruction* 25–26; translation slightly altered)

According to Sebald, there is a radical incommensurability between the unprecedented experience of witnessing total destruction and the descriptive capacities of everyday language to comprehend and represent this experience. Far from simply unrepresentable, new forms of narration and new techniques of representation are needed to convey the enormity of the modernist event. As Ōta Yōko asks, with regard to the impossibility of comprehending the atomic bombing of Hiroshima, in her testimonial *City of Corpses*: "How could everything in our vicinity have been so transformed in one instant? We hadn't the slightest idea. Perhaps it hadn't been an air raid. In my daze, I had a different idea: that it might have no connection to the war, that it might be something that occurs at the end of the world, when the globe disintegrates."[69] The extreme punctuality and instantaneousness of the destruction of Hiroshima at seventeen seconds after 8:15 in the morning on August 6, 1945, could not have been derived in any way from prior reality, for it radically contravened all historical, linguistic, and existential experience. Rather than resorting to clichés to describe the atomic bombing, she begins with a recognition of the utter disjunction between experience and comprehension caused by the modernist event.[70]

In arguing that the accounts of the aerial bombing of Germany given by eyewitnesses are "of only qualified value" and need to be supplemented by a "synoptic and artificial view," Sebald is proposing that this specific, largely repressed part of German history might be elucidated by the encompassing perspectives offered by those *without* direct memories of the experience and the representational practices of fiction. In other words, literature—particularly the techniques of literary modernism—might contribute to our understanding of history and the representation of the modernist event, even though—or precisely because—literature is fictional.[71] As he says in his reflections on the lectures, "I do not doubt that there were and are memories of those nights of destruction; I simply do not trust the form—including the literary form—in which they are expressed, and I do not believe they were a significant factor in the public consciousness of the new Federal Republic in any sense except as encouraging the will to reconstruction" (*Destruction* 81).

Because the history of the air war has essentially been banished from collective German memory and, when it is mentioned, invoked in an instrumental fashion as the impetus behind the "economic miracle" of the 1950s, Sebald sees new and necessary possibilities for expression and representation in literature written by those without direct memories of the catastrophe. These forms of expression must not, however, try to pass themselves off as something that they can never be, namely, authentic voices or literal representations of what happened: To do so would be, as White has argued, to fall back into the naively realist modes of representation characteristic of nineteenth century history writing. "How," then, Sebald asks, "ought a natural history of destruction to begin?" (*Destruction* 33). His answer, it seems, would be to begin with a form of emplotment that recognizes the contingency of encountering and narrating what remains of the past in the present. Although his own life only touches the history of the air war at a few insignificant, perhaps even random points, these encounters with the remains of the past form the beginnings of a narrative, one that takes its point of departure in the history of the present. As Sebald writes, he does not need to return to Germany "to make present [*vergegenwärtigen*] the period of destruction." Instead,

> It is often called to mind [*in Erinnerung gerufen*, literally, "called to remembering"] where I live now. Many of the seventy airfields from which the war of annihilation was waged against Germany were in the county of Norfolk. Some ten of them are still military bases, and a few others are now used by flying clubs, but most were abandoned after the war. Grass has grown over the runways, and the dilapidated control towers, bunkers, and corrugated iron huts stand in an often eerie landscape where you sense the dead souls of men who never came back from their missions, and of those who perished in the vast fires. I live very close to Seething airfield. I sometimes walk my dog there, and imagine what the place was like when aircraft took off with their heavy freight and flew out over the sea, making for Germany. Two years before these flights began, a Luftwaffe Dornier plane crashed in a field not far from my house during a raid on Norwich. One of the four crew members who lost their lives, Lieutenant Bollert, shared a birthday with me and was the same age as my father.   (*Destruction* 77–78)[72]

To be sure, as he clearly acknowledges, these points of connection are "entirely insignificant in themselves" (*Destruction* 78); however, they do form the basis of an encounter with the past, which is mediated, as Hirsch argues, through imaginative investment and is experienced, I would add, in the contingency of the present. How then might a modernist form of narration be derived from this layered history of the present? Or, to put it in Benjamin's language, what would this history look like as an image, as a dialectic at a standstill, "wherein what has been comes together in a flash with the now to form a constellation" (AP 462)?

Rather than attempting to imagine an exterior point of view from which to observe and describe the catastrophe, something that would ostensibly make sense for someone who was not there, Sebald creates a narrative form in which the narrator is connected to the catastrophe through its remains in the present and inside the processes of describing through the very artificiality and contingency of his limited perspective. Such a form of narration does not create a spectator (or the effect of a spectator) who observes a catastrophe from the sidelines and attempts to recount what happened from an outside, objective, or transcendental perspective. Citing Hans Blumenberg's *Shipwreck with Spectator* directly, Sebald sees the "emphatic configuration in which shipwreck at sea is set beside the uninvolved spectator on dry land"[73] as a fundamentally flawed epistemological and ethical stance. In other words, unlike traditional realist modes of representation, we cannot describe the experience of the catastrophe from the safety of external spectatorship. With regard to this desire to observe the catastrophic from the safety of distance and solid ground, Sebald says: "It is certainly a question of one of the fundamental conditions of artistic work itself: that one stands on the edge of the catastrophe, looking and reporting how it is, how it was. It is obvious that this results in a certain moral problematic for the author or spectator. In this constellation, one warms one's hands on the misfortune of others, one somehow feels happy—although this would never be confessed—that one was not there."[74] The catastrophe cannot simply be experienced and represented from the inviolable position of terra firma. Unlike Goethe's fantasy, as we saw in chapter 3, to stand on a solid cliff, safe and sound, and "let the furious tumult pass [him] by," Sebald refuses this exteriority of the bystander: Spectatorship from a distance always places the subject on dubious moral and epistemological grounds, benefiting from the misfortune of others if only by the recognition that the spectator is not involved.

To see how Sebald turns this conviction into a representational practice, I would now like to examine what I consider to be Sebald's most compelling work, *Austerlitz*, starting with his construction of the perspective of the German narrator. The novel begins with this unnamed narrator telling about one of his trips from England to Belgium during the 1960s. On one such trip he met a man named Austerlitz in Antwerp's Centraal train station's Salle des pas perdus who, at the time, reminded him of the German hero Siegfried in Fritz Lang's *Nibelungen* film. It quickly becomes clear that the narrator is describing an encounter from the past, one constituted by a complex history of documents, photographs, memories, and stories later assembled and reworked by the narrator some thirty years later. When they first met in 1967, the narrator later conveys to us, Austerlitz was a lecturer from a university in London, working on a comparative architectural history of the capitalist era, what was to be a study of "the compulsive sense of order and the tendency towards monumentalism evident in law courts and penal institutions, railway stations and stock exchanges, opera houses and lunatic asylums, and the dwellings built to rectangular grid patterns for the labor force" (33). The Belgian railway station where they met, with its "great domed hall" and "mighty clock" with six-foot hands, was erected, Austerlitz tells the narrator, by King Leopold as an emblem of "inexorable progress" and the world-historical dominance of the Belgian colonial enterprise (8–9). Mobility is, once again, revealed in its dialectical complexity, the emblem of progress and domination, of freedom and enslavement.

The "family likeness" of the railway station leads Austerlitz to the history of the fortification: "it is often our mightiest projects that most obviously betray the degree of our insecurity" (14), he says. He mentions the fortress of Breendonk, a gigantic cement structure completed shortly before the outbreak of World War I. The structure lies halfway between Antwerp and Brussels and was used by the German SS between 1940 and August 1944 as a reception and penal camp (19). The reader learns about the history of the fortification during the Second World War through several photographs of the structure, ground plans, and the conversation between the narrator and Austerlitz. Upon visiting the fort of Breendonk, a decision motivated solely, he says, by Austerlitz's chance mentioning of it the previous evening, the narrator's perceptions mix with his relatively idyllic memories of his childhood: "As I stared at the smooth, gray floor of this pit, which seemed to me to be sinking further and further, the grating over the drain in the middle of it and the metal pail standing beside the drain, a picture of our laundry room at home in W. rose from the abyss and with it, suggested perhaps by the iron hook hanging on a cord from the ceiling, the image of the butcher's shop I always had to pass on my way to school" (25). The narrator continues by adding that he could only guess "at the kind of third-degree interrogations which were being conducted here around the time I was born, since it was only a few years later that I read Jean Améry's description of the dreadful physical closeness between torturers and their victims, and of the tortures that he himself suffered in Breendonk" (26).

In this scene Sebald mixes fact and fiction, autobiography and literature, and photography and narrative to create a space of terra infirma that destabilizes both memory and spectatorship. Within the parameters of the novel the narrator's own memories are layered like Freudian screen memories:

memories from a later period (his reading of Améry's memoirs) are amalgamated with earlier memories in 1967, which in turn are mixed with childhood memories in Germany, as if they were formed in 1944, when Améry was tortured, and all these are narrated together from the perspective of the late 1990s. However, far from falsifying memory or somehow contesting historical truth, Sebald's prose opens up a new space for both the evocation of memory and the practice of history through literature. Through the "artificial" and the "synoptic" perspective of literature, he creates a narrative space for a history of the present in which the modernity of the German/Jewish encounter comes to the foreground.

Although it should not be simply assumed that the German narrator represents the author himself, there are, as in his other novels, especially *The Emigrants*, a number of important parallels that bear upon Sebald's conception of narrating catastrophic history. Like Sebald, the narrator in *Austerlitz* was born in Germany around 1944 and grew up in the provincial town of W. (Sebald's birthplace is Wertach), where he stayed until the age of twenty when he left Germany to study in England. Austerlitz, a Jew who was sent by his mother from Prague in 1939 to safety in England, is about ten years older than the narrator. The story that Sebald writes is that of a German/Jewish encounter, the tale of the German narrator conveying his understanding of Austerlitz's search for his destroyed family history. From the perspective of Austerlitz, the novel is the story of a recovered memory and the struggle to find traces of his past in the present. From the perspective of the narrator, it is a story of postmemory, mediated by imaginative investment and creation. But, unlike a simple German-Jewish symbiosis, the encounters between Austerlitz and the narrator occur in what Andreas Huyssen has aptly called "a gray zone of identification and transference that allows for a reciprocal mimetic approximation without blurring the distinction between German narrator and Jewish protagonist."[75]

While the identities of the German narrator and the Jewish protagonist never blur together, Austerlitz and the narrator need each other in fundamental ways. In fact, the story only exists because of their connection with one another, and, hence, their pasts become inextricably bound up in the contingent space of the present. As Austerlitz conveyed to the narrator and as the narrator conveys to the reader immediately before recounting his story: "he [Austerlitz] must find someone to whom he could relate his own story, a story which he had learned only in the last few years and for which he needed the kind of listener I [the narrator] had once been in Antwerp, Liège, and Zeebrugge" (43–44). Austerlitz's story not only needed a listener, but it also needed someone to record it, to arrange the thoughts, experiences, and photographs into a narrative. The narrator takes on this tremendous task: "I sat until almost three in the morning at a secretaire faintly illuminated by the street lighting—the cast-iron radiator clicked quietly, and only occasionally did a black cab drive past outside in Liverpool street—writing down, in the form of notes and disconnected sentences, as much as possible of what Austerlitz had told me that evening" (97). Austerlitz's story exists precisely because the narrator preserved it by listening to it and writing it down. In so doing, Sebald has essentially created a novel that takes the modernity of the German/Jewish dialectic as both its historical content and its organizational principle.

But the narrator, like Sebald himself, never "owns" the memories and experiences of the Jewish protagonist. Instead they become grafted onto his own by the way in which he receives them as he listens to Austerlitz's story and encounters them in the physical remains of the past. Indeed, the narrator does not share any of these "direct experiences"—and this is precisely the point. He was not at Fort Breendonk in 1944 and did not personally experience the torture suffered by someone like Améry. There is a fundamental gap between what the narrator experienced upon visiting the fort in 1967 (and subsequently remembering and organizing this experience into a narrative of words and pictures) and what Améry experienced in 1944.[76] Sebald in no way wants to overcome or sublate this experiential and historical gap and, for this reason, he forgoes all attempts at representing or recreating the past of 1944 as it really was or might have been. Instead his concern is with the present, with what people born after the catastrophe know of what happened, how they gain knowledge of the catastrophe, what sorts of memories they create about it, and what kind of relationships they have to it—in other words, how they encounter, recall, and narrate the remains of the catastrophic past in the present. This is the critical role and perhaps even the ethical obligation of Sebald's German narrator.

It is not that Sebald's works simply blur the boundaries between fact and fiction, history and literature, autobiography and biography, German and Jewish; the very form of narration is itself marked by an inexpungeable uncertainty: the experiences of the past might be lost; the story might not be right; the narrator might have forgotten to write down vital pieces or lost crucial photographs. But, even more important, the narrator in the present cannot replicate the reality of the past in an authoritative or definitive sense. As Sebald explained in an interview:

> [This] whole process of narrating something which has a kind of reas-suring quality to it is called into question. That uncertainty which the narrator has about his own trade is then, I hope, imparted to the reader who will, or ought to, feel a similar sense of irritation about these mat-ters. I think that fiction writing, which does not acknowledge the un-certainty of the narrator himself, is a form of imposture and which I find very, very difficult to take. Any form of authorial writing, where the narrator sets himself up as stagehand and director and judge and executor in a text, I find somehow unacceptable.[77]

At the same time, this uncertainty of the narrator and the generic status of the text never question the historical truth of the Holocaust; instead Se-bald consciously draws our attention to the fundamental limits of narrative to capture the past. *Austerlitz* is a history of the present told from the arti-ficial and synoptic perspective of contingent encounters with what remains of the Holocaust. For this reason Sebald's prose is very different from that of Holocaust survivors. In a critical essay on the work of Améry,[78] for exam-ple, Sebald insists that Améry's writing represents one of "the few authentic voices" on the Holocaust (*Destruction* 145) because it is literally "based on the most ponderous insights into the irreparable condition of the victims, and that it is from such insights alone that the true nature of the terror visited on them can be extrapolated with some precision" (*Destruction* 147; translation modified). Here Sebald applauds the realism and authenticity of Améry's memoir but will himself never transgress this limit and pre-sume to represent what Améry or any other victim experienced, felt, or observed. This is because Sebald's realism is concerned with something else: he is not attempting to represent accurately the reality of the past but rather to create a reality effect of the present in all its uncertainty and contin-gency. Significantly, when the narrator in *Austerlitz* sees the iron hook upon which Améry was hoisted by his arms tied behind his back, it reminds him of the butcher in his hometown. This is not a flippant association but an acknowledgment of the limits of both knowability and narrative strategy: Sebald refuses to restage, reproduce, or represent Amèry's or any victim's suffering realistically. Not even Améry can describe the pain inflicted on his body, because those feelings "mark the limit of the capacity of language to communicate. If someone wanted to impart this physical pain, he would be forced to inflict it and thereby become a torturer himself."[79] While Améry conveys, with the most objective sobriety, the truth of the torture he experienced, Sebald's writing begins with what it means today—in the space of the present—to read Améry's testimony, to visit Fort Breendonk, to look at photographs from the 1930s and early 1940s, and to walk among the remains of concentration camps and other places of torture. In so doing, he rejects the historicist injunction of authoritatively reenacting the extremity of the past in favor of a modernist staging of what remains in the present.

In this respect, *Austerlitz* could be read as a history of the present, intimately connected to and motivated by the uncertainty and contingency of the German/Jewish remains of the catastrophic past. For Sebald these remains range from material objects such as photographs, railway stations, bunkers, concentration camps, gravestones, and the objects of everyday life such as bowls and vases to the remains of language, memories, individual stories, words, letters, numbers, and, as with Austerlitz, encounters with victims. Although they may appear to subsist outside of or cut off from time, remains are deeply wed to a given present, bound to a moment of legibility and recognizability, which at any minute could disappear. To recall Benjamin's postulation, *the Abfall der Geschichte*—the remains or trash of history—is "bound to a time-kernel [*Zeitkern*]" because remains do not simply belong to the past or subsist as unchanged in the present; they enter into and out of legibility at a specific time, under particular circumstances in the present.[80] Far from having a claim to some kind of transcendental presence, architecture and literature will also, one day, be nothing more than remains.

Within Sebald's novels the photographs are arguably the most precarious of remains. Their truth or falsehood can never be adjudicated with any degree of certainty because the modernist narrative—a composite of text and image—has been divorced from its capability to literally reproduce the past while, seemingly paradoxically, extending our knowledge and memory of the past. Sometimes the photographs "gloss" the text, and sometimes they do not; sometimes the photographs offer testimony or historical evidence, and sometimes they do not; sometimes the photographs prove or ground reality, and sometimes they do not. But, in every case, the photographs attest to their own finitude. While they may appear to arrest the fugitive and the contingent, their intelligibility and materiality remain time bound, finite, and fleeting. Far from evoking permanence or transcendence, the photograph, as Roland Barthes argued in his famous reflections on photography, *Camera Lucida*, is quickly transformed into "refuse": "Not only does it commonly have the fate of paper (perishable), but even if it is attached to more lasting supports, it is still mortal: like a living organism, it is born on the level of the sprouting silver grains, it flourishes a moment, then ages. . . . Attacked by light, by humidity, it fades, weakens, vanishes."[81] Thus, while they appear to suspend time, photographs are marked by finitude and transience.

Unlike Barthes, who continues by suggesting that "there is nothing left to do but throw it away" when the photograph fades, Sebald believes that old photographs are closely bound with the very possibility of narrative and imagination:

> [They] have something spectral about them. It seems as if the people who appear in these pictures are kind of fuzzy on the edges, very much like ghosts which you may encounter in any of those streets out there. . . . It's less the sense of nostalgia but that there is something utterly mysterious in old photographs, that they are almost designed to be lost, they're in an album which vanishes in an attic or in a box, and if they come to light they do accidentally, you stumble upon them. The way in which these stray pictures cross your paths, it has something at once totally coincidental and fateful about it. Then of course you begin to puzzle over them, and it's from that that much of the desire to write about them comes.[82]

Photographs are found objects, remains of a past, that cannot be identified with certainty but impel the desire to tell their story. As he adds in another interview: "It has always struck me that these photographs make a monstrous appeal, a demand on the observer to narrate or imagine what one could narrate proceeding from these pictures [*was man, von diesen Bildern ausgehend, erzählen könnte*]."[83] Photography is not just about the narration of a story but about the very possibility of narrative, about what one *could* narrate. As a modernist form of emplotment, we might see these impulses as overlapping in Sebald's prose: photography demands the possibility of narrative, and narrative demands the possibility of photography.

Sebald's understanding of photography as the possibility of narrative is thus an adamant rejection of the historicist's belief in the unbleached recovery of the past as something that can be attained like the so-called objectivity or literalness of a photograph. As Sebald writes in *Austerlitz* about the inability to recreate the fullness of the past: "We try to reproduce the reality, but the harder we try, the more we find the pictures that make up the stock-in-trade of the spectacle of history forcing themselves upon us: the fallen drummer boy, the infantryman shown in the act of stabbing another, the horse's eye starting from its socket, the invulnerable Emperor surrounded by his generals, a moment frozen still amidst the turmoil of battle. Our concern with history [*Geschichte*] . . . is a concern with pre-formed images [*Bilder*] already imprinted on our brains" (71–72).[84] Here Sebald is explicitly glossing one of Benjamin's central ideas of historical materialism, namely, the injunction that "history breaks down into images, not into stories" ("Geschichte zerfällt in Bilder nicht in Geschichten"; AP 476; translation modified). In this aphorism Benjamin plays off the double meaning of *Geschichte* as both history (in the sense of what happened) and story (in the sense of *Historie* or the narrative of history)[85] in order to make the point that "what happened" (*die Geschichte* or *das Geschehen*) does not correspond to its narrative rendition; rather history breaks down into constellations of images. It is the task of the historical materialist to arrange these images into a montage or a composition of word and image, as Sebald does, and thereby produce an explosive tension between a given past and a given present.

Photography, as Eduardo Cadava has argued in his "theses on the photography of history," is uniquely suited to arresting the flow of history and turning it from a temporal continuum into a spatial constellation: "Within this condensation of past and present, time is no longer to be understood as continuous and linear, but rather as spatial, an imagistic space that Benjamin calls a 'constellation' or a 'monad.' . . . It interrupts history and opens up another possibility of history, one that spaces time and temporalizes space."[86] Writing history, then, does not mean to represent the presence of the past as a kind of narrative rehabilitation; instead the historical articulation of the past means the seizure of an image in a moment of interruption, danger, and standstill.

It is in this sense that Sebald refuses to represent the reality of the past as a singular narrative. While looking for the traces of his murdered mother in the town of Terezín, Austerlitz discovers an "Antikos Bazar" with hundreds of seemingly frozen objects on display in a storefront window. In an extraordinary set of three photographs the small objects of everyday life, replete with intricate details, come back to life in the present and are rescued for a moment of recognizability. Austerlitz, as relayed by the narrator, wonders:

7.6 © W. G. Sebald, *Austerlitz*, trans. Anthea Bell (Hamish Hamilton, 2001), 194–95. *Reproduced by permission of Penguin Books Ltd.*

7.7 © W. G. Sebald, *Austerlitz*, trans. Anthea Bell (Hamish Hamilton, 2001), 196. *Reproduced by permission of Penguin Books Ltd.*

7.8 © W. G. Sebald, *Austerlitz*, trans. Anthea Bell (Hamish Hamilton, 2001), 197. *Reproduced by permission of Penguin Books Ltd.*

What secret lay behind the three brass mortars of different sizes, which had about them the suggestion of an oracular utterance, or the cut-glass bowls, ceramic vases, and earthen-ware jugs, the tin advertising sign bearing the words *Theresienstädter Wasser* ... the outsize Russian officer's cap and the olive-green uniform tunic with gilt epaulettes that went with it, the fishing rod, the hunter's bag, the Japanese fan, the end-less landscape painted round a lampshade in fine brushstrokes, show-ing a river running quietly through perhaps Bohemia or perhaps Bra-zil? ... They were all as timeless as that moment of rescue, perpetuated but forever just occurring, these ornaments, utensils, and mementoes stranded in the Terezín bazaar, objects that for reasons one could never know had outlived their former owners and survived the process of destruction, so that I could now see my own faint shadow image barely perceptible among them.   (195–97)

The remains of history appeared timeless not in the sense of eternal preser-vation or permanent knowledge but in the sense of being without time pre-cisely because they are recursive, like the river in some unknown landscape that flows back onto itself. These objects have become detached or dislo-cated from time by surviving their former owners and temporarily flouting destruction, something that is conveyed to the reader through their pho-tographic doubling. Perhaps these objects belonged to Jews who were in-terned and killed in Terezín, perhaps they belonged to the perpetrators who left them behind, or perhaps they preceded the Holocaust entirely. If they are rescued from oblivion, it is not a permanent salvation or an endowment of knowledge but a momentary one, contingent upon the curiosities, inter-ests, desires, and wishes of the present. That Austerlitz's (or Sebald's) face is barely visible in the reflection off the glass as he raises his camera to his face in the third picture is thus highly significant. The remains of the past are never finally "saved" or "stored" but rather encountered and recognized—if at all—in the temporality and subjectivity of the present.[87]

The reader of Sebald's prose encounters these remains of the past as pho-tographic reproductions with an uncertain status: one might wonder wheth-er these objects were actually found in the town of Terezín, when these pho-tographs were taken, or if they were taken by Sebald himself. These kinds of questions, however, are of only secondary importance. What matters is the possibility of narrative—what one could narrate from these pictures—and the imaginative investment of these images for history and memory in the present. As Sebald explained with respect to the photographs in his work: "[They have] a very real nucleus and around this nucleus is a gigantic space of nothingness. One does not know the context in which a person [in a photograph] is standing, what kind of landscape it is. . . . One must begin to think hypothetically. . . . One recognizes possibilities in writing, to proceed in a narrative fashion from the pictures, to enter into pictures by way of narrative."[88] It is in this gigantic space of nothingness that Sebald finds the possibility of narration. The story that emerges, like the photograph that is taken, cannot be adjudicated on a true/false spectrum stretching from uncontested factuality to outright fabrication. It partakes in both and, in so doing, extends historical knowledge through its representation of and engagement with the desires, anxieties, hopes, and claims of the present.

At the same time that Austerlitz is haunted by the presence of material remains, he entertains a wish for complete preservation, an almost Freudian wish to be, in his words, "outside time" (101). While visiting the Royal Observatory in Greenwich, the historical origin of the temporal organization of the modern world, Austerlitz conveys a wish for nothing to pass away:

> I have always resisted the power of time out of some internal compulsion which I myself have never understood, keeping myself apart from so-called current events in the hope, as I now think, said Austerlitz, that time will not pass away, has not passed away, that I can turn back and go behind it, and *there I shall find everything as it once was, or more precisely I shall find that all moments of time have co-existed simultaneously*, in which case none of what history tells us would be true, past events have not yet occurred but are waiting to do so at the moment when we think of them, although that, of course, opens up the bleak prospect of everlasting misery and neverending anguish.   (101; my emphasis)

Not unlike Freud's metaphor of the simultaneous existence of Rome's layered histories in which "nothing has passed away," Austerlitz desires to halt the flow of time, to go behind it in order to "find everything as it once was." Whereas the historicist fantasy presumes to be able to reconstruct the past as it really was by eliminating all difference and distance between what happened and its subsequent representation, Sebald, through his conception of the relationship between the modernist event and modernist narration, and Freud, through his conception of the relationship between the unconscious and memory, insist upon an insurmountable difference between what happened and the representation of the past, between the atemporality of complete preservation and the temporality of remains, whether memories, dreams, photographs, or objects. The incompleteness and tentativeness of the latter never replicates the fullness of the former. In other words, the fantasy of complete preservation does not indicate how close we are to the past but how far we remain. Rather than reproducing or replicating the fullness or truth of the past, memory and history—by virtue of their mobility, openness, and uncertainty—can only deliver us over to interpretations and remains.

As Amir Eshel has pointed out in his astute analysis of the "poetics of suspension" in *Austerlitz*, Sebald's choice to stage this monologue against time at the Royal Observatory in Greenwich was hardly coincidental.[89] After all, it was at the end of the nineteenth century that Greenwich was chosen as the zero meridian for the purpose of dividing the earth into twenty-four time zones, establishing the precise length of the day, and standardizing time across the globe: Greenwich effectively represented a locus of modernity.[90] As we have already seen, the exigencies of world industrialization demanded a uniform coordination of the many heterogeneous local times in order to facilitate worldwide communication and schedule train transportation. As Germany's most famous proponent of standard time, Helmuth von Moltke, argued in his last speech delivered before the Prussian House of Lords in 1891, the maintenance of the multiplicity of local time zones would only continue to impede strategic military planning.[91]

Just a few years later, the world-historical significance of Greenwich—the symbol of an ever expanding, outwardly realized modernity—was recognized during the evening of February 15, 1894, when a young anarchist named Martial Bourdin set off a bomb on the hill leading up to the Royal Observatory. The idea was to blow up the Greenwich observatory; instead the bomb killed him. "The Greenwich Bomb Outrage," as it was later dubbed around the world, was much more than an isolated anarchist act. It was the repudiation of a decidedly modern organization of time, with all its economic, social, political, and technological consequences, whereby experience and expectation were progressively and reliably linked to one another via what Reinhart Koselleck, calls "a temporal coefficient of change."[92] The symbol of world standard, new time was to be blown up; that is to say, modernity was quite literally to be killed, ended.[93]

The institution and destruction of world standard time represents a critical aspect of Sebald's articulation of the dialectic of modernity: The promise of world standard time was, on the one hand, the hope of global

communication and unity and, on the other hand, the horror of coordinated destruction and disunity achieved on a global scale. Standardized
timetables for railway travel not only facilitated an unprecedented mobility and emancipatory freedom but, as von Moltke predicted, also enabled
an unprecedented expansion of military power and means of subjugation
and oppression. Like Benjamin, Sebald distills the dialectical history of
modernity as a problem of mobility. In responding to what he regards as
the catastrophic, Sebald said: "One of the fundamental principles that has
to do with migration, immigration and emigration and all these things, is
mobility [*die Mobilität*], which, from an economical-technical perspective,
seemed to be something positive. Now it turns, like every phenomenon, on
a dialectical point and becomes catastrophic."[94] Indeed, *Austerlitz* might be
understood as an extended meditation on the relationship between memory, mobility, and the possibilities of narrating the German/Jewish dialectic
of modernity.

In the novel the railway system, the embodiment of Austerlitz's "early
fascination with the idea of the network" (33), represents the material instantiation of this dialectic of modernity—the progressive hopes of German national unification in the early nineteenth century and the means
for deporting and destroying the Jews of Europe in the mid twentieth. In
its remains the futures past—that is to say, the dreams and horrors of modernization—are still legible.[95] As Benjamin famously suggested in the *Arcades Project,* historical materialists study an epoch by looking at the ways
in which the hopes, desires, dreams, and fears generated by the epoch lay
buried in its leftover remains. These remains—from architectural achievements to literary forms, from works of art to cultural ephemera—offer up
the "physiognomy" of the epoch from the perspective of the contingency of
the present. For Benjamin the outmoded "passage" or arcade represented
the quintessential material witness of the physiognomy of nineteenth century Paris; for Sebald the railway would have to be the material witness of
the physiognomy of the twentieth. Both the passage and the railway are material witnesses to bygone epochs, the embodiments of a dialectic of dream
and terror; at the same time, they are also figures for the finitude of any
kind of historical practice.

It is no coincidence that the very first conversation between the narrator
and Austerlitz begins in the Salle des pas perdus in the Centraal Station of
Antwerp, and their final conversation ends with "the most mysterious of all
the railway terminals of Paris" (292), the gare d'Austerlitz, a train station

dedicated to the memory of Napoleon's victory over the Austrian Empire in 1805. The first station, inspired by the Lucerne train station in Switzerland, was the embodiment of the nineteenth century hopes of material progress, speed, and the secularized totality of religious dreams: "When we step into the entrance hall we are seized by a sense of being beyond the profane, in a cathedral consecrated to international traffic and trade. . . . In Antwerp Station the elevated level from which the gods looked down on visitors to the Roman Pantheon should display, in hierarchical order, the deities of the nineteenth century—mining, industry, transport, trade, and capital" (10–12). Railway construction was essentially the religion of modernity, an observation that resonates closely with Benjamin's material history of nineteenth century Paris. As he quotes the Saint-Simonian Michel Chevalier, "If it is true, as we hear, that the word 'religion' comes from *religare*, 'to bind' . . ., then the railroads have more to do with the religious spirit than one might suppose. There has never existed a more powerful instrument for . . . rallying the scattered populations."[96]

For Sebald the dialectical underbelly of this religious zeal to unite and rally the scattered populations is the mass exodus and mass deportations of the Jews of Europe, paradigmatically represented by Austerlitz's arrival in Liverpool on a *Kindertransport* and, at the novel's conclusion, the overdetermined gare d'Austerlitz. Sebald reveals a part of the layered space of the British train station through the fact that it was built upon a former cemetery uncovered by archaeologists in 1984 during a round of demolition work. In the novel, images of the calcified dead are critically juxtaposed by Sebald with images of the railway lines that "on the engineers' plans [look] like muscles and sinews in an anatomical atlas" (132). For Austerlitz these embodied images of construction and destruction, sedimented in the layers of the railway station, confirm the dialectic of modernity, which for him, is a "vision of imprisonment and liberation" (135). Once again history (*Geschichte*) not only breaks down into images but is endowed with a specific spatiality—as in *Schichten* or layers, which are impacted, as remains or trash, in the space of the present. It is in these layers that the dialectic of modernity can be recognized, if only for a fleeting moment in a kernel of time.

In describing the gare d'Austerlitz, Sebald converts its chronological history into a space of simultaneity by revealing the layered topographies around the train station "superimposed on each other to form the carapace of the city" (288): The new library building of the Bibliothèque Nationale intersects with the railway yards of the train station, which intersects with the warehousing complex erected by the SS to stockpile goods looted from Jewish homes during the 1940s:

> On the waste land [*Ödland*] between the marshaling yard of the gare d'Austerlitz and the pont de Tolbiac where this Babylonian library now rises, there stood until the end of the war an extensive warehousing complex to which the Germans brought all the loot they had taken from the homes of the Jews of Paris. I believe they cleared some forty thousands apartments at that time, said Lemoine [the librarian at the Bibliothèque Nationale], in an operation lasting months, for which purpose they requisitioned the entire pantechnicon fleet of the Paris Union of Furniture Removers, and an army of no fewer than fifteen hundred removal men was brought into action. . . . In the years from 1942 onwards everything that our civilization has produced, whether for the embellishment of life or merely for everyday use, from Louis XVI chests of drawers, Meissen porcelain, Persian rugs and whole libraries, down to the last saltcellar and pepper mill, was stacked there in the Austerlitz-Tolbiac storage depot. . . . No one will now admit to knowing where [the objects] went, for the fact is that the whole affair is buried in the most literal sense beneath the foundations of our pharaonic President's Grande Bibliothèque.   (288–89)

This station, from which Austerlitz imagines his father being deported, was also used to collect, organize, and redistribute the material belongings of Jews sent to concentration camps. Its history is hidden in the layered topographies of the city that Sebald dissects through his emplotment of Austerlitz's story.

At no point, however, does Sebald reveal the "truth" of the gare d'Austerlitz by unpacking and organizing the layers of its buried pasts into a realist history. Instead he creates a narrative form in which the German/Jewish layers of history exist simultaneously and are pulled apart for a moment of visibility and then are quickly dissolved again into their ultimate unknowability. Within this complex of simultaneous histories Sebald presents three photographs: the first a snapshot of the view from the promenade deck of the Bibliothèque Nationale; the second a reproduction of a photograph from an American architecture journal found in the reading room of the library depicting the records room of Terezín, where the files on all the prisoners are still kept today; and the third an eerily still picture of the interior of the

7.9 (*left*) © W. G. Sebald, *Austerlitz*, trans. Anthea Bell (Hamish Hamilton, 2001), 279. *Reproduced by permission of Penguin Books Ltd.*

7.10 (*above*) © W. G. Sebald, *Austerlitz*, trans. Anthea Bell (Hamish Hamilton, 2001), 284-85. *Reproduced by permission of Penguin Books Ltd.*

7.11 © W. G. Sebald, *Austerlitz*, trans. Anthea Bell (Hamish Hamilton, 2001), 290-91. *Reproduced by permission of Penguin Books Ltd.*

gare d'Austerlitz. As palimpsests of one another the photographs might be seen as the possibility of simultaneous narration, and, at the same time, simultaneous narration might be seen as the possibility of photography. The photographs, like the narrative, cannot be resolved into a linear, historical chronology; instead, through their "real nucleus" surrounded by a "gigantic space of nothingness," they evoke simultaneous possibilities. Through intersections and cuts that fold back on themselves, the narrative moves almost all at once between Austerlitz's search for traces of his father, the archives at the Bibliothèque Nationale, the building's massive expansion, the land around the gare d'Austerlitz and its horrific history, Austerlitz's present vision of his father being sent away on a transport, the off-hand remark to the narrator that "part of the railway network had been paralyzed by a strike last Wednesday" (291), the narrator's own memory of Austerlitz's story, and the recounting of this story, perhaps with the narrator's own selection of photographs, to the reader.

Sebald once described this decidedly modernist technique of narration as "periscopic writing," something that he attributed to the Austrian writer Thomas Bernhard. He explains: "Everything that the narrator relates is mediated through sometimes one or two other stages, which makes for quite complicated syntactical labyrinthine structures and in one sense exonerates the narrator, because he never pretends that he knows more than is actually possible."[97] In his prose the narrator is divested of a position of certainty and exterior knowledge. Since he is not a spectator of the catastrophe, he cannot arrange the past according to any kind of objective chronology of what happened; instead he is placed within the processes of narration, which are themselves mediated by a multiplicity of German/Jewish encounters as well as refracted through the stratified remains of the past in the present. Not unlike the modernism of Freud's dream interpretation, the past, according to Sebald, can never be represented in its wholeness or endowed with a stability that can be passed down from one generation to another, as if it were a kind of ontological totality. Instead the artificial closures, the narrative ruptures, the simultaneous histories, the periscopic narration, and the breakdown of the distinction between real and imaginary—in effect, modernist techniques of representation—offer up a history of the present from the standpoint of the contingency of what remains of the past. For both Freud and Sebald the railway system embodies the cultural metaphor, the material reality, and the modernist epistemology for conceptualizing a theory of memory and a practice of history. It is where Sebald tracks the dialectic of modernity, its emancipatory hopes and destructive nightmares. And it is on this *terra infirma* that Sebald and Freud extend what memory and historical knowledge can be.

In conclusion, Sebald's *Austerlitz* unlinks literature from the domain of the imaginary and unlinks history from the literal reproduction of the past. In the same way that Freud divorced memory from the factual recall of what happened, Sebald produces a narrative form, which divorces history from the factual replication of what happened. Sebald uses literature—in his particular modernist form of combining word and image, blurring the real and the imaginary, and dissecting, if only for a moment, the simultaneously layered remains of the German/Jewish past—to extend historical knowledge and interrogate what history is and can be. It is not that Sebald simply blurs the distinction between fact and fiction; he does this while using the fictive to contribute to the factual and thereby produce a new kind of historical knowledge whose meaning cannot be, in the final analysis, definitively adjudicated. At stake in his prose, then, is not simply the historical (*geschichtlich*) status of the Holocaust; rather it is the possibility of creating a new, imagistic narrative form (*Historie*) whose very existence is mediated by the entanglement of the German narrator and the Jewish protagonist, Freud's dream interpretation and Sebald's periscopic narration in the modernist geographies of the present.

CONCLUDING REMARKS

"Geography wrests history from the cult of necessity in order to stress the irreducibility of contingency."[1]

AT THE END of their last conversation the narrator recounts that Austerlitz decided to set off from Paris to find the remains of a camp in the Pyrenean foothills where his father may have been interned: "I don't know, said Austerlitz, what all this means, and so I am going to continue looking for my father" (292). Before departing, he invites the narrator to stay at his home in England for as long as he wishes as well as visit a small Ashkenazi cemetery he had just discovered behind a wall of the adjoining house. They take leave of each other at the Glacière Métro station. The story of their relationship ends at this moment, or, more precisely, starts at this moment since it is at this point that the narrator first begins to compose the story of Austerlitz telling the narrator the story of his life. Over the course of the years that go by, he is entrusted with Austerlitz's photographs, which, he thinks, "one day, would be all that was left of his life" (293). The narrator visits the Ashkenazi cemetery and sets off on his own journey to search for more traces of the violently vanished past. Once again the German narrator becomes geographically bound—in the contingent space of the present—to the remains of the Jewish past.

Sebald's novel takes the simultaneously progressive hopes and destructive nightmares of modernity, ingrained in the physiognomy of its railway ruins, as the starting and ending point for articulating the German/Jewish dialectic. In the same way that the material ruins of the Anhalter Bahnhof reveal a crystallization of modernity, the photographs of the empty railway station, the decomposing gravestones in the Ashkenazi cemetery, and the blurred image of the narrator's reflection in the shop window at Terezín represent a crystallization of the German/Jewish dialectic. Benjamin underscores the historiographic insight: "Indeed, to discover in the analysis of the small individual moment the crystal of the total event" (AP 461).

While navigating through and attempting to find an orientation in these ruins of modernity, the Jewish protagonist and the German narrator become inextricably bound to one another. After all, Austerlitz's story would not exist without the German narrator listening to it and writing it down;

without Austerlitz the German narrator would have no living connection to the remains of the past. But, rather than yielding a definitive history, a final resolution, or an ultimate symbiosis, the novel ends with both the fracture and the binding together of past and present, near and far, German and Jewish. And while their identities remain deeply connected to one another, even overlapping in certain places in the story, the narrator and Austerlitz are never simply combined together or elevated into a third, higher term; instead their relationship is left radically unresolved, in tension, at a kind of standstill. Celan once remarked in the notes he composed for his Meridian speech that *Gegenüber ist unaufhebbar* (that which stands across cannot be sublated),[2] a dictum that appositely describes the German/Jewish dialectic in Sebald's *Austerlitz*.

Sebald's novel can thus be considered part of a much longer and complicated problematic, in which German and Jewish are entangled with and fundamentally bound to one another. It is a problematic, I would suggest, that has only become visible (and viable) after a significant amount of time has elapsed to allow us to reject Scholem's famous encapsulation of German-Jewish history as an unrequited love affair and a dialogue that never took place. Now, instead of a failed dialogue and strict opposition, we can begin to recognize the complex constellations and dialectical images that comprise German/Jewish modernity. This is not a project of simply "reinserting" Jews into German history or demonstrating the significance of their various "contributions." Nor is it a revisionist history, which seeks to highlight the "good" Germans and downplay the "bad" Germans. Instead it is the articulation of a persistent problematic specific to the intellectual history of modernity: the encounter of German and Jewish in constructive, critical, and violent tension. The history of this tension betrays, emblematically, the possibilities and pitfalls of the dialectic of modernity.

To be sure, Sebald's novel is unique in the historiography that I lay out in this book insofar as it is constructed as the explicit rejection of Scholem's model of failed dialogue: *Austerlitz* is entirely a German/Jewish dialogue in which the German narrator listens to the Jewish protagonist, perceives him for what he is and what he represents, and responds to him.[3] The cultural geography that I mapped here was scarcely such a dialogue. However, the point, as I insisted earlier, is not "dialogue"—a criterion that is simply too narrow—but rather the multiplicity of expressions, encounters, and relationships, both constructive and destructive, between German and Jewish. In other words, the point is the possibility of reconceiving and reimagining the dialectical unity between German and Jewish, the complex ways in which the one adds to, enriches, and replaces the other.

In this regard, Hannah Arendt's formulation of "the Jew as Pariah"—written in 1944—is a much more helpful way of imagining the relationship between German and Jewish than Scholem's model of failed dialogue.[4] Although unabashedly essentializing in treating Jews as "a pariah people," she draws our attention to the creative and critical possibilities of being an outcast and thereby conceives of Jewishness as an attack on any sort of social and political hegemony. To be Jewish, for Arendt, has less to do with a particular religious or linguistic identity and more to do with a critical perspective, position, and point of view. As she explains, this perspective results in a "shifting of the accent, from this vehement protest on the part of the pariahs, from this attitude of denying the reality of the social order and of confronting it, instead, with a higher reality."[5] Her examples of Jewish pariahs include Heine, Kafka, Bernard Lazare, and Charlie Chaplin, the last of whom was not a Jew but "epitomized in an artistic form a character born of the Jewish pariah mentality."[6] We might even say that critical theory—a tradition that would include thinkers such as Benjamin, Adorno, and Arendt as well as Kafka and Heine—is not only Jewish in Arendt's sense but also—and perhaps more precisely—German/Jewish in the entangled sense that I argue for in this book. This is because the Jewish and the German, the German and the Jewish form, if only for a moment, a constellated image, a dialectic at a standstill, that allows us to reassess and reinterpret the culture from which they came.

This attention to entanglement demands a new approach to writing the intellectual history of German/Jewish modernity, an approach that recognizes the multiplicity of expressions and relationships between the two terms, particularly the ways in which they condition and move with respect to one another. To articulate this entanglement, I chose several moments in which the two terms come together to form a dialectic saturated with tension. Indeed there are many more such moments—one may think of Goethe/Varnhagen, Dohm/Mendelssohn, Bauer/Marx, Wagner/Schönberg, Rosenzweig/Heidegger, and others—and that is precisely the point: the German/Jewish dialectic has just recently begun to be mapped.[7] It is still a project of the future.

With the rejection of developmental or teleological models of history, the encounters between each of the thinkers are motivated by constellations of simultaneity or contiguity that were mapped onto the cultural geography of the railway system. One of the key consequences of this is that a new Germany and a new German emerges, one that is not bound to the geographic borders of the nation or even the linguistic territory of the *Kulturnation*. It finds its borders between Berlin and Delos, Sicily and New York City, the North Sea, Nuremberg-Fürth-Palestine, Auschwitz, and, finally, Vienna-Rome-Prague-Antwerp-Paris. And it finds its representation in the thought of those travelers, wanderers, exiles, insiders and outsiders such as Heidegger, Celan, Goethe, Kafka, Hegel, Heine, List, Herzl, Arendt, Sebald, Freud, and Benjamin. Chronology, necessity, and nationality have been replaced by spatiality, contingency, and mobility to yield a new cultural geography of German/Jewish modernity.

Not unlike the argument that Scott Spector produced in *Prague Territories*, a "deterritorialized" modernity comes into existence, one that is not slavishly derived from nationality but rather from spatiality, mobility, exchange, and encounter.[8] Spector's cultural history of fin-de-siècle Prague, indebted to the recent attention by social theorists to the production of space as a powerful discursive system and complex matrix of socially mediated and mediating relations, examines the ways in which culture is bound—materially and metaphorically—to the articulation of territory and space. As spatial counterpoints to Benjamin's temporal or historical terms, Spector's spatial constellations ("territorialization and flight, self and other, here and there") coincide to reveal a "middle Europe" as dialectics at a standstill.[9]

It is here that we may see another set of priorities, models, and questions emerging in German-Jewish studies, one that moves the field beyond the paradigms of trauma and memory studies that have positively defined its contours for the past two decades. Building on the work on Hess, Gordon, Hahn, Spector, and others, new research questions have begun to emerge that do not take the Holocaust as the *Urtext* for understanding and commemorating German-Jewish modernism. The goal of this book was to demonstrate the fundamental entanglement of German modernity and Jewish modernity without reducing the relationship to one of failed dialogue or negative symbiosis. To do so, I introduced the emerging field of mobility studies—the analysis of cultures in transit—to German-Jewish studies. Drawing on the insights of transnational literary studies and cultural geography, I sought to develop a model for writing cultural criticism in which the contingency of location, language, and transmission comes to the forefront of the analyses.[10] Rather than writing a traditional cultural history organized by the linearity of chronology and culminating in the negativity of the Holocaust, I have produced a broader account of modernity that focuses on the complex dialectics of mobility and the material spaces of exchange between German and Jewish. Complementing the recent work in transnational cultural studies and inspired by a Benjaminian approach to historiography, the result is a constellated cultural geography derived from the figure par excellence of German/Jewish modernity: the Jew on a train.

NOTES

1. Dialectics at a Standstill

1. Walter Benjamin, *Berliner Kindheit um Neunzehnhundert* (Frankfurt: Suhrkamp, 1992), 94. All translations are my own unless otherwise stated.

2. Among other places, Derrida tracks the operations of the separatrix (*le trait*) in *Of Grammatology*, trans. Gayatri Chakravorty Spivak (Baltimore: Johns Hopkins University Press, 1974), and *Dissemination*, trans. Barbara Johnson (Chicago: University of Chicago Press, 1981). For a good overview of the operations of the separatrix, see Jeffrey Kipnis, "Twisting the Separatrix," *Assemblage* 14 (1991), 31–61.

3. Kipnis, "Twisting the Separatrix," 32.

4. A transcription of the talk, "Rede über die jiddische Sprache" (Speech on the Yiddish language), is reprinted in Franz Kafka, *Gesammelte Werke*, ed. Max Brod (New York: Schocken, 1953), 421–26. All quotations will be documented parenthetically as Y followed by the page number. With regard to the genesis of the speech, Kafka writes in his diaries that he received a card from Oskar Baum asking him to give a "talk at the evening for the Eastern Jews" on February 18, 1912. In his diaries he notes that he "was overpowered by uncontrollable twitchings, the pulsing of my arteries sprang along my body like flames," but he reassures himself: "I shall, of course, give a good lecture, that is certain, besides, the restlessness itself, heightened to an extreme on that evening, will pull me together in such a way that there will not be room for restlessness and the talk will come straight out of me as though out of a gun barrel." *Diaries, 1910–1923*, ed. Max Brod (New York: Schocken, 1976), 179–80. For a discussion of Kafka "talking on Yiddish," see Noah Isenberg, *Between Redemption and Doom: The Strains of German-Jewish Modernism* (Lincoln: University of Nebraska, 1999), 42–50.

5. Four years earlier, in 1908, the first international conference on the Yiddish language took place in Czernowitz. In addition to resolving Yiddish to be "a national language of the Jews," the conference sought to address the standardization of Yiddish, including grammar, spelling, the entry of foreign words and new words into the language, and the establishment of a Yiddish dictionary. Although Kafka may have been right when he declared that Yiddish had no grammatical structure and that it consisted entirely of foreign words, the movement to standardize the language had already begun.

6. With regard to the fear of Yiddish by German speakers, Giuliano Baioni argues that the arbitrariness of Yiddish represents an affront to the bourgeois, rational work ethic of the West. See his essay, "Zionism, Literature, and the Yiddish Theater," in

Mark Anderson, ed., *Reading Kafka: Prague, Politics, and the Fin-de-Siècle* (New York: Schocken, 1989), 95–115.

7. Derrida describes the double logic of the supplement as follows: "The supplement adds itself, it is a surplus, a plenitude enriching another plenitude, the *fullest measure* of presence. . . . But the supplement supplements. It adds only to replace. It intervenes or insinuates itself *in-the-place-of*; if it fills, it is as if one fills a void. If it represents and makes an image, it is by the anterior default of a presence. Compensatory [*suppléant*] and vicarious, the supplement is an adjunct, a subaltern instance which take*s-(the)-place.*" *Of Grammatology*, 144-45.

8. Gilles Deleuze and Félix Guattari, *Kafka: Toward a Minor Literature*, trans. Dana Polan (Minneapolis: University of Minnesota Press, 1986), 25. Deleuze and Guattari developed the concept of deterritorialization to describe the revolutionary displacements of a major language by a minority. These displacements not only occur when new modes of expression are introduced in a major language but also when the "place" of expression shifts, such as Jews speaking Prague German. Following Kafka's own reflections on a minor literature, Deleuze and Guattari explain that "a minor literature doesn't come from a minor language; it is rather that which a minority constructs within a major language. . . . [In a minor literature] language is affected with a high coefficient of deterritorialization" (16). For an excellent discussion of Deleuze and Kafka, see Scott Spector, *Prague Territories: National Conflict and Cultural Innovation in Franz Kafka's Fin de Siècle* (Berkeley: University of California Press, 2000), 27ff.

9. In the conclusion to chapter 2, I suggest that Celan's "Gespräch im Gebirg" functions in much the same way: He essentially writes Yiddish in German, thereby undermining the separatrix between the two.

10. Gershom Scholem, "Against the Myth of the German-Jewish Dialogue," in *On Jews and Judaism in Crisis: Selected Essays*, ed. Werner J. Dannhauser (New York: Schocken, 1976), 61–64; here 62.

11. There are many good studies addressing this problematic. See, for example, Jehuda Reinharz and Walter Schatzberg, eds., *The Jewish Response to German Culture: From the Enlightenment to the Second World War* (Hanover, NH: University Presses of New England, 1985). In his book, *German Jews Beyond Judaism* (Bloomington: Indiana University Press, 1985), George L. Mosse famously countered Scholem's argument by showing how German and German-Jewish intellectuals mutually embraced the ideal of *Bildung*. Mosse certainly extended the historical record of "dialogue" through his own work. For a reassessment of Scholem's position, see the collection by Klaus Berghahn, ed., *The German-Jewish Dialogue Reconsidered: A Symposium in Honor of George L. Mosse* (New York: Lang, 1996).

12. Michael Löwy prefers the term *elective affinities* in his study of Jewish libertarian thought. Very much in accord with the relationship of German/Jewish that I am describing, he defines an elective affinity as "a very special kind of dialectical relationship that develops between two social or cultural configurations, one that cannot be reduced to direct casuality [*sic*] or to 'influences' in the traditional sense. Starting from a certain structural analogy, the relationship consists of a convergence, a mutual attraction, and active confluence, a combination that can go as far as fusion." *Redemp-*

tion and Utopia: Jewish Libertarian Thought in Central Europe, A Study in Elective Affinity, trans. Hope Heaney (London: Athlone, 1992), 6.

13. Berghahn, "Introduction," *The German-Jewish Dialogue Reconsidered*, 2.

14. Peter Eli Gordon, *Rosenzweig and Heidegger: Between Judaism and German Philosophy* (Berkeley: University of California Press, 2003), xxii. Further citations are documented parenthetically. Also Michael Brenner, *The Renaissance of Jewish Culture in Weimar Germany* (New Haven: Yale University Press, 1996).

15. Paul Mendes-Flohr, *German Jews: A Dual Identity* (New Haven: Yale University Press, 1999). All citations will be documented parenthetically as GJ followed by the page number.

16. This is something also treated in Paul Reitter's forthcoming book, "The Soul of Form: Karl Kraus and the Dialectics of German-Jewish Identity."

17. Moritz Goldstein's article was originally published in the literary magazine, *Der Kunstwart*, as "Deutsch-jüdischer Parnass," 25 (1912): 281–94. The quotation comes from Steven Aschheim's entry, "The publication of Moritz Goldstein's 'The German-Jewish Parnassus' sparks a debate over assimilation, German culture, and the 'Jewish spirit,'" in Sander L. Gilman and Jack Zipes, eds., *Yale Companion to Jewish Writing and Thought in German Culture, 1096–1996* (New Haven: Yale University Press, 1997), 299–305; here 299.

18. Max Horkheimer and Theodor W. Adorno, *Dialectic of Enlightenment*, trans. John Cumming (New York: Continuum, 1993), 3. All citations will be documented parenthetically as DE followed by the page number.

19. For an excellent discussion of the dialectic of Enlightenment vis-à-vis anti-Semitism, see Anson Rabinbach, *In the Shadow of Catastrophe: German Intellectuals Between Apocalypse and Enlightenment* (Berkeley: University of California Press, 1997).

20. Walter Benjamin, "Theses on the Philosophy of History," in *Illuminations*, trans. Harry Zohn (New York: Schocken, 1968), 256.

21. Breaking with the paradigm of modernity as a hegemonic monolith in which Jews were essentially "silent victims of the modern state's quest to produce a homogenous citizenry," Jonathan Hess has cogently demonstrated how Jews and Germans actively contested Enlightenment universalism and challenged the terms of emancipation and progress. In his important book, *Germans, Jews, and the Claims of Modernity* (New Haven: Yale University Press, 2003), he investigates "the discourse of Jewish emancipation from 1781 to 1806" in order to shed light on "a dynamic tradition of debate within modernity about the promise, contradictions, and the limits of universalism" (8–9). Citing a trend in German-Jewish studies including the work of Paul Mendes-Flohr, David Sorkin, and Shulamit Volkov, Hess seeks to recover—contra Adorno and Horkheimer—the agency of Jewish intellectuals in fashioning both their own identities and, more broadly, the terms and limits of modernity. Cf. Sorkin, *The Transformation of German Jewry, 1780–1840* (New York: Oxford University Press, 1987); Volkov, *Das jüdische Projekt der Moderne: Zehn Essays* (Munich: Beck, 2001). By arguing that German modernity must be understood as German/Jewish modernity, I see my own work contributing to this reevaluation of modernity.

22. Jacques Derrida, *Positions*, trans. Alan Bass (London: Continuum, 2002), 56–7.

23. In its traditional sense, cultural geography tries to answer the questions of "how the world looks," "how the world works," and "what the world means." Cf. Kenneth E. Foote, Peter J. Hugill, Kent Mathewson, and Jonathan Smith, eds., *Re-reading Cultural Geography* (Austin: University of Texas Press, 1994). See the introductory essay by Hugill and Foote, "Re-reading Cultural Geography," 9–23.

24. Carl O. Sauer, "Cultural Geography," in Philip L. Wagner and Marvin W. Mikell, eds., *Readings in Cultural Geography* (Chicago: University of Chicago Press, 1962), 30–34; here 32–3.

25. Cf. Carl O. Sauer, "The Agency of Man on the Earth," ibid., 539–57.

26. "General Introduction," ibid., 1.

27. Peter Jackson, *Maps of Meaning: An Introduction to Cultural Geography* (London: Unwin Hyman, 1989).

28. Without implying their agreement with one another, see Dennis Cosgrove, "Towards a Radical Cultural Geography: Problems of Theory," *Antipodes* 15 (1983): 1–11; David Harvey, *Spaces of Capital: Towards a Critical Geography* (New York: Routledge, 2001); Edward Soja, *Postmodern Geographies: The Reassertion of Space in Critical Social Theory* (London: Verso, 1989).

29. In this regard my work differs methodologically from what we might call standard cultural and literary histories such as those of Ritchie Robertson, *The Jewish Question in German Literature, 1749–1939* (Oxford: Oxford University Press, 1999); Amos Elon, *The Pity of It All: A Portrait of German Jews, 1743–1933* (London: Lane, 2002); and Ruth Wisse, *The Modern Jewish Canon: A Journey Through Language and Culture* (New York: Free, 2000).

30. Elon, *The Pity of It All*, 11.

31. Michael André Bernstein, *Foregone Conclusions: Against Apocalyptic History* (Berkeley: University of California Press, 1994), 16. As a way of avoiding the fallacies of "foreshadowing" and "backshadowing" in historical writing, Bernstein develops the concept of "sideshadowing" to show how the future is rife with possibilities in any given present. My attention to cultural geography seeks to augment this approach.

32. Barbara Hahn, *The Jewess Pallas Athena: This Too a Theory of Modernity*, trans. James McFarland (Princeton: Princeton University Press, 2005), 13.

33. Spector, *Prague Territories*. While quite different from Spector, Till van Rahden's social history of Jewish Breslau is also grounded in a concrete spatial matrix: *Juden und andere Breslauer: Die Beziehungen zwischen Juden, Protestanten und Katholiken in einer deutschen Grossstadt von 1860 bis 1925* (Göttingen: Vandenhoeck and Ruprecht, 2000).

34. Hess, *Germans, Jews, and the Claims of Modernity*; Gordon, *Rosenzweig and Heidegger*.

35. Walter Benjamin, *Das Passagen-Werk*, ed. Rolf Tiedemann, 2 vols. (Frankfurt: Suhrkamp, 1983). I will quote from the English translation, with references to the German as necessary: *The Arcades Project*, trans. Howard Eiland and Kevin McLaughlin (Cambridge: Harvard University Press, 1999), 461. Further citations will be documented as AP followed by the page number.

36. Perhaps unfairly, the name Leopold von Ranke is traditionally associated with the historicist dictum of representing the past "wie es eigentlich gewesen" (as it really was). He proclaimed these famous words in the preface to his *Histories of the Romantic and Germanic Peoples* (1824). Benjamin's strongest critiques of historicism can be found in Convolute N of *The Arcades Project* and in "Theses on the Philosophy of History."

37. Benjamin, "Theses on the Philosophy of History," 262.

38. Ibid., 262.

39. Ibid., 257.

40. Rolf Tiedemann, "Dialectics at a Standstill: Approaches to the *Passagen-Werk*," trans. Gary Smith and André Lefevere, AP 929–45; here 942.

41. Ibid., 943.

42. Benjamin, "Exposé of 1935, section V," quoted ibid., 943.

43. Ibid., 943.

44. Max Pensky, *Melancholy Dialectics: Walter Benjamin and the Play of Mourning* (Amherst: University of Massachusetts Press, 1993), 213–14.

45. Susan Buck-Morss, *The Dialectics of Seeing: Walter Benjamin and the Arcades Project* (Cambridge: MIT Press, 1991), 210.

46. Michael W. Jennings, *Dialectical Images: Walter Benjamin's Theory of Literary Criticism* (Ithaca: Cornell University Press, 1987), 37.

47. Benjamin, "Theses on the Philosophy of History," 262.

48. Ibid., 263.

49. Theodor Adorno, *Minima Moralia: Reflections from Damaged Life*, trans. E. F. N. Jephcott (London: Verso, 1999), 152.

50. Stephen Greenblatt, "Racial Memory and Literary History," *PMLA* 16, no. 1 (January 2001): 48–63; here 60.

51. Ibid., 62.

52. For the best studies of contingency as a defining attribute of cultural production and historical analysis, cf. Barbara Herrnstein Smith, *Contingencies of Value: Alternative Perspectives for Critical Theory* (Cambridge: Harvard University Press, 1988); and Hayden White, *Figural Realism: Studies in the Mimesis Effect* (Baltimore: Johns Hopkins University Press, 1999).

53. For a thorough discussion of historical narrative and the emplotment of time, see the seminal work of Paul Ricoeur, *Time and Narrative*, trans. Kathlene Blamey and David Pellauer, 3 vols. (Chicago: University of Chicago Press, 1988), vol. 3. Also see the intriguing discussions of the changing concept of historical time by Reinhart Koselleck in *The Practice of Conceptual History: Timing History, Spacing Concepts,* trans. Todd Samuel Presner and others (Stanford: Stanford University Press, 2002). In his most recent work Koselleck employs the term *Zeitschichten* (layers of time) to indicate how time is always spatially layered. For more on this, see my discussion in chapter 7 on Freud and Sebald. Also, see Koselleck, "The Unknown Future and the Art of Prognosis" (chapter 8) in *The Practice of Conceptual History.*

54. Franco Moretti, *Atlas of the European Novel, 1800–1900* (London: Verso, 1999), 3.

55. See, for example, Dennis Hollier, ed., *A New History of French Literature* (Cambridge: Harvard University Press, 1994), and David E. Wellbery, Judith Ryan, Hans Ulrich Gumbrechtt, Anton Kaes, Joseph Leo Koerner, Dorothea E. von Mückech, eds., *New History of German Literature* (Cambridge: Harvard University Press, 2004).

56. Some of the essential works include Margaret Cohen and Carolyn Dever, eds., *The Literary Channel: The Inter-National Invention of the Novel* (Princeton: Princeton University Press, 2002); Caren Kaplan, *Questions of Travel: Postmodern Poetics of Displacement* (Durham: Duke University Press, 1996); James Clifford, *Routes: Travel and Translation in the Late Twentieth Century* (Cambridge: Harvard University Press, 1997); Homi Bhabha, *The Location of Culture* (London: Routledge, 1994); Paul Gilroy, *The Black Atlantic: Modernity and Double Consciousness* (Cambridge: Harvard University Press, 1993). For a fascinating study of British modernism and technologies of mobility, see Andrew Thacker, *Moving Through Modernity: Space and Geography in Modernism* (Manchester: Manchester University Press, 2003). Two recent special issues of *PMLA* have addressed the relationships between mobility and globalization within literary studies: "Globalizing Literary Studies" (coordinated by Giles Gunn), 116, no. 1 (January 2001) and "Mobile Citizens, Media States" (coordinated by Emily Apter, Anton Kaes, and D. N. Rodowick), 117, no. 1 (January 2002).

57. Emily Apter, "Afterword: From Literary Channel to Literary Chunnel" in Cohen and Dever, *The Literary Channel*, 286–293; here 288.

58. Paul Gilroy, for example, recognizes this and even tries to bring Jewish scholars back into the discussion of transnationality and culture in the conclusion to his book, *The Black Atlantic*. He notes that the concept of diaspora comes from Jewish thought and that "the themes of escape and suffering, tradition, temporality, and the social organization of memory have a special significance in the history of Jewish responses to modernity" (205). Although there have been a handful of excellent studies of Jewish literature and culture over the past few years that draw attention to the significance of mobility vis-à-vis the concepts of exile and diaspora, they have yet to significantly impact the fields of transnational cultural and literary studies. See, for example, Sidra DeKoven Ezrahi, *Booking Passage: Exile and Homecoming in the Modern Jewish Imagination* (Berkeley: University of California Press, 2000); Howard Wettstein, ed., *Diasporas and Exiles: Varieties of Jewish Identity* (Berkeley: University of California Press, 2002).

59. James Clifford, "Traveling Cultures," in Lawrence Grossberg, Cary Nelson, and Paula A. Treichler, eds., *Cultural Studies* (New York: Routledge, 1992), 96–112. The arguments in this article are developed at more length in his book, *Routes: Travel and Translation in the Late Twentieth Century* (Cambridge: Harvard University Press, 1997).

60. As Clifford notes, the term *spatial practice* is derived from Michel de Certeau, *The Practice of Everyday Life*, trans. Steven Rendall (Berkeley: University of California Press, 1984). Arguably the most influential theorist to examine culture in spatial terms is Fredric Jameson. See, for example, the idea of cognitive mapping developed, among other places, in *The Geopolitical Aesthetic: Cinema and Space in the World System* (Bloomington: Indiana University Press, 1992).

61. Clifford, "Traveling Cultures," 105. He argues that studies limited to localization and dwelling fail to account for "the wider global world of intercultural import-ex-

port in which the ethnographic encounter is always already enmeshed" (100). Cultural anthropologists need to focus on the ways in which people leave home and variously return by considering travel in its widest possible sense: Not simply the bourgeois, heroic traveler but also the coerced traveler, the servants, helpers, merchants, tourists, translators, and laborers, among others. This attention to travel in all its expressions and possibilities demonstrates, he argues, how hybridity and cosmopolitanism produce new types of cultural agency that resist the leveling power of both "localism" and global capitalism: "Cultures of displacement and transplantation are inseparable from specific, often violent, histories of economic, political and cultural interaction, histories that generate . . . *discrepant cosmopolitanisms*" (108). In this respect the study of mobility and the forms of agency produced are also the study of how ideologies become displaced and political resistance is leveraged.

62. Homi Bhabha, "The Postcolonial and the Postmodern," in *The Location of Culture*, 172.

63. For more on this, see Arjun Appadurai, *Modernity at Large: Cultural Dimensions of Globalization* (Minneapolis: University of Minnesota Press, 1996).

64. Bhabha, "The Postcolonial and the Postmodern," 172–73.

65. Gilroy, *The Black Atlantic*, 15. All further citations will be documented parenthetically as BA followed by the page number.

66. In the wake of Gilroy, a new trend has begun to emerge within literary studies in which spaces, such as the sea or the railway system, are examined for their contribution to both cultural production and new models for literary criticism. See, for example, the work of Margaret Cohen on the novel and the sea, Andrew Thacker's studies of British modernism, and Cesare Casarino's *Modernity at Sea: Melville, Marx, Conrad in Crisis* (Minneapolis: University of Minnesota Press, 2002). Also, the collection *Geographies of Modernism: Literatures, Cultures, Spaces*, ed. Peter Brooker and Andrew Thacker (London: Routledge, 2005). This trend can also be seen in the attention to language and linguistic dispersion by cultural geographers such as Jackson, *Maps of Meaning*, especially chapters 6–7.

67. In Clark's words: "It is just because the 'modernity' that modernism prophesied has finally arrived that the forms of representation it originally gave rise to are now unreadable . . . The intervening (and interminable) holocaust was modernization." T. J. Clark, *Farewell to an Idea: Episodes from a History of Modernism* (New Haven: Yale University Press, 1999), 2–3.

68. Theodor Adorno, *Negative Dialectics*, trans. E. B. Ashton (New York: Continuum, 1983), 33.

2. Berlin and Delos

1. Quoted in Christine Roik-Bogner, "Der Anhalter Bahnhof: Askanischer Platz 6–7," in Helmut Engel, Stefi Jersch-Wenzel, Wilhelm Treue, eds., *Geschichtslandschaft Berlin—Orte und Ereignisse,* vol. 5: Kreuzberg (Berlin: Nicolai, 1994), 52–69; here 59.

2. Summary from Alan Cowell, "Suspect in Nazi Massacre Arrested in Germany," *New York Times*, March 5, 1998.

3. Josef Joffe, quoted from an interview given on National Public Radio, March 4, 1998.

4. The archival collection, *Ein Denkmal für die ermordeten Juden Europas: Dokumentation 1988–1995* (Berlin: Bürgerinitiative Perspektive Berlin, 1995), provides many newspaper and magazine articles on the debate over the "form" of the memorial and the motivations for remembering in Berlin. It also contains the winners of the original competition for the memorial, both rejected by Helmut Kohl in 1995. A new competition commenced in 1996 and the winners of this competition, a joint submission by Peter Eisenman and Richard Serra, were announced in early 1998. After contentious political debates, Eisenman's redesigned memorial (without Serra) was finally given the green light in 1999, when construction began on the site. An extensive documentation is to be found in Ute Heimrod, Günter Schlusche, Horst Seferens, eds., *Der Denkmalstreit – Das Denkmal? Die Debatte um das 'Denkmal für die ermordeten Juden Europas' – Eine Dokumentation* (Bodenheim: Philo, 1999). One of the best critical essays on the Holocaust memorial debate is James Young, "Germany's Holocaust Memorial Problem—and Mine," in *At Memory's Edge: After-Images of the Holocaust in Contemporary Art and Architecture* (New Haven: Yale University Press, 2000), 184–223.

5. "Wo das Holocaust-Mahnmal geplant ist," *Berliner Morgenpost*, March 9, 1998.

6. The terms for this analysis resonate with Jacques Derrida's *Specters of Marx: The State of Debt, the Work of Mourning, and the New International*, trans. Peggy Kamuf (New York: Routledge, 1994).

7. Cf. Ernst Bloch, *Heritage of Our Times*, trans. Neville and Stephen Plaice (Cambridge: Polity, 1991).

8. David Blackbourn and Geoff Eley, *The Peculiarities of German History: Bourgeois Society and Politics in Nineteenth-Century Germany* (Oxford: Oxford University Press, 1984), 239.

9. Reinhart Koselleck, "'Neuzeit': Remarks on the Semantics of the Modern Concepts of Movement," in *Futures Past: On the Semantics of Historical Time*, trans. Keith Tribe (Cambridge: MIT Press, 1985), 231–66.

10. Of the immense literature on the so-called *Vergangenheitsbewältigung*, Charles S. Maier's *The Unmasterable Past: History, Holocaust, and German National Identity* (Cambridge: Harvard University Press, 1988), remains one of the best.

11. Susan Buck-Morss, *The Dialectics of Seeing: Walter Benjamin and the Arcades Project* (Cambridge: MIT Press, 1991), 55. She points out that "philosophical history" or "philosophy of history" rather inadequately translates the term *Geschichtsphilosophie* since Benjamin's point was not to construct "a philosophy *of* history but philosophy *out* of history." She suggests that "philosophical history" might be a less misleading translation of the term.

12. The full quote is from Hamlet, "time is out of joint." The quote serves as the exergue to Derrida's *Specters of Marx*.

13. Perhaps an exception might be the concentration camps, of which all the major camp ruins are still extant, many with extensive museums documenting the horror.

However, they are hardly forever immune to "disposal"—for the argument runs: "fifty years *have* past, is this not enough time to 'reclaim' this land for 'normal' activities again?" In Fürstenburg, for example, residents decided to have a supermarket built on a portion of the acreage belonging to the former concentration camp Ravensbrück. The "Supermarkt-Skandal" (as reported in the *Frankfurter Allgemeine Zeitung*, March 9 and 18, 1993) indicates one element of a larger *Schlußstrich-Mentalität* ("drawing a line to demarcate the past"), that the residents no longer want to "live with" a concentration camp in "their backyards." As one sympathetic commentator put it, "Fifty years after the liberation, the city of Fürstenburg had to work to establish a new beginning. . . . Finally something happened that looked like a normal life." Jürgen Dittberner, "Ravensbrück 50 Jahre nach der Befreiung: Ein Neuer Anfang," in Jürgen Dittberner and Antje von Meer, eds., *Gedenkstätten im Vereinten Deutschland* (Berlin: Hentrich, 1994), 41–45; here 42–43.

14. Reprinted in Jürgen Habermas, *Die neue Unübersichtlichkeit* (Frankfurt: Suhrkamp, 1996), 261–68.

15. Jürgen Habermas, "1989 im Schatten von 1945: Zur Normalität einer künftigen Berliner Republik," in *Die Normalität einer Berliner Republik* (Frankfurt: Suhrkamp, 1995), 167–88. In 1999 the city of Weimar sponsored an "International Essay Prize Question" on the topic "Liberating the Past from the Future? Liberating the Future from the Past?" One can understand the formulation of this question precisely along the lines analyzed by Habermas.

16. Walser used this phrase in his 1998 *Friedenspreisrede* with respect to what he saw to be the overemphasis of the Holocaust in Germany. For a discussion of the ensuing debate between Walser and Bubis, see Amir Eshel, "Vom eigenen Gewissen: Die Walser-Bubis Debatte und der Ort des Nationalsozialismus im Selbstbild der Bundesrepublik," in *Deutsche Vierteljahresschrift für Literaturwissenschaft und Geistesgeschichte* 2 (June 2000): 333–60.

17. Although a more extensive discussion of the very complex processes of musealization is beyond the scope of this chapter, some important questions would surely need to engage the possibility that museums are hardly hegemonic institutions of reification (whether of historical events or art objects despite Adorno's famous criticism "Valéry Proust Museum"), particularly along the lines of fractured, nonlinear representations of space and history. Daniel Libeskind's Jewish Museum in Berlin as well as Peter Zumthor's design for the museum building on the site of the former Gestapo headquarters are both innovative and striking examples of the latter. The anthology edited by Wolfgang Zacharias, *Zeitphänomen Musealisierung: Das Verschwinden der Gegenwart und die Konstruktion der Erinnerung* (Essen: Klartext, 1990), contains a number of apropos articles on this issue. See also Zumthor's published writings on his design in *Stabwerk: Internationales Besucher- und Dokumentationszentrum 'Topographie des Terrors'* (Berlin: Aedes, 1995).

18. The 1946 film *Irgendwo in Berlin* depicts both the shock and fascination of ruins in a devastated Berlin. The film was shot in Berlin during the months after the end of World War II. Young children are shown cavorting on the rubble, fascinated by the tattered landscape. They supposedly represent innocence and liberation since they have no haunting memories of Nazism.

19. I am referring to Bataille's influential essay "The Notion of Expenditure," in *Visions of Excess: Selected Writings, 1927–1939* (Minneapolis: University of Minnesota, 1985). "Productive expenditure" refers to instrumental rationality, capitalist exchange, and commodification whereas "excess" refers to the possibility of transgression, the fact of waste, remains, leftovers, and loss. Benjamin's critiques of historicism can be found most pointedly in Convolute N of *The Arcades Project* and in the "Theses on the Philosophy of History." The brand of historicism most heavily critiqued by Benjamin is that in which the past is pursued as worthy in itself such that continual development and progress is enabled by its amenability to narrative rehabilitation.

20. Derrida articulates the famous notion of *différance* in an essay by the same name in *Margins of Philosophy,* trans. Alan Bass (Chicago: University of Chicago Press, 1986), 1–27.

21. Walter Benjamin, "Theses on the Philosophy of History" in *Illuminations*, trans. Harry Zohn (New York: Schocken, 1968), 256.

22. Ibid., 257.

23. The literature on the Heidegger-Celan relationship is immense. Some of the key texts include Otto Pöggeler's *Spur des Wortes: Zur Lyrik Paul Celans* (Freiburg: Alber, 1986) and his *Heidegger in seiner Zeit* (Munich: Fink, 1999); Philippe Lacoue-Labarthe, *La Poésie comme experience* (Paris: Bourgeois, 1986); Véronique M. Fóti, *Heidegger and the Poets* (New Jersey: Humanities Press International, 1992), chapters 6 and 7; Christopher Fynsk, *Language and Relation . . . That There Is Language* (Stanford: Stanford University Press, 1996), chapter 4. For recent accounts, see Amir Eshel's thought-provoking essay, "Paul Celan's Other: History, Poetics, and Ethics," in *New German Critique* 91 (Winter 2004): 57–77; and James K. Lyon, *Paul Celan and Martin Heidegger: An Unresolved Conversation, 1951–1970* (Baltimore: Johns Hopkins University Press, 2006). The latter appeared after this book went into production.

24. The full poem appears in Paul Celan, *Gesammelte Werke in fünf Bänden* (Frankfurt: Suhrkamp, 1983), 2:255.

25. Martin Heidegger, *Aufenthalte* (Frankfurt: Klostermann, 1989), 3. Pagination is in accordance with Heidegger's hand-numbered pages. All further citations will be documented parenthetically as H followed by the page number.

26. Celan's poem was first published in the collection *Die Niemandsrose* (Frankfurt: Suhrkamp, 1963), 80–81. The poem is dated September 19, 1962. For biographical details I am particularly indebted to Jean-Marie Winkler's interpretation of the poem in Jürgen Lehmann, ed., *Kommentar zu Paul Celans 'Die Niemandsrose'* (Heidelberg: Winter, 1997), 331–39.

27. Translation of "Bread and Wine" from Friedrich Hölderlin, *Selected Poems and Fragments,* ed. Jeremy Adler, trans. Michael Hamburger (New York: Penguin Books, 1998), 153.

28. German original and translation of "Bread and Wine," ibid., 152–53.

29. Heidegger is calling on a distinction that he articulated in his *Discourse on Thinking,* trans. John M. Anderson and E. Hans Freund (New York: Harper and Row, 1966). The original is *Gelassenheit* (Pfullingen: Neske, 1959). "Calculative thinking" (*rechnendes Denken*) is technological in nature because it seeks to quantify thought into stable units or objects. "Meditative thinking" (*besinnliches Denken*), on the other

hand, is characterized as "the releasement toward things" (*Gelassenheit*) and associated with opening the world up to mystery and memory (*Andenken*).

30. Cf. Martin Heidegger, "Brief über den Humanismus," in *Wegmarken* (Frankfurt: Klostermann, 1996), 313–64. The translation appears as "Letter on Humanism" in Martin Heidegger, *Basic Writings*, ed. David Farrell Krell (New York: Harper and Row, 1977), 189–242.

31. Heidegger, *Discourse on Thinking*, 43 (translator's note).

32. Cf. Amir Eshel, *Zeit der Zäsur: Jüdische Dichter im Angesicht der Shoah* (Heidelberg: Winter, 1999).

33. Paul Celan, *Der Meridian: Endfassung, Entwürfe, Materialen*, eds. Bernhard Böschenstein and Heino Schmull (Frankfurt: Suhrkamp, 1999), 102.

34. Celan's "Der Meridian" (October 22, 1960) is the most pointed rejection of poetry as a kind of "art" or practice of "representation." The poem is not an attempt to "mimic" a reality "out there" but is "reality" by virtue of its sedimented time and space as well as by virtue of its relational or ethical dimension. *Gesammelte Werke in fünf Bänden*, 3:187–202. All references to the Meridian speech will be documented parenthetically as M followed by the page number. For an excellent discussion of the speech, see Fynsk, *Language and Relation*, chapter 4.

35. Martin Heidegger, "Erläuterungen zu Hölderlins Dichtung," in *Gesamtausgabe*, 102 vols. (Frankfurt: Klostermann, 1981), 4:28.

36. Martin Heidegger, "What Are Poets For?" (1946), in *Poetry, Language, Thought*, trans. Albert Hofstadter (New York: Harper and Row), 142.

37. Cf. Martin Heidegger, *Gesamtausgabe*, vol. 4 ("Andenken") and vol. 53 ("Der Ister"). Fóti, *Heidegger and the Poets*, 47. Also see Beda Allemann, *Hölderlin und Heidegger* (Zurich: Atlantis, 1954).

38. Quoted in Fóti, *Heidegger and the Poets*, 47–48.

39. Celan, *Der Meridian*, 158.

40. Ibid., 125.

41. Ibid., 93, 132.

42. Benjamin, *Das Passagen-Werk*, I:577–578. The English translation reads: "bound to a nucleus of time" (AP 463)

43. Paul Celan, "Ansprache anlässlich der Entgegennahme des Literaturpreises der freien Hansestadt Bremen" (1958), in *Gesammelte Werke in fünf Bänden*, 3:185–86.

44. Paul Celan, "Gespräch im Gebirg" (1959), *Gesammelte Werke in fünf Bänden*, 3:169–173.

45. Ibid., 173. Translation by John Felstiner, *Paul Celan: Poet, Survivor, Jew* (New Haven: Yale University Press, 1994), 143–44.

46. Celan, *Der Meridian*, 145. Although she does not deal with the Meridian notes, Barbara Hahn introduces "the Jewess Pallas Athena" with a late Celan poem which begins "If I know not, know not / without you, without you, without a You, / they all come, / the / freebeheaded, who / lifelong brainlessly sang / of the tribe / of the You-less / Aschrej." Hahn explains that "the tribe of the You-less injects its words, rather than giving them to a You, rather than making room with its calling for a You." *The Jewess Pallas Athena: This Too a Theory of Modernity*, trans. James McFarland (Princeton: Princeton University Press, 2005), 4–5.

47. Celan, *Der Meridian*, 96.

48. In writing it is known that Heidegger mentioned the Nazi concentration camps twice. The first mention comes in a 1948 response Heidegger sent to Herbert Marcuse on the charge that his philosophy identified with "a regime that has killed millions of Jews." Heidegger's simple response is that if Marcuse had written "East Germans" instead of Jews, "the same [would hold] true." Cited in Richard Wolin, ed., *The Heidegger Controversy: A Critical Reader* (New York: Columbia University Press, 1991), 160–64; here 163. The second time comes in his Bremen lectures of 1949: "Agriculture is now a motorized food industry: in essence, the same thing as the fabrication of corpses in gas chambers and death camps, the same thing as blockades and the starvation of countries, the same thing the fabrication of hydrogen bombs." The lectures are entitled "Einblick in das was ist" and reproduced in Heidegger's *Gesamtausgabe*, 79:27. I will discuss these lectures and Heidegger's thoughts on mass death in chapter 6.

49. There has emerged a sort of cottage industry around Heidegger scholarship dedicated to precisely this task. Spurred by Victor Farías's *Heidegger and Nazism* (1987), two of the earliest and critical engagements with Heidegger's work were undertaken by Jacques Derrida and Jean-François Lyotard: See, respectively, *Of Spirit: Heidegger and the Question*, trans. Geoffrey Bennington and Rachel Bowlby (Chicago: University of Chicago Press, 1989); and *Heidegger and "the jews,"* trans. Andreas Michel and Mark Roberts (Minneapolis: University of Minnesota, 1990). Derrida believes Heidegger realized the error of his ways in his post-1945 work and tries to show through an elegant—but, in my opinion, ultimately unsatisfying and sometimes forced—argument that Heidegger himself performed the necessary "deconstruction." For discussions of Heidegger and Nazism, see Berel Lang, *Heidegger's Silence* (Ithaca: Cornell University Press, 1996); and Hans Sluga, *Heidegger's Crisis: Philosophy and Politics in Nazi Germany* (Cambridge: Harvard University Press, 1993).

50. Martin Heidegger, "Die Bodenständigkeit des heutigen Menschen ist im Innersten bedroht," *Gelassenheit*, 18. I will quote from the English translation, "Memorial Address," in *Discourse on Thinking*, 49.

51. Heidegger, "Memorial Address," 48. A little later in the memorial speech Heidegger even laments how "farming and agriculture, for example, now have turned into a motorized food industry" (54). In the memorial speech of 1955 he has already forgotten "the manufacture of corpses in gas chambers."

52. In the "Letter on Humanism" Heidegger writes that young Germans who knew Hölderlin's poetry (such as "Heimkunft") died for something much greater than the war itself; they died for the sake of overcoming the "loss of being" (*Seinsverlassenheit*), 218–19. Heidegger mentions the destruction of the atomic bomb numerous times in his writings about poetry and the possibility of dwelling after 1945: cf. "Das Ding" (1950), translated as "The Thing" in *Poetry, Language, Thought*, 166, 170. Here the atomic bomb is considered "the final emission of what has long since taken place, has already happened [namely, the loss of being]" (166); "The Discourse on Thinking," 49, 52. Among other places, his disgust with the "Americanization" of the world is mentioned in *Aufenthalte*, 8, "What Are Poets For?" 113, and in an essay on Hölderlin's "Der Ister": "Ameri-

canism is determined to annihilate Europe, which is to say, its homeland. . . . The entry of America into this planetary war is not an entry into history, but is already the final American act of American ahistory and self-devastation." *Gesamtausgabe*, 53:68.

53. Heidegger, "Memorial Address," 57.

54. Heidegger, "Letter on Humanism," 219, 242.

55. Celan, *Der Meridian*, 53.

56. Maurice Blanchot, *The Writing of the Disaster*, trans. Ann Smock (Lincoln: University of Nebraska, 1995), 2 and 75.

3. Sicily, New York City, and the Baranovich Station

1. This history of the Anhalter Bahnhof draws on the following studies: Peter Bley, *150 Jahre Berlin-Anhaltische Eisenbahn* (Düsseldorf: Alba, 1990); Helmut Maier, *Berlin Anhalter Bahnhof* (Berlin: Ästhetik und Kommunikation, n.d.); Rainer Knothe, *Anhalter Bahnhof* (Berlin: Ästhetik und Kommunikation, 1987); Christine Roik-Bogner, "Der Anhalter Bahnhof: Askanischer Platz 6–7," in Helmut Engel, Stefi Jersch-Wenzel, Wilhelm Treue, eds., *Geschichtslandschaft Berlin—Orte und Ereignisse*, vol. 5: Kreuzberg (Berlin: Nicolai, 1994), 52–69; and Alfred Gottwaldt, *Berlin: Anhalter Bahnhof* (Düsseldorf: Alba, 1994).

2. *Handbuch der deutschen Eisenbahnstrecken: Eröffnungsdaten 1835–1935. Streckenlängen, Konzessionen, Eigentumsverhältnisse*, introduction by Horst-Werner Dumjahn (Mainz: Dumjahn, 1984).

3. Bley, *150 Jahre Berlin-Anhaltische Eisenbahn*, 33.

4. Maier, *Berlin Anhalter Bahnhof*, 123.

5. Ibid., 135–36.

6. Ibid., 154–66.

7. Bley, *150 Jahre Berlin-Anhaltische Eisenbahn*, 52.

8. Heinrich Heine, *Lutezia. Zweiter Teil*, in *Werke: Schriften Über Frankreich*, ed. Eberhard Galley, 4 vols. (Frankfurt: Insel, 1968), 3:509–10.

9. Ibid., 3:509.

10. Ibid.

11. Ibid.

12. Reinhart Koselleck, *Futures Past: On the Semantics of Historical Time*, trans. Keith Tribe (Cambridge: MIT Press, 1985), especially the essay "'Neuzeit' Remarks on the Semantics of the Modern Concepts of Movement," 231–66; also "The Eighteenth Century as the Beginning of Modernity," in *The Practice of Conceptual History: Timing History, Spacing Concepts*, trans. Todd Samuel Presner and others (Stanford: Stanford University Press, 2002), 154–69.

13. Reinhart Koselleck, "'Space of Experience' and 'Horizon of Expectation': Two Historical Categories," in *Futures Past*, 267–88; here 279.

14. In his essay "Crash (Speed as the Engine of Individuation)," Jeffrey Schnapp has explored the ways in which speed contributed to the formation of a modern form of subjectivity and individuation. *Modernism/Modernity* 6, no. 1 (January 1999): 1–49.

15. Besides Koselleck, Michel Foucault, Hans Ulrich Gumbrecht, and Friedrich A. Kittler have also argued that a new conception of historicity and temporality emerged in this period: Catalyzed by the French Revolution, an eschatological notion of time became replaced by a "modern" notion of temporality in which the future was imagined as a space of indeterminacy, possibility, and openness. See, for example, Michel Foucault, *The Order of Things* (New York: Vintage, 1975); Hans Ulrich Gumbrecht, "Modern, Modernität, Moderne," in Otto Brunner, Werner Conze, and Reinhart Koselleck, eds., *Geschichtliche Grundbegriffe* (Stuttgart: Klett-Cotta, 1978), vol. 4, 93–131; and Friedrich A. Kittler, *Discourse Networks, 1800/1900,* trans. Michael Metteer, with Chris Cullens (Stanford: Stanford University Press, 1990).

16. Heine, *Lutezia,* 510.

17. Carriage travel from Paris to Germany normally took several days. Ludwig Börne, "Die Bedeutung der 'Idées sur les réformes,'" in Friedrich List, *Werke,* ed. Artur Sommer and Wilhelm V. Sonntag (Berlin: Hobbing, 1935), 9:190. For a detailed, comparative history of carriage travel vis-à-vis the primacy placed on speed, cf. Schnapp, "Crash."

18. Heine, *Lutezia,* 510.

19. Heine did make a short trip to England in 1827, and he published some of his observations in 1828. These were republished in 1831 under the title "Englische Fragmente" and included in the fourth volume of the *Reisebilder.* See Chapter 4.

20. Derek Howse, *Greenwich Time and the Discovery of the Longitude* (Oxford: Oxford University Press, 1980), 87.

21. Ibid., 86–88.

22. John Langton and R. J. Morris, eds., *Atlas of Industrializing Britain: 1780–1914* (London: Methuen, 1986), 89.

23. François Caron, *Histoire des chemins de fer en France,* vol. 1: *1740–1883* (Paris: Fayard, 1997); Hans-Henning Gerlach, *Atlas zur Eisenbahngeschichte: Deutschland, Österreich, Schweiz* (Zürich: Orell Füssli, 1986), xxi.

24. David Landes, *Revolution in Time: Clocks and the Making of the Modern World* (Cambridge: Harvard University Press, 1983).

25. In his classic cultural and social history of the railway, Wolfgang Schivelbusch briefly discusses Heine and his comments about the annihilation of space and time. *The Railway Journey* (Berkeley: University of California Press, 1977), 33–44.

26. In 1884 members from twenty-five countries convened in Washington, D.C. to establish Greenwich as the zero meridian, to determine the exact length of the day, and to divide the earth into twenty-four time zones. However, as a result of political resistances and national differences, Greenwich mean time was not immediately adopted everywhere. Germany adopted it in 1892, but France, for instance, continued to use "Paris time" until just prior to World War I. For this history, see Stephen Kern, *The Culture of Time and Space: 1880–1918* (Cambridge: Harvard University Press, 1983), 10–15; Gerhard Dohrn-van Rossum, *Geschichte der Stunde: Uhren und moderne Zeitordnung* (Munich: Hanser, 1992), 315–21.

27. According to Marx, the emphasis on regularity, expectation, rationalization, and timing—all part and parcel of the quantification of units of work and the invention of the workday—necessitated a spatialization of time into infinitely divisible and

repeatable segments. Cf. Karl Marx, "The Working Day," *Capital*, trans. Ben Fowkes, 2 vols. (New York: Penguin, 1990), 1:340–416.

28. Edmund Husserl, *The Crisis of European Sciences and Transcendental Phenomenology*, trans. David Carr (Evanston: Northwestern University Press, 1970).

29. For a discussion of the trauma of the railway accident and the inability to control all contingencies, cf. Schivelbusch, *The Railway Journey*, 129–49.

30. Niklas Luhmann, *Social Systems*, trans. John Bednarz Jr., with Dirk Baecker (Stanford: Stanford University Press, 1995), 24.

31. Niklas Luhmann, "Contingency as Modern Society's Defining Attribute," in *Observations on Modernity*, trans. William Whobrey (Stanford: Stanford University Press, 1998), 44–62.

32. Kafka and Brod were themselves intensively occupied with travel literature between 1909 and 1912, from Fontane and Hebbel to Flaubert and Goethe, and, during this time, traveled by train to Northern Italy, Paris, Weimar, and Zurich (where Kafka spent time nearby in a sanatorium)—but Kafka never left Europe. The accounts of America and his knowledge of American geography in *Der Verschollene* come entirely from secondary sources, not first-hand experiences. Franz Kafka, *Reisetagebücher* (Frankfurt: Fischer, 1994). The best book to date on Kafka and travel literature is John Zilcosky's *Kafka's Travels: Exoticism, Colonialism, and the Traffic of Writing* (New York: Palgrave, 2003). I also draw on Malcolm Pasley's important article, "Kafka als Reisender," in Wendelin Schmidt-Dengler, ed., *Was Bleibt von Kafka? Positionsbestimmung Kafka-Symposium, Wien 1983* (Vienna: Braumüller, 1985), 1–15; here 3.

33. Franz Kafka, *The Diaries, 1910–1923*, ed. Max Brod, trans. Joseph Kresh (New York: Schocken, 1976), 56 (translation modified).

34. In terms of its attention to space and travel in the work of Kafka, this chapter draws on the insightful discussions in Scott Spector's *Prague Territories* and John Zilcosky's *Kafka's Travels*.

35. *Italienische Reise* is the general title given to the body of writings that Goethe wrote and collected about his trip to Italy. Goethe wrote some of these documents in the form of letters and diary entries during the trip itself, which he regularly sent back to Charlotte von Stein. From the onset of the trip he planned to use these to write about the journey upon returning to Weimar. Although a couple of travel sketches on Italy were published in 1789 and 1790, most notably an illustrated book called *The Roman Carnival*, Goethe did not begin working on the composition of the *Italienische Reise* until 1813, and the first two volumes were not published until 1816 and 1817. Following Stuart Atkins, in order to avoid confusion, when referring to the first two volumes individually, I will use *Reise I* and *Reise II*, respectively, and refer to the 1786/87 trip itself as the Italian journey (without italics). In the *Ausgabe letzter Hand*, these writings are designated as *Italiänische Reise. I, II*. The third volume, composed and published in 1829, differs markedly in form and content from the first two, and is given a separate title by Goethe, *Zweyter Aufenthalt in Rom*, which is also how I will refer to it. In general, I will use the broader title *Italienische Reise* to refer to the collected corpus of writings on the trip. For more on the history of this work, see Stuart Atkins, "*Italienische Reise* and Goethean Classicism," in

Jane K. Brown and Thomas P. Saine, eds., *Essays on Goethe* (Columbia, SC: Camden House, 1995), 182–97.

36. Johann Wolfgang von Goethe, *Tagebücher, Historisch-kritische Ausgabe. 1775–1787*, ed. Wolfgang Albrecht and Andreas Döhler (Stuttgart: Metzler, 2000), 1.1:164. This is also the same line Goethe would use in the published version of his *Italienische Reise I* (1816): *Italienische Reise*, in *Sämtliche Werke,* ed. Christoph Michel and Hans-Georg Dewitz, 40 vols. (Frankfurt: Deutscher Klassiker, 1993), 14:9. Unless otherwise noted, I will quote from the standard English translation of the latter: Johann Wolfgang von Goethe, *Italian Journey*, in *Goethe's Collected Works,* ed. Thomas P. Saine and Jeffrey L. Sammons, introduction and notes, Thomas P. Saine, trans. Robert R. Heitner, 12 vols. (New York: Suhrkamp, 1989), 6:13. All further citations will be documented parenthetically. My historical background is indebted to Saine's thorough introduction.

37. Goethe's diary (*Tagebücher*) covers the first two months of his Italian journey, from leaving Germany on September 3, 1786, through his departure for Rome at the end of October 1786. Much of the 1816 reworking of the first two months of his journey simply replicates and expands upon the diary entries. The later parts of his journey, however, are significantly more indebted to letters and retrospective memories than contemporaneously recorded data. For this reason, I do not think it is necessary to overly insist upon the distance of conceptualization for the early parts of the Italian journey. There are certainly important historical and biographical reasons to acknowledge the fact that Goethe's *Italienische Reise* was composed and published retrospectively, and this is particularly important for the third part, *Zweyter Aufenthalt in Rom*, since it was produced at the end of Goethe's life and differs markedly, in content and structure, from the other two parts.

38. Erich Schmidt, ed. *Tagebücher und Briefe Goethes aus Italien an Frau von Stein und Herder,* 2 vols. (Weimar: Goethe-Gesellschaft, 1886), vol. 2.

39. Gerhard Schulz, "Goethe's *Italienische Reise,*" in Gerhart Hoffmeister, ed., *Goethe in Italy, 1786–1986* (Amsterdam: Rodopi, 1988), 5–19; here 6.

40. Caren Kaplan, "Transporting the Subject: Technologies of Mobility and Location in an Era of Globalization," in *PMLA* (special topic, "Mobile Citizens, Media States," coordinated by Emily Apter, Anton Kaes, and D. N. Rodowick) 117.1 (January 2002): 32–42; here 36.

41. James Clifford, *Routes: Travel and Translation in the Late Twentieth Century* (Cambridge: Harvard University Press, 1997), 36.

42. Ibid., 35.

43. Cf. Koselleck's *The Practice of Conceptual History* and his *Futures Past*.

44. Friedrich A. Kittler, *Discourse Networks, 1800/1900*.

45. We might recall the spatial and mobile terms in which Cicero classically defines metaphor in *De Oratore*: Metaphorical words are "those that are transferred and placed, as it were, in an alien place [*eis quae transferuntur et quasi alieno in loco collocantur*]."

46. In Plato's *Statesman*, for example, the stranger relates a creation story to Socrates with God as the pilot of the metaphorical ship of the universe. In order to avoid cosmic chaos, God must rescue his creation from shipwreck: "Beholding its troubles, and anxious for it lest it sink racked by storms and confusion, and be dissolved again in

the bottomless abyss of unlikeness, he takes control of the helm once more" (273e). Less grandly, but more persistently, the ship and the ship journey are also metaphors for the state or a civic leader, as Goethe remarks in his visit to the "ship of Venice" on October 5, 1786: Goethe writes that the state barge, *Bucentaur* (destroyed in 1797 by Napoleon), is "a true monstrance for displaying the nation's leaders to it in great magnificence.... The ornate ship is a real bit of stage property, which tells us what the Venetians were and considered themselves to be" (*Italian Journey*, 68). The history of the ship as state (*Staatsschiff*) metaphor has been traced in detail by Eckart Schäfer, "Das Staatsschiff: Zur Präzision eines Topos," in Peter Jehn, ed., *Toposforschung: Eine Dokumentation* (Frankfurt: Athenäum, 1972), 259–93.

47. Paul Gilroy's *The Black Atlantic: Modernity and Double Consciousness* (Cambridge: Harvard University Press, 1993) shows how the ship, as both a historical reality and literary metaphor, structures the dialectical underside of modernity. He argues that "the ship is the first of the novel chronotopes ... to rethink modernity via the history of the black Atlantic and the African diaspora into the Western hemisphere" (17).

48. As Georges Van Den Abbeele has argued, the "voyage," while certainly counting as one of the most banal motifs in Western letters, is also the basis of many of Western culture's "dearest notions," ranging from progress, the quest for knowledge, freedom as freedom to move, self-awareness, and salvation. *Travel as Metaphor: From Montaigne to Rousseau* (Minneapolis: University of Minnesota Press, 1992), xv.

49. Hans Blumenberg, *Shipwreck with Spectator: Paradigm of a Metaphor for Existence*, trans. Steven Rendall (Cambridge: MIT Press, 1997).

50. Ibid., 17.

51. Ibid., 10.

52. Ibid., 26.

53. *Wilhelm Meisters Lehrjahr* (1795–1796) was a revision of an earlier work, the *Theatralische Sendung*, conceived between 1777 and 1786. He put the latter work on hold during his trip to Italy and returned to it after coming back to Weimar.

54. One is reminded of Novalis's famous characterization of the circularity of the bildungsroman: "Where is the journey of maturation and discovery leading? '*Immer nach Hause*' [always heading home]." Quoted in Michael Minden, *The German Bildungsroman: Incest and Inheritance* (Cambridge: Cambridge University Press, 1997), 1.

55. Zilcosky briefly discusses Goethe's impulse to "find oneself" by staging such a "view from above" in his *Kafka's Travels*, 54–55.

56. Immanuel Kant, *Critique of Judgment*, trans. Werner S. Pluhar (Indianapolis: Hackett, 1987 [1790]), 120. Quotations will be cited parenthetically.

57. Edmund Burke, *A Philosophical Enquiry Into the Origin of Our Ideas of the Sublime and the Beautiful* (London: Routledge, 1958 [1757]), 46.

58. Goethe, *Gedenkausgabe der Werke: Briefe und Gespräche*, ed. Ernst Beutler, 24 vols. (Zurich: Artemis, 1948–1971), 22:454; quoted in Blumenberg, *Shipwreck with Spectator*, 48 (my emphasis).

59. In book 11 of Homer's *Odyssey* the Cimmerians refer to a distant people who live in fog and clouds. This is the first of several important references that Goethe will make to the *Odyssey*, in this case linking Germans to Cimmerians.

60. Homi Bhabha, *The Location of Culture* (London: Routledge, 1994), 143.

61. Dohrn-van Rossum, *Geschichte der Stunde*, 315–17.

62. *The Roman Carnival* was inserted verbatim by Goethe in the third part of the *Italienische Reise* in 1829. The essay by M.M. Bakhtin is "The *Bildungsroman* and Its Significance in the History of Realism (Toward a Historical Typology of the Novel)," in *Speech Genres and Other Late Essays*, trans. Vern W. McGee (Austin: University of Texas Press, 1986), 10–59.

63. Bakhtin, "The *Bildungsroman*," 39.

64. Goethe, *Annals;* quoted in Bahktin, "The *Bildungsroman*," 48.

65. Benedict Anderson, *Imagined Communities: Reflections on the Origins and Spread of Nationalism* (London: Verso, 1991), 26.

66. Goethe, *Wilhelm Meisters Lehrjahre* (Stuttgart: Reclam, 1982). I will quote from the standard English translation, in *Goethe's Collected Works, Wilhelm Meister's Apprenticeship*, ed. and trans. Eric A. Blackall, 12 vols. (Princeton: Princeton University Press, 1995), 9:27.

67. Goethe, *Wilhelm Meister's Apprenticeship*, 306 and 307; translation slightly altered. The German is *Wilhelm Meisters Lehrjahre,* 526.

68. Goethe, *Wilhelm Meister's Apprenticeship*, 165.

69. See the excellent discussion by Minden, *The German Bildungsroman*.

70. Cf. Reinhart Koselleck, "On the Anthropological and Semantic Structure of *Bildung*," in *The Practice of Conceptual History*, 170–207.

71. Goethe, *Wilhelm Meister's Apprenticeship*, 345.

72. Ibid., 346.

73. Max Horkheimer and Theodor W. Adorno, *Dialectic of Enlightenment*, trans. John Cumming (New York: Continuum, 1993), 3.

74. See, particularly, Koselleck's essays "The Eighteenth Century as the Beginning of Modernity" and "'Space of Experience' and 'Horizon of Expectation': Two Historical Categories" in *Futures Past*. Even where Koselleck gives evidence for the definitive "rupture in continuity" (281), as he calls it, mitigating evidence also exists: At the century's turn, for instance, Goethe wrote to Schiller, "I sincerely enjoyed closing out the year and also the century with you yesterday evening, as we were once ninety-niners. Let the end be like the beginning, and the future like the past." *Brief an Friedrich Schiller*, January 1, 1800, *Goethes Werke: Herausgegeben im Auftrage der Grossherzogin Sophie von Sachsen: IV. Abtheilung: Goethes Briefe, 1800-1801*, vol. 15, ed. Hermann Böhlau (Weimar, 1894). Once again, Goethe underscores a circular continuity precisely where one might expect to see a rupture in experience. This, of course, is not meant to negate the force of "new time," but it does indicate the coexistence of more than one experience of temporality during the critical *Sattelzeit* period. I thank Hinrich Seeba for this kind reference. Wellbery's argument was delivered as a talk at Stanford University on January 22, 2001: "Temporal Semantics and Poetological Conception: On the Unity of Goethe's Thought."

75. The argument could be made, however, that the third part of the *Italienische Reise*, composed and published by Goethe in 1829, does evidence the ruptures of modernity in its montage format. In the *Zweyter Aufenthalt in Rom*, Goethe organizes

the return journey back through Rome not by place, as in *Reise I–II*, but roughly by month, beginning in June 1787 and ending in April 1788. Goethe breaks up the narrative continuity by inserting actual letters, reports, and short essayistic prose pieces into the description of his journey. The dates are not always sequential, and Goethe deliberately ruptures the narrative with intrusions such as his "Intruding Meditations on Nature" (300–1) or even lengthy excerpts from essays that were published after the journey took place (for example, an excerpt from the *German Mercury* of 1791).

76. As Irad Malkin has written, "The word *nostos*, possibly expressing at once a spatial dimension and the human undertakings, occurs already in the Odyssey itself, where it signifies both the action of returning and the hero who returns . . . and the story or song about him." *The Returns of Odysseus* (Berkeley: University of California Press, 1998), 2–3. Goethe is quite self-consciously fashioning himself into precisely this tradition: He returns to Weimar as a hero and writes the very story of his voyage of discovery.

77. Goethe, *Conversations with Eckermann, 1823–1832,* trans. John Oxenford (San Francisco: North Point, 1984), 227.

78. Rainer Fremdling, *Eisenbahnen und deutsches Wirtschaftswachstum, 1840–1879.* This is also confirmed by David Blackbourn and Geoff Eley, two of the most suspicious critics of the German *Sonderweg* theories: David Blackbourn and Geoff Eley, *The Peculiarities of German History: Bourgeois Society and Politics in Nineteenth-Century Germany* (Oxford: Oxford University Press, 1984).

79. Quoted ibid., 189, note 45.

80. After the urging of Rabbi Isaac Löwi, the rabbi of Fürth, Jews bought 31 percent of the railway stock purchased by the citizens of Fürth. Later, in 1866, Jewish factories in Fürth manufactured exactly half of the fourteen steam engines in use. This information comes from Gerd Walther, "Die Juden im Fürther Wirtschaftleben," and Werner J. Heymann, "Die erste Deutsche Eisenbahn und die Fürther Juden," in Werner J. Heymann, ed., *Kleeblatt und Davidstern: Aus 400 Jahre jüdischer Vergangenheit in Fürth* (Emskirchen: Mümmler, 1990), 133, 162, respectively.

81. Jack Wertheimer, *Unwelcome Strangers: East European Jews in Imperial Germany* (Oxford: Oxford University Press, 1987), 11–15; Steven E. Aschheim, *Brothers and Strangers: The East European Jew in German and German Jewish Consciousness, 1800–1923* (Madison: University of Wisconsin Press, 1982), especially chapter 2; Mark Wischnitzer, *To Dwell in Safety: The Story of Jewish Migration Since 1800* (Philadelphia, Jewish Publication Society of America, 1948), chapters 3–4; David Berger, *The Legacy of Jewish Migration: 1881 and Its Impact* (New York: Columbia University Press, 1983).

82. Aschheim, *Brothers and Strangers,* 34.

83. The best book to detail this complex history is Jack Wertheimer's *Unwelcome Strangers,* and my historical summary is indebted to his invaluable study.

84. Walter Benjamin, *The Arcades Project,* trans. Howard Eiland and Kevin McLaughlin (Cambridge: Harvard University Press, 1999), 602.

85. Sholem Aleichem, Yiddish for "hello there" (traditionally, "peace be onto you"), is the pen name of Sholem Y. Rabinovich (1859–1916). The *Railroad Stories* were written in Yiddish in two cycles, one between 1902–1903 and the other between 1909–1910,

and first published in 1911 as *Ayznban geshikhtes: Ksovim fun a komivoyazher* (Railroad stories: Tales of a commerical traveler). I will refer to the standard English translation by Hillel Halkin in *Tevye the Dairyman and the Railroad Stories* (New York: Schocken, 1987).

86. Since the 1880s, government-backed pogroms and anti-Semitic decrees in the Pale of Settlement had increased dramatically. For this reason, between 1881 and 1914, as many as three million Jews left the Russian Empire, many for Western Europe and the United States. The modernization of Russia not only meant railway construction and economic growth but also forced expulsions, more pogroms, and Cossacks who traveled by train to terrorize Jews. Cf. Hans Rogger, *Russia in the Age of Modernisation and Revolution, 1881–1917* (London: Longman, 1983); and Wischnitzer, *To Dwell in Safety*.

87. The term *diasporic consciousness* comes from Daniel Boyarin and Jonathan Boyarin, "Diaspora: Generation and the Ground of Jewish Identity," *Critical Inquiry* 19 (Summer 1993): 693–725; here 713.

88. Kafka worked on and completed the second draft of the novel in September, October, and November of 1912. *Der Verschollene,* ed. Jost Schillemeit, in *Schriften, Tagebücher, Briefe: Kritische Ausgabe,* ed. Jürgen Born, Gerhard Neumann, Malcolm Pasley, and Jost Schillemeit (New York: Schocken, 1983). For translations I used the following version and made corrections or clarifications as noted: Franz Kafka, *Amerika,* trans. Willa and Edwin Muir (New York: Schocken, 1996). All quotations will give references to the German edition followed by the page of the English translation.

89. Both Goethe and Kafka were indebted to "actual" guidebooks for their accounts of travel, the former primarily to J. J. Volkmann's three-volume *Historical and Critical News of Italy* (first published in Leipzig in 1770–1771) and the latter to a number of descriptions of America, most notably, Arthur Holitscher's *Amerika: Heute und Morgen* (1911–1912) and Frantisek Soukup's lecture and travel book on the disenfranchisement of American immigrant workers. Goethe, *Italian Journey,* 450, note 26. Unlike Goethe, who did, of course, travel through Italy, Kafka never made it to America. As Mark Anderson and others have noted, Holitscher's influential text first appeared in installments in the *Neue Rundschau.* Anderson, "Kafka and New York: Notes on a Traveling Narrative" in Andreas Huyssen and David Bathrick, eds., *Modernity and the Text: Revisions of German Modernism* (New York: Columbia University Press, 1989), 142–61; here 147. Kafka attended Soukup's lecture on June 1, 1912, from which, according to his diary he learned about "the Czechs in Nebraska, [that] all officials in America are elected . . . Roosevelt . . . threatened a farmer who had made an objection, [and that] street speakers . . . carry a small box with them to serve as a platform" (June 2, 1912). *The Diaries, 1910–1923,* 203.

90. This passage parallels a dream, which Kafka wrote about in his diaries (September 11, 1912), of landing in New York's harbor: "In the direction of New York my glance slanted downwards a little, in the direction of the sea it slanted upwards. I now noticed the water rise up near us in high waves on which was borne great cosmopolitan traffic." *The Diaries, 1910–1923,* 209.

91. Interestingly, the Muirs literalize this in their translation of the last sentence, "And behind them all rose New York, and its skyscrapers stared at Karl with their hundred thousand eyes" (12). But Kafka uses the word *Fenstern* here, not *Augen*. Indeed, the metaphor of the window as a supposed portal of clarity onto the world has a long tradition in both literature and art history. E. T. A. Hoffmann's story *Des Vetters Eckfenster* (1822), for example, depicts an invalid, confined to his bed, who teaches the "art of seeing" from his bedroom window. He considers the window a "framed canvas" from which he can see the whole panorama of Berlin's Gendarmenmarkt "in a single glance." In both Goethe and Hoffmann the window is a metaphor for seeing, and, more important, a world that can be visually mastered exists beyond the window. Kafka, however, breaks with this tradition: Even when Karl sees beyond or outside of the window frame, the world is just as impenetrable and recalcitrant as before. In Kafka's world the window offers no clarity and the gazing subject gains no mastery.

92. For example, Joseph Freiherr von Eichendorff's short drama, *Das Incognito*, depicts the runaway train as the devil. Walter Benjamin analyzed the theological dimensions of the faith in progress and the nineteenth-century enthusiasm for building railways in Convolute U of the *Arcades Project*, "Saint-Simon, Railroads."

93. While Kafka is giving literary form to what Sidra DeKoven Ezrahi calls "the transformative power of the ethos of immigration," I think this ethos is subsumed within a critical assessment of the relationship between modernity and mobility. See her brief discussion of *Der Verschollene* in *Booking Passage: Exile and Homecoming in the Modern Jewish Imagination* (Berkeley: University of California Press, 2000), 116.

94. Some critics such as Mark Anderson and Wolfgang Jahn have identified a correlation between this epistemological confusion and Kafka's linguistic complexity, paradigmatically illustrated by the confusing syntactical structure of this sentence. Anderson, in his article "Kafka and New York: Notes on a Traveling Narrative," has termed Kafka's linguistic technique "the traveling narrative." His argument, certainly in consonance with parts of mine, is that Kafka's text can best be understood by examining the multiple valences of the term *Verkehr* (traffic). These include the representation of complex traffic patterns in the narrative, the layered linguistic structure of the sentences, and the sexual connotations of intercourse contained in the term *Verkehr*. He considers the montagelike narrative to have cinematic qualities, as Wolfgang Jahn first argued in his seminal study *Kafkas Roman 'Der Verschollene' ('Amerika')* (Stuttgart: Metzler, 1965), especially 52–67.

95. In a short essay published in 1906 called "On Apperception," Kafka first noted the epistemological consequences of mobility for perception. His essay, "Über Apperzeption," is available in Max Brod's *Der Prager Kreis* (Stuttgart: Kohlhammer, 1966), 94–95. Kafka posits that perceptions are always new, even of ostensibly the same objects: "[Since] all objects are located in a constantly changing time and light, and since we spectators no less so, we always encounter these objects in a different place.... Hence, apperception is not a state but a movement" (94–95). I am indebted to Mark Anderson for this reference (I modified his translation).

96. Albert Einstein's "On the Electrodynamics of Moving Bodies" and "Special Theory of Relativity" were first published in 1905. In her astute comparative study of

modernist literature and modern science, N. Katherine Hayles argues that Einstein's theory of relativity "contains two fundamental and related implications . . . : first, that the world is an interconnected whole . . .; and second, that there is no such thing as observing this interactive whole from a frame of reference removed from it. Relativity implies that we cannot observe the universe from an Olympian perspective." N. Katharine Hayles, *The Cosmic Web: Scientific Field Models and Literary Strategies in the Twentieth Century* (Ithaca: Cornell University Press, 1984), 49.

97. Rendered literally, "I am an American citizen with my entire soul."

98. This is, of course, taken to an extreme in Kafka's description of the legal system in *The Trial*. Along quite the same lines as I have argued with respect to *Der Verschollene*, we might interpret the operation of the legal system in *The Trial*: It is a complex, horizontally differentiated system of power that is linked together by utterly contingent, inscrutable, and incomprehensible connections. In fact, everything and everyone in this system is linked in one way or another to Josef K.'s case; however, he himself can never penetrate or discern the nature of the connections or the logic of the system's totalitarian operation. As the famous parable attests, he is always "before the law," waiting to be granted an admission that will never come.

99. The Muirs correct Kafka's supposed misunderstanding of American geography by changing "Boston" to "Brooklyn" and the "Hudson" to the "East River." Stanley Corngold discusses the significance of these "translation mistakes" in his *Lambent Traces: Franz Kafka* (Princeton: Princeton University Press, 2004), chapter 10, "On Translation Mistakes, with Special Attention to Kafka in Amerika."

100. In this respect, I disagree with the attempts by certain critics to read *Der Verschollene* as a kind of bildungsroman, even if in a "special" or "unique" way. As I tried to make clear, I do not think that Kakfa is in any way extending this tradition. See, for example, Jürgen Pütz, *Kafkas 'Verschollener': Ein Bildungsroman? Die Sonderstellung von Kafkas Romanfragment 'Der Verschollene' in der Tradition des Bildungsromans* (Frankfurt: Lang, 1983). In a suggestive (but, in my opinion, unconvincing) article, Gerhard Neumann tries to show how *Der Verschollene* can be "read as a late form of the German Bildungsroman" because it fits within the tradition of the "Adventure-, migration-, and exile-novel." But what he fails to account for is the complete lack of subject formation, guidance, growth, or even change in Karl Rossmann. Moreover, he gives inadequate attention to the real issues of "modernity" in the novel, namely, the structures and systems of power, which Karl consistently runs up against. "Ritual und Theater: Franz Kafkas Bildungsroman 'Der Verschollene,'" in *Franz Kafka: Der Verschollene. Le Disparu/L'Amérique—Écritures d'un nouveau monde?* (Strasbourg: Presses Universitaires de Strasbourg, 1997), 51–78; here 77.

101. Derived from Aristotle, Luhmann's definition of contingency is that which is "neither necessary nor impossible." *Observations on Modernity*, 45; also *Social Systems*, 106.

102. If anything, *Der Verschollene* can be read as a negation of the bildungsroman tradition. Although he dose not discuss the novel, this is also the argument in Minden's conclusion to his *The German Bildungsroman*, 245–48.

103. "Alles . . . nicht einem 'Faden' mehr folgt, sondern sich in einer unendlich verwobenen Fläche ausbreitet [Everything . . . no longer follows a 'thread' but rather

spreads out into an infinitely interwoven space]." Robert Musil, *Der Mann ohne Eigenschaften* (Berlin: Rowohlt, 1930), 1044. For a thorough discussion of Musil vis-à-vis the question of narrative strategy and nationality, see Stefan Jonsson, *Subject Without Nation: Robert Musil and the History of Modern Identity* (Durham: Duke University Press, 2001).

104. In this particularly overdetermined moment, Karl confesses his disenfranchisement by allying himself with black Americans. Rather than calling himself "Jewish," he calls himself "Negro." As Paul Gilroy indicates in his discussion of Jews and blacks in the final chapter of *The Black Atlantic*, certain black intellectuals, such as Edward Blyden, developed "a sense of the affinity between Jews and blacks based around the axes provided by suffering and servitude" (210). Through the figure of Karl, Kafka is extending this affinity.

105. As is well known, Kafka's *Der Verschollene*, like both his other novels, was left uncompleted. Thus any definitive arguments about the novel's end must be avoided. Nevertheless, given the structure of the novel as it is, there is no indication that Karl was to return "home" or, for that matter, that anything more than perpetual wandering would come to fruition. That Kafka intended "The Nature Theatre of Oklahoma" to be the final, inclusive chapter, a chapter that Kafka apparently quite enjoyed, is confirmed by Max Brod: "Afterword," *Amerika*. What is more uncertain, however, is that Brod also says: "In enigmatic language Kafka used to hint smilingly, that within this 'almost limitless' theatre his young hero was going to find again a profession, a standby, his freedom, even his old home and his parents, as if by some celestial witchery" (299–300). Even if this last statement is true, the sheer outrageousness of Karl being reunited with his home and parents while traveling through Oklahoma seems to still underscore my claim about the radical contingency of the narrative structure. As the novel stands, however, no hints whatsoever are given that anything like Brod reports will take place.

106. In his lifetime Kafka published only the first chapter of *Der Verschollene*, "Der Heizer" (The stoker) in May 1913. Janouch's assessment of Karl Rossmann comes from this piece.

107. Gustav Janouch, *Conversations with Kafka*, trans. Goronwy Rees (New York: Quartet, 1985), 30. Although Kafka does indicate in his letters a number of conversations that he had with Janouch in the early 1920s, the reliability of this source is still somewhat questionable.

108. Ibid., 30.

109. This has been done, for example, by Gershon Shaked, *The Shadows Within: Essays on Modern Jewish Writers* (Philadelphia: Jewish Publication Society, 1987); Gerhard Neumann, "Der Wanderer und der Verschollene: Zum Problem der Identität in Goethes 'Wilhelm Meister' and in Kafkas 'Amerika-Roman,'" in P. Stern and J. J White, eds., *Paths and Labyrinths* (Atlantic Highlands: Humanities, 1985), 43–65. For a highly suggestive and insightful discussion of the influence of Yiddish theater on the development of *Der Verschollene* in general, see Evelyn Torton Beck, *Kafka and the Yiddish Theater: Its Impact on His Work* (Madison: University of Wisconsin Press, 1971), 122–35.

110. While Zilcosky discusses the influence of Goethe and his travel writings on Kafka, he does not mention the influence of Jewish travel writing, such as that of Sholem Aleichem; cf. *Kafka's Travels*, 44ff.

111. See, for example, Arnold Eisen's *Galut: Modern Jewish Reflections on Homelessness and Homecoming* (Bloomington: Indiana University Press, 1986); and Ezrahi's *Booking Passage*.

112. Kafka, *The Diaries, 1910–1923*, 81 and 175. Kafka was preparing to give his "Little Introductory Speech on the Yiddish Language" in late January and early February of 1912, when he produced this outline of Yiddish literature. For more on Kafka's encounters with Yiddish, cf. Beck, *Kafka and the Yiddish Theater*.

113. For examples of these different types of comparisons, cf. Ezrahi's *Booking Passage*. Also Ruth R. Wisse, *The Modern Jewish Canon: A Journey through Language and Culture* (New York: Free, 2000). In her decision to bring Sholem Aleichem and Kafka together, Wisse writes: "Kafka follows so naturally after Sholem Aleichem that one might think his comic vision had derived from the older kin's. The moral and cognitive breakdown that always threatens Sholem Aleichem's characters overtakes Kafka's fiction from the very first" (20).

114. Walter Benjamin, "The Storyteller," in *Illuminations*, trans. Harry Zohn (New York: Schocken, 1968), 83–109; here 83.

115. David G. Roskies, *A Bridge of Longing: The Lost Art of Yiddish Storytelling* (Cambridge: Harvard University Press, 1995), 178.

116. Both novellas are translated in *A Shtetl and Other Yiddish Novellas*, ed. Ruth R. Wisse (Detroit: Wayne State University Press, 1986).

117. Wisse, *The Modern Jewish Canon*.

118. "The Travels of Benjamin the Third" appears in English in Mendele Moykher-Sforim, *Tales of Mendele the Book Peddler: Fishke the Lame and Benjamin the Third*, ed. Dan Miron and Ken Frieden, trans. Hillel Halkin (New York: Schocken, 1996). The best critical work on Mendele and the emergence of Yiddish literature is Dan Miron, *A Traveler Disguised: A Study in the Rise of Modern Yiddish Fiction in the Nineteenth Century* (New York: Schocken, 1973).

119. Sholem Aleichem, *Tevye the Dairyman and the Railroad Stories*, 163.

120. Ibid., 186.

121. As the flipside to the equation of modernity with speed and transcendence, Sholem Aleichem taps into the slowly destructive capacities of a mundane modernity. For the former, see Paul Virilio, *Speed and Politics: An Essay on Dromology*, trans. Mark Polizzotti (Cambridge: MIT Press, 1986).

122. Aleichem, *Tevye the Dairyman and the Railroad Stories*, 193.

123. Roskies, *A Bridge of Longing*, 181–82.

124. Boyarin and Boyarin, "Diaspora."

125. Ibid., 701.

126. Ibid., 721.

127. James Clifford, "Diasporas," in *Cultural Anthropology* 9, no. 3 (1994): 302–38; here 321.

4. The North Sea

1. Walter Benjamin analyzed railway construction side by side with the religious zeal of Saint Simon in Convolute U, "Saint-Simon, Railroads," in *The Arcades Project*, trans. Howard Eiland and Kevin McLaughlin (Cambridge: Harvard University Press, 1999), 571–602.

2. Susan Buck-Morss, *The Dialectics of Seeing: Walter Benjamin and the Arcades Project* (Cambridge: MIT Press, 1991), 91.

3. Michel Chevalier, "Chemins de fer," quoted in Walter Benjamin, "Saint Simon, Railroads," 598.

4. Walter Benjamin, *One-Way Street and Other Writings* (London: Verso, 1979, 81–82.

5. Walter Benjamin, "Theses on the Philosophy of History," in *Illuminations*, trans. Harry Zohn (New York: Schocken, 1968), 255–56; here 255.

6. Ibid., 255.

7. Ibid., 255.

8. G. W. F. Hegel, "Der Geist des Christentums und sein Schicksal," in *Werke*, ed. Eva Moldenhauer and Karl Markus Michel, 20 vols. (Frankfurt: Suhrkamp, 1969–71), 1:297.

9. *Reisebilder* (Pictures of travel) is the term given by Heine to his four collections of travel writings. The first, *Reisebilder I: Die Heimkehr, Die Harzreise, Die Nordsee. Erste Abteilung* (Pictures of travel I: The homecoming, The Harz journey, The North Sea, part one), was published in 1826; the second, *Reisebilder II: Die Nordsee. Zweite Abteilung, Die Nordsee. Dritte Abteilung, Ideen. Das Buch Le Grand, Briefe aus Berlin* (Pictures of travel II: The North Sea, part two, The North Sea, part three, Ideas: The book Le Grand, Letters from Berlin), was published in 1827; the third, *Reisebilder III: Reise von München nach Genua, Die Bäder von Lucca* (Pictures of travel III: The journey from Munich to Genoa, The baths of Lucca), was published in 1830; the last, *Reisebilder IV: Die Stadt Lucca, Englische Fragmente* (Pictures of travel IV: The town of Lucca, English fragments), was published in 1831. All four books are published together as volume 2 of Heinrich Heine, *Sämtliche Schriften*, ed. Klaus Briegleb, 6 vols. (Munich: Hanser, 1968–1975).

10. Although Heine did not, of course, use the term *deconstruction* to describe his *Reisebilder*, I am arguing that the *Reisebilder* effectively do just that, namely, deconstruct Hegel's universality of world history by mimicking the travel narrative as "history with a Jewish difference." Because the *Reisebilder* present a history of particularity and betray a specifically Jewish consciousness of history, they can be productively read next to and against Hegel's systematic idea of world history. I will use the term *deconstruction* to mean this kind of doubled reading of Hegel, both next to and against his system from within. Derrida's most important engagement with Hegelian ideas comes in his own "doubled reading" of Hegel and Genet, the universal and the particular, respectively. Cf. Jacques Derrida, *Glas*, trans. John P. Leavey Jr. and Richard Rand (Lincoln: University of Nebraska Press, 1986).

11. Jeffrey L. Sammons, *Heinrich Heine: A Modern Biography* (Princeton: Princeton University Press, 1978), 78; Jost Hermand, *Der frühe Heine: Eine Kommentar zu den 'Reisebildern'* (Munich: Winkler, 1976), 108.

12. For an overview of the Science of Judaism in the context of the German-Jewish Enlightenment (*Haskalah*), see Michael A. Meyer, ed., *German-Jewish History in Modern Times*, vol. 2: *Emancipation and Acculturation, 1780–1871* (New York: Columbia University Press, 1997), chapter 4; also Michael A. Meyer, *The Origins of the Modern Jew: Jewish Identity and European Culture in Germany, 1749–1824* (Detroit: Wayne State University Press, 1967), chapter 6.

13. The three lectures delivered by Gans between 1821 and 1823 are reprinted in Norbert Waszek, *Eduard Gans (1797–1839): Hegelianer-Jude-Europäer. Texte und Dokumente* (Frankfurt: Lang, 1991), 55–85. Gans also wrote the forward to both Hegel's *Grundlinien der Philosophie des Rechts* in 1833 and *Vorlesungen über die Philosophie der Geschichte* in 1837. For an excellent discussion of Gans and Hegel, see Norbert Waszek, "'Wissenschaft und Liebe zu den Seinen'—Eduard Gans und die hegelianischen Ursprünge der 'Wissenschaft des Judentums,'" in *Eduard Gans (1797–1839): Politischer Professor zwischen Restauration und Vormärz*, ed. Reinhard Blänkner, Gerhard Göhler, and Norbert Waszek (Leipzig: Leipziger Universitätsverlag, 2002), 71–103.

14. Georg Lukács, *Deutsche Realisten des 19. Jahrhunderts* (Berlin: Francke, 1952).

15. "On the History of Religion and Philosophy and Germany" and "The Romantic School" were intended to be published together as a singe work, as they appeared in French under the title *De l'Allemagne*, a clear reference to Germaine de Staël's 1810 work of the same title. Heine's *Geständisse* (Confessions) were written in the winter of 1854 and contain numerous references to Hegel, mostly concerning his personal attempts to come to terms with Hegel. For instance, Heine writes: "How difficult it is to understand Hegel's writings and how easy it is for one to be led astray and believe oneself to understand him having only learned to construct dialectical formulas." *Sämtliche Schriften*, 6.1:473.

16. Harold Mah, "The French Revolution and the Problem of German Modernity: Hegel, Heine, and Marx," *New German Critique* 50 (1990): 3–20; here 10. As Mah and others have indicated, Heine wrote a new preface to this work in 1852, essentially repudiating his earlier claims and rejecting Hegelianism. Moreover, it is worth noting that Mah's argument is also inflected by Lukács's periodization and focuses exclusively on the post-1831 Heine.

17. Eduard Krüger, *Heine und Hegel: Dichtung, Philosophie und Politik bei Heinrich Heine* (Kronberg: Scriptor, 1977).

18. Ibid., 111–39. Space does not permit for an evaluation of the details of Krüger's argument; however, it should be noted that he does not simply replicate Lukács's argument without spelling out the changing ideological and philosophical commitments of Marx and Heine during this period. It should also be noted that Marx also penned his notorious essay "On the Jewish Question" in 1844. Anita Bunyan has even suggested that the negative portrayal of Jews as money hungry may have come from Marx's readings of Heine's *The Baths of Lucca*. See "Heinrich Heine and Karl Marx Meet" in *Yale Companion to Jewish Writing and Thought in German Culture, 1096–*

1996, ed. Sander L. Gilman and Jack Zipes (New Haven: Yale University Press, 1997), 171–77; here 177.

19. Between December 1843 and early 1845, Heine and Marx had several meetings and exchanges. Krüger does briefly mention Heine's 1822–23 text "Über Polen" (On Poland), which was published around the time Heine heard Hegel's lectures on the philosophy of world history. Krüger detects a "dialectical treatment of history" in Heine's articulation of the "political destiny of the Poles," but he does not provide any further details. Krüger, *Heine und Hegel*, 49.

20. Klaus Briegleb has productively posed the question of history in Heine's poetry and his reception of Hegel in his article "Abgesang auf die Geschichte? Heines jüdisch-poetische Hegelrezeption," in Gerhard Höhn, ed., *Heinrich Heine: Ästhetisch-politische Profile* (Frankfurt: Suhrkamp, 1991), 17–37. More recently, in his *Bei den Wassern Babels: Heinrich Heine, jüdische Schriftsteller in der Moderne* (Munich: DTV, 1997), Briegleb has shown how Heine's reception of Hegel informed a range of critical responses over the course of Heine's career.

21. Briegleb, *Bei den Wassern Babels*, 140, 139.

22. Ibid.,138.

23. Multiple versions of these lectures exist: the earliest, *Vorlesungen über die Philosophie der Geschichte*, was edited by Eduard Gans in 1837. The version by Karl Hegel, *Vorlesungen über die Philosophie der Geschichte* (1840), is the standard edition, volume 12 of Hegel's *Werke*. Recently, another reconstruction of the lectures was published, based on three sets of lecture notes from the same winter semester 1822–23: *Vorlesungen über die Philosophie der Weltgeschichte*, ed. Karl Heinz Ilting, Karl Brehmer, and Hoo Nam Seelmann, vol. 12 (Hamburg: Meiner, 1996). I will refer to both the standard edition and this reconstruction since the latter is probably closest to what Heine heard.

24. These lectures formed the basis of his 1821 double publication, G. W. F. Hegel, *Naturrecht und Staatswissenschaft im Grundrisse* and *Grundlinien der Philosophie des Rechts*, in *Werke*, vol. 7.

25. G. W. F. Hegel, *Vorlesungen über die Philosophie des Rechts*, eds. Emil Angehrn, Martin Bondeli, and Hoo Nam Seelmann (Hamburg: Meiner, 2000), 14:198. This book represents the reconstructed lectures given in Berlin during 1819–20.

26. Hegel, *Werke*, 7:503. The original formula, "Die Weltgeschichte ist das Weltgericht," came from a 1784 poem by Schiller called "Resignation," and it makes its first Hegelian appearance in the *Heidelberger Enzyklopädie* (1817). The Hegelian formulation was the topic of the Hegel Congress in 1999 and the proceedings are available in *Die Weltgeschichte – das Weltgericht?* ed. Rüdiger Bubner and Walter Mesch (Stuttgart: Klett-Cotta, 2001).

27. For an attempt to articulate Hegel's relationship to colonialism and views on Africa, cf. Robert Bernasconi, "Hegel at the Court of Ashanti," in *Hegel After Derrida*, ed. Stuart Barnett (London: Routledge, 1998), 41–63.

28. According to Charles Taylor, the "Germanic world" does not refer to Germany, per se, but rather to the "barbarians who swarmed over the Roman empire at its end and founded the new nations of Western Europe. There is no particular chauvinism in this use of the word German." *Hegel* (London: Cambridge University Press, 1975), 398.

29. Jews have no freedom—the hallmark of Christianity and crucial to the progress of world history—because they are dogmatically bound to their own laws. Hegel's argument is remarkably similar to Horkheimer and Adorno's explanation of the origins of anti-Semitism in the *Dialectic of Enlightenment*: Because Jews have their own laws, particularly the *Bildverbot*, they do not need the laws of civilization in order to "control mimesis." Jews are hated precisely because they have their own laws, and are, hence, condemned to be always already "outside" civilization. In the same way, Hegel disparages the Jews because of their laws, which he sees as antithetical to the formation of civil society. Cf. Max Horkheimer and Theodor W. Adorno, *Dialectic of Enlightenment* trans. John Cumming (New York: Continuum, 1993), 180–81.

30. Kierkegaard reads Abraham in precisely this way, but not in order to deprecate his willingness to transcend the law but rather to praise his radically individual commitment to faith. For Hegel, Jews represent a kind of slave mentality because their laws are enforced by a rigidly abstract code of morality, with no connection to the formation of civil society, family, or state. Cf. Søren Kierkegaard, *Fear and Trembling*, trans. Alastair Hannay (New York: Penguin, 1985).

31. Cf. Meyer, *The Origins of the Modern Jew*, 165–67.

32. Eduard Gans, "Erste Rede vor dem 'Kulturverein," in Waszek, *Eduard Gans*, 55–62; here 57.

33. Ibid., 57.

34. Ibid., 57–58.

35. Eduard Gans, "Halbjähriger Bericht im Verein für Cultur und Wissenschaft der Juden," in Waszek, *Eduard Gans*, 62–75; here 65.

36. Ibid., 66.

37. Ibid., 66–67.

38. Eduard Gans, "Dritter Bericht im Verein für Cultur und Wissenschaft der Juden," in Waszek, *Eduard Gans*, 75–85; here 80–81.

39. After the dissolution of the Verein in 1824, the strong Hegelianism of the founders of *Wissenschaft des Judentums* was replaced by an effort to resist assimilation. As Susannah Heschel has argued using postcolonial theory, Abraham Geiger's study of Judaism, for example, was motivated by the attempt "to subvert Christian hegemony and establish a new position for Judaism within European history and thought." Heschel, "Revolt of the Colonized: Abraham Geiger's *Wissenschaft des Judentums* as a Challenge to Christian Hegemony in the Academy," *New German Critique* 77 (1999): 61–85; here 64. I thank Leslie Adelson for drawing my attention to this reference.

40. Although Heine was a member of the *Verein* from August 4, 1822, until he left Berlin in May of 1823, his understanding of "Judaism" and its place in Europe was never inflected by such a resolutely Hegelian philosophy of history, nor did he ever pursue a "scientific" study of Judaism. Moreover, the members of the *Verein* cannot even be said to have espoused a consistent philosophy on the "scientific" study of Judaism. Isaac Marcus Jost, for instance, contended that Jews were not even a people and, hence, could not be studied as if they were, despite the protestations of Zunz or Gans. For more on Heine's relationship to the members of the *Verein*, cf. Edith Lutz, *Der 'Verein für Cultur und Wissenschaft der Juden' und sein Mitglied H. Heine* (Stuttgart: Metzler, 1997).

41. S. S. Prawer, *Heine's Jewish Comedy: A Study of his Portraits of Jews and Judaism* (Oxford: Oxford University Press, 1983), 10–40.

42. Part of the reason for Heine's and Gans's baptism is that Heine was hoping to find and Gans already had an academic teaching position in a Prussian institution of higher education. However, in the late 1810s and early 1820s, a growing institutional anti-Semitism largely prevented Jews from acquiring such teaching positions in public colleges, and this sentiment was codified into law in 1822.

43. The twenty-four poems are published in Heine's *Sämtliche Schriften* as part 1 of the *Reisebilder*.

44. Prawer remarks that Heine's depiction of Christ here is "the irenic Christ" whose sure sign of his Judaism, as Heine relates elsewhere, is his circumcision; cf. Prawer, *Heine's Jewish Comedy,* 114–15. In the third part of his writings on the North Sea, Heine's narrator discusses his ironic rapprochement with Christianity: "The Lord knows I am a good Christian, and am often even prepared to visit his house, but by some mishap, I am always hindered in my good intentions. Generally, this is done by some chatty gentleman who holds me up on the way there, and even if I get to the gate of the temple, some jocular, irreverent thought comes to mind, and then I regard it as sinful to enter. Last Sunday . . . an extract from Goethe's *Faust* came into my head." *Sämtliche Schriften* 2:217–18.

45. Sammons, *Heinrich Heine,* 117.

46. Fritz Strich, *Goethe und die Weltliteratur* (Bern: Francke, 1957), 69.

47. See also Pierre Grappin's commentary on the poem in *Heinrich Heine, Historisch-kritische Gesamtausgabe der Werke,* ed. Manfred Windfuhr, 16 vols. (Hamburg: Hoffmann, 1986), 1.2:1054–57.

48. This image of world history appearing in a glass also comes up in *Die Harzreise,* when Heine describes an evening spent drinking with patriotic Germans. He relentlessly ridicules their patriotism and even advises one to write bad poetry, full of "ragged verse," in order to better represent the morasses and crooked paths of the Teutonic forest where the mythical Hermann battle took place. *Sämtliche Schriften* 2:149–50.

49. Jacques Derrida, "Violence and Metaphysics: An Essay on the Thought of Emmanuel Levinas," *Writing and Difference,* trans. Alan Bass (Chicago: University of Chicago Press, 1978), 153.

50. "An Jules Michelet in Paris," January 20, 1834, *Werke, Briefwechsel, Lebenszeugnisse: Säkularausgabe* (Berlin: Akademie; Paris: Cars, 1970), 21:74.

51. Aristotle, *The Poetics,* trans. Ingram Bywater (New York: McGraw, 1984), 234–35.

52. Leopold von Ranke proclaimed these famous words in the preface to his *Histories of the Romantic and Germanic Peoples* (1824). Quoted in Georg G. Iggers, *The German Conception of History: The National Tradition of Historical Thought from Herder to the Present* (Middletown: Wesleyan University Press, 1983), 67. To be sure, the complexity of Ranke's ideas cannot be reduced to this single dictum. Nevertheless, the scientific treatment of the past as a recoverable object is certainly crucial to his critical project. In Walter Benjamin's trenchant analysis of his pervasive method-

ological influence, he assessed Ranke's historicism to be "the strongest narcotic of the [nineteenth] century." Walter Benjamin, *The Arcades Project*, 463.

53. In Derrida's analysis of Marx, he analyzes the ways in which ghosts disjoin or disrupt the progression of time using the famous declaration of Hamlet, "Time is out of joint." Heine is doing something quite similar. Cf. Jacques Derrida, *Specters of Marx: The State of Debt, the Work of Mourning, and the New International*, trans. Peggy Kamuf (New York: Routledge, 1994).

54. Cf. Sammons, *Heinrich Heine*; Hermand, *Der Frühe Heine*.

55. Precisely by avoiding any kind of "systematic" writing, Hinrich C. Seeba has cogently argued analogously that Heine's *Briefe aus Berlin* (1822) present the seemingly innocent urban stroll as "a political venture in disguise." What is more important than what Heine says is what he does not say, and, hence, "seeing what is not written and what must not be questioned [is] an oppositional act that defies censure." "'Keine Systematie': Heine in Berlin and the Origin of the Urban Gaze," in Jost Hermand and Robert C. Holub, eds., *Heinrich Heine's Contested Identities: Politics, Religion, and Nationalism in Nineteenth-Century Germany* (New York: Lang, 1999), 89–108; here 100.

56. As Amir Eshel has recently argued in "Cosmopolitanism and Searching for the Sacred Space in Jewish Literature," many of Heine's works, ranging from the *Reisebilder* to *Deutschland: Ein Wintermärchen* and his famous poem "Jehuda ben Halevy," "can be read as a constant attempt to inhabit places poetically in the European cosmos" by a poet who "does not have and will not have a home to which he can return." *Jewish Social Studies* 9.3 (2003): 121–38; here 126–27.

57. Letter to Moses Moser, October 14, 1826, *Werke* 20:265.

58. Theodor W. Adorno's essay "Heine: The Wound" is the classic—and not unproblematic—attempt to understand Heine's German-Jewish identity as a "homelessness" or "wound" vis-à-vis the German tradition after Goethe. The essay appears in his *Notes on Literature*, trans. Shierry Weber Nicholson, 2 vols. (New York: Columbia University Press, 1991), 1:80–90. For a thoughtful reflection on Heine's *Zerrissenheit*, see Peter Uwe Hohendahl's chapter "Language, Poetry, and Race: The Example of Heinrich Heine," in his *Prismatic Thought: Theodor W. Adorno* (Lincoln: University of Nebraska Press, 1995), chapter 5.

59. Derrida attempts to enact a similar deconstruction in *Glas* by performing a double reading of Hegel against Genet. Hegel's idea of the universal development of *Weltgeist* is shown to be a Christian ghost story, which grounds its legitimacy in the rejection the "Abrahamic cut." *Glas*, 41.

60. Quoted in Prawer, *Heine's Jewish Comedy*, 100–1.

61. Cf. Seeba, "'Keine Systematie.'"

62. Jost Hermand has also pointed out the way that these dialectical tensions offer a pointed alternative to an all-consuming Hegelian philosophy of history. As he writes, Heine's "dialectical view of history . . . stretches back to the Indians, Persians, Greeks, Middle Ages, indeed to all cultural circles and the reception of these traditions . . . [such that] everything is inserted in, over, and through antitheses and enumerations." Hermand sees these "antitheses" and multiple contradictions as "the poetic expression of a consciousness of history which synthetically blends together." Although I do not think that Heine's consciousness of history can be said to be "synthetic," he does

mix together and reassemble the "raw material" of the past in a volatile, dialectical constellation with his present. *Der Frühe Heine*, 110–11.

63. See Jost Hermand's commentary in *Heinrich Heine*, 6:836–37.

64. Theodor W. Adorno, *Negative Dialectics*, trans. E. B. Ashton (New York: Continuum, 1983), 22.

65. Ibid., 142.

66. Ibid., 144.

67. As Derrida wrote in *Specters of Marx*: "[The] deconstructive procedure . . . consisted from the outset in putting into question the onto-theo- but also archeo-teleological concept of history—in Hegel, Marx, or even in the epochal thinking of Heidegger. Not in order to oppose it with an end of history or an anhistoricity, but, on the contrary, in order to show that this onto-theo-archeo-teleology locks up, neutralizes, and finally cancels historicity. It was then a matter of thinking another historicity . . . another opening of event-ness as historicity that permitted one not to renounce, but on the contrary to open up access to an affirmative thinking of the messianic and emancipatory promise as promise: as *promise* and not as onto-theological or teleo-eschatological program or design" (74–75).

68. Benjamin, "Theses on the Philosophy of History," 254.

5. Nuremberg-Fürth-Palestine

1. Ferdinand Avenarius, "Aussprachen mit Juden," *Der Kunstwart*, 25, no. 22 (2 August 1912): 226. Qtd. in Paul Mendes-Flohr, "The Berlin Jew as Cosmopolitan," in *Berlin Metropolis: Jews and the New Culture, 1890–1918*, ed. Emily D. Bilski (Berkeley: University of California Press; New York: Jewish Museum, 1999), 20. I thank Juliet Koss for the kind reference.

2. Waltraud Schade, "Hotel Excelsior: Stresemannstrasse 78," in Helmut Engel, Stefi Jersch-Wenzel, Wilhelm Treue, eds., *Geschichtslandschaft Berlin—Orte und Ereignisse*, vol. 5: Kreuzberg (Berlin: Nicolai, 1994), 70–83; Helmut Maier, *Berlin Anhalter Bahnhof* (Berlin: Ästhetik und Kommunikation, n.d.), 255–58; Rainer Knothe, *Anhalter Bahnhof* (Berlin: Ästhetik und Kommunikation, 1987), 59–60. The stores included a winery, flower shop, bakery, and stationary store.

3. Max Grunwald, "Juden als Rheder und Seefahrer," *Ost und West* 7 (July 1902): 479–86. The article was also published as a small pamphlet under the same title in 1902. Further citations will be documented parenthetically as JR followed by the page number.

4. Johann Gottfried Herder, "The Hebrews," in *On World History: An Anthology*, eds. Hans Adler and Ernest A. Menze, trans. Ernest A. Menze, with Michael Palma (Armonk, NY: Sharpe, 1997), 263.

5. For an assessment of the significance of Herder's coinage of the Jew as parasite metaphor, see Alex Bein's *Die Judenfrage. Biographie eines Weltproblems*, 2 vols. (Stuttgart: Deutsche-Verlags-Anstalt, 1980), 2:93–95; and Bein's essay "The Jewish Parasite: Notes on the Semantics of the Jewish Problem, with special Reference to Germany," *Leo Baeck Year Book* 19 (1964): 3–40.

6. Houston Stewart Chamberlain, *Die Grundlagen des neunzehnten Jahrhunderts,* 5th ed., 2 vols. (1899; Munich: F. Bruckmann, 1904) 1:454 (my emphasis). Further references are documented parenthetically.

7. For a fascinating account of the vibrancy of Jewish seafaring in antiquity, see Raphael Patai's *The Children of Noah: Jewish Seafaring in Ancient Times* (Princeton: Princeton University Press, 1998). For a discussion of the tradition of the wandering Jew in its many cross-cultural variants, see Galit Hasan-Rokem and Alan Dundes, eds., *The Wandering Jew: Essays in the Interpretation of a Christian Legend* (Bloomington: Indianapolis University Press, 1986); in particular, the essay by R. Edelman, "Ahasuerus, The Wandering Jew: Origin and Background," 1–10.

8. Georges Van Den Abbeele, *Travel as Metaphor: From Montaigne to Rousseau* (Minneapolis: University of Minnesota Press, 1992), xv.

9. As Susanne Zantop has shown, German colonial fantasies existed long before Germany actually became a colonial nation under Bismarck. While it was more limited in terms of both time span and global reach than that of other Western European countries, German colonialism perpetrated some of the worst atrocities, including the Herero genocide of 1904, in its brief existence. An extensive literature on German colonialism has developed in recent years. In addition to Zantop's *Colonial Fantasies: Conquest, Family, and Nation in Precolonial Germany, 1770–1870* (Durham: Duke University Press, 1997), some of the key studies include Sara Friedrichsmeyer, Sara Lennox, and Susanne Zantop, eds., *The Imperialist Imagination: German Colonialism and Its Legacy* (Ann Arbor: University of Michigan, 1998); Russell Berman, *Enlightenment or Empire: Colonial Discourse in German Culture* (Lincoln: University of Nebraska Press, 1998); Alexander Honold und Oliver Simons, eds., *Kolonialismus als Kultur: Literatur, Medien, Wissenschaft in der deutschen Gründerzeit des Fremden* (Tübingen: Francke, 2002); John K. Noyes, *Colonial Space. Spatiality in the Discourse of German South West Africa 1884–1915* (Reading: Harwood, 1992). For an argument showing the long-term development of German colonial discourse, see George Steinmetz, "Precoloniality and Colonial Subjectivity: Ethnographic Discourse and Native Policy in German Overseas Imperialism, 1780s–1914," *Political Power and Social Theory* 15 (2001): 135–228.

10. J.G. Fichte, *Reden an die deutsche Nation* (Leipzig: Meiner, 1944 [1808]); *Addresses to the German Nation*, trans. R.F. Jones and G.H. Turnbull (Westport: Greenwood, 1979); all references will be documented parenthetically as *Addresses* followed by the page number.

11. Zantop, *Colonial Fantasies.*

12. J.G. Fichte, *Gesamtausgabe*, ed. Reinhard Lauth and Hans Gliwitzky, 10 vols. (Stuttgart-Bad Cannstatt: Frommann, 1988), vol. 7. For more on Fichte's ideas, see "Fichte's Blueprint for Autarky," in Michael A. Heilperin, *Studies in Economic Nationalism* (Geneva: Droz, 1960), 82–96.

13. J.G. Fichte, *Der geschloßne Handelsstaat*, in *Gesamtausgabe*, vol. 7. 139.

14. Friedrich List, *Le Système Naturel d'Économie Politique/Das Natürliche System der Politischen Ökonomie* (1837), in *Werke,* ed. Artur Sommer and Wilhelm V. Sonntag, 10 vols. (Berlin: Hobbing, 1935), 4:519–27.

15. Ibid., 4:397. Further citations to List's *Werke* will be documented parenthetically as List followed by the volume and page number.

16. Barrie Axford, *The Global System: Economics, Politics and Culture* (New York: St. Martins, 1995), 27.

17. This goes for a wide range of studies on globalization, from the most sophisticated cultural analyses, such as Frederick Buell's *National Culture and the New Global System* (Baltimore: Johns Hopkins University Press, 1994), to popular celebrations such as Nicholas Negroponte's *Being Digital* (New York: Vintage, 1995) or Frances Cairncross, *The Death of Distance: How the Communications Revolution Will Change Our Lives* (Boston: Harvard Business School Press, 1997). One of the most comprehensive books to buck the trend and embed the concept of globalization within historical networks of change, ranging from the scientific to the financial, environmental to the social, is David Held, Anthony G. McGrew, David Goldblatt, and Jonathan Perraton, eds., *Global Transformations: Politics, Economics and Culture* (Stanford: Stanford University Press, 1999). For critically skeptical assessments, cf. Jean-Marie Guéhenno, *The End of the Nation-State*, trans. Victoria Elliott (Minneapolis: University of Minnesota Press, 1995); or Masao Miyoshi, "A Borderless World? From Colonialism to Transnationalism and the Decline of the Nation-State," in *Critical Inquiry* 19.4 (Summer 1993): 726–51.

18. Cairncross, *The Death of Distance*; Stanley D. Brunn and Thomas R. Leinbach, eds., *Collapsing Space and Time: Geographic Aspects of Communication and Information* (London: Harper Collins Academic, 1991).

19. Cf. Néstor García Canclini, *Hybrid Cultures: Strategies for Entering and Leaving Modernity*, trans. Christopher L. Chiappari and Silvia L. López (Minneapolis: University of Minnesota Press, 2005).

20. Negroponte, *Being Digital*, 230, 238.

21. Cairncross, *The Death of Distance*, 279.

22. Jürgen Habermas, "The European Nation-State and the Pressures of Globalization," trans. G. M. Goshgarian, *New Left Review* 235 (May/June 1999): 40–59. Although an advocate of a so-called postconventional identity (that is, an identity not grounded in nationality), Habermas does not suggest that globalization is the panacea for overcoming nationalism and identities derived from national heritages and histories.

23. Friedrich List, "Eisenbahnen und Canäle, Dampfboote und Dampfwagentransport," in *Staats-Lexikon oder Encyclopädie der Staatswissenschaften*, ed. Carl von Rotteck and Carl Welcker, 15 vols. (Altona: Hammerich, 1837), 4:650–778; here 659–60.

24. Ibid., 4:660.

25. Bernhard Siegert gives a short discussion of Klüber in his book *Relays: Literature as an Epoch of the Postal System*, trans. Kevin Repp (Stanford: Stanford University Press, 1999), 57–59.

26. Ludwig Klüber, *Das Postwesen in Teutschland, Wie es war, ist, und seyn könnte* (Erlangen, 1811).Further citations will be documented parenthetically as PT followed by the page number.

27. Siegert, *Relays*, 57.

28. In a second book on the relationship between the world postage system and German nationality, Klüber further argued that "global" communication, far from incompatible with patriotism and national feelings, would actually help to promote both of the latter: Ludwig Klüber, *Patriotische Wünsche: Das Postwesen in Teutschland betreffend* (Weimar, 1814).

29. Heinrich von Kleist, "Useful Inventions: Project for a Cannonball Postal System," in *An Abyss Deep Enough*, ed. and trans. Philip B. Miller (New York: Dutton, 1982), 245–48.

30. Ibid., 245.

31. Ibid., 246.

32. Wolfgang Schivelbusch, "Railroad Space and Railroad Time," in *The Railway Journey: The Industrialization of Time and Space in the Nineteenth Century* (Berkeley: University of California Press, 1986).

33. Michael S. Batts, *A History of Histories of German Literature, 1835–1914* (Montreal: McGill-Queen's University Press, 1993). My history of German literary histories produced during this period also draws on the following studies: Jürgen Fohrmann, *Das Projekt der deutschen Literaturgeschichte: Entstehung und Scheitern einer nationalen Poesiegeschichtsschreibung zwischen Humanismus und Deutschem Kaiserreich* (Stuttgart: Metzler, 1989); Sibylle Ohly, *Literaturgeschichte und politische Reaktion im Neunzehnten Jahrhundert: A. F. C. Vilmars 'Geschichte der deutschen National-Literatur'* (Göppingen: Kümmerle, 1982).

34. Ludwig Wachler, *Vorlesungen über die Geschichte der teutschen Nationalliteratur*, 2 vols. (Frankfurt, 1818–1819).

35. Johann Wilhelm Schaefer, *Grundriß der Geschichte der deutschen Literatur* (1836), quoted in Batts, *A History of Histories of German Literature*, 6.

36. Ibid.

37. Georg Gottfried Gervinus, *Neuere Geschichte der poetischen National-Literatur der Deutschen*, 5 vols. (Leipzig: Engelmann, 1843–48); Wolfgang Menzel, *Die deutsche Literatur*, 3 vols. (Stuttgart: Hallberger, 1836).

38. For critical overviews of Young Germany, cf. Jeffrey L. Sammons, *Six Essays on the Young German Novel* (Chapel Hill: University of North Carolina, 1972); Gert Mattenklott and Klaus R. Scherpe, eds., *Demokratisch-revolutionäre Literatur in Deutschland: Vormärz* (Kronberg: Scriptor, 1974); Joseph A. Kruse and Bernd Kortländer, eds., *Das Junge Deutschland: Kolloquium zum 150. Jahrestag des Verbots von 10. Dezember 1835* (Hamburg: Hoffmann und Campe, 1987).

39. One could certainly see the decision of "die deutsche Bundesversammlung" to outlaw particular works by Heine, Gutzkow, Mundt, Wienbarg, and Laube as one of the first steps in securing a unified German cultural tradition. According to the joint ruling, all these authors stand accused of defiling social relations, destroying morality, and, most of all, regarding Christianity with disdain. Heine is even accused of propagating a *Weltreligion* in his salon writings through his expression of enthusiasm for Saint Simonism. "Der Beschluß des Bundestages" is reproduced in Jost Hermand, ed., *Das Junge Deutschland: Texte und Dokumente* (Stuttgart: Reclam, 1966), 331–34.

40. Wolfgang Menzel, "Unmoralische Literatur" (1835), reprinted in *Politische Avantgarde, 1830–1840. Eine Dokumentation zum 'Jungen Deutschland,'* ed. Alfred Estermann, 2 vols. (Frankfurt: Athenäum, 1972), 1:56–64; here 62.

41. Sammons, *Six Essays on the Young German Novel*, 51.

42. Friedrich List, *Über ein sächsisches Eisenbahn-System als Grundlage eines allgemeinen Deutschen Eisenbahn-Systems und insbesondere über die Anlegung einer Eisenbahn von Leipzig nach Dresden* (Leipzig, 1833). The pamphlet is also reproduced in List, *Werke* 3.1:155–95.

43. As early as 1819, List had publicly advocated, against Metternich's wishes, for the formation of a German customs union in order to foster free trade between the German states and, in his analysis, economically strengthen Germany. Understandably, Metternich viewed a unified Germany as a potential threat to the economic and political clout of Austria-Hungary. Cf. Roman Szporluk, *Communism and Nationalism: Karl Marx Versus Friedrich List* (New York: Oxford University Press, 1988), 105; W. O. Henderson, *Friedrich List: Economist and Visionary, 1789–1846* (London: Cass, 1983), 46–48.

44. Despite the clear economic and national benefits of railways, List spent the last decade of his life—largely in vain—trying to convince politicians to construct railway lines connecting together the various German cities and states. Although he met with countless politicians and financiers as well as published scores of articles and pamphlets on the beneficial effects of railway, List only succeeded in convincing two states to build railways: Saxony in 1837 and Thuringia in 1841. Unrecognized and largely scorned, he took his own life in 1846. For more biographical details, see Henderson, *Friedrich List*.

45. Ibid., 79.

46. The state as body metaphor has a long prehistory that goes back to Aristotle and plays a significant role in modern discourses on state formation, such as in Hobbes and Kant. In taking up this metaphor, Fichte and List are building on its valences of regeneration. At the beginning of the nineteenth century the concept of regeneration had broken away from its strict uses in medicine and theology and came to designate rebirth in all its respects—physical, moral, and political. It was explicitly linked with its antonym, degeneration, and gained explanatory power as part of the Enlightenment belief in progress and the perfectibility of the human race. Not only could individual bodies be regenerated, but the larger social or political body could also be reborn, renewed, and perfected. Regeneration had gained a revolutionary corporeal meaning. See the discussions by Jonathan Hess, *Reconstituting the Body Politic: Enlightenment, Public Culture and the Invention of Aesthetic Autonomy* (Detroit: Wayne State University Press, 1999); and Antoine de Baecque, *The Body Politic: Corporeal Metaphor in Revolutionary France, 1770–1800*, trans. Charlotte Mandell (Stanford: Stanford University Press, 1997).

47. Here Fichte is reworking the biblical story of cutting up and distributing the parts of the body to the twelve tribes of Israel, a reference that his contemporary, Heinrich von Kleist, also used in his drama of nationalism, *Hermannsschlacht*.

48. Hinrich C. Seeba, "Auferstehung des Geistes: Zur religiösen Rhetorik nationaler Einheit," in Thomas Müller, Johannes G. Pankau, Gert Ueding, eds., *"Nicht al-*

lein mit den Worten." *Festschrift für Joachim Dyck zum 60. Geburtstag* (Stuttgart-Bad Cannstatt: Frommann-Holzboog, 1995), 266–82; here 278.

49. Gervinus, *Geschichte der poetischen National-Literatur der Deutschen,* 1835ff. All references will be documented parenthetically as G followed by the volume and page number; here 4:6–7.

50. James J. Sheehan, *German History, 1770–1866* (Oxford: Oxford University Press, 1994), 616.

51. Quoted ibid.

52. Goethe, Conversation (July 15, 1827), in *Conversations with Eckermann, 1823–1832,* trans. John Oxenford (San Francisco: North Point, 1984), 175; also in Fritz Strich, *Goethe und die Weltliteratur* (Bern: Francke, 1957), 369.

53. Goethe, quoted in Strich, *Goethe und die Weltliteratur,* 371.

54. Ibid., 372.

55. Karl Gutzkow, *Ueber Göthe: Im Wendepunkte zweier Jahrhunderte* (1836) (Frankfurt am Main: Athenäum, 1973), 230.

56. Goethe, *Conversations with Eckermann,* 227 (translation modified). For a discussion of the concept of world literature, see David Damrosch, *What Is World Literature?* (Princeton: Princeton University Press, 2003).

57. Sheehan, *German History,* 502.

58. List, quoted in Szporluk, *Communism and Nationalism,* 103–4.

59. Goethe, *Conversations with Eckermann, 1823–1832,* 227–28.

60. Menzel, *Die Deutsche Literatur.* All references will be cited parenthetically as M followed by the volume and page number. Translations were adapted from Wolfgang Menzel, *German Literature,* trans. C. C. Felton, 3 vols. (Boston: Hilliard, Gray, 1840).

61. Many of the German states, owing to their small size and desire to retain autonomy, refused to let any private entrepreneurs finance the first railways. It was feared that foreign capitalists, particularly the Rothschilds, would exert an "undue economic influence" over their state. This was, for example, precisely the reasoning of the Baden parliament in 1838. Cf. Henderson, *Friedrich List: Economist and Visionary,* 138.

62. List, quoted in Niall Ferguson, *The World's Banker: The History of the House of Rothschild* (London: Weidenfeld and Nicolson, 1998), 273, 439–40. After the first decade of railway construction in Germany, private Jewish bankers and Jewish entrepreneurs played an ever increasing role in investing the needed capital for the expansive railway development during the 1850s and 1860s. Outside of the Rothschild family, Bethel Henry Strousberg and Joseph Mendelssohn (of the Berlin banking family) played prominent roles. Cf. W. E. Mosse, *Jews in the German Economy: The German-Jewish Economic Elite, 1820–1935* (Oxford: Oxford University Press, 1987), 100–18; Joachim Borchart, *Der europäische Eisenbahnkönig Bethel Henry Strousberg* (Munich: Beck, 1991).

63. Ferguson, *The World's Banker,* 451. To be sure, France was hardly immune to a vitriolic anti-Semitic backlash during this time. As Ferguson shows, a growing number of books, pamphlets, and newspapers emerged during the 1840s to denounce the private, Jewish railway monopolies in France. Of these, Alphonse Toussenel's *The Jew-*

Kings of the Epoch: A History of Financial Feudalism codified the image of the Jewish railway baron as an exploitive capitalist; cf. Ferguson, 453–54. But, unlike in Germany, railways were hardly coded in France as the means of attaining "national unity."

64. No imperial governing authority existed to grant concessions for the construction of railways, and, hence, as Anselm Rothschild explained his lack of involvement in 1838, "here in Germany, railways get off the ground only with a great deal of effort." Quoted in Ferguson, *The World's Banker*, 439.

65. Ludwig Börne, *Briefe aus Paris*, in *Sämtliche Schriften*, 5 vols. (Düsseldorf: Melzer, 1964), 3:758.

66. Wolfgang Menzel, "Die jeune allemagne in Deutschland," *Literaturblatt*, no. 1 (January 1, 1836), 4.

67. Ibid.

68. Wolfgang Menzel, "Die jeune allemagne in Deutschland," *Literaturblatt*, no. 2 (January 4, 1836), 8.

69. List, "Idées sur les réformes économiques, commerciales et financières applicables à la France" in *Revue Encyclopédique* (March, April, November 1831), in *Werke* 5:59–91. List argued that a national "railway system" would help strengthen France by fostering internal commerce and the centralization of political authority.

70. Edward Whiting Fox, *History in Geographic Perspective: The Other France* (New York: Norton, 1972), 131.

71. M. Charié-Marsaines, "Mémoire sur les chemins de fer considérés au point de vue militaire" (Paris, 1862).

72. Ibid., 4.

73. Ibid., 14, 23.

74. Although beyond the scope of my project here, it would be interesting to comparatively examine the emergence and transformation of the concept of nationality in the nineteenth century by paying attention to the role of railways in national unification, particularly in countries such as Russia, Italy, and the United States, where "traditional" unification cannot be presupposed. The essays by Alexander Gerschenkron, collected in *Economic Backwardness in Historical Perspective* (Cambridge: Harvard University Press, 1962), offer the classic (economic) interpretative framework for doing this. In the United States the debate over railways and economic development has raged since Robert Fogel, in his seminal book *Railroads and American Economic Growth* (Baltimore: Johns Hopkins University Press, 1964), argued that railways were not nearly as pivotal for American development as had been previously thought. In his analysis of the economics of German railways in the nineteenth century, Rainer Fremdling has demonstrated that Fogel's thesis cannot be accurately applied to Germany, where, in fact, "a single innovation" (namely, railways) was "vital for economic growth in the nineteenth century." See Rainer Fremdling, "Railroads and German Economic Growth: A Leading Sector Analysis with a Comparison to the United States and Great Britain," *Journal of Economic History* 37, no. 3 (September 1977): 583–604; here 601. Another, more recent, nation-specific account is Albert Schram's *Railways and the Formation of the Italian State in the Nineteenth Century* (Cambridge: Cambridge University Press, 1997).

75. The primary works to initiate the *Sonderweg* theory are A. J. P. Taylor's *The Course of Germany History* (1945) and Helmuth Plessner's *Die verspätete Nation* (1959), both of which explain German history by pointing to its unique failures (the failure of a proper bourgeois revolution, Germany's supposed hostility to modernization). The best critical account of the history of the *Sonderweg* argument is still David Blackbourn and Geoff Eley's *The Peculiarities of German History: Bourgeois Society and Politics in Nineteenth-Century Germany* (Oxford: Oxford University Press, 1984). As Blackbourn rightly argues, we must "question assumptions about German peculiarity, while at the same time indicating what was actually distinctive about the German nineteenth-century experience" (165). I share this view.

76. Otto von Bismarck, *Werke in Auswahl*, ed. Gustav Adolf Rein et al., 8 vols. (Stuttgart: Kohlhammer, 1965), 3:3.

77. Cf. John Westwood, *Railways at War* (San Diego: Howell North, 1980), 7; Wolfgang Klee, *Preussische Eisenbahngeschichte* (Stuttgart: Kohlhammer, 1982), 97–113.

78. *Handbuch der deutschen Eisenbahnstrecken: Eröffnungsdaten, 1835–1935. Streckenlängen, Konzessionen, Eigentumsverhältnisse,* introduction by Horst-Werner Dumjahn (Mainz: Dumjahn, 1984), 28.

79. Klee, *Preussische Eisenbahngeschichte,* 224.

80. James M. Brophy, *Capitalism, Politics, and Railroads in Prussia, 1830–1870* (Columbus: Ohio State University Pres, 1998), 169.

81. Although the particulars of the so-called *Eisenbahnpolitik* are beyond the scope of my concerns here, it is worth pointing out, as Fritz Stern has done, that Bismarck's enthusiasm for nationalizing the railroads was also sustained by his own personal financial investments in the railroads. Cf. Fritz Stern, *Gold and Iron: Bismarck, Bleichröder, and the Building of the German Empire* (New York: Knopf, 1977), 210–17; for more on the Reich's railway law and the mandatory sale of privately held railway lines, cf. Rudolf Morsey, *Die oberste Reichsverwaltung unter Bismarck, 1867–1890* (Münster: Aschendorff, 1957), 139–60.

82. Michel Chevalier, "Chemins de fer," quoted in Walter Benjamin, *The Arcades Project,* trans. Howard Eiland and Kevin McLaughlin (Cambridge: Harvard University Press, 1999), 598.

83. Helmuth von Moltke, "On the Bill Relating to the Acquisition of Several Private Railways for the State," in *Essays, Speeches, and Memoirs,* trans. Charles Flint McCumpha (New York: Harper, 1893), 2:37 (translation modified).

84. Stern, *Gold and Iron,* 217.

85. Bismarck, quoted in Stern, *Gold and Iron,* 203.

86. For an insightful conceptual history of the ship of state metaphor, cf. Eckart Schäfer, "Das Staatsschiff: Zur Präzision eines Topos," in Peter Jehn, ed., *Toposforschung: Eine Dokumentation* (Frankfurt: Athenäum, 1972).

87. Although Bismarck famously rejected the need for Germany to have colonies, he changed his mind in 1884–85, outlining the economic and political necessity of establishing *Schutzgebiete* (protectorates) in a series of speeches given at the Reichstag between June 26, 1884, and March 16, 1885. These speeches are reprinted in Bismarck,

Werke in Auswahl, vol. 7. Otto Pflanze argues that Bismarck's support of German colonies reflects a kind of "Torschlusspanik," namely a fear that Germany would be shut out of the global market as new geographies of world politics took shape. For a thorough discussion of Bismarck and the colonial question, see Otto Pflanze, *Bismarck and the Development of Germany* (Princeton: Princeton University Press, 1990), vol. 3.

88. Theodor Herzl, *Briefe und Tagebücher: Zionistisches Tagebuch, 1895–1899*, ed. Alex Bein, et al., 7 vols. (Berlin: Propyläen, 1983), vols. 2–3; here 2:142. All further references to Herzl's letters and diaries will be documented parenthetically as T, followed by the volume and page number.

89. For more on the historical and political context of the development of Herzl's ideas, cf. Carl E. Schorske, *Fin-de-Siècle Vienna: Politics and Culture* (New York: Vintage, 1981), chapter 3.

90. Cf. Benedict Anderson, *Imagined Communities: Reflections on the Origins and Spread of Nationalism* (London: Verso, 1991); Homi Bhabha, *The Location of Culture* (London: Routledge, 1994).

91. Hinrich C. Seeba, "'Einigkeit und Recht und Freiheit': The German Quest for National Identity in the Nineteenth Century," in *Concepts of National Identity: An Interdisciplinary Dialogue/Interdisziplinäre Betrachtungen zur Frage der nationalen Identität*, ed. Peter Boerner (Baden-Baden: Nomos, 1986), 153–66; here 164–65.

92. About a half of year later, Herzl uses almost the same explanation in the preface to *Der Judenstaat*: "I say that this force, when correctly used, is strong enough to run a great machine and transport human beings and goods. The machine may look however one wants." Herzl is certainly drawing a parallel between the "machine" of Zionism and railways, something that will emerge in his ideas as the necessary prerequisite for the practical realization of Zionism. *Der Judenstaat* is reproduced in Theodor Herzl, *Gesammelte Zionistische Werke*, 5 vols. (Tel Aviv: Ivrith, 1934), 1:19–105; here 20. All further references to *Der Judenstaat* will be documented parenthetically as J followed by the page number to this edition.

93. In a feuilleton he wrote for the *Neue Freie Presse* on May 31, 1896, "Das lenkbare Luftschiff" (The guidable airship), Herzl presented an allegory of Zionism using the metaphor of the zeppelin. The article is reprinted in *Philosophische Erzählungen* (Berlin: Harz, 1919), 25–39.

94. Alex Bein, *Theodor Herzl: A Biography of the Founder of Modern Zionism*, trans. Maurice Samuel (New York, Atheneum, 1970), 179.

95. Ibid., 184.

96. Herzl's leadership of the masses was, however, far from undisputed. In trying to secure a location for the First Congress, growing protests, largely from the assimilated Jewish communities in Western Europe, forced Herzl to move the conference from Munich to Basel. The Executive Committee of the Association of Rabbis in Germany, consisting of five rabbis from Berlin, Frankfurt, Breslau, Halberstadt, and Munich, published a protest article in the *Berliner Tageblatt* rejecting Zionism because "Judaism obligates its adherents to serve the fatherland to which they belong with full devotion and to further its national interests with all their hearts and all their strength."

Quoted in Bein, *Theodor Herzl,* 221. Building on his airship allegory, Herzl's response was that "Zionism is not a party. One can come to Zionism from any party; in the same way, Zionism embraces all the factions in the life of the people. Zionism is the Jewish people *in movement* [*unterwegs*]" (my emphasis). Herzl, "Protestrabbiner," in *Gesammelte Zionistische Werke,* 1:169–74; here 170.

97. Schorske, *Fin-de-Siècle Vienna,* 167.

98. For more on the French political context of LeBon's work, cf. Robert A. Nye, "Introduction," to Gustav LeBon, *The Crowd* (New Brunswick: Transaction, 1995 [1895]), 1–26. Also, for the growth of mass politics and anti-Semitism in France during the Dreyfus affair, see Nancy Fitch, "Mass Culture, Mass Parliamentary Politics, and Modern Anti-Semitism: The Dreyfus Affair in Rural France," *American Historical Review* 97 (February 1992): 55–95.

99. LeBon, *The Crowd,* 34.

100. Quoted in Bein, *Theodor Herzl,* 231–32.

101. Michael Berkowitz has also intimated a link between Herzl and LeBon in his astute analysis of the cultural creation of Zionism in his *Zionist Culture and West European Jewry Before the First World War* (Cambridge: Cambridge University Press, 1993), 30.

102. In *Der Judenstaat,* he rhetorically asks, "Who among us knows enough Hebrew to buy a railway ticket in that language?" (J 94).

103. Herzl, "Mauschel," in *Gesammelte Zionistische Werke,* 1:209–15; here 209.

104. Ibid., 211.

105. Ibid., 214.

106. Ibid., 212.

107. Ibid., 215.

108. Friedrich Schiller, *Wilhelm Tell* (1804), quoted in Seeba, "Auferstehung des Geistes," 267.

109. Herzl, "The Family Affliction" (originally published in *The American Hebrew*), in *Zionist Writings: Essays and Addresses,* trans. Harry Zohn, 2 vols. (New York: Herzl, 1975), 2:43–47; here 45.

110. Ibid.

111. Max Nordau, *Entartung* (Berlin: Duncker and Humblot, 1892–1893). For translations I used the following English edition: *Degeneration,* 7th ed. (New York: Appleton, 1895), 560.

112. Nordau, *Degeneration,* 38–39 (translation modified).

113. Ibid., 557. The violence of Nordau's imagery of crushing the degenerate "vermin" to death had, of course, a disturbing afterlife in the fervid adoption of race science and eugenics in the service of state formation and state purification. Moreover, throughout the twentieth century, the concept of the *Ungeziefer* has consistently indicated the abject of society, the absolutely vile deviation from the norm. Franz Kafka famously thematized this in his short story *Die Verwandlung* (*The Metamorphosis*), in which Gregor Samsa wakes up to find himself transformed into an *Ungeziefer* and is ultimately killed by his family for the sake of preserving bourgeois society. More ominously, the association of Jews with parasites and vermin was a persistent topos of

Nazi propaganda, something that was given a direct visual association in the virulently anti-Semitic Nazi film, *The Eternal Jew* (1940). For a more extensive discussion of Nordau, see my "'Clear Heads, Solid Stomachs, and Hard Muscles': Max Nordau and the Aesthetics of Jewish Regeneration," *Modernism/Modernity* 10.2 (2003): 269–96.

114. Nordau, *Degeneration*, 550.

115. Nordau's original call for a "muscular Judaism" was given at the second annual Zionist Congress in 1898. His article "Muskeljudentum" was first published in the *Jüdische Turnzeitung* of June 1900. The article is reprinted in Max Nordau, *Zionistische Schriften*, ed. Zionistischen Aktionskomitee (Cologne/Leipzig: Jüdischer, 1909), 379–81; here 380.

116. For a thorough discussion of the figure of the muscle Jew, see my "'Clear Heads, Solid Stomachs, and Hard Muscles'" and my book, *Muscular Judaism: The Jewish Body and the Politics of Regeneration* (London: Routledge, 2007).

117. Although Germany never carried out a full-fledged colonial program in the Middle East analogous to its efforts in Southwest Africa, German colonies were established in Palestine as outposts of European civilization and Bildung. Unlike the ethnographic and genealogical studies on race mixing that the Germans undertook in Africa, something that, as Russell Berman points out, informed key aspects of Nazi racial thought, the colonies in Palestine were founded primarily with cultural-imperial, missionary goals in mind. This was also the rationale given for the kaiser's visit to Palestine in 1898. After German unification in 1871, he writes, "the mission to the Jews played a not insignificant role in the reconstruction of national representations. The image of Prussian liberalism would finally give way to a religious Prussia with a benevolent, if unctuous, orientation toward Palestine. Such was the ideological background of the pilgrimage of Wilhelm II, the imperialist kaiser, at the end of the century." *Enlightenment or Empire*, 109.

118. Theodor Herzl, *Altneuland*, in *Gesammelte Zionistische Werke*, 5: 125–420. All citations will be documented parenthetically as A followed by the page number to this edition.

119. The Zionist Jew arriving from the sea or even being born from the sea is a critical part of Israeli self-fashioning: First the pioneer arrives from the sea and, then, proceeds to regenerate the desolate land. In so doing, he is turned into a new "Sabra" Jew. This recursivity of building and being rebuilt is captured in the opening line of S.Y. Agnon's novel, *Only Yesterday* (1945): "Like all our brethren of the Second Aliya, the bearers of our Salvation, Isaac Kumer left his country and his homeland and his city and ascended to the Land of Israel to build it from its destruction and to be rebuilt by it." trans. Barbara Harshav (Princeton: Princeton University Press, 2000), 3. The trope of the pioneer arriving from the sea appears in countless works of literature and film, perhaps most emblematically articulated by Moshe Shamir who declares that his hero, Elik, "was born from the sea." For a discussion of the seafaring Zionist Jew in Israeli cinema, see Ella Shohat, *Israeli Cinema: East/West and the Politics of Representation* (Austin: University of Texas Press, 1989). For a timely reassessment of this trope, see Hannan Hever, "We Have Not Arrived from the Sea: A Mizrahi Literary Geography," *Social Identities* 10.1 (2004). 31–51.

120. Daniel Boyarin, *Unheroic Conduct: The Rise of Heterosexuality and the Invention of the Jewish Man* (Berkeley: University of California Press, 1997), 303. Boyarin continues by arguing that Zionism "is *almost, but not quite*, colonialism," instead favoring an analysis of its "mimicry" of European colonialism (307–8).

121. Moritz Goldstein, *Begriff und Programm einer jüdischen Nationalliteratur* (Berlin: Jüdischer Verlag, n.d.), 20. All quotations will be documented parenthetically. The pamphlet was most likely published in 1912, the same year he published his classic (and notorious) essay "The German-Jewish Parnassus."

6. Auschwitz

1. I draw on the following sources for this historical material: Alfred Gottwaldt, *Berlin: Anhalter Bahnhof* (Düsseldorf: Alba, 1994), 97; Christine Roik-Bogner, "Der Anhalter Bahnhof: Askanischer Platz 6–7," in Helmut Engel, Stefi Jersch-Wenzel, Wilhelm Treue, eds., *Geschichtslandschaft Berlin—Orte und Ereignisse*, vol. 5: Kreuzberg (Berlin: Nicolai, 1994), 63–65.

2. Norbert Wollheim quoted in Mark Jonathan Harris and Deborah Oppenheimer, *Into the Arms of Strangers: Stories of the Kindertransport* (New York: Bloomsbury, 2000), 99.

3. Heinz Knobloch, *Meine liebste Mathilde: Die beste Freundin der Rosa Luxemburg* (Berlin: Morgenbuch, 1994), 305–12.

4. Ibid.

5. For the former, see Elzbieta Ettinger, *Hannah Arendt/Martin Heidegger* (New Haven: Yale University Press, 1995); for the latter, see Richard Wolin, *Heidegger's Children: Hannah Arendt, Karl Löwith, Hans Jonas, and Herbert Marcuse* (Princeton: Princeton University Press, 2001); and Dana R. Villa, *Arendt and Heidegger: The Fate of the Political* (Princeton: Princeton University Press, 1996). Moreover, the correspondence between Heidegger and Arendt was recently published: *Hannah Arendt/Martin Heidegger: Briefe 1925 bis 1975 und andere Zeugnisse*, ed. Ursula Ludz (Frankfurt: Klostermann, 2002).

6. Hannah Arendt, *The Origins of Totalitarianism* (New York: Harcourt Brace, 1979 [1951]). Further citations will be documented parenthetically as OT followed by the page number.

7. Martin Heidegger, "Bremer und Freiburger Vorträge" in *Gesamtausgabe*, 102 vols. (Frankfurt: Klostermann, 1994), 79:27. All further citations will be documented parenthetically as BV followed by the page number.

8. Ludz, ed., *Hannah Arendt/Martin Heidegger*, 94. Barbara Hahn briefly discusses this quote in her book, *The Jewess Pallas Athena: This Too a Theory of Modernity*, trans. James McFarland (Princeton: Princeton University Press, 2005), 161–62.

9. For a discussion of this topic, see the collection by Alan Milchman and Alan Rosenberg, eds., *Martin Heidegger and the Holocaust* (New Jersey: Humanities, 1997).

10. Jean-François Lyotard, *Heidegger and "the jews,"* trans. Andreas Michel and Mark Roberts (Minneapolis: University of Minnesota, 1990), 82.

11. There is an immense body of literature on Heidegger and the Nazi question. Some of the key works include Hans Sluga, *Heidegger's Crisis: Philosophy and Politics in Nazi Germany* (Cambridge: Harvard University Press, 1993); Berel Lang. *Heidegger's Silence* (Ithaca: Cornell University Press, 1996); and Julian Young, *Heidegger, Philosophy, Nazism* (Cambridge: Cambridge University Press, 1997). Jacques Derrida's *Of Spirit: Heidegger and the Question* is probably the most widely cited of the extraordinary defenses of Heidegger.

12. Martin Heidegger, *Being and Time* (1926), trans. John Macquarrie and Edward Robinson (New York: Harper and Row, 1962). All citations will be documented parenthetically as BT followed by the page number.

13. Following Edith Wyschogrod, I use the term *mass death* to refer to anonymous death suffered in great numbers. It is a general concept that includes the Holocaust as well as embraces other instances of extermination and mass murder. See her book: *Spirit in Ashes: Hegel, Heidegger, and Man-Made Mass Death* (New Haven: Yale University Press, 1985). In order to unpack the conceptual trajectory of Heidegger's thinking about death and dying, I chose the term *mass death* (rather than *mass murder*) since he is not concerned with acts of killing. Mass death, of course, obscures the agency involved in killing—and this is precisely my point and one of my central critiques of Heidegger. For an important argument underscoring the agency of genocide and mass murder, see Norman M. Naimark, *Fires of Hatred: Ethnic Cleansing in Twentieth-Century Europe* (Cambridge: Harvard University Press, 2001).

14. Giorgio Agamben, *Remnants of Auschwitz: The Witness and the Archive,* trans. Daniel Heller-Roazen (New York: Zone, 1999); Wyschogrod, *Spirit in Ashes.*

15. As we will see below, Heidegger accorded a very specific meaning to *sterben* (to die) and differentiated it from other seemingly synonymous terms such as *ableben* (to demise) and *verenden* (to perish). He writes: Dasein "can end without authentically dying, though on the other hand, *qua* Dasein, it does not simply perish. . . . Let the term '*dying*' stand for the *way of Being* in which Dasein *is towards* its death" (BT 291).

16. In philosophy a thorough discussion of this tripartite temporality is found in Jean-Paul Sartre's *Being and Nothingness* (1943), trans. Hazel Barnes (New York: Simon and Schuster, 1956); cf. part 2, "Being-for-Itself," in which the "for-itself" (Sartre's concept of an authentic human) is a temporal being who is simultaneously what it has been (past), what it is not (present nihilation), and what it projects to be (future). Sartre's notions of temporality are largely adapted from Heidegger's *Being and Time* (1926), where an analogous argument informs his characterization of Dasein's temporality.

17. Wyschogrod, *Spirit in Ashes.* According to Wyschogrod and derived from Husserl, the "life-world" is a set of cultural and social meanings that render our lives and relationships to others intelligible, meaningful, and coherent. As a pregiven dimension of human experience, the life-world represents the spatial and temporal constitution and extension of our world. The "death-world"—the concentration camps, for example—is a new social form in which the meaninglessness of death is its supreme and singular purpose.

18. Wyschogrod, *Spirit in Ashes,* 57.

19. In addition to Wyschogrod, William Haver, Giorgio Agamben, and Wolfgang Sofsky have written astute analyses of mass death and modernity. Through a striking parallel analysis of the atomic bombings and the AIDS crisis, Haver articulates the challenges of narrating the disaster in his *The Body of This Death: Historicity and Sociality in the Time of AIDS* (Stanford: Stanford University Press, 1996); Agamben articulates the aporias of bearing witness to the "Muselmann" in his *Remnants of Auschwitz: The Witness and the Archive;* and Sofsky articulates the space and time of the world of the concentration camp in his *The Order of Terror: The Concentration Camp*, trans. William Templer (Princeton: Princeton University Press, 1997). I draw on their conceptual and theoretical insights in this chapter.

20. Heidegger will argue in *Being and Time* that "the conceptions of 'future,' 'past,' and 'present' have first arisen in terms of the inauthentic way of understanding time" (BT 374). He prefers to characterize Dasein and the structure of care according to the "ecstases of temporality," calling upon the literal sense of the term as a kind of standing out from time (BT 377). Dasein is "thrown" into a situation (hence, its historicity) as a project, which moves toward or anticipates what is not by present nihilation.

21. Edmund Husserl, *The Crisis of European Sciences and Transcendental Phenomenology*, trans. David Carr (Evanston: Northwestern University Press, 1970), 138. The German original is *Gesammelte Werke*, ed. Walter Biemel (The Hague: Nijhoff, 1954), vol. 6.

22. Ibid.,144 (translation modified); ibid., 6:147.

23. Ibid., 142 (translation modified); ibid., 6:145.

24. Ariès, who calls himself a "historian of death," has written extensively about Western conceptions of death, including how the death of the individual and its meaning changed from the Middle Ages to the present. *Western Attitudes Toward Death*, trans. P. M. Ranum (Baltimore: Johns Hopkins University Press, 1974). I draw on this history here.

25. Philippe Ariès, *The Hour of Death*, trans. H. Weaver (Oxford: Oxford University Press, 1990).

26. Heidegger mentions Tolstoy's story in footnote xii on page 495 of *Being and Time*.

27. Rainer Maria Rilke, *Die Aufzeichnungen des Malte Laurids Brigge* (Zurich: Niehans and Rokitansky, 1948). I thank Andreas Huyssen for drawing my attention to the affinity between Heidegger's and Rilke's concepts of death. In the secondary literature on Heidegger, this connection has received surprisingly little attention. A key exception, which I discuss below, is an essay by Maurice Blanchot, "Rilke and Death's Demand," in *The Space of Literature*, trans. Ann Smock (Lincoln: University of Nebraska Press, 1982), 120–70. Agamben also indicates, along the same lines, a connection between Rilke and Heidegger in his *Remnants of Auschwitz*, 72–73.

28. Rilke, *Die Aufzeichnungen des Malte Laurids Brigge*, 12.

29. Ibid., 20.

30. Blanchot, "Rilke and Death's Demand," in *The Space of Literature*, 122–23.

31. Ibid., 128.

32. Ibid., 129.

33. Rilke, Letter to Fürsten Alexander von Thurn und Taxis (October 4, 1914), in *Briefe aus den Jahren 1914 bis 1921*, ed. Ruth Sieber-Rilke and Carl Sieber (Leipzig: Insel, 1938), 17.

34. The "tomb of the unknown soldier" originated in World War I because individuals could no longer be identified and buried as such. For more on this, see Jay Winter, *Sites of Memory, Sites of Mourning: The Great War in European Cultural History* (Cambridge: Cambridge University Press, 1995). For a comparative focus, cf. Ken Inglis, "Entombing Unknown Soldiers: From London and Paris to Baghdad," *History and Memory* 5 (1993): 7–31.

35. Reinhart Koselleck, "War Memorials: Identity Formations of the Survivors," trans. Todd Presner, in *The Practice of Conceptual History: Timing History, Spacing Concepts* (Stanford: Stanford University Press, 2002). Quite in consonance with the argument I am making here about how death changed in modernity, Koselleck has traced how the transformation of death (from individuals dying as heroes or martyrs to anonymous, mass death) impacted possibilities for representation. War memorials, he argues, changed from figurative representations of single individuals to abstract monuments commemorating the magnitude and senselessness of mass death.

36. The term *traumatic unconscious* comes from Anton Kaes and his recent work on the heritage of World War I in the cultural and intellectual life of Weimar thinkers.

37. Thomas Mann, *Doktor Faustus*, trans. H. T. Lowe-Porter (New York: Knopf, 1965), 352.

38. Ibid., 491 (translation modified). The original is *Doktor Faustus*, in *Gesammelte Werke in Zwölf Bänden* (Oldenburg: 1960), 6:651.

39. Mann, *Doktor Faustus*, 452.

40. Paul Valéry, "La Crise de l'esprit," in *Variety*, trans. Malcolm Cowley (New York: 1927), 7.

41. Walter Benjamin, *Understanding Brecht*, trans. Anna Bostock (London: NLB, 1973), 44.

42. Paul Valéry, "La Crise de l'esprit," 3–4 (translation modified).

43. Ibid., 12–13.

44. Primo Levi, *The Drowned and the Saved* (New York: Vintage, 1989), 75.

45. Sofsky, *The Order of Terror*, 73.

46. Ibid., 86.

47. Ibid., 81.

48. Reinhart Koselleck, "Terror and Dream: Methodological Remarks on the Experience of Time during the Third Reich," in *Futures Past: On the Semantics of Historical Time*, trans. Keith Tribe (Cambridge: MIT Press, 1985), 224.

49. Levi, *The Drowned and the Saved*, 83.

50. Agamben, *Remnants of Auschwitz*, 34.

51. Ibid.

52. Sofsky, *The Order of Terror*, 199. He continues: "In a final stage of emaciation, their skeletons were enveloped by flaccid, parchmentlike sheaths of skin, edema had formed on their feet and thighs, their posterior muscles had collapsed. Their skulls

seemed elongated; their noses dripped constantly, mucus running down their chins. Their eyeballs had sunk deep into their sockets; their gaze was glazed. Their limbs moved slowly, hesitantly, almost mechanically. They exuded a penetrating, acrid odor; sweat, urine, liquid feces trickled down their legs."

53. Primo Levi, *Survival in Auschwitz*, trans. Stuart Woolf (New York: Collier, 1993), 90. Agamben discusses this passage on page 44 of his *Remnants of Auschwitz*.

54. The original essay, entitled "What Is Existenz Philosophy?" (1946), was published in the *Partisan Review*. In 1948 she published the essay in German, and it is reprinted in English translation as "What Is Existential Philosophy?" in Hannah Arendt, *Essays in Understanding, 1930–1954*, ed. Jerome Kohn (New York: Harcourt Brace, 1994), 163–87. All further citations will be documented parenthetically as WEP followed by the page number to this edition.

55. Cf. Søren Kierkegaard, *The Sickness Unto Death: A Christian Psychological Exposition for Upbuilding and Wakening*, trans. Howard V. Hong and Edna H. Hong (Princeton: Princeton University Press, 1980).

56. Paul Celan, *Der Meridian: Endfassung, Entwürfe, Materialen*, ed. Bernhard Böschenstein and Heino Schmull (Frankfurt: Suhrkamp, 1999), 145.

57. Theodor Adorno, *The Jargon of Authenticity*, trans. Knut Tarnowski and Frederic Will (Evanston: Northwestern University Press, 1973), 152.

58. Arendt also used the phrase "the fabrication of corpses" in an interview that she gave in 1964 with Günther Gaus. She described learning about the Holocaust: "*This ought not to have happened.* And I don't mean just the number of victims. I mean the method, the fabrication of corpses and so on—I don't need to go into that. This should not have happened. Something happened there to which we cannot reconcile ourselves. None of us ever can." "What Remains? The Language Remains: An Interview with Günther Gaus." Reprinted in *Essays in Understanding*, 14.

59. In his discussion of Heidegger in *Remnants of Auschwitz*, Agamben also quotes a portion of this speech. I consulted his translation and his insightful discussion of the first part of this passage but offer my own translation and analysis here. *Remnants of Auschwitz*, 73–74.

60. Heidegger's critique of modern technology was given further expression in the lectures he gave in the 1950s, which were later published in *Die Technik und die Kehre* (Pfullingen: Günter Neske, 1962). Two of these essays were published in English in the volume *The Question Concerning Technology and Other Essays*, trans. William Lovitt (New York: Harper and Row, 1977).

61. Heidegger, "The Question Concerning Technology," in *The Question Concerning Technology and Other Essays*, 15. I discussed the memorial speech in chapter 2.

62. Ibid.

63. Arendt, *The Human Condition* (Chicago: University of Chicago, 1958), 248.

64. Ibid., 250–51.

65. Heidegger, "The Age of the World Picture," in *The Question Concerning Technology and Other Essays*, 128. This essay was originally given as a lecture in 1938. His critique of the "world picture" also appears in the Rilke essay of 1946, "What Are Poets For?" In the latter, he writes: "Man places before himself the world as the whole of

everything objective, and he places himself before the world. Man sets up the world toward himself, and delivers Nature over to himself" (110).

66. Heidegger, "The Age of the World Picture," 129.

67. Agamben, *Remnants of Auschwitz*, 73.

68. Levi, *Survival in Auschwitz*, 90.

69. Agamben, *Remnants of Auschwitz*, 71–72.

70. Arendt, *The Human Condition*, 19.

7. Vienna-Rome-Prague-Antwerp-Paris

1. W. G. Sebald, *On the Natural History of Destruction*, trans. Anthea Bell (New York: Random House, 2003), 39–40.

2. *Frankfurter Allgemeine Zeitung*, February 1961.

3. The exhibition was entitled *Mythos Berlin*. Cf. the exhibition catalogue, *Mythos Berlin: Eine szenische Ausstellung auf dem Anhalter Bahnhof* (Berlin: Ästhetik und Kommunikation, 1987).

4. Christa Wolf, *A Model Childhood*, trans. Ursule Molinaro and Hedwig Rappolt (London: Virago, 1982), 335.

5. As Saul Friedlander argued in his introduction to a pathbreaking collection of essays, *Probing the Limits of Representation*, "postmodern thought's rejection of the possibility of identifying some stable reality or truth beyond the constant polysemy and self-referentiality of linguistic constructs challenges the need to establish the realities and truth of the Holocaust." "Introduction," in *Probing the Limits of Representation: Nazism and the "Final Solution,"* ed. Saul Friedlander (Cambridge: Harvard University Press, 1992), 1–21; here 4–5.

6. Both Ginzburg's paper, "Just One Witness" (82–96), and White's paper, "Historical Emplotment and the Problem of Truth" (37–53), are reproduced in *Probing the Limits of Representation*. A revised version of White's essay, "Historical Emplotment and the Problem of Truth in Historical Representation," is printed in *Figural Realism: Studies in the Mimesis Effect* (Baltimore: John Hopkins University Press, 1999), 27–42. I will quote White's essay from this edition.

7. Pierre Vidal-Naquet, quoted in Ginzburg, "Just One Witness," 86 (my emphasis). Ginzburg continues his argument by accusing White of dissolving the distinction between fiction and history, of putting the reality of the Holocaust in question, and, through a reconstruction of White's intellectual trajectory, partaking in some decidedly unsavory, almost fascist company. It is beyond the scope of this chapter to evaluate the merits of Ginzburg's argument or his representation of Hayden White's position. For a thorough discussion of the terms of the debate, I recommend the essays collected in Friedlander's *Probing the Limits of Representation*, especially those by Friedlander, Christopher Browning, Perry Anderson, Amos Funkenstein, Martin Jay, and Berel Lang.

8. White, "Historical Emplotment and the Problem of Truth," 27.

9. Ibid., 39.

10. Hayden White, "The Modernist Event," in *Figural Realism*, 66–86; here 70.

11. Ibid., 81.

12. I discuss White's position, together with Sebald, at more length in my article, "'What a Synoptic and Artificial View Reveals': Extreme History and the Modernism of W.G. Sebald's Realism," *Criticism*, special issue, "Extreme and Sentimental History," 46.3 (Summer 2004): 341–60.

13. W.G. Sebald, *Die Ausgewanderten: Vier lange Erzählungen* (Frankfurt: Eichborn, 1992); *Austerlitz* (Munich: Hanser, 2001). Unless otherwise stated, I will quote from the English translations: *The Emigrants*, trans. Michael Hulse (New York: New Directions, 1997); *Austerlitz*, trans. Anthea Bell (New York: Modern Library, 2001). All references to *Austerlitz* will be documented parenthetically.

14. Interview with W.G. Sebald, "Ich fürchte das Melodramatische," in *Der Spiegel*, March 12, 2001, 228–34.; here 228. In an article by Maya Jaggi, "Recovered Memories," Sebald gives the name of the woman as Susie Bechhofer and adds that her life, "with child abuse in a Calvinist Welsh home, [was] far more horrific than anything in *Austerlitz*. But I didn't want to make use of it because I haven't the right. I try to keep at a distance and never invade." *Guardian*, September 22, 2001. Andreas Huyssen speculates that the other half of Austerlitz is Sebald himself. Cf. his article "*Austerlitz*: Gray Zones of Remembrance," in David Wellbery, Judith Ryan, Hans Ulrich Gumbrecht, Anton Kaes, Joseph Leo Koerner, Dorothea E. von Mücke, eds., *A New History of German Literature* (Cambridge: Harvard University Press, 2004), 970–75.

15. Sebald, "Ich fürchte das Melodramatische," 228.

16. The most important critique of the affinities between the claims of photography and the claims of historicist thought remains Siegfried Kracauer's essay "Photography." Kracauer writes that historicists "believe . . . that they can grasp historical reality by reconstructing the course of events in their temporal succession without any gaps. Photography presents a spatial continuum; historicism seeks to provide the temporal continuum. . . . Historicism is concerned with the photography of time." *The Mass Ornament: Weimar Essays*, trans. Thomas Y. Levin (Cambridge: Harvard University Press, 1995), 49–50.

17. In the short period between December 1896 and the writing of the *Interpretation of Dreams* in 1899, Freud completely reconceptualized how memory functions. Memory is not the recollection of the reality of the past as such but rather something that is retrospectively produced within a given present. This shift in Freud's thought has been often remarked upon, and hefty debates have focused on the significance of Freud's rejection of the seduction theory for explaining hysteria and establishing the truth of childhood molestation. One of the most polemical attacks came from Jeffrey Moussaieff Masson, who argued that the early Freud was right in privileging the actual occurrence of the physical trauma, whereas the post-1897 Freud "is in covert collusion with what made [his patient] ill in the first place" because he seemed to characterize the patient's memories as mere fantasies. See Jeffrey Moussaieff Masson, *The Assault on Truth: Freud's Suppression of Seduction Theory* (New York: Farrar, Straus, and Giroux, 1984), 185. I do not think this assessment of Freud is fair: As I argue in

this chapter, I think that Freud is giving up the logocentrism of his former theory in favor of a praxis of interpretation and meaning construction. This does not mean that the trauma is simply turned into a "mere fantasy," but it does mean that the past is no longer recoverable and reproducible as he had earlier imagined it to be. For one account of the debate, see William McGrath, *Freud's Discovery of Psychoanalysis: The Politics of Hysteria* (Ithaca: Cornell University Press, 1986). For a thorough discussion of its significance within Freud's intellectual development and personal biography, see Peter Gay, *Freud: A Life for Our Time* (New York: Norton, 1998), 87–102; and Ernest Jones, *The Life and Work of Sigmund Freud*, vol. 1: *The Formative Years and the Great Discoveries, 1856–1900* (New York: Basic, 1953).

18. Unless otherwise stated, all citations to Freud's work will come from *The Standard Edition of the Complete Psychological Works of Sigmund Freud,* trans. James Strachey, 24 vols. (London: Hogarth, 1966–73). Citations will be abbreviated as SE followed by the volume and page number. Freud's most widely cited works on trauma are "Remembering, Repeating, and Working-Through" (SE 12), "Mourning and Melancholia" (SE 14), and *Beyond the Pleasure Principle* (SE 18). Building off of Freudian (and Kleinian) theory, a vast body of literature on trauma theory has emerged over the past decade. Some of the important studies include Ruth Leys, *Trauma: A Genealogy* (Chicago: University of Chicago Press, 2000); Cathy Caruth, *Unclaimed Experience: Trauma, Narrative, and History* (Baltimore: Johns Hopkins University Press, 1997); and the collection edited by Cathy Caruth, *Trauma: Explorations in Memory* (Baltimore: Johns Hopkins University Press, 1995). Caruth does not, however, discuss Sebald in either of these works. For a critique of "trauma studies" see Dominick LaCapra, *History and Memory After Auschwitz* (Ithaca: Cornell University Press, 1998).

19. Within the field of psychoanalysis extensive work has been done on "recovered memories." The theories behind this range from the attempt to resurrect the wholeness of the past or what "actually happened" to ones that take the lability of memory and all representations of the past as their starting point. In contrast, for example, to the literalism of Binjamin Wilkomirski's claims about his recovered "Holocaust memories," Austerlitz's memories, as we will see, are tentative, contingent, and always a function of the layered spaces of the present. For an assessment of Wilkomirski and the patently false nature of his memories, see Daniel Ganzfried and Sebastian Hefti, eds., *Alias Wilkomirski: Die Holocaust-Travestie: Enthüllung und Dokumentation eines literarischen Skandals* (Berlin: Jüdische Verlagsanstalt, 2002). For an insightful discussion of the malleability of memories from a sociological and clinical perspective, see Jeffrey Prager's *Presenting the Past: Psychoanalysis and the Sociology of Misremembering* (Cambridge: Harvard University Press, 1998). Prager argues, in line with my thinking here, that memory is "as much a product of the present as of the past" (11).

20. As Andreas Huyssen notes, this modernist breakdown of language in *Austerlitz* is also a citation of Hugo von Hofmannthal's *Lord Chandos Brief* (1902), a fictional letter recounting, paradoxically, the disintegration of language and the facility to use language. Huyssen, "*Austerlitz:* Gray Zones," 971.

21. In this nascent formulation of the work of psychoanalysis, Freud is not concerned with articulating a theory of the difference between the origin and the reproduction: There exists an originary trauma and the cure to hysteria is to be found in its literal reproduction. Several years later, particularly in "Screen Memories" (1899), Freud gives up this single-minded search for origins and begins to articulate the thesis that there may only be reproductions with no recoverable origin. I will discuss this shift in more detail below.

22. Friedrich Kittler points out that these metaphors conform to the wider scientific practices of his day: "The *Project* provided the very model of contemporary models; the soul became a black box. One need only compare the hypothetical pathways, discharges, cathexes, and (of course discrete) neurons of Freud's text with statements about the material of brain psychology, which, since Sigmund Exner, had described the brain as a 'street system' with more or less deeply engraved 'driving tracks,' or as a network of telegraphic 'relay stations' with more or less prompt connections. Freud's mental apparatus, which has recently been interpreted as protostructuralist, merely conforms to the scientific standards of its day." *Discourse Networks 1800/1900*, trans. Michael Metteer, with Chris Cullens (Stanford: Stanford University Press, 1990), 278–79.

23. Derrida briefly discusses the concept *Bahnung* in his essay, "Freud and the Scene of Writing," in *Writing and Difference*, trans. Alan Bass (Chicago: University of Chicago Press, 1978), 196–231. He is interested in how Freud's use of writing metaphors develops from the *Project* to the "Note on the 'Mystic Writing-Pad'" such that the "configuration of traces . . . can no longer be represented except by the structure and functioning of writing" (200). He does not, however, consider the shift in Freud's thinking that I am discussing here.

24. Jones points out that Exner published his *Entwurf zu einer physiologischen Erklärung der psychischen Erscheinungen* (Leipzig: Deuticke, 1894) the year before Freud wrote the *Project for a Scientific Psychology* and that "it was Exner who developed the conception of Bahnung (facilitation of the flow of excitation)." Jones, *The Life and Work of Sigmund Freud*, 1:381.

25. Ibid., 1:385.

26. It is not until Freud famously discovers the "mystic writing-pad" (*der Wunderblock*) in 1924 that he finds an apparatus capable of representing or modeling memory, although the desire for finding such a model clearly goes back to 1895. The mystic writing-pad models the mnemic apparatus because it satisfies both of Freud's demands: unlimited receptive capacity (that is, it can always receive fresh impressions) and retention of permanent traces (that is, nothing is lost). "A Note on the 'Mystic Writing-Pad,'" in SE 19:226–32. For a brilliant discussion of this essay and the conceptual context of the development of Freud's concept of memory, see Mary Ann Doane's *The Emergence of Cinematic Time: Modernity, Contingency, the Archive* (Cambridge: Harvard University Press, 2002), 33–68. See also the discussion in Derrida, "Freud and the Scene of Writing," 220–29.

27. The German version of the *Project* is published in Sigmund Freud, *Aus den Anfängen der Psychoanalyse: Briefe an Wilhelm Fließ, Abhandlungen und Notizen aus den Jahren 1887–1902* (Frankfurt: Fischer, 1950), 297–384; here 331.

28. Letter of Sigmund Freud to Wilhelm Fliess, September 23, 1895, in *The Complete Letters of Sigmund Freud to Wilhelm Fliess, 1887–1904*, ed. and trans. Jeffrey Moussaieff Masson (Cambridge: Harvard University Press, 1985), 140.

29. Letter of Sigmund Freud to Wilhelm Fliess, October 8, 1895, ibid., 141. He repeats his discovery in the October 15, 1895, letter: "Have I revealed the great clinical secret to you, either orally or in writing? Hysteria is the consequence of a presexual *sexual shock*. Obsessional neurosis is the consequence of a presexual *sexual pleasure*, which is later transformed into [self-]*reproach*. 'Presexual' means actually before puberty, before the release of sexual substances; the relevant events become effective only as *memories*" (144).

30. Letter of Sigmund Freud to Wilhelm Fliess, October 20, 1895, ibid., 146.

31. This formulation of exorcising ghosts represents Freud in the position of the *Aufklärer*, a role that unequivocally describes his early scientific work but that also runs, in one way or another, throughout his entire career. However, as Derrida points out, Freud also learned to live with ghosts and never completely drove out the specters through his investment in science and rationalism. For this reason, it is possible to consider psychoanalysis as a kind of "hauntology," rather than a meaning-determinate ontology. For an elaboration of this difference with respect to Marx, see Derrida's *Specters of Marx: The State of Debt, the Work of Mourning, and the New International*, trans. Peggy Kamuf (New York: Routledge, 1994). With respect to Freud, Derrida writes: "It is known that Freud did everything possible to not neglect the experience of haunting, spectrality, phantoms, ghosts. He tried to account for them. Courageously, in as scientific, critical, and positive a fashion as possible. But by doing that, he also tried to conjure them. Like Marx." *Archive Fever: A Freudian Impression*, trans. Eric Prenowitz (Chicago: University of Chicago Press, 1995), 85. To my mind, the *Studies of Hysteria* represents Freud's preeminent conjuring of ghosts.

32. Letter of Sigmund Freud to Wilhelm Fliess, December 6, 1896, in *The Complete Letters of Freud to Fliess*, 207. The German can be found in Sigmund Freud, *Aus den Anfängen der Psychoanalyse*, 151.

33. Derrida, "Freud and the Scene of Writing," 206.

34. Richard Terdiman, *Present Past: Modernity and the Memory Crisis* (Ithaca: Cornell University Press, 1993), 292.

35. Freud's new understanding of the relationship between psychoanalysis and the telling of "historical truth" has been astutely analyzed by Peter Brooks, *Psychoanalysis and Storytelling* (Oxford: Oxford University Press, 1994); and Donald Spence, *Narrative Truth and Historical Truth: Meaning and Interpretation in Psychoanalysis* (New York: Norton, 1982).

36. The German version is Sigmund Freud, *Die Traumdeutung*, in *Gesammelte Werke*, 18 vols. (London: Imago, 1942), vols. 2–3; here 3:286.

37. The dream is first mentioned on page 269 of the standard edition of *The Interpretation of Dreams* (SE 4). Freud gives the dream content and his analysis on pages 441–44 (SE 5).

38. Yosef Hayim Yerushalmi, *Freud's Moses: Judaism Terminable and Interminable* (New Haven: Yale University Press, 1991), 40.

39. Freud, *Die Traumdeutung*, 3:444. In his essay, "Freud's Passover Dream Responds to Herzl's Zionist Dream," Ken Frieden points out that James Strachey's translation of *freizügig* as "can move across frontiers" captures the imbrication of mobility and Jewish emancipation but that the term also refers to a "liberal education" in the sense of being open-minded and cosmopolitan. The essay appears in Sander L. Gilman and Jack Zipes, eds., *Yale Companion to Jewish Writing and Thought in German Culture, 1096–1996* (New Haven: Yale University Press, 1997), 240–48.

40. The literature on Freud and Judaism is immense. In addition to Yerushalmi's book cited above, some of the most important book-length studies include Sander Gilman, *The Case of Sigmund Freud: Medicine and Identity at the Fin de Siècle* (Baltimore: Johns Hopkins University Press, 1993); Sander Gilman, *Freud, Race, and Gender* (Princeton: Princeton University Press, 1993); Peter Gay, *A Godless Jew: Freud, Atheism, and the Making of Psychoanalysis* (New Haven: Yale University Press, 1987).

41. Peter Loewenberg, "A Hidden Zionist Theme in Freud's 'My Son, the Myops . . .' Dream," *Journal of History of Ideas* 31 (1970): 129–32.

42. Ken Frieden, *Freud's Dream of Interpretation* (Albany: State University of New York Press, 1990), 120–22.

43. Perhaps the most suggestive is Yerushalmi's book, in which he concludes his "monologue with Freud" with the fateful question—posed to Freud's specter—whether psychoanalysis is a "Jewish science." See his *Freud's Moses*, 99–100. Responding to this decisive question, Derrida offers a powerful, deconstructive reading of Yerushalmi's monologue in his *Archive Fever*.

44. For one of the best accounts of this problematic in Freud, see Daniel Boyarin, *Unheroic Conduct: The Rise of Heterosexuality and the Invention of the Jewish Man* (Berkeley: University of California Press, 1997).

45. Frieden makes the compelling argument that *Schriftgelehrten* is better translated as "rabbinic scholars" than as "philologists." See his "Freud's Passover Dream," 242.

46. Yerushalmi, *Freud's Moses*, 69.

47. Frieden, "Freud's Passover Dream," 247.

48. This is articulated most clearly in Niklas Luhmann's *Social Systems*, trans. John Bednarz Jr., with Dirk Baecker (Stanford: Stanford University Press, 1995), and *Observations on Modernity*, trans. William Whobrey (Stanford: Stanford University Press, 1998).

49. Luhmann, *Social Systems*, 24.

50. Interestingly, this rendition of the reach of the "greater" German Empire includes Poland, Denmark, Austro-Hungary, and eastern France.

51. Freud, *Die Traumdeutung*, 3:535.

52. Archaeological metaphors can be found in Freud's earliest work on hysteria, such as "On the Aetiology of Hysteria" (SE 3), through his case studies—for example, the fate of Pompeii as a metaphor for repression in "The Rat Man" (SE 10)—up through his anthropological works, such as *Totem and Taboo* and *Civilization and Its Discontents*, to his "historical novel," *Moses and Monotheism* (SE 23). In his early work the fantasy of uncovering and deciphering the ruins of the past illustrates the work

of psychoanalysis; later the total preservation of the past functions as a conceptual analogue to the functioning of the "archaic" unconscious.

53. As Terdiman and others have pointed out, Freud never gave up this phylogenic conception of the unconscious, something for which he has been extensively criticized. See Terdiman, *Present Past*, 280–82. Although I find the biological investment in phylogeny dubious, Freud's hypothesis of an "archaic memory" can be used, following Herbert Marcuse, "for its symbolic value" in elucidating the dialectics of domination and civilization. See his chapter, "The Origin of Repressive Civilization (Phylogenesis)," in *Eros and Civilization: A Philosophical Inquiry into Freud* (Boston: Beacon, 1966), 55–77.

54. Terdiman, *Present Past,* 273.

55. Yerushalmi, *Freud's Moses*, 95.

56. Derrida, *Archive Fever*, 74.

57. Yerushalmi, *Freud's Moses*, 100.

58. Derrida, *Archive Fever*, 51.

59. Derrida's critique of Yerushalmi is layered in its complexity, and I cannot do it justice by responding to only one part. He essentially is arguing the following: "Yerushalmi undoubtedly thinks, and his book seems in any case to aim at demonstrating, that psychoanalysis is a Jewish science. It seems to aim for it in an original sense. Proposing a rigorous and 'scientific' renewal of reading, he bases himself on an archive sometimes archaic (the oldest biblical or talmudic tradition), sometimes recently published." Besides accusing Yerushalmi of a kind of "archive fever" in his revelation of a "private document" (the inscription in the Bible given by Jakob Freud to his son) to determine Freud's Jewishness and the Jewishness of psychoanalysis in general, he wants to elicit a confession from Freud himself, "that he [Freud] avows and proclaims, in an irreducible performance, that psychoanalysis should honor itself for being a Jewish science. A performative by which he would as much determine science, psychoanalytic science, as the essence of Jewishness, if not Judaism." *Archive Fever*, 46–47.

60. See, for example, Linda Woodbridge, "Afterword: Speaking with the Dead" in *PMLA* 118.3 (May 2003): 597–603.

61. W. G. Sebald, *Luftkrieg und Literatur. Mit einem Essay zu Alfred Andersch* (Munich: Hanser, 1999). The English translation includes two additional essays, one on Jean Améry and the other on Peter Weiss; *On the Natural History of Destruction*, trans. Anthea Bell (New York: Random House, 2003). The lectures were originally delivered in 1997 and reworked for publication. Although I find Bell's translation of *Austerlitz* masterful, I had to often provide my own translations of *Luftkrieg und Literatur* in order to convey Sebald's argument as precisely as possible. I will cite Bell's translation parenthetically as *Destruction* followed by the page number and make emendations as necessary; here vii.

62. Sebald, *Luftkrieg und Literatur,* 5 (my translation). The English translation reads somewhat pallidly: "this catastrophe had nonetheless left its mark on my mind," viii.

63. Sebald, *Luftkrieg und Literatur,* 83; I have altered this translation in several places.

64. Pierre Nora, "Between Memory and History: Les Lieux de Mémoire," *Represen-tations* 26 (Spring 1989): 7–25.

65. J.J. Long, "History, Narrative, and Photography in W.G. Sebald's *Die Ausge-wanderten,*" *Modern Language Review* 98.1 (January 2003): 117–37.

66. Marianne Hirsch, *Family Frames: Photography, Narrative, and Postmemory* (Cambridge: Harvard University Press, 1997), 22.

67. White, *Figural Realism,* 81.

68. Sebald, *Luftkrieg und Literatur,* 34. The English translation is "rather unreal effect" (*Destruction* 24).

69. Ōta Yōko, "City of Corpses" in *Hiroshima: Three Witnesses,* trans. Richard H. Minear (Princeton: Princeton University Press, 1990), 185.

70. Unlike the paucity of literature on the air war in Germany, an extensive body of Japanese literature has emerged on the bombing of Hiroshima and Nagasaki. For an excellent overview of this literature and its formal innovations, cf. John Whittier Treat, *Writing Ground Zero: Japanese Literature and the Atomic Bomb* (Chicago: University of Chicago Press, 1995). For a fascinating comparative discussion of catastrophe and representation, see William Haver, *The Body of This Death* (Stanford: Stanford University Press, 1997).

71. I make this argument more fully in my article, "'What a Synoptic and Artificial View Reveals.'"

72. Sebald, *Luftkrieg und Literatur,* 90 (English translation slightly emended).

73. Hans Blumenberg, *Shipwreck with Spectator: Paradigm of a Metaphor for Existence,* trans. Steven Rendall (Cambridge: MIT Press, 1997), 10.

74. W.G. Sebald, "Katastrophe mit Zuschauer: Ein Gespräch mit dem Schriftsteller W.G. Sebald," *Neue Züricher Zeitung* (November 22, 1997), 52.

75. Huyssen, "*Austerlitz*: Gray Zones," 972.

76. Jean Améry's experiences of torture at Fort Breendonk are conveyed in his memoir, *At the Mind's Limits,* trans. Sidney Rosenfeld and Stella P. Rosenfeld (Bloomington: Indiana University Press, 1980).

77. James Wood, "An Interview with W.G. Sebald," in *Brick: A Literary Journal* 58 (Winter 1998): 23–29; here 26.

78. W.G. Sebald, "Against the Irreversible: On Jean Améry," in *On the Natural History of Destruction,* 143–67. The original essay, "Mit den Augen des Nachtvogels: Über Jean Améry," is reprinted in W.G. Sebald, *Campo Santo,* ed. Sven Meyer (Munich: Hanser, 2004).

79. Améry, *At the Mind's Limits,* 33.

80. AP 463; translation modified. In an earlier section Benjamin insists: "For the historical index of the images not only says that they belong to a particular time; it says, above all, that they attain legibility only at a particular time" (462).

81. Roland Barthes, *Camera Lucida: Reflections on Photography,* trans. Richard Howard (New York: Hill and Wang, 1981), 93.

82. Wood, "An Interview with W.G. Sebald," 27.

83. W.G. Sebald interview with Christian Scholz, "Aber das Geschriebene ist ja kein wahres Dokument," in *Neue Züricher Zeitung* 48 (February 26, 2000): 51.

84. The first part of the English translation (although approved by Sebald) differs from the German original and conveys a somewhat different impression: "Wir versuchen, die Wirklichkeit wiederzugeben, aber je angestrengter wir es versuchen, desto mehr drängt sich uns das auf, was auf dem historischen Theater von jeher zu sehen war" ("We try to reproduce the reality, but the harder we try, the more we find that what was seen in the historical theater always forces itself upon us"). Sebald, *Austerlitz*, 105. Here Sebald relates history not to reality but to theater, preserving the sense that it is something staged, enacted, and visualized.

85. For more on this distinction, see Reinhart Koselleck's "Geschichte, Historie," in Otto Brunner, Werner Conze, and Reinhart Koselleck, eds., *Geschichtliche Grundbegriffe* (Stuttgart: Klett, 1975), 2:593–718.

86. Eduardo Cadava, *Words of Light: Theses on the Photography of History* (Princeton: Princeton University Press, 1997), 60–61.

87. We might read Benjamin's famous dictum on history in much the same way: "The past can be seized only as an image which flashes up at the instant when it can be recognized and is never seen again.... For every image of the past that is not recognized by the present as one of its own concerns threatens to disappear irretrievably." Walter Benjamin, "Theses on the Philosophy of History," in *Illuminations*, trans. Harry Zohn (New York: Schocken, 1968), 255.

88. W. G. Sebald interview with Christian Scholz, 51.

89. Amir Eshel, "Against the Power of Time: The Poetics of Suspension in W. G. Sebald's *Austerlitz*," *New German Critique* 88 (Winter 2003): 71–96. I thank Eshel for graciously sharing his research on Sebald with me.

90. Cf. Stephen Kern, *The Culture of Time and Space: 1880–1918* (Cambridge: Harvard University Press, 1983), 10–15.

91. Helmuth von Moltke's speech, "Third Debate on the Imperial Budget—Imperial State Railways—Standard Time," was given on March 16, 1891, in the Reichstag. *Essays, Speeches, and Memoirs of Field Marshal Count Helmuth von Moltke*, trans. Charles Flint McClumpha, 2 vols. (New York: 1893), 2:39–43.

92. Reinhart Koselleck, *Futures Past: On the Semantics of Historical Time*, trans. Keith Tribe (Cambridge: MIT Press, 1985), and *The Practice of Conceptual History: Timing History, Spacing Concepts*, trans. Todd Samuel Presner and others (Stanford: Stanford University Press, 2002).

93. Joseph Conrad's novel *The Secret Agent* (1906) is the most famous literary rendition of the history of the Greenwich bombing.

94. Interview with W. G. Sebald, "Wie kriegen die Deutschen das auf die Reihe?" in *Wochenpost*, June 17, 1993, 1–2.

95. Koselleck uses the term *futures past* to describe the ways in which past epochs imagined the openness or closure of the future. As such, through the practice of conceptual history, he examines the ways in which a given past imagined what the future would look like and bring.

96. Michel Chevalier, "Chemins de fer," quoted in Walter Benjamin, "Saint Simon, Railroads," in AP 598; ellipses are Benjamin's.

97. Wood, "An Interview with W. G. Sebald," 28.

Concluding Remarks

1. Gilles Deleuze and Félix Guattari, "Geophilosophy," in *What Is Philosophy?* trans. Hugh Tomlinson and Graham Burchell (New York: Columbia University Press, 1994), 96.

2. Paul Celan, *Der Meridian: Endfassung, Entwürfe, Materialen,* ed. Bernhard Böschenstein and Heino Schmull (Frankfurt: Suhrkamp, 1999),104.

3. Gershom Scholem, "Against the Myth of the German-Jewish Dialogue," in *On Jews and Judaism in Crisis: Selected Essays,* ed. Werner J. Dannhauser (New York: Schocken, 1976), 61–64; here 61–62.

4. Hannah Arendt, "The Jew as Pariah: A Hidden Tradition," in *The Jew as Pariah: Jewish Identity and Politics in the Modern Age,* ed. Ron H. Feldman (New York: Grove, 1978), 67–90.

5. Ibid., 72.

6. Ibid., 69.

7. See, for example, Peter Eli Gordon, *Rosenzweig and Heidegger: Between Judaism and German Philosophy* (Berkeley: University of California Press, 2003); and the fascinating study by Michael Mack, which argues that the figure of the Jew and the history of anti-Semitism are central to the narratives and counternarratives of German philosophy: *German Idealism and the Jew: The Inner Anti-Semitism of Philosophy and German Jewish Responses* (Chicago: University of Chicago, 2003).

8. Scott Spector, *Prague Territories: National Conflict and Cultural Innovation in Franz Kafka's Fin de Siècle* (Berkeley: University of California Press, 2000).

9. Spector explicitly invokes Benjamin's concept of dialectics at a standstill in his conclusion, ibid., 239–40. Very much in line with my thinking here, Spector argues for the centrality of the Jew in German modernism in his article "Modernism Without Jews: A Counter-Historical Argument," forthcoming in Amir Eshel and Todd Presner, eds., *Modernism/Modernity* 13.4 (2006).

10. In addition to the seminal works by Paul Gilroy, Homi Bhabha, Clifford Geertz, James Clifford, and Arjun Appadurai, see the recent studies on cosmopolitanism, flexible citizenship, transnationality, and transmigration by Avtar Brah, *Cartographies of Diaspora: Contesting Identities* (London: Routledge, 1996); Aihwa Ong, *Flexible Citizenship: The Cultural Logic of Transnationality* (Durham: Duke University Press, 1999); Smadar Lavie and Ted Swedenburg, eds., *Displacement, Diaspora, and Geographies of Identity* (Durham: Duke University Press, 1996); and Margaret Cohen, "Traveling Genres," *New Literary History* 34 (2003): 481–99.

INDEX

"The German-Jewish Parnassus" (Goldstein), 8, 293*n*17, 332*n*121
German/Jewish specters of history,
33–44
German-Jewish studies, 14–15, 288
*Germans, Jews, and the Claims of Moder-
nity* (Hess), 293*n*21
Germany: capitalism and, 61, 149, 156,
161, 172; carriages between France
and, 304*n*17; Christianization of, 120;
as closed nation, 155–56, 172, 177–78;
colonialism and, 153–56, 197, 322*n*9,
331*n*117; deterritorialized, 13, 107;
France and, 120, 155, 170, 175, 178–79;
Greece and, 47–48, 56, 149–52; industrialization and modernization
of, 61, 90–91, 161; Italy v., 75, 80–85,
94; Jewish children sent out of, from
Anhalter Bahnhof, 2, *205*, 206; as
"land of two rivers" (*Zweistromland*),
8; railway systems of, 61–62, *63*, *167*,
167–70, *169*, 180–84, 327*n*69; space of,
113; trains between France and, 61;
unification of, 24, 28, 57–58, 90, 155–
57, 160–61, 163, 166–72, 174–75, 179–83,
192, 325*nn*43–44, 327*n*69, 327*n*74
Gerschenkron, Alexander, 327*n*74
Gervinus, Georg, 165–66, 170–74
"Gesang des Deutschen" (Song of the
German)(Hölderlin), 47, 55–56
Geschichte (history), 273, 279, 295*n*53
*Geschichte der poetischen National-Lit-
eratur der Deutschen* (Gervinus),
165–66, 171
Geschichtslosigkeit (historylessness), of
Holocaust, 53
Geschichtsphilosophie (philosophical his-
tory), 120, 298*n*11
Geseres (imposed sufferings or doom),
252–55
"Gespräch im Gebirg" (Conversation in
the mountains)(Celan), 53–54
Geständisse (Confessions)(Heine),
316*n*15

Gestapo headquarters, 34, 235
Gestapo member, confession of, 33–35
Ghost stories, German/Jewish, 130–46
Ghosts, 247–48, 341*n*31; *see also* German/
Jewish specters of history
Gilroy, Paul, 23–24, 296*n*658, 297*n*66,
307*n*47, 313*n*104
Ginzburg, Carlo, 236, 337*n*7
Gleichzeitigkeit des Ungleichzeitigen (si-
multaneity of the nonsimultaneous),
35–36, 235
Global anxieties, national fantasies and,
156–79
Globalization: cosmopolitanism and,
160, 161, 163, 201; mobility and,
296*n*56; nationalism and, 160, 323*n*22;
nationality and, 28, 158–79; railways
and, 159–61, 164, 166–70, 172–77, 179;
studies on, 323*n*17; transnationality
and, 21
Goebbels, Joseph: bunker of, 34–36;
non-Jews evacuated by order of, 206
Goethe, Johann Wolfgang, 26, 288; "An
Schwager Kronos," 88; Battle of Jena,
Luden and, 78–79; bildungsroman
and, 158; death of, 89, 173; diaries of,
69–70, 306*n*37; on Germany's unification and railways, 90; Hegel and, 132;
Heine and, 117–18, 131–32, 138; Italian
journey of, 66–89, 131, 305*n*35, 306*n*37;
Kafka and, 6, 13, 15, 65–68, 72, 93–98,
100–101, 104, 106, 113, 310*n*89, 314*n*110;
modes of mobility used by, 69; *The
Roman Carnival*, 83, 305*n*35, 308*n*62;
spectatorship and, 65–66, 75–79, 95,
136, 138, 266; steering to port on a
tempestuous sea, 68–89; on subject
formation, 66–67, 72, 83, 86–88;
Varnhagen and, 287; on Vesuvius,
76–77, 79, 94–95; on world literature,
161, 172–73, 177; *Zweyter Aufenthalt
in Rom*, 69, 305*n*35, 306*n*37, 308*n*62,
309*n*75; *see also Italienische Reise;
Wilhelm Meister*